# A
# Treasury
# of
# Catholic Thinking

*By the Author*

A Treasury of Inspiration

A Treasury of Catholic Thinking

The Family Reader of American Masterpieces

# A
# Treasury
# of
# Catholic Thinking

*Compiled and Edited by*

## RALPH L. WOODS

*Introduction by*

## REV. JAMES M. GILLIS, C.S.P.

NEW YORK

## THOMAS Y. CROWELL COMPANY

NIHIL OBSTAT:
Rev. Thomas W. Smiddy, S.T.L.
*Censor Librorum*

IMPRIMATUR:
Most Rev. Thomas E. Molloy, S.T.D.
*Archbishop—*
*Bishop of Brooklyn, New York*

July 18, 1953

# *Acknowledgments*

The editor and the publisher are grateful to the following copyright owners, publishers, authors, and agents for their splendid cooperation in granting permission to use in this book selections from the works mentioned below.

GERTRUDE ALGASE: Fulton J. Sheen's paper in *The Modern Social and Economic Order*, copyright 1939 by *Our Sunday Visitor*, Huntington, Indiana.

Archbishop Karl J. Alter: an address by John T. McNicholas, "No Wall Between God and Child," April 1947; an address by Archbishop Alter, Xavier University, Cincinnati, Ohio, 1953. The America Press, Inc.: *What is the Catholic Attitude?* by William J. Smith, S.J.; *No Pope Can Be Wrong in Teaching Doctrine,* by Martin J. Scott, S.J., copyright 1941 by The America Press; *The Philosophy of Catholic Education* by William J. McGucken, S.J.; *Equal Rights for Children* by Robert C. Hartnett, S.J.; Address to the Fordham Faculty by George Bull, S.J., 1933; *Education for International Understanding* by William L. Lucey, S.J., and Paul W. Facey, S.J., edited by Robert C. Hartnett, S.J. American Academy of Political and Social Science: paper by John Courtney Murray, S.J., in *The Annals,* March, 1948. Appleton-Century-Crofts, Inc.: Fulton J. Sheen's *Philosophy of Religion,* copyright 1948 by Fulton J. Sheen, reprinted by permission of the publishers, Appleton-Century-Crofts, Inc. *The Atlantic Monthly:* Robert Hugh Benson's "Catholics and the Future," vol. CCVI, 1910; Alfred E. Smith's letter to Charles G. Marshall, May, 1927. The Ave Maria Press: John J. Cavanaugh's *The Blasphemous Thing,* copyright 1939 by The Ave Maria Press.

Bruce Publishing Company: Brother Benignus' *Nature, Knowledge and God,* copyright 1947 by Brother Benignus of Jesus, F.S.C. Burns Oates and Washbourne, Ltd.: John Cuthbert Hedley's *The Light of Life;* Sir Bertram C. A. Windle's *A Century of Scientific Thought;* Dom Bruno Webb's *Why Does God Permit Evil?*

Cassel and Co. Ltd.: from Eric Gill's *Art Nonsense and Other Essays.* Catholic Association for International Peace, Washington, D.C.: *Secularism's Attack on World Order,* report by John La Farge, S.J. and The Ethics Committee and the Religion and Culture Subcommittee, 1944; *Timeless Rights in Modern Times,* by Wilfrid Parsons, S.J., John M. Paul, S.C.P., and The Ethics Committee of the C.A.I.P. *The Catholic Mind:* sermon by Benjamin L. Masse, S.J., Gary, Indiana, Labor Day, 1949, issue of October, 1949. Catholic Truth Society of Ireland: M. J. Browne's *The Sacred Roman Rota.* Catholic Truth Society of London, England: Ronald A. Knox's *Miracles; What The Catholic Church Is and What She Teaches,* by E. R. Hull, S.J. Catholic University of America Press: *Better Men for Better Times,* by The Commission on American Citizenship, The Catholic University of America, copyright 1943 by The Catholic University of America Press. *The Commonweal:* William P. Clancy's "The Liberal Catholic," copyright July 11, 1952; Victor White's "The Analyst and the Confessor," copyright July 23, 1948. Confraternity of the Precious Blood: Martin J. Healey's in *My Way of Life,* by Walter Farrell and Martin J. Healey, copyright 1952 by Confraternity of the Precious Blood. Ignatius W. Cox, S. J.: *God, Man and Redemption,* Catholic Hour Radio Sermons, 1933. Archbishop Richard J. Cushing: sermon, Boston, Massachusetts, April 14, 1952.

Christopher Dawson: paper in *The Dublin Review,* July, 1942. Devin-Adair Company: Eric Gill's *Autobiography;* Columba Cary-Elwes' *Law, Liberty and Love,* 1951. Ditchling Press, Ltd.: Jacques Maritain's *The Philosophy of Art,* translated by John O'Connor, 1923. E. P. Dutton and Company, Inc.: Baron Friedrich von Hugel's *Essays and Addresses on the Philosophy of Religion.*

*The Ensign,* Montreal, Canada: Etienne Gilson's paper, issues of March 15 and 22, 1952.

FARRAR, STRAUSS AND YOUNG, INC.: François Mauriac's *The Woman of the Pharisees,* a Pellegrini and Cudahy book, Farrar, Strauss and Young, Inc., publishers. FIDES PUBLISHERS, Chicago, Illinois: Emanuel Cardinal Suhard's *Growth or Decline? The Church Today,* translated by James J. Corbett, copyright 1948 by Fides Publishers. FUNK AND WAGNALL COMPANY: William J. Kerby's paper in *The Encyclopedia of Social Reform,* edited by Wm. D. P. Bliss. PAUL HANLEY FURFEY: paper before the fourth annual meeting, American Catholic Philosophical Association, 1929.

JAMES M. GILLIS, C.S.P.: excerpt from *The Catholic World,* July, 1928; *If Not Christianity, What?,* Catholic Hour Radio Sermons, 1935. GRUNE AND STRATTON, INC.: Thomas Verner Moore's *Personal Mental Hygiene,* copyright 1944 by Grune and Stratton, Inc.

DANIEL U. HANRAHAN: sermon, September, 1951. HARPER AND BROTHERS: James M. O'Neill's *Catholics and American Freedom,* copyright 1952 by Harper and Brothers. ROBERT C. HARTNETT, S.J.: radio address, January 20, 1952, published in *The Catholic Mind,* September, 1952. HARVARD UNIVERSITY PRESS: *The Apostolic Fathers,* edited and translated by Kirsopp Lake for The Loeb Classical Library, 1912. B. HERDER BOOK COMPANY: Robert Howard Lord's "Introduction" to Dom Poulet's *A History of the Catholic Church,* translated by Sidney A. Raemers, copyright 1939 by B. Herder Book Company. HENRY HOLT AND COMPANY, INC.: *The Mind and Heart of Love* by Martin C. D'Arcy, S.J., copyright 1947 by Henry Holt and Company, Inc., used by permission of the publishers.

KNIGHTS OF COLUMBUS: pamphlets titled *Yes, I Condemned the Catholic Church; What Do You Mean—Only One True Church; Let Us Judge Catholics by the Bible.*

JOHN LA FARGE, S.J.: lecture at University of North Carolina, April 24, 1952, published in *The Catholic Mind,* November, 1952. LA SALLE PROVINCILATE OF THE CHRISTIAN BROTHERS, from Brother Benignus' *Nature, Knowledge and God,* copyright 1947 by Brother Benignus of Jesus, F.S.C. LONGMANS, GREEN AND COMPANY, INC.: Patrick A. Sheehan's *Parerga;* Christopher Hollis' *The Noble Castle; The Church of Christ* by Peter Finlay, S.J.; Dietrich von Hildebrand's *Transformation in Christ,* copyright 1948 by Longmans, Green and Company, Inc.; Rosalind Murray's *The Good Pagan's Failure;* Lecomte du Noüy's *Human Destiny,* copyright 1947 by Lecomte du Noüy; Gerald Vann's *The Heart of Man,* copyright 1945 by Gerald Vann, O.P. A. C. McCLURG AND COMPANY: John Lancaster Spalding's *Glimpses of Truth.* LAURENCE J. McGINLEY, S. J.: address, University of Detroit, May 25, 1952.

THE MACMILLAN COMPANY: John A. O'Brien's *Truths Men Live By,* copyright 1946 by The Macmillan Company; Karl Adam's *The Spirit of Catholicism,* translated by Dom Justin McCann, copyright 1929 by The Macmillan Company; Georges Bernanos' *The Diary of a Country Priest,* translated by Pamela Morris, copyright 1938 by The Macmillan Company; *Philosophy for the Millions,* by J. A. McWilliams, S.J., copyright 1942 by The Macmillan Company. McMULLEN BOOKS, INC., Antonin Gilbert Sertillanges' *Recollection,* published by McMullen Books, Inc., New York, 1950. *The Month,* London, England: "Dogmatic Intolerance and Civil Toleration," by Max Pribilla, S.J., issue of October, 1950. EDWARD CARDINAL MOONEY: address, Milwaukee, Wisconsin, 1938; address, Detroit, Michigan, August, 1944. JOHN COURTNEY MURRAY, S.J.: address, American Academy of Political and Social Science, published in *The Annals,* March, 1948.

NATIONAL CATHOLIC WELFARE COUNCIL: John A. Ryan's *The Norm of Morality,* copyright 1944 by Rt. Rev. John A. Ryan. NATIONAL CONFERENCE OF CATHOLIC CHARITIES: Bryan J. McEntegart's paper in *Catholic Charities Review,* June, 1926. NATIONAL COUNCIL OF CATHOLIC MEN: *God, Man and Redemption* by Ignatius W. Cox, S.J.; *If Not Christianity, What?* by James M. Gillis, C.S.P.; volumes of radio sermons delivered in 1933, 1935, on the National Broadcasting Company's "The Catholic Hour." NEW DIRECTIONS: Thomas Merton's *Figures For an Apocalypse,* copyright 1947 by New Directions. THE NEWMAN PRESS: Antonin Gilbert Sertillanges' *The Intellectual Life,* published by The Newman Press, Westminster, Maryland.

ARCHBISHOP PATRICK A. O'BOYLE: address, Boston, Massachusetts, October, 1948. OUR SUNDAY VISITOR, INC.: *The Modern Social and Economic Order, A Symposium;* papers by Francis J. Haas, Ben W. Palmer, Fulton J. Sheen, copyright 1939 by Our Sunday Visitor, Inc. OXFORD UNIVERSITY PRESS: *St. Thomas Aquinas—Philosophical Texts,* selected and translated by Thomas Gilby, O.P., 1951; *Documents of the Christian Church,* selected and edited by Henry Bettenson, Oxford Galaxy Edition, 1947.

THE PAULIST PRESS: Hilaire Belloc's *Europe and the Faith,* copyright 1920, 1939, by The Missionary Society of St. Paul the Apostle in the State of New York; Adolph Dominic Frenay's *Is Life Worth Living,* 1933; John A. Ryan's *Citizen, Church and State,* copyright 1941 by The Missionary Society of St. Paul the Apostle in the State of New York; John B. Harney's *Sin,* copyright 1949 by The Missionary Society of St. Paul the Apostle in the State of New York. PRINCETON UNIVERSITY PRESS: Emmet John Hughes' *The Church and The Liberal Society,* copyright 1944 by The Princeton University Press.

RANDOM HOUSE, INC.: *The Basic Writings of St. Thomas Aquinas,* edited and translated by Anton C. Pegis, copyright 1945 by Random House, Inc. *The Record,* Louisville, Kentucky: Alfred F. Horrigan's editorial, May 9, 1952. HENRY REGNERY COMPANY: William Aylott Orton's *The Challenge of Christian Liberalism,* copyright 1946 by Human Events, Inc.

ST. ANTHONY'S GUILD PRESS: Luigi Sturzo's *The True Life,* translated by Barbara Barclay Carter, copyright 1943 by St. Anthony's Guild Press. CHARLES SCRIBNER'S SONS: Francis Cardinal Spellman's *Action This Day,* copyright 1943 by Charles Scribner's Sons, copyright 1943 by Crowell-Collier Publishing Co.; Etienne Gilson's *The Spirit of Medieval Philosophy,* translated by A. H. C. Downes, copyright 1936 by Charles Scribner's Sons; Jacques Maritain's *True Humanism,* 1936; Jacques Maritain's *Ransoming the Time,* translated by Harry Lorin Binsse, copyright 1941 by Charles Scribner's Sons; Jacques Maritain's *Christianity and Democracy,* translated by Doris Anson, copyright 1945 by Charles Scribner's Sons; Etienne Gilson's *The Unity of Philosophy Experience,* copyright 1937 by Charles Scribner's Sons. SHEED AND WARD INC.: Christopher

Dawson's *Progress and Religion,* published by Sheed and Ward, Inc., New York, 1938; Christopher Dawson's *Beyond Politics,* published by Sheed and Ward, Inc., New York, 1934; Jacques Maritain's *Freedom in the Modern World,* translated by Richard O'Sullivan, published by Sheed and Ward, Inc., New York, 1935; Paul Claudel's *Ways and Crossways,* translated by John O'Connor, published by Sheed and Ward, Inc., New York, 1933; Douglas Jerrold's *The Future of Freedom,* copyright 1938 by Sheed and Ward, Inc., New York; Rudolph Aller's *The Psychology of Character,* translated by E. B. Strauss, copyright 1943 by Sheed and Ward, Inc., New York; Alfred Noyes' *The Unknown God,* published by Sheed and Ward, Inc., New York, 1934; *Essays in Order,* edited by Christopher Dawson and T. F. Burns, copyright 1939 by Sheed and Ward, Inc., New York; *Complete Works of St. Teresa,* translated by E. Allison Peers, published by Sheed and Ward, Inc., New York, 1946. SIMON AND SCHUSTER, INC.: Thomas F. Woodlock's *The Catholic Pattern,* copyright 1942 by Thomas F. Woodlock.

JOSEPH F. WAGNER, INC.: *Christian Apologetics,* by W. Devivier, S.J., copyright 1924 by Joseph F. Wagner, Inc.; Juan Donoso Cortés' *An Essay on Catholicism, Authority and Order,* translated by Madeleine Vincent Goddard, copyright 1925 by Joseph F. Wagner, Inc. MRS. JOHN A. WARNER: Alfred E. Smith's Letter to Charles G. Marshall, *Atlantic Monthly,* May, 1927.

UNIVERSITY OF CHICAGO PRESS: from Jacques Maritain's *Man and the State,* copyright 1951 by The University of Chicago.

YALE UNIVERSITY PRESS: Etienne Gilson's *God and Philosophy,* copyright 1941 by Yale University Press.

Since no one person could hope to explore so vast a field of literature unaided, I cannot omit mention of the guidance afforded me by the valuable collections compiled and edited by George N. Schuster, the Reverend Francis B. Thornton, and the Reverend Benjamin L. Masse, S.J.

It is a pleasure to acknowledge helpful suggestions from E. J. Woods, H. F. Woods, Jr., Patricia Joan Woods, W. O. Lightfoot, Nathaniel Hicks and the Reverend Edwin B. Broderick. Lillias Watt Woods did considerable checking of manuscript and proofs and helped with the indexing. Lois Dwight Cole, associate editor of Thomas Y. Crowell Company, made excellent suggestions and generally shepherded the project with skill and admirable restraint.

Finally, I must express my deep appreciation of the Reverend James M. Gillis' kindness in introducing this book.

R. L. W.

*Port Washington, New York*

To my wife

LILLIAS WATT WOODS

# Introduction

by JAMES M. GILLIS, C.S.P.

THE PROFESSED intention of the compiler of this anthology or, as he prefers to call it, "treasury," is "to give the Catholic view of life in all its aspects in the world today." "A tolerably sizable task" as a non-Catholic friend said when I told him that the Church has hopes of making America Catholic. There may be some—even Catholics—who feel that Catholic thought is ambitious when it ventures into fields not strictly religious. They fail to realize that religion must of necessity touch life in this world at all points. Faith itself is not merely one aspect of life. "Religion's all or nothing," says Robert Browning. Those who hold that the preacher must, as they express it, "stick to the Gospel," remain inside the altar rail, or, as the French say, be *"prêtre de sacristie"* are really suggesting that the concern of the Church must be with prayer, worship, liturgy, catechism, and that it must have no place in affairs political, social, economic.

The wide range of subjects discussed in this "treasury" indicates that Catholicism is not content with any limitations. The poet Virgil, in some respects a precursor of Catholicism, says, "Mind working in the members gives life and motion to the entire body." I venture to capitalize the word "Mind *(Mens)*" in the supposition that it may mean "God." Another Roman poet says that man must think of nothing as alien to himself. What those wise Romans said of God and of man we may say of the Church; she is concerned with all things, human and divine. *Verbum Dei non est alligatum* says St. Paul; "the word of God is not in chains."

Mr. Woods in the following pages has called upon a great number of writers, some of them creative thinkers, others—as they themselves would be the first to protest—only adapters and popularizers.

The resultant is indeed a "treasury." It contains gold and silver and many gems of great value. The mere sight of them, it may be hoped, will lead many to dig deep into the mines from which the treasures have been unearthed.

# Preface

THE PURPOSE of this collection is to give authoritatively, simply, and forcefully the Catholic view of life in all its aspects in the world today. The contents have been chosen carefully from writings of many periods that state Catholic beliefs and attitudes, especially those writings in which the teachings of the Church relate to life as it is lived by active men and women today.

It seems well to emphasize that this volume does not attempt or pretend to comprise all the doctrines, beliefs, and teachings of the Church. Dogma, doctrine, and theology are, of course, touched upon and discussed by some of the writers in the collection, but the book is not intended to be either a guidebook or a textbook on these subjects. Moreover, although there are numerous philosophical passages included, it is not a collection of Catholic philosophy or meditation or inspiration. But it does give the Catholic view on many of the problems that beset us all.

The table of contents accurately reflects both the scope and the orderly development of the book. And although this volume emphasizes the problems of our day, it often goes back to great Catholics of earlier centuries to illustrate the immutability of Catholic truths and the far-ranging wisdom of Catholic teachings; repeatedly the Church deals with and judges contemporary problems in the light of its eternal principles.

There will also be found in the book many carefully reasoned discussions of why and to what extent the Church's teachings reach into many aspects and phases of life and secular activity that may seem to non-Catholics beyond the province of the Church. Care has been taken always to choose writings that state the reasoning, or the philosophical basis, upon which rests the Catholic position on the many problems with which the book deals.

One cannot end so challenging a task as this without regretting the omission of much fine thinking and writing. I can only regret that it has been impossible to explore all the treasures of almost two thousand years of Catholic writings, and that it has been impossible to include all of the pertinent and forceful writing that research uncovered. For the omissions caused by limitations of space, or of ignorance, I hope for the reader's forgiveness.

Since this collection carries an Imprimatur, it might be well to make clear that this does *not* mean that every word in the book is official Catholic doctrine. It does not even mean that those granting the Imprimatur agree with all the statements and opinions in the book, though no doubt they agree with many. The Imprimatur means only that there is nothing in the volume contrary to Catholic dogma on faith and morals.

As I complete the selections for this book I am acutely reminded of Jacques Maritain's observation that "A Catholic writer is tortured and terrified by the thought that Catholicism may, perhaps, be judged by the standard of his own insufficiency." When so profound and scholarly a Catholic thinker as Maritain has trepidations, a mere compiler and editor of Catholic thinking can only be most diffident. However, I am happy that I have been able to draw upon so many great Catholic thinkers who have cogently and brilliantly stated the views of our Church.

R. L. W.

xiv

# Contents

THE final joy of man consists in the superlative activity of his supreme power, namely the activity of mind engaged with incomparable truth.

ST. THOMAS AQUINAS

MAN is but a reed, the most feeble thing in nature; but he is a thinking reed. . . . All our dignity consists, then, in thought. By it we must elevate ourselves, and not by space and time which we cannot fill. Let us endeavor, then, to think well; this is the principle of morality.

BLAISE PASCAL

THERE are still too many Catholics hardly more than in name. There are too many who fulfill more or less faithfully the more essential obligations of the religion they boast of professing, but have no desire of knowing it better, of deepening their inward convictions.

PIUS XI, March 19, 1937

# A
# Treasury
## of
# Catholic Thinking

# I

# God

*The proofs of His existence. His nature, attributes, and powers. His intervention in human affairs. Man's obligation to worship Him. The spiritual suicide of atheism.*

## ST. PAUL TO THE ATHENIANS

WHAT therefore you worship without knowing it, that I preach to you: God, who made the world and all things therein; he, being Lord of heaven and earth, dwelleth not in temples made with hands; neither is he served with men's hands, as though he needed anything; seeing it is he who giveth to all life and breath and all things: And hath made of one, all mankind, to dwell upon the whole face of the earth, determining appointed times and the limits of their habitation. That they should seek God, if happily they may feel after him or find him, although he be not far from every one of us: For in him we live, and move, and are; as some also of your own poets said: *For we are also his offspring.*

Being therefore the offspring of God, we must not suppose the divinity to be like unto gold or silver or stone, the graving of art and device of man. And God indeed having winked at the times of this ignorance, now declareth unto men, that all should everywhere do penance. Because he hath appointed a day wherein he will judge the world in equity, by the man whom he hath appointed; giving faith to all, by raising him up from the dead.

(ACTS, xvii, 23–31)

I

"Seek ye God, and your soul shall live." It is because He is hidden that He must be sought in order to be found; and being found He must still be sought because of His immensity. . . . For He satisfies the seeker in the measure of his capacity and He makes the finder to have greater capacity so that he may again seek to be filled when his ability to receive has grown.

ST. AUGUSTINE (ca. 415)

# THAT THE NON-EXISTENCE OF GOD IS INCONCEIVABLE

## ST. ANSELM (OF CANTERBURY)

So truly dost thou exist, O Lord my God, that thou canst not be conceived not to exist. For this there is the highest reason. For, if any mind could conceive of anything better than thou art, then the creature could ascend above the Creator, and become his judge; which is supremely absurd. Everything else, indeed, which exists besides thee, can be conceived not to exist. Thou alone, therefore, of all things, hast being in the truest sense, and consequently in the highest degree; for everything else that is, exists not so truly, and has, consequently, being only in an inferior degree. . . .

Thou alone, O Lord, art what thou art and who thou art. For that which is one thing in its whole and another in its parts, and in which there is anything mutable, is not what it is, in an absolute sense. And that which begins from non-existence and can be conceived of as not existing, and which unless it subsist through something else, must return to non-existence; also whatever has a past which is now no longer, and a future, which is yet to come, this does not exist in proper and absolute sense. But thou art what thou art; because whatsoever thou art at any time, or in any manner, thou art this at all times and absolutely. And thou art who thou art properly and simply; because thou has neither past nor a future, but only a present, neither canst thou be conceived of as not existing at any moment.

(ca. 1075)

# MAN'S NATURE INCLINES
# HIM TO GOD

## ST. THOMAS AQUINAS

To know that God exists in a general and confused way is implanted in us by nature, inasmuch as God is man's beatitude. For man naturally desires happiness, and what is naturally desired by man is naturally known by him. This, however, is not to know absolutely that God exists; just as to know that someone is approaching is not the same as to know that Peter is approaching, even though it is Peter who is approaching; for there are many who imagine that man's perfect good, which is happiness, consists in riches, and others in pleasures, and others in something else.

Perhaps not everyone who hears this name *God* understands it to signify something than which nothing greater can be thought, seeing that some have believed God to be a body. Yet, granted that everyone understands that by this name *God* is signified something than which nothing greater can be thought, nevertheless, it does not therefore follow that he understands that what the name signifies exists actually, but only that it exists mentally. Nor can it be argued that it actually exists, unless it be admitted that there actually exists something than which nothing greater can be thought; and this precisely is not admitted by those who hold that God does not exist.

(1272)

# "SPONTANEOUS NATURAL
# THEOLOGY"

## ETIENNE GILSON

QUITE apart from any philosophical demonstration of the existence of God, there is such a thing as a spontaneous natural theology. A quasi-instinctive tendency, observable in most men, seems to invite them to wonder from time to time if, after all, there is not such an unseen being as the one we call God. The current objection that such a feeling is but a survival in us of primitive myths, or our own early religious education, is not a very strong one. Primitive myths do not

3

account for the human belief in the existence of the Divinity; obviously it is the reverse which is true. Early religious education is not a sufficient explanation for the questions which sometimes arise in the minds of men concerning the reality or unreality of God. Some among us have received a decidedly antirelegious education; others have had no religious education at all; and there are even quite a few who, having once received a religious education, fail to find in its memory any incentive to think too seriously of God. The natural invitations to apply his mind to the problem come to man from quite different sources. These are the very selfsame sources which once gave rise not only to Greek mythology but to all mythologies. God spontaneously offers himself to most of us, more as a confusedly felt presence than as an answer to any problem, when we find ourselves confronted with the vastness of the ocean, the still purity of mountains, or the mysterious life of a midsummer starry sky. Far from being social in essence, these fleeting temptations to think of God usually visit us in our moments of solitude. But there is no more solitary solitude than that of a man in deep sorrow or confronted with the tragic perspective of his own impending end. "One dies alone," Pascal says. That is perhaps the reason why so many men finally meet God waiting for them on the threshold of death.

What do such feelings prove? Absolutely nothing. They are not proofs but facts, the very facts which give philosophers occasion to ask themselves precise questions concerning the possible existence of God. Just as such personal experiences precede any attempt to prove that there is a God, they survive our failures to prove it.

(1941)

# MAN'S INBORN BELIEF IN A GOD

### THE REV. JAMES M. GILLIS, C.S.P.

ALMOST all atheists seem to imagine that a group of theologians met together in secret session and said to one another, "Let us concoct a dogma and impose it on the people." And lo, they came forth from the hall of conspiracy with a formula which they taught men, women, and children, to say: "I believe in God." But theologians didn't invent God. Man—simple man, not perhaps the man in the street for there weren't any streets, but the man in the woods, the man on the

4

mountain, the man under the starry sky, the man on the shore of the sea—came to the instant conclusion that there must be a God, for the self-same reason and by the same instinctive logic as Robinson Crusoe came to the swift realization that there must be a man on the island because he saw a human foot-print. God didn't make the world, couldn't make the world, without leaving all over it hints, suggestions, tell-tale evidence that He had been here. "The heavens shew forth the glory of God," says the Psalmist, "and the firmament declareth the work of His hands."

Man, primitive man, as yet unspoiled with curious, intricate, impossible philosophies, had a firm grasp on the fundamental principle of science: "Nothing comes from nothing; whatever is made had a maker." . . .

One thing is certain: the human heart is incurably religious. If by coercion or ridicule you compel man to surrender belief in the One True Holy God, he will create for himself a hundred, or a thousand other gods, filthy gods, monstrous gods, gods of lust, and blood, Molechs, Baals, Venuses, Astarthes. If you take away Ormuzd, the god of light, man will turn to Ahriman, the god of darkness.

Good God or bad god, true God or false God, kind God or cruel god, man will have some god. The God-idea is indestructible. Believers in God may take heart in that fact; unbelievers should take warning. You can no more blot out God than you can snuff out the light of the sun as if it were a candle.

(1935)

## THE FIVE PROOFS OF THE
## EXISTENCE OF GOD

### ST. THOMAS AQUINAS

THE existence of God can be proved in five ways.

The first and more manifest way is the argument from motion. It is certain, and evident to our senses, that in the world some things are in motion. Now whatever is moved is moved by another, for nothing can be moved except it is in potentiality to that towards which it is moved; whereas a thing moves inasmuch as it is in act. For motion is nothing else than the reduction of something from potentiality to actuality. But nothing can be reduced from potentiality to actuality, except by something in a state of actuality. Thus that which is actually hot, as fire, makes wood, which is potentially hot, to be actually hot, and thereby moves and changes it. Now it is not possible that the same thing should be at once in actuality and potentiality in the same respect, but only in different respects. For what is actually hot cannot simultaneously be potentially hot; but it is simultaneously potentially cold. It is therefore impossible that in the same respect and in the same way a thing should be both mover and moved, i.e., that it should move itself. Therefore, whatever is moved must be moved by another. If that by which it is moved be itself moved, then this also must needs be moved by another, and that by another again. But this cannot go on to infinity, because then there would be no first mover, and, consequently, no other mover, seeing that subsequent movers move only inasmuch as they are moved by the first mover; as the staff moves only because it is moved by the hand. Therefore it is necessary to arrive at a first mover, moved by no other; and this everyone understands to be God.

The second way is from the nature of efficient cause. In the world of sensible things we find there is an order of efficient causes. There is no case known (neither is it, indeed, possible) in which a thing is found to be the efficient cause of itself; for so it would be prior to itself, which is impossible. Now in efficient causes it is not possible to go on to infinity, because in all efficient causes following in order, the first is the cause of the intermediate cause, and the intermediate is the cause of the ultimate cause, whether the intermediate cause be several, or one only. Now to take away the cause is to take away the effect. Therefore, if there be no first cause among efficient causes, there will be no ultimate, nor any intermediate, cause. But if in efficient causes it is possible to go on to infinity, there will be no first efficient cause; neither will there be an ultimate effect, nor any intermediate efficient causes; all of which is plainly false. Therefore it is necessary to admit a first efficient cause, to which everyone gives the name of God.

The third way is taken from possibility and necessity, and runs thus. We find in nature things that are possible to be and not to be, since they are found to be generated, and to be corrupted, and consequently, it is possible for them to be and not to be. But it is impossible for these always to exist, for that which can not-be at some time is not. Therefore, if everything can not-be, then at one time there was nothing in existence. Now if this were true, even now there would be nothing in existence, because that which does not exist begins to exist only through something already existing. Therefore, if at one time nothing was in existence, it would have been impossible for anything to have begun to exist; and thus even now nothing would be in existence—which is absurd. Therefore, not all beings are merely possible, but there must exist something the existence of which is necessary. But every necessary thing either has its necessity caused by another, or not. Now it is impossible to go on to infinity in necessary things which have their necessity caused by another, as has been already proved in regard to efficient causes. Therefore we cannot but admit the existence of some being having of itself its own necessity, and not receiving it from another, but rather causing in others their necessity. This all men speak of as God.

The fourth way is taken from the gradation to be found in things. Among beings there are some more and some less good, true, noble and the like. But *more* and *less* are predicated of different things according as they resemble in their different ways something which is the maximum, as a thing is said to be hotter according as it more nearly resembles that which is hottest; so that there is something which is truest, something best, something noblest, and, consequently, something which is most being, for those things that are greatest in truth are greatest in being, as it is written in *Metaph.* ii. Now the maximum in any genus is the cause of all in that genus, as fire, which is the maximum of heat, is the cause of all hot things, as is said in the same book. Therefore there must also be something which is to all beings the cause of their being, goodness, and every other perfection; and this we call God.

The fifth way is taken from the governance of the world. We see that things which lack knowledge, such as natural bodies, act for an end, and this is evident from their acting always, or nearly always, in the same way, so as to obtain the best result. Hence it is plain that they achieve their end, not fortuitously, but designedly. Now whatever lacks knowledge cannot move towards an end, unless it be directed by some being endowed with knowledge and intelligence; as the arrow is directed by the archer. Therefore some intelligent being exists by whom all natural things are directed to their end; and this being we call God.

(1272)

## PIUS XII

TRUE science discovers God in an ever-increasing degree—as though God were waiting behind every door opened by science. We would even say that from this progressive discovery of God, which is realized in the increase of knowledge, there flow benefits not only for the scientist himself when he reflect as a philosopher—and how can he escape such reflection?—but also for those who share in these new discoveries or make them the object of their own considerations. . . .

Thus stimulated and guided, the human intellect approaches that demonstration of the existence of God which Christian wisdom recognizes in those philosophical arguments which have been carefully examined throughout the centuries by giants in the world of knowledge, and which are already well known to you in the presentation of the "five ways" which the Angelic Doctor, St. Thomas, offers as a speedy and safe road to lead the mind to God. . . .

If the primitive experience of the ancients could provide human reason with sufficient arguments to demonstrate the existence of God, then with the expanding and deepening of the field of human experiments, the vestiges of the Eternal One are discernible in the visible world in even more striking and clearer light. . . .

Just as in a picture done in chiaroscuro, the figures stand out on a background of darkness, and only in this way achieve the full effect of form and life, so also the image of the Eternally Immutable Being emerges clear and resplendant from the torrent which snatches up and carries off with itself all the material things of the macrocosm and the microcosm in an intrinsic mutability which knows no pause. The scientist who stops on the bank of this immense torrent finds rest in that cry of truth with which God defined Himself, "I am who am." . . .

How . . . faithful a reflection of limitless visions is the language of an outstanding modern scientist, Sir Edmund Whittaker, member of the Pontifical Academy of Science, when he speaks of the above-mentioned inquiries into the age of the world: "These different calculations point to the conclusion that there was a time, some nine or ten billion years ago, prior to which the cosmos, if it existed, existed in a form totally different from anything we know and this form constitutes the very last limit of science. We refer to it, perhaps not improperly, as creation. It provides a unifying background, suggested by geological evidence, for that explanation of the world according to which every organism existing on the earth had a beginning in time."

What, then, is the importance of modern science for the argument for the existence of God based on the mutability of the cosmos? By means of exact and detailed research into the macrocosm and the microcosm, it has considerably broadened and deepened the empirical foundation on which the argument rests, and from which it concludes to the existence of an "Ens a Se," immutable by His very nature. It has, besides, followed the course and the direction of cosmic developments and just as it was able to get a glimpse of the term toward which these developments were inexorably leading, so also has it pointed to their beginning in time some five billion years ago. Thus, with that concreteness which is characteristic of physical proofs, it has confirmed the contingency of the universe and also the well-founded deduction as to the epoch when the cosmos came forth from the hands of the Creator.

Hence, creation took place in time. Therefore, there is a creator. Therefore, God exists! Although it is neither explicit or complete, this is the reply we were awaiting from science.

(November 22, 1951)

MATTER cannot be eternal; but God, if a man takes in the idea at all, cannot be thought of as other than eternal. He who is the Eternal Existence has created the first matter; He who has life in Himself has created life; and He who is the Supreme Lawgiver has subjected matter and life to the laws they obey.

AUBREY DE VERE (1887)

## THE ULTIMATE EXPLANATION

### ETIENNE GILSON

WHEN a man falls to wondering whether there is such a being as God, he is not conscious of raising a scientific problem, or hoping to give it a scientific solution. Scientific problems are all related to the knowledge of *what* given things actually are. An ideal scientific explanation of the world would be an exhaustive rational explanation of *what* the world actually is; but *why* nature exists is not a scientific

9

problem, because its answer is not susceptible of empirical verification. The notion of God, on the contrary, always appears to us in history as an answer to some existential problem, that is, as the *why* of a certain existence. The Greek gods were constantly invoked in order to account for various "happenings" in the history of men as well as in that of things. A religious interpretation of nature never worries about what things are—that is a problem for scientists—but it is very much concerned with the questions why things happen to be precisely what they are, and why they happen at all. The Jewish-Christian God to whom we are introduced by the Bible is there at once posited as the ultimate explanation for the very existence of man, for the present condition of man upon the earth, for all the successive events that make up the history of the Jewish people as well as for these momentous events: the Incarnation of Christ and the Redemption of man by Grace. Whatever their ultimate value, they are existential questions. As such, they cannot possibly be transposed into terms of science, but only in terms of an existential metaphysics.

(1941)

# THE UNIVERSE'S PROOF OF GOD

### THE REV. JOHN A. O'BRIEN

What do we mean by God? God is not a mere dream, not an hypothesis, nor the projection of our hopes and aspirations upon the frail canvas of illusion. He is the meaning of the universe and the hope of humanity. . . .

God is the Supreme Ruler of the universe. He is the omniscient Mind Who thought out the myriad laws of nature and the omnipotent Power Who flung the uncounted planets, stars and galaxies out into the vastness of immeasurable space. He is the Architect not only of the stupendous universe but also of the heart and mind and soul of man. . . .

If a person walking along a seashore comes suddenly upon a watch, he will conclude that there must be a watchmaker. Why? Because as he looks at the mechanism of the watch, with its springs, its cogwheels, its hour hand and its minute hand, with its crystal and its face, with the movement of the minute hand so co-ordinated that it travels precisely twelve times faster than the hour hand, he knows that this could not have happened by accident or by blind chance. The adaptations of parts and the co-ordinations of movements reflect unmistakably the work of a thinking agent who arranged the whole to achieve a definite, previsioned end. There is blinding evidence here of plan, purpose, order and design, which leaves him in no uncertainty.

Suppose you were to say to such a person: There is no evidence of a thinking agent behind that bit of mechanism. Those parts are simply an aggregation of bits of metal and glass, and were blown together by the winds of chance. Earth, sea, wind, sun, sky, air and the blind forces of nature explain the making of that watch. Would he not conclude that you were either joking or that you were a lunatic? Would he not say: Surely you cannot expect an intelligent person to believe so wild a fairy tale. Even a child of six would scorn such an explanation as an insult to his intelligence. There is woven into that watch an artistry of power and intelligence which convinces me that nothing on this planet could account for that watch except a human being who has mastered the craft of the watchmaker.

Let us now glance at the marvelous universe in which our earth is as a tiny speck. The whole is arranged with wonderful order and design. Our earth rotates on its axis once in twenty-four hours, bringing to us night and day. The earth revolves around the sun once in the course of a year, bringing to us with unfailing regularity the four seasons of the year. This planet of ours, with its great cities teeming with millions of inhabitants, with its lofty skyscrapers, with its vast emporiums of trade and commerce, with its mountains, rivers and valleys, is shooting through space at the startling velocity of 68,400 miles per hour. Yet so smoothly does it move, that it disturbs not a babe in its cradle, nor brings a tremor to the wings of the bee nestling on the frail petals of an autumn rose. . . .

Here then is order, plan, purpose and design which cries out not less imperiously than the watch found at the seashore for an intelligent and adequate cause.

Inescapable then is the simple conclusion: As the watch implies a watchmaker, so the universe implies a God. As the watch demands adequate cause in the form of an intelligent horologist, so the universe, vastly greater in size, complexity of organization, and adjustment of parts, demands an adequate cause in the form of a Being of vastly greater power and intelligence. This is the Being Whom we call by the venerable name of God. . . .

The great astronomer, Kirchner, had a friend who experienced doubts about the existence of God. Knowing that a simple illustration would be more effective than a long argument, Kirchner made a globe and placed it in his study. When his friend called to see him, he noticed the new globe, and asked:

"Who made this globe?"

"Why," replied Kirchner, "it made itself."

His friend laughed heartily at the joke. Whereupon Kirchner said: "You laugh at that as absurd, and rightly so. But it would be a thousand times easier to believe that this little globe made itself than that the large one on which we live made itself." . . .

Moreover, the number of stars and solar systems floating about in the regions of interstellar space seems to be almost unlimited. The millions and billions of stars in the Milky Way are but a tiny fragment of the myriad worlds coursing through space. The most powerful photographic cameras are continually catching glimpses of new galaxies of stars beyond the outermost rim of the previously charted stellar universe. Professor Shapley of the Harvard Observatory has recently reported "island universes" of stars, far outside the main sidereal system. These globular clusters are over a million light years distant. In other words they are so far distant that light traveling at the rate of 186,000 miles per second would take more than a million years to reach our earth.

For all that astronomers have been able to discover, this may be but the nearest fringe, the vestibule of a universe that stretches out with its planets, suns, and stars into immeasurable and boundless space. Indeed, the question of the finitude or infinity of the physical universe vexes the minds of astronomers, and remains with them a moot question. Truly does the mind reel and stagger under the weight of such stupendous distances, such unimaginable sizes and such baffling complexity of galaxies of worlds seemingly without number. . . .

The findings of modern astro-physicists concerning the immensity and the grandeur of the universe serve therefore to emphasize the truth uttered by the Psalmist centuries before the dawn of the Christian era: "The heavens show forth the glory of God, and the firmament declareth the work of His hands." . . .

The atom is viewed as a small solar system. Around its central nucleus of positive electricity called a proton, the electrons revolve as the planets revolve about the sun. The movements, however, apparently follow no fixed path or orbit. While the atom is so small as to be invisible to the naked eye, science has measured the speed of these electrons and tells us that they move in an orbit of less than one-millionth of a inch in diameter, faster than an airplane or a bullet from a revolver. Thus the average electron revolves around its central nucleus several thousand million million times every second, with a velocity of hundreds of miles a second. This amazing orbital speed which is greater than that of the planets or even of the stars, is achieved in spite of the infinitesimally small chamber in which it is imprisoned —namely less than one-millioneth of an inch in diameter. . . .

In the light of these discoveries of modern physics, a speck of dust and a grain of sand become teeming worlds of marvel and of mystery. In a speck of dust so small as to be beyond our naked vision are more particles than there are inhabitants upon our planet. They are moving in their atomic orbits, so silently as to be inaudible, with a velocity which bewilders our imagination. Science with its huge cyclotron, or atom crusher, is able occasionally to split an atom. Science has not been able as yet, however, to penetrate deep enough into the depths of the atom to ferret out the network of laws which stretch from the heart of an atom to the galaxy of the farthest stars. These laws hold the whole vast universe together and support the stars in their courses, much as milady's clothesline holds securely the whole family washing flapping in the summer breeze. . . .

Dr. George L. Clark, Professor of X-ray Chemistry at the University of Illinois and a world authority in that field, threw upon the screen an X-ray picture of a particle of soot. I can still remember the expressions of wonderment and awe which came spontaneously from my students as they perceived the beauty and the symmetry of the molecular arrangements therein disclosed. Like flakes of snow on a window pane tracing out geometric figures of remarkable symmetry and wonderful diversity, so these figures stood revealed like frozen pieces of glorious architecture. Indeed within a speck of soot which an individual will flip disdainfully from his white kid glove, there is a perfection of symmetry in the arrangement of the molecules and an embodiment of mathematical precision which would make the Taj Mahal of India or St. Peter's Cathedral in Rome seem like child's play in comparison.

That is why the scientist who has peered even a little way into the unfathomed and mysterious depths of a particle of matter, will stand with reverent eyes and uncovered head before a particle of dust or a grain of sand. Like Moses standing before the burning bush, he too hears the voice which says: "Put off thy shoes from thy feet, for the place whereon thou standest is holy ground." To him there is no common clay. For every particle of matter is aglow with miracle and with mystery, singing a refrain in homage to that Infinite Power from Whose creative hands it came. . . .

Truly, indeed, the world of the infinitesimally small is not less wonderful than the world of the infinitely large. Nor does it speak less cogently nor less eloquently of a Supreme Ruler of the universe. "In all the vast and the minute," as the poet, Cowper, says, "we see the unambiguous footsteps of the God Who gives its luster to the insect's wings and wheels His throne upon the rolling worlds." . . .

When we reach the mind of man, we reach the pinnacle of all creation. It is the apex in the pyramid of values to be found in the universe. It is this which constitutes the dignity of man as a moral personality, and makes him a being of surpassing worth. . . .

While the material universe, as disclosed to us by modern astronomy, is indeed marvelous in its order and staggering in its immensity, still more marvelous is the mind of man which no scale can measure, because it transcends the properties of matter and reaches into the world of spirit. How wonderful, indeed, is the mind of man which measures the girth of Betelgeux and weighs stars a million light years from our planet! There is the supreme evidence of design, and the crowning argument of God's existence.

Man . . . is a walking argument of God's existence, a moving advertisement of God's power, an articulate herald of God's intelligence. As man is the crowning work of God, so we affirm man is the supreme argument and the blinding evidence of God's existence. . . . For only in God do we find a suitable Cause for the mysterious power of human reason. Among all the objects in the visible universe, the mind of man sounds the loudest and the most eloquent note proclaiming the existence of a Supreme Being, an Omniscient Mind, and an Infinite God, Who is, in the words of St. Paul, "the Alpha and the Omega, the beginning and the end of all things." . . .

To know God, mere intellectual groping is not enough. More helpful in seeing God than intellectual subtlety is a pure heart and a clean conscience. When Ignatius, Bishop of Antioch, was being led to martyrdom, a Roman soldier asked him leeringly: "Who is this Christian God of yours?" Gazing into his sensual, brutal face, Ignatius replied: "You shall know Him when you are worthy of Him."

The person who suffers persecution for justice' sake, who sacrifices

14

for truth, who hungers for righteousness, who lives a godly life, penetrates to the deepest understanding of God. Virtue is more important than knowledge in enriching one's vision of God. Live a holy life and God will dwell in you and make Himself known to you. "God's thoughts," observes George Macdonald, "His will, His love, His judgments are all man's home. To think His thoughts, to choose His will, to love His loves, to judge His judgments, and thus to know that He is in us, is to be at home."

When God dwells in the soul of a person, a radiance shines in his face, a spiritual resonance in his voice, and peace fills his heart. Nothing in the universe can supply the radiance lost when God is banished from a human life. The experience of humanity the world over verifies the finding of St. Theresa: "Where God is, there is Heaven. Where God is not, there is Hell." Plato too caught a glimmering of this mighty truth when he declared: "To escape from evil we must be made, as far as possible, like God; and this resemblance consists in becoming just, holy, and wise."

God then is the answer to the cry of the human soul for happiness. In the partial possession of God in this life, we catch glimmerings of that supreme ecstasy which the soul will experience when it will be in intimate union with infinite Beauty, Truth, and Love, when the unveiled majesty of the eternal King will ravish the soul with beauty and still its restless yearning with a love that knows no ending.

(1946)

GOD expresses Himself in the visible and recognizes Himself in us. Our striving after the visible is God seeking Himself. We ourselves seek Him by our moral life, by our mysticism, by love, by philosophy, by science and art—and we find Him when these things are well ordered.

THE REV. ANTONIN SERTILLANGES, O.P. (1950)

## THAT WHICH HAS EXISTED ALWAYS

### THE REV. IGNATIUS W. COX, S.J.

THERE is a natural logic which leads the open mind to God. Last summer I was walking around a little estate on Long Island Sound with a philosopher who was as profound as he was simple. "How would you propose a popular argument for the existence of God," I asked. "That is easy," he replied. "Imagine that in the beginning there was no existing thing, an absolute blank, absolutely nothing. In that absurd hypothesis, there would be nothing existing today. Start with nothing existent and you end with nothing existent. Something must have existed always and that something is God." . . .

The proof of my friend was at once an argument for God's existence and a rejection of materialism and pantheism. Materialists say that the something which existed from the beginning was matter. To which my philosopher would reply: "That cannot be; for matter is changeable and the original something had all its existence at once, is unchangeable." "Perhaps God is part and parcel of the universe," says the pantheist; "All things are God and God is all things." To this my philosopher would answer with a smile: "That cannot be, for the universe is in constant change and God is unchangeable."

This eternal, unchangeable thing then is God. Without His eternal existence we cannot explain ourselves or the world around us. He is the cause of the world and He is a person, because He is intelligent. The universe around us is an open book wherein is written the greatest of mystery stories and wherein is disclosed the intelligence of its Author.

(1933)

To ask the question, Who caused God, or Who caused the first cause, is to ask that a first cause be at one and the same time a secondary cause, which is a contradiction.

MOST REV. FULTON J. SHEEN (1948)

## "PURE ACT"

### DÉSIRÉ JOSEPH CARDINAL MERCIER

THAT which changes cannot possess within itself the adequate reason of its change. Now the universe changes. Therefore the universe has not in itself the adequate reason for its changing existence.

It follows then that there exists, outside this everchanging world, a Being who is not Himself subject to change, and who can thus account for the origin of all the changes of the universe. This Being metaphysicians call a *Pure Act;* by which they mean that His reality is exempt from all potentiality, from all capacity of receiving further actuation, and is therefore immutable, eternal, all-perfect. . . .

The principle on which we have based our argument, and on which rests the theology of Aristotle, of St. Thomas Aquinas, and of all the great thinkers of the School, has therefore the character of an axiom: *That which changes has not in itself the adequate reason of its change, and therefore does not itself account fully for that change.* Whence the following conclusion emerges: Beyond and above all beings subject to change we must affirm, under pain of contradicting ourselves, the existence of a Being whose nature is exempt from the change to which all the things of our experience are subject. This Supreme Being, this Pure Actuality, we call God. . . .

Passing next from the study of vicissitudes of the external world and of our own physical activity, to the consideration of our interior life, we detect there an aspiration, constant and imperious, towards an absolute moral good, a good which once more forces upon us, under a new aspect, the great truth of the existence of God. From the dawn of reason, that is, from the time man becomes conscious of his personal responsibility, he feels himself bound to subordinate his will and his desires to an end which is higher and nobler than the self-interest of the passing moment. He has obligations towards his neighbor, towards his family, towards his country, towards society. But society itself exists, as an organised whole, only to safeguard more effectually the mutual interests of all its members; from which it results that man, conscious of his moral obligations, must search necessarily and instinctively, high above the social entity which envelops him and of which he is himself a factor, for an absolute, ultimate Good, a selfsubsisting End,—in a word, for God, the keystone of the moral edifice.

How comes it then that humanity thus gravitates around a fixed centre, without finding in itself the end and the *raison d'être* of the movement that carries it along? What then is this human nature? Man has had a beginning in time, each individual is born on a certain day into the world, then grows and develops, and finally disappears. Man is a "contingent being" as the philosophers say: which means that he possesses existence indeed, but that of himself he cannot conserve it, nor, consequently have originated it. We must then look elsewhere, beyond him, for the explanation of this contingent existence of his. Were we to seek such a reason in beings anterior to himself, but contingent like himself, we should merely be shifting the difficulty backward instead of solving it. We are forced therefore to conclude that above and beyond the beings whose existence is contingent there is a first Being whose existence is in no wise contingent; in other words, a Being whose very essence is existence, whom metaphysicians call the Self-subsisting Being—the *Ens a se,*—the Necessary Being. Thus the affirmation of the existence of a Necessary Being, First Principle of all contingent existences, appears once more as the only way to escape self-contradiction.

(1912)

LIFE passes away, riches fly away, popularity is fickle, the senses decay, the world changes, friends die. One alone is constant; One alone is true to us; One alone can be true; One alone can be all things to us; One alone can supply our needs; One alone can train us up to our full perfection; One alone can give a meaning to our complex and intricate nature; One alone can give us tune and harmony; One alone can form and possess us.

JOHN HENRY CARDINAL NEWMAN (1836)

## THE DIVINE GOODNESS

### ST. THOMAS AQUINAS

THERE is something first which is essentially being and essentially good which we call God. . . . Hence from the first being, essentially being and good, everything can be called good and a being inasmuch as it participates in the first being by way of a certain assimilation. . . . Everything is therefore called good from the divine goodness, as from the first exemplary, effective, and final principle of all goodness. Nevertheless, everything is called good by reason of the likeness of the divine being belonging to it, which is formally its own goodness, whereby it is denominated good. And so of all things there is one goodness, and yet many goodnesses.

(1272)

WHEN we say, *God is good,* the meaning is not, *God is the cause of goodness,* or *God is not evil;* but the meaning is, *Whatever good we attribute to creatures pre-exists in God,* and in a higher way. Hence

18

it does not follow that God is good because He causes goodness; but rather, on the contrary, He causes goodness in things because He is good.

ST. THOMAS AQUINAS (1272)

BOETHIUS introduces a philosopher who asks: *"If there be a God, whence comes evil?"* He should have argued; *"If there is evil, there is God."* For there would be no evil if the order of good were removed, the privation of which is evil; and there would be no such order, if there were no God.

ST. THOMAS AQUINAS (1260)

## THE BEAUTY OF GOD

### JACQUES MARITAIN

GOD is beautiful. He is the most beautiful of all beings, because, as set forth by Denys the Areopagite and St. Thomas, His Beauty is without change or vicissitude, without increase or diminution; and because it not like that of things, which all have a particularized beauty, *particulatam pulchritudinem, sicut et particulatam naturam* (a particularised beauty as also a particularised nature). He is beautiful by Himself and in Himself, beautiful absolutely.

He is surpassingly beautiful (*superpulcher*) because in the perfectly simple unity of His nature pre-exists in a manner passing excellent the wellspring of all beauty.

He is beauty itself, because he gives beauty to all created being, according to the property of each, and because He is the cause of all unison and all clarity. Indeed every form, that is to say every light, is "a certain irradiation coming out of the primal clarity," "a sharing in the divine clarity." And every unison, or every harmony, every concord, every friendship and every unison whatsoever between beings comes forth from the divine Beauty, the primitive and supereminent type of all unison, which likens all things to one another, and calls them all unto itself, well deserving therein "the name of καλός which derives from calling." Thus the "beauty of the creature is none other than a similitude of the divine Beauty shared among things," and, moreover, every form being a principle of being and

19

every unison or harmony being a preserver of being, we can say that the Beauty of God is the cause of the Being of all that is. *Ex divina pulchritudine esse omnium derivatur.*

(1923)

WE can know what God is not, but we cannot what He is.

ST. AUGUSTINE (ca. 397)

GOD's own being is not only conformed to his intellect, but His act of understanding is the measure and cause of every other being and of every other intellect, and He is Himself His own existence and act of understanding. Whence it follows not only that Truth is in Him, but He is Truth itself, and the Sovereign and First Truth.

ST. THOMAS AQUINAS (1272)

## BEATITUDE IN GOD

### ST. THOMAS AQUINAS

BEATITUDE . . . is the perfect good of an intellectual nature. Thus it is that, as everything desires the perfection of its nature, so an intellectual nature desires naturally to be happy. Now that which is most perfect in any intellectual nature is the intellectual operation, by which in some sense it grasps everything. Whence the beatitude of every created intellectual nature consists in understanding. Now, in God, to be and to understand are one and the same thing, differing only in the manner of our understanding them. Beatitude must therefore be attributed to God according to His intellect.

(1272)

## ALL THINGS NEED GOD

### ST. THOMAS AQUINAS

GOD's omnipotence does not imply that He can make two contradictories true at the same time. Now the statement that God can produce a thing which does not need to be upheld by Him involves a contradiction. For we have already proved that every effect depends upon its cause in so far as it is its cause. Accordingly, the statement that a thing does not need God to uphold its existence implies that it is not created by God; while the statement that such a thing is produced by God implies that it is created by Him. Wherefore, just as it would involve a contradiction to say that God produced a thing that was not created by Him, even so it would involve a contradiction were one to say that God made a thing that did not need to be kept in existence by Him.

(1272)

# THE SUPREMACY OF THE WILL OF GOD

BROTHER BENIGNUS, F.S.C.

MANY moderns argue that if God freely causes all the events of nature, then nothing in nature is due to natural causes, and science is a futile pursuit. Unwilling to give up science, they reject the Christian idea of a free creating God. The argument, as St. Thomas formulates it in the *Summa Theologica*, runs thus:

"No other cause except the will of the agent may be assigned for those things that are produced by a voluntary agent who wills things without his own will having any cause. But as has been shown above, the will of God is the cause of all things. If, therefore, there is no cause of His will, no other cause may be sought for all natural things except the divine will alone. In that case all sciences would be vain which seek to assign causes for any effects. This is unacceptable. Therefore, some cause ought to be assigned for the divine will."

The answer of St. Thomas is just as good today as it was seven centuries ago; indeed, the blindnesses of contemporary naturalism give it added point:

"Since God wills effects to exist in such a way that they proceed from definite causes so that the order among beings may be preserved, it is not vain to seek other causes in addition to the will of God. *It would, however, be vain, if the other causes were sought as primary and not depending upon the divine will.* So spoke St. Augustine (*De Trinitate*, Book III, Chapter 2): 'It pleases the vanity of the philosophers to attribute contingent effects to other causes, since they are altogether unable to see the cause which is superior to all others, that is to say, the will of God.'"

(1947)

He who has once detected in his conscience the outline of a Lawgiver and Judge, needs no definition of Him, whom he dimly but surely contemplates there, and he rejects the mechanism of logic, which cannot contain in its grasp matters so real and so recondite. . . . Conscience is nearer to me than any other means of knowledge.

JOHN HENRY CARDINAL NEWMAN (1870)

# THE FIRST AND THE LAST

JOHN HENRY CARDINAL NEWMAN

THE word "God" is a Theology in itself, indivisibly one, inexhaustibly various, from the vastness and simplicity of its meaning. Admit a God, and you introduce among the subjects of your knowledge, a fact encompassing, closing in upon, absorbing, every other fact conceivable. How can we investigate any part of any order of Knowledge, and stop short of that which enters into every other order? All true principles run over with it, all phenomena converge to it; it is truly the First and the Last. In word indeed, and in idea, it is easy enough to divide Knowledge into human and divine, secular and religious, and to lay down that we will address ourselves to the one without interfering with the other; but it is impossible in fact. Granting that divine truth differs in kind from human, so do human truths differ in kind one from another. If the knowledge of the Creator is in a different order from knowledge of the creature, so, in like manner, metaphysical science is in a different order from physical, physics from history, history from ethics. You will soon break up into fragments the whole circle of secular knowledge if you begin the mutilation with divine. . . .

According to the teachings of Monotheism, God is an Individual, Self-dependent, All-perfect, Unchangeable Being; intelligent, living, personal, and present; almighty, all-seeing, all-remembering; between whom and His creatures there is an infinite gulf; who has no origin, who is all-sufficient from Himself; who created and upholds the universe; who will judge every one of us, sooner or later, according to that Law of right and wrong which He has written on our hearts. He is One who is sovereign over, operative amidst, independent of,

22

the appointments which He has made; One in whose hands are all things, who has a purpose in every event, and a standard for every deed, and thus has relations of His own towards the subject-matter of each particular science which the book of knowledge unfolds; who has with an adorable, never-ceasing energy implicated Himself in all the history of creation, the constitution of nature, the course of the world, the origin of society, the fortune of nations, the action of the human mind, and who thereby necessarily becomes the subject-matter of a science, far wider and more noble than any of those which are included in the circle of secular Education.

This is the doctrine which belief in a God implies in the mind of a Catholic; if it means anything, it means all this, and cannot keep from meaning all this, and a great deal more. . . .

Nothing is easier than to use the word, and mean nothing by it. The heathens used to say, "God wills," when they meant "Fate," "God provides," when they meant "Chance," "God acts," when they meant "Instinct," or "Sense"; and "God is everywhere," when they meant "The Soul of Nature." The Almighty is something infinitely different from a principle, or a centre of action, or a quality, or a generalization of phenomena. If, then, by the word, you do but mean a Being who keeps the world in order, who acts in it, but only in the way of general Providence, who acts towards us only through what are called laws of Nature, who is more certain not to act at all than to act independent of those laws, who is known and approached indeed, but only through the medium of those laws; such a God it is not difficult for anyone to conceive, not difficult for anyone to endure. . . . Then is He but coincident with the laws of the universe; then is He but a function, or correlative, or subjective reflection and mental impression, of each phenomenon of the material or moral world, as it flits before us. . . .

I understand, in that case, how it is that the religious sense is but a "sentiment," and its exercise a "gratifying treat," for it is like the sense of the beautiful or the sublime. I understand how the contemplation of the universe "leads onward to *divine* truth," for divine truth is not something separate from Nature, but it is Nature with a divine glow upon it.

(1852)

23

# AN ULTIMATE GROUND

ETIENNE GILSON

CALL it Matter, with Democritus, the Good with Plato, the self-thinking thought with Aristotle, the One with Plotinus, Being with all Christian philosophers, Moral Law with Kant, the Will with Schopenhauer, or let it be the absolute idea with Hegel, the Creative Duration of Bergson and whatever else you may cite, in all cases the metaphysician is a man who looks behind and beyond for an ultimate ground of all real and possible experience. Even restricting our field of observation to the history of Western civilization, it is an objective fact that men have been aiming at such knowledge for more than twenty-five centuries and that after proving that it should not be sought, and swearing that they would not seek it any more, men have always found themselves seeking it again. A law of the human mind that rests on an experience of twenty-five centuries is at least as safely guaranteed as any empirically established law.

(1936)

# CHRISTIAN BELIEF IN DIVINE
# INTERVENTION

CHRISTOPHER HOLLIS

DOES God intervene in the affairs of men? Are there ways in which we can obtain His assistance? Let us turn first to the evidence of the pre-Christian and the non-Christian world. We find not indeed a unanimous opinion but certainly an overwhelming majority opinion, that God does intervene in the affairs of men, and that there are ways in which His assistance may be obtained. It is true that it may be objected that the gods, of, say, the Homeric Olympus are preternatural forces rather than, properly speaking, divine beings. They have more of the nature of the witches of Macbeth than of the Redeemer of the Universe, and a belief in them implies only a belief that there are forces acting in this world other than those of flesh and blood and daily experience. But, wherever you find belief in such forces, you also find belief in darker but diviner forces behind them—forces which they are able to tap—

24

> Gods behind the gods,
> Gods that are best unsung.

Christianity, then, when it claimed that God intervened in the affairs of men, was making no hitherto unheard-of claim. Men had believed in the possibility of such intervention, since the beginning of time. . . . The pre-Christian pagan believed, as most of us would think, in an excess of divine intervention in the affairs of men. God, or the gods, were constantly intervening—intervening often, as would seem to us, in ways that were very unworthy and ridiculous—but nevertheless intervening. Man has, as a matter of fact, always believed in Divine intervention in the workings of the world. There is no novelty in the claim. The only question to be asked is whether it is justified.

The fact that it has been so widely held is in itself an argument in its favour. *Consensus universalis*—general consent—is a good argument. *Securus iudicat orbis terrarum.* The world can judge unquestioned. Yet let us consider the arguments by which the sceptics sought to explain it away. They are two—that of scientific ignorance and that of wishful thinking. The savage believed that, when it thundered, God was angry, and man comforted himself illegitimately with the thought that God would help him because without such illusive comfort he could not bear to face the evils of life.

The two arguments clearly to some extent cancel one another out. The pagan savage, who believed in the Divine interventions in his life, did not at all believe that the God who intervened was a nice God. He feared his gods far more than he loved them. So far from being wishful for such acts of intervention, he would much rather not have had them, if he could, and it was as a liberator from evil that the great Roman poet Lucretius saw himself when he attacked the power of religion.

> Tantum religio potuit suadere malorum.
> (To so much evil can religion persuade us.)

Whatever may be true of the primitively pure religions, which are lost in the mists of antiquity, the pagans of historical times—debased pagans as they may have been—knew much of the power of God and very little of His love. The Christian may justly be accused of "wishful thinking," if he cannot persuade his critic that his claims are true. For he does frankly proclaim that his news is good news. But there was very little good news in pagan theology. . . .

25

So I think we are justified in saying that the fact that men have always believed in the possibility of Divine intervention is much more striking than attempts to explain that belief away are convincing. But why should God wish to intervene? The gaping defect in Pagan metaphysics was clearly not so much in their belief that Zeus was acting, when he thundered, as in their belief that he was angry. For God cannot clearly be angry—at least in the crude sense of being in a rage, and losing his temper and throwing things at people—for to suffer such anger is a limitation, and God is unlimited. And yet, if God does intervene in the affairs of men, it can only be because he wishes to establish some sort of relationship with His creatures. If the cold, rational Aristotelian Supreme Being who "thinks himself, and his thinking is a thinking of thinking" were what God was and were all that God was, there would be no reason why He should wish to intervene in order to manifest Himself to man. What quality then is there, the possession of which is not at all a limitation, and which is wholly worthy of Divinity? For it is in that quality that the relationships between the human and Divine must necessarily be found. . . .

The existence of compassion in Man proves the existence of compassion in God. And, yet since there cannot be suffering in the merely unlimited, the full nature of God requires the possession by Him of a plural personality. Nothing else will suffice, but, in order that all may be fulfilled, the unlimited must take to itself limitation, the immortal must put on mortality. In one moment of blinding vision he foresees the necessity of the Incarnation, and in that clear vision at last the whole meaning of the Creation is clear to him. . . .

It was beyond the power of the pre-Christian to guess at the bounty with which his demand for "something more" was to be granted. But it was not beyond his power to accept by pure reason the truth and the necessity of monotheism, and, then, having accepted it, to be dissatisfied with mere monotheism, to feel—though he could not guess how sense could be made of such talk—that, even though God was one, yet His personality could not be single. The mere knowledge of a single God was not enough. We need more. There must be something more coming. . . .

Natural religion has already shown us, whether Christianity be true or false, that God created man and created him with a certain nature. And it is surely significant, if we can find that his nature was such that, even when he lacked the Christian revelation, he was continually groping out towards, and dimly guessing at, the great Chris-

26

tian truths. If the whole burden of the greatest of the pre-Christian religions and of pagan thought is "We cannot see very clearly, but it seems to us that things must be something like this, or else they do not make sense," and if then the Christian revelation comes along and says, "Yes, indeed they are like that. I, who speak with authority, tell you that it is so and that your faint trusting in the larger hope was justified"—that all is surely an argument for Christianity—how strong an argument may be debated—but, in so far as it goes, certainly an argument for Christianity.

Thus the modern scholars tell us that there are most striking parallels between the mythology of Mithraism and the historical claims of Christianity. Indeed we can find the notion of the atonement playing its part in almost every Oriental religion from India to Egypt. Generations and nations that had never heard of Adam and that could not have heard of Christ, yet believed that Man was fallen but not irredeemable. It is most interesting to learn such things but who is it who is expected to be surprised at them? What are they supposed to prove? What do they prove save that Man has at the very depth of his strange nature the double feeling that he is separated from God by a gap of sin, and that yet that gap is not unbridgeable? To the Christian there is nothing surprising in that discovery. It has throughout been his contention that Christian teaching came to answer the most profound and enduring needs of the human heart. It was the Victorian agnostics who said that morality was "plain and simple" and "theology" was invented by priests, who with misplaced ingenuity delighted to confuse mankind with subtle rubbish concerning which sensible people had no cause to bother their heads. It is not we, the Christians, who are surprised to learn that Man had discovered the sad news that he was a miserable sinner before he learnt the glad news that he had been redeemed from his sins.

Again, if it be true, as the learned tell us, that the notion of the Trinity is by no means original to Christianity but can be found, embedded in the theology of the Greeks and the Hindoos and other people, what does this indicate but that the mind of Man, whom God created, in some mysterious but natural way seems to gravitate to Trinitarianism, when it meditates upon His nature,—that man knows not how but he finds a triple nature irretrievably stamped upon the face of all Creation. The more freely we admit that the Christian Doctrine of the Trinity is a mystery, undiscoverable by the unaided natural reason, the more interesting is it to learn of these non-Christian minds, who have caught a glimpse of it. Indeed, we are logically forced to admit, the finger of God was there.

There is, of course, all the difference in the world between the mythological belief and the historical claim. Nobody pretended that it was on such and such a date that Demeter set out to find her stolen child, that Isis started to collect together the limbs of Osiris or that the lament was raised for beautiful Adonis. These were myths—symbols of the way in which creation worked—true of all time and no particular time. And, if you asked their devotees whether they had actually happened, they would hardly have understood what your question meant. But why then did they wish to dress up their philosophical notions in the form of a story? They could not tell. But surely we can tell. Surely the reason was—little though they guessed it—that it was a story—a story to which they could not give a date because it had not yet happened. But on such and such a date in the City of Jerusalem, and when the Emperor Tiberius was on the Roman throne, the Mother of God, like Demeter, was going to be left desolate of her Divine Son. His disciples were to lament for the death of God, as they lamented for Adonis. They would bury him, like Osiris, but, like Persephone, He would come again from the world below, triumphant over death and the lord of light.

People sometimes speak as if the Christian was under some form of obligation to deny any glimmer of discovered truth to thinkers who do not play their part in the Christian story. It is hard to see whence such a notion can have been derived. On the contrary, it is most obvious Christian teaching that all mankind, Christian or pre-Christian, was created by God, and all creation was for a purpose. The pre-Christians had their part to play in witnessing to the greater glory of God. It would be both blasphemy and heresy to think otherwise, and almost a greater blasphemy to think that the generations were created merely to minister to the comfort of their more enlightened descendants by being always wrong. On the contrary, if we believe that the Incarnation was assigned by Almighty God to such a date and such a place, it is but natural to ask why it was so delayed and placed. And, even if this be a question which only a fool can expect to be able fully to answer, nevertheless he is a yet greater fool who for that reason never stays to ask it. Why was it that the Incarnation was delayed? It is perhaps possible to say that God delayed his fuller revelation until Man had come to confess his own insufficiency and to ask for something more. . . .

If we accept the truth of the Incarnation, it follows inevitably in logic that all other events in history derive ultimately their importance only from their relation to that supreme event. We accept this on faith. It must necessarily be so. But of many of history's events we cannot ourselves say what was the part that they played in the divine scheme. So, too, of the precursors of the faith. None knew the full truth of that at which he hinted. The great thinker and poet who hoped humbly that God might give something more had no notion of the full richness with which his request was to be satisfied. And, when we turn from the realm of thought to that of action, we see that it is even more clearly true that those, who built, built more greatly than they knew. God might have become incarnate at any time and at any place, but He did choose to become incarnate in the Roman world in the early days of Rome's world empire. This was then His plan. And, that being so, when a great pre-Christian thinker like Virgil wonders whether it was not for some special destiny that Providence raised up the mighty empire of Rome, we can answer, as Dante answered with confidence, that indeed it was. There might have been a church without a Roman Empire, but without the Roman Empire it could not have shaped itself as it did in secondary details. All those who played their part in building up the Roman power were then, little though they guessed it, playing their part also in building up a greater power even than that of Rome.

(1941)

# IMPLICATIONS OF BELIEF IN
## CHRIST'S DIVINITY

JOHN HENRY CARDINAL NEWMAN

IF we really believe that our Lord is God, we believe all that is meant by such a belief; or, else, we are not in earnest, when we profess to believe the proposition. In the act of believing it at all, we forthwith commit ourselves by anticipation to believe truths which at present we do not believe, because they have never come before us;—we limit henceforth the range of our private judgment in prospect by the conditions, whatever they are, of that dogma. Thus the Arians said that they believed in our Lord's divinity, but when they were pressed to confess His eternity, they denied it: thereby showing in fact that they never had believed in His divinity at all. In other words, a man who really believes in our Lord's proper divinity, believes *implicité* in His eternity.

And so, in like manner, of the whole *depositum* of faith, or the revealed word:—If we believe in the revelation, we believe in what is revealed, however it may be brought home to us, by reasoning or in any other way. He who believes that Christ is the Truth, and that the Evangelists are truthful, believes all that He has said through them, though he has only read St. Matthew and has not read St. John. He who believes in the *depositum* of Revelation, believes in all the doctrines of the *depositum;* and since he cannot know them all at once, he knows some doctrines, and does not know others; he may know only the Creed; but, whether he knows little or much, he has the intention of believing all that there is to believe whenever and as soon as it is brought home to him, if he believes in Revelation at all. All that he knows now as revealed, and all that he shall know, and all that there is to know, he embraces it all in his intention by one act of faith; otherwise, it is but an accident that he believes in this or that, not because it is a revelation. This virtual, interpretative, or prospective belief is called a believing *implicité* and it follows from this, that, granting that the Canons of Councils and the other ecclesiastical documents and confessions, to which I have referred, are really involved in the *depositum* or revealed word, every Catholic, in accepting the *depositum,* does *implicité* accept those dogmatic decisions.

(1870)

REASON acknowledges that it is worthy of God that, in His dealings with man, whether through natural religion or revelation, He should both show Himself and shroud Himself—disclose Himself to men of good-will, who can walk humbly and bravely in His light, and veil Himself from those to whom the revelation abused would prove but a woe. God shows Himself, and He shrouds Himself, alike in His Word and in His Works. "The heavens are His garment;" and it is the office of a garment both to indicate and to conceal what it invests.

AUBREY DE VERE (1887)

# MAN'S MORAL OBLIGATION TO WORSHIP GOD

### THE REV. JOHN A. O'BRIEN

Is there a duty upon all mankind to render homage and worship to God? "No," reply some, "that is a privilege which may be exercised or not according to the whim or option of the individual." True, man is physically free to worship God or not. Likewise the legislation of virtually every State grants its citizens the right to engage in religious worship, but refrains from any enactment compelling them to do so.

The fact is, however, that there exists a stern moral obligation upon every human being to render homage and adoration to God. Why? Since man owes his very existence to the Creator, that man should acknowledge this dependence upon God, proclaim his gratitude to Him, and express by appropriate action God's sovereign and absolute dominion over him. This is a law of nature. This is a dictate of reason. This is a command of God. The failure to make such an acknowledgement constitutes a serious violation of the whole moral order. . . .

We are dependent upon the Creator from Whom all life proceeds. Our dependence is, however, even more absolute and universal. We are dependent upon God for body and soul, for every breath we take, for every movement we make, for every thought of our mind, for every decision of our will, and for every aspiration of our soul. All the faculties of the soul and all the powers of the body come to us as gifts from the Creator's bounty. We are indebted to the divine Omnipotence not only for their existence but for their actions as well.

Withdraw the sustaining power of God for but a moment, and we would cease to be. . . .

Does God really want our homage? What does He gain from it? We are so small. God is so great. Isn't it somewhat presumptuous to think that the God of a million worlds and of the immeasurable spaces would be interested and pleased by our expressions of reverence and love? The answer is simple and direct. God does want our worship and our love. He has proclaimed that time after time in Holy Scripture. This is the burden of the prophets and the focal point in the Saviour's message to mankind. This is the duty proclaimed in the first of the ten commandments, given by God to Moses amidst the thunders on Mount Sinai. "I am the Lord, thy God. . . . Thou shalt not have strange gods before Me."

A doctor of the law asked Christ: "Master, which is the great commandment in the law?"

Jesus replied: "Thou shalt love the Lord thy God with thy whole heart, and with thy whole soul, and with thy whole mind. *This is the greatest and the first commandment.*" . . .

The fact that man is *physically* free to worship God or not, should never be construed to mean that he is morally free to ignore his Creator. We are physically free to commit theft or murder. But we are under a *moral* restraint. So it is with the worshiping of God. While physically free to turn our backs upon Him, we are under the most serious and compelling moral obligation to render to Him the homage of gratitude, worship and love due Him in strict justice.

This truth above all others, needs to be driven home to the people of America. . . .

It is time for the American people to remember that man does not live by bread alone, but by every word that proceedeth from the mouth of God. It is time to remember that they have souls as well as bodies. It is time to remember the God Who has showered such riches, wealth and prosperity upon our land as no other nation in all history has ever known.

(1944)

## "THE BLESSED SEE THE
## ESSENCE OF GOD"

### ST. THOMAS AQUINAS

Since everything is knowable according as it is actual, God, who is pure act without any admixture of potentiality is in Himself supremely knowable. But what is supremely knowable in itself may not be knowable to a particular intellect, because of the excess of the intelligible object above the intellect; as, for example, the sun, which is supremely visible, cannot be seen by the bat by reason of its excess of light.

Therefore some who considered this held that no created intellect can see the essence of God. This opinion, however, is not tenable. For the ultimate beatitude of man consists in the use of his highest function, which is the operation of the intellect. Hence, if we suppose that a created intellect could never see God, it would either never attain to beatitude, or its beatitude would consist in something else besides God; which is opposed to faith. For the ultimate perfection of the rational creature is to be found in that which is the source of its being; since a thing is perfect so far as it attains to its source. Further, the same opinion is also against reason. For there resides in every man a natural desire to know the cause of any effect which he sees. Thence arises wonder in men. But if the intellect of the rational creature could not attain to the first cause of things, the natural desire would remain vain. Hence it must be granted absolutely that the blessed see the essence of God.

(1272)

# THE SPIRITUAL SUICIDE OF ATHEISM

### JACQUES MARITAIN

EVERY will, even the most perverse, desires God without knowing it. They may choose other final ends, decide for other loves, but it is always and everywhere God that they desire under errant forms and despite their own choice.

Atheism, *if it could be lived down to its ultimate roots* in the will, would disorganize and kill the will metaphysically. It is not by accident, it is by a strictly necessary effect, written in the nature of things, that every absolute experience of atheism, if it is conscientiously and rigorously followed, ends by provoking its psychical dissolution, in suicide.

One may cite in witness the heroic and tragic experience of Nietzsche; or the profound intuition of Dostoevsky, as shown in the character of Kirilov. Kirilov precisely incarnates in Dostoevsky's eyes the effort of a man to live atheism down to its metaphysical roots, in its deepest ontological implications. Consider in *The Possessed* the conversation between Kirilov and Peter Stepanovitch, a few minutes before Kirilov's suicide. "If God exists," says Kirilov, "all things depend on Him and I can do nothing outside His will. If He does not exist, all depends on me and I am bound to display my independence. . . . For three years I have been seeking for the attribute of my divinity and I've found it; the attribute of my divinity is independence. That

33

is all I can do to prove in the highest point my autonomy and my new and terrible freedom. For it is very terrible. I shall kill myself to prove my independence and my terrible new freedom." Though he had not read St. Thomas Aquinas Dostoevsky was well aware that the profoundest metaphysical attribute of the Deity is *aseitas*. And it is this attribute which Kirilov, because he is an actual atheist, must manifest in himself:—subordinating his own existence to his own absolute independence.

(1936)

# II

# Man's Origin, Nature,
# and Destiny

*His creation. His biological evolution. His inheritance from
Adam. His dual nature. His soul. God's purpose in creating
man. Man's vocation. Man's happiness. Man's immortality.
Earthly life and eternal ends. Self-knowledge through God.*

SINCE the sciences of civics, sociology and economics deal with individual and collective human welfare, they cannot escape from the
philosophical and religious implications of man's origin, nature and
destiny. If they ignore God, they can never hope to understand adequately the creature which He formed in his own image and likeness,
and whom He sent His own Divine Son to redeem.

PIUS XI (September 21, 1938)

## CREATION

### ETIENNE GILSON

IT is a fact that there is something which is not God. Men, for instance, are not such an eternal act of absolute existence. There are
therefore some beings that are radically different from God at least
in this that, unlike him, they might have existed, and still may, at
a certain time, cease to exist. Thus to be, or exist, is not at all to be,
or exist, as God himself is, or exists. It is therefore not to be an inferior sort of god; rather, it is not to be a god at all. The only possible

35

explanation for the presence of such finite and contingent beings is that they have been freely given existence by "Him who is," and not as parcels of his own existence, which, because it is absolute and total, is also unique, but as finite and partial imitations of what He himself eternally is in his own right. This act whereby "He who is" causes to exist something that, of itself, is not, is what is called, in Christian philosophy, "creation." Whence there follows, that whereas all that which the Christian God begets must of necessity share in the oneness of God, all that which does not share in his oneness must of necessity be not begotten but created.

(1941)

# THE BIOLOGICAL EVOLUTION
# OF MAN

### THE REV. JOHN A. O'BRIEN

WHAT . . . is the outstanding religious truth taught us in Genesis? Simply this: The universe and all living things owe their existence in some way to the creative power of God.

> *The earth is the Lord's and the fulness thereof;*
> *The world and they that dwell therein.*

The detailed processes by which the planets were formed, the hills fashioned, and living creatures brought into being, are part of the legitimate subject-matter of natural science. In other words, Genesis in no text-book of geology, astronomy, botany or zoology or any of the other sciences. Certainly no person who is even slightly familiar with the findings of geology thinks of creation as completed in six literal days.

How about evolution when applied to man? Here a distinction is necessary. In regard to the soul of man, it is the common teaching of theologians that God creates directly and immediately the soul of each individual human being. In regard to the body of man, the evidence of evolution from antecedent animal life is most impressive, and in the judgment of most scientists, overwhelming. The Church leaves the individual free to accept or reject this view in accordance with his judgment as to the weight of evidence behind it. . . .

Evolution fits in admirably with the principle of the divine utilization of secondary causes to attain a purposed end—a principle generally accepted by the greatest theistic thinkers. In simple language this means that God is not to be conceived as constantly interfering with the laws and processes of nature to attain the objectives purposed in the divine plan, but that He endows nature and her laws with a potency and direction adequate to achieve her ends. In accordance with this principle, the concept of biological evolution on our earth and the evolution of the entire universe into a harmonious whole under the reign of natural laws would admirably reflect the unity, power, and wisdom of the Divine Being. . . .

The Bible gives no revelation concerning the subject matter of science but reveals only spiritual and religious truths. Thus it does not encroach in any way upon the freedom and autonomy of the human intellect in its investigation of the structure, organization, and functioning of the material universe and of the laws which are embedded alike in the grain of sand and in the most distant star. Evolution may well serve as a ladder upon which the student of nature climbs to a deeper and more penetrating insight into the creative power of God that unfolds itself in every living creature from the lowest to the highest. . . .

Evolution renders more imperative than ever before the need of a great intelligence to explain the progressive march of life from the lowest to the highest forms. Instead of the crude concept of a Deity working as a master mechanic constantly interfering with natural processes to make needed adjustments, evolution gives us a more sublime concept of a God who operates through the laws of nature which He has established and which hold universal sway throughout the entire universe from the tiny amoeba to the most distant star.

(1946)

Surely no one is bound to admit that Adam's body was *created* in the proper sense of the term. In our rigid interpretation of Genesis, we are accustomed to refer to it as having been *formed* from the earth. The only part of man that is immediately *created* is the human soul. Exponents of the new (evolutionist) opinion call attention to the fact that the decree [of the Biblical Commission in 1909] doesn't specify the *first man*: whence these authors deduce that the decision applies not only to Adam but to all men.

THE REV. P. H. KEHOE, O.S.A. (1937)

37

THE evolution of the body of man from some inferior animal and its subsequent endowment in the body from God of a rational soul is antagonistic to no dogma of faith and may be shown to be in harmony with the teaching of St. Thomas.

THE REV. JOHN A. ZAHM, C.S.C. (1895)

THIS is the difference between a Divine Agent and a human natural agent, that the natural agent is the cause only of the motion, while the Divine Agent is the cause of the being.

ST. THOMAS AQUINAS (1272)

## MAN'S INABILITY TO COMPREHEND
## HIS ORIGIN AND DESTINY

### BLAISE PASCAL

WHAT is man in nature? A nothing in comparison with the Infinite, an All in comparison with the Nothing, a mean between nothing and everything. Since he is infinitely removed from comprehending the extremes, the end of things and their beginning are hopelessly hidden from him in an impenetrable secret; he is equally incapable of seeing the Nothing from which he was made, and the Infinite in which he is swallowed up. . . .

All things proceed from the Nothing, and are borne towards the Infinite. Who will follow these marvellous processes? The Author of these wonders understands them. None other can do so. . . .

And what completes our incapability of knowing things, is the fact that they are simple, and that we are composed of two opposite natures, different in kind, soul and body. For it is impossible that our rational part should be other than spiritual; and if any one maintains that we are simply corporeal, this would far more exclude us from the knowledge of things, there being nothing so inconceivable as to say that matter knows itself. It is impossible to imagine how it should know itself.

(1661)

FOR God the whole fullness of intellectual knowledge is contained in one object, namely the divine essence, in which He knows all things.

Rational creatures achieve a lower and less simple completeness. What He knows in single simplicity they know in many forms. How a less exalted mind needs more ideas is partly illustrated by the fact that people of lower intelligence need to have things explained to them point by point in detail, while those of stronger mind can grasp more from a few hints.

ST. THOMAS AQUINAS (1272)

WHAT is this mysterious being formed of a body that passes away and a soul that lives on? By what law is it governed? . . . The principle that gives life to man, that is, his soul, is placed midway, as it were, between God and things of the corporeal world: when it turns towards God it is enlightened, ennobled, perfected: but when it stoops to creatures it is blinded, degraded, corrupted.

ST. THOMAS AQUINAS (1272)

## MAN'S INHERITANCE FROM ADAM

### PAUL CLAUDEL

THE first man, disobeying his Author, preferred his own will to the Will of God. He preferred himself to God. He preferred his own welfare to that of God. He deliberately broke the pact which united him with his Creator. He acted, so to speak, in a revolutionary manner. He declared his independence. There was divorce. There was a break-up of the initial state of things. God withdrew His impulse, His co-operation, which was Grace; the state of commonweal and in-division with that son who pretends to have evermore attained his majority, is at an end. God gives him back his portion, that "Substance" mentioned in the Parable of the Prodigal Son, to use it at his pleasure. . . .

When man thus sets up in his new estate and condition, exercises his powers, he no longer exercises them in the name of God, with Whom he has rescinded his contract. He exercises them in his own name. Now among his powers is the Creative power. When he calls another being into life, he no longer calls it in the name of God, but calls it in his own name. He no longer calls it forth in the name of something Infinite; he calls it forth in the name of something finite. He no longer calls it forth in the image of God, but in the image of

39

Adam. He cannot give him more than he has himself. He cannot give him life everlasting because it is not his to give, and because he has renounced this inheritance which has no *contingence* with him. He can only give him a finite and transitory life. He cannot give him the impossibility of sinning because that is beyond his powers. He cannot give him the power and the knowledge of God, because they are not his to give. He can but give him finite strength and light, like his own. . . .

Such is Original Sin. It has the character of an inheritance. Man transmits to man an inheritance in which all is oriented naturally towards the good of the *estate* by means of the resources placed at his disposal. Everything is made for a finite man whose end is set within himself and all is oriented towards that end.

But . . . man is not an end in himself; he is not capable of himself providing an end for nature. He has that which permits nature to go right to its end which is God. . . .

God made man His steward over all nature. He gave it to him to cultivate and to husband so that it might yield homage unto Him. He gave it into his hands as the means of his complete self-realisation, and in order to have a sacrifice and a priest. But man, as we have seen by Original Sin, departed from God. God on one side, and man on the other. He claimed the *division,* the immediate surrender of the portion of traditional inheritance which falls to him, and by virtue of which he maintains his own existence in time. When he dies without baptism, without repentance, without reconciliation, without the restoration of his lawful and reasonable position as child of God, he dies as it were consolidated in that personal and independent world which he has made for himself by help of the means put at his disposal. Only after death the scene is changed. The body is gone, has done its work. The soul is naked. The veil which separated it from God is vanished, and the means of self-defense which the outer world gave him, the means of maintaining that state of separation and independence all alike are gone. The soul is now given over defenseless to the gaze of its Creator and its Judge who demands its account. "Render account of thy Stewardship," says the parable. Vainly would she strive to say, "Give me a little time." *Time is no more.* Before the Face of God she enters on a state of things in which time as we know it here below is no more an element. She is in the position of a debtor, eternal insolvent; for the resources which she could use, on which she could draw while the world was at her disposal, fail her now.

There is nothing now that lets her fulfil between Creator and creation her function of intermediary, Priest-Oblator. She no longer provides to God any communication with His work. She no longer is of any use to Him. Let her burn then, like that barren fig-tree which cumbereth the ground. Behold man, all alone, weighted with a debt which he can never more discharge, which God can never cease to claim. Let Him then, as the vulgar saying is in French "take it out of the beast"! He has placed himself in a state of finality. He hinders God. He will not let Him pass. He now has nothing behind him, nothing that can *back* him. . . .

When instead of seeking solely the service of God, the fulfilment of His law, which the Gospel calls "The Kingdom of God," we set ourselves to seek our pleasure or our personal advantage, we are guilty of a *contradiction;* we draw to ourselves, unruly and chance-covetous of their enjoyment, the objects of which our senses give us knowledge and desire, instead of referring them to God to Whom they belong. Thus we modify our moral organism. We turn it back upon ourselves. We make things serve an end, we make them move in a direction, which is not theirs—bent backwards, and there results for us in this life, morally, intellectually, and even physically, all manner of disorder. But when we die, we present to God a creature entirely oriented and worn smooth to its personal advantage, absolutely incapable of giving to God the straightforward service which evermore He exacts, of making normal use of the new surroundings into which it finds itself plunged. God bears upon her, and she can no longer bear upon her surroundings. Then she goes on fire within herself, and since God has made her indestructible, and moreover, *time is no more,* she burns everlastingly without being consumed. Instead of satisfying Love by the fire which makes it light, splendour, spirit, she satisfies justice by that same fire which without end questions, analyses, calcines her, strips her nature bare, shows her her vocation and her failure in the inexorable light of evidence. That is what the Prophet Ezekiel utters when he makes God say to the King of Tyre, meaning Satan: "I will cause to break out in the midst of thee a devouring fire."

(1933)

SOME people believe that the Church is the enemy of the body! Why, she immortalizes it. Even here and now she divinizes it as the "temple of the Holy Ghost." She only forbids it to upset everything by the violence of its instincts, and the abuse of its own powers.

The Church would not subscribe to that verse of Victor Hugo: "My God, how great is the soul and how small is man!"

It is the whole man which is great. The work of God is not divisible.

THE REV. ANTONIN SERTILLANGES, O.P. (1950)

# WHAT IS MAN?

## JACQUES MARITAIN

IN answer to our question, then, "What is man?" we may give the Greek, Jewish and Christian idea of man: man as an animal endowed with reason, whose supreme dignity is in the intellect; and man as a free individual in personal relation with God, whose supreme righteousness consists in voluntarily obeying the law of God; and man as a sinful and wounded creature called to divine life and to the freedom of grace, whose supreme perfection consists of love.

From the philosophical point of view alone the main concept to be stressed here is the concept of human personality. Man is a person, who holds himself in hand by his intelligence and his will. He does not merely exist as a physical being. There is in him a richer and nobler existence; he has spiritual superexistence through knowledge and love. He is thus, in some way, a whole, not merely a part—he is a universe unto himself, a microcosm in which the great universe in its entirety can be encompassed through knowledge. And through love he can give himself freely to beings who are to him, as it were, other selves; and for this relationship no equivalent can be found in the physical world.

If we seek the prime root of all this, we are led to the acknowledgment of the full philosophical reality of that concept of the soul, so variegated in its connotations, which Aristotle described as the first principle of life in any organism and viewed as endowed with supramaterial intellect in man, and which Christianity revealed as the dwelling place of God and as made for eternal life. In the flesh and bones of man there exists a soul which has a greater value than the whole physical universe. Dependent though he may be upon the slightest accidents of matter, the human person exists by virtue of the existence of his soul, which dominates time and death. It is the spirit which is the root of personality.

The notion of personality thus involves that of wholeness and independence. To say that a man is a person is to say that in the depths of his being he is more a whole than a part and more independent than servile. It is this mystery of our nature which religious thought designates when it says that the person is the image of God. A person possesses absolute dignity because he is in direct relationship with the realm of being, truth, goodness, and beauty, and with God, and it is only with these that he can arrive at his complete fulfilment. His spiritual fatherland consists of the entire order of things which have absolute value, and which reflect, in some manner, a divine Absolute superior to the world and which have a power of attraction toward this Absolute. . . .

The same man, the same entire man who is, in one sense, a person or a whole made independent by his spiritual soul, is also, in another sense, a material individual, a fragment of a species, a part of the physical universe, a single dot in the immense network of forces and influences, cosmic, ethnic, historic, whose laws we must obey. His very humanity is the humanity of an animal, living by sense and instinct as well as by reason. Thus man is "a horizon in which two worlds meet." . . .

The chief aspirations of a person are aspirations to freedom—I do not mean that freedom which is free will and which is a gift of nature in each of us, I mean that freedom which is spontaneity, expansion, or autonomy, and which we have to gain through constant effort and struggle. And what is the more profound and essential form of such a desire? It is the desire for inner and spiritual freedom. In this sense Greek philosophy, especially Aristotle, spoke of the independence which is granted to men by intellect and wisdom as the perfection of the human being. And the Gospel was to lift up human perfection to a higher level—a truly divine one—by stating that it consists of the perfection of love, and, as St. Paul put it, of the freedom of those who are moved by the divine Spirit.

(1943)

MAN is multiple and each of us is a separate specimen of mankind; God is in all men; let us have the wisdom to honour man and to respect God in ourselves.

THE REV. ANTONIN SERTILLANGES, O.P. (1920)

# THE ORIGIN OF THE SOUL

RT. REV. MSGR. EDWARD B. JORDAN

PSYCHOLOGY holds that the origin of the soul can be attributed only to direct creation on the part of God; and this conclusion is based on the nature of the soul, which is a simple, spiritual entity, as may be deduced from an analysis of its operations. The Church in her ordinary teaching adheres to this conclusion of philosophy, but she has made no dogmatic pronouncement in the matter. She has indeed defined the creation of the human soul, but she has not defined exactly *how* it is created, though the general tenor of her traditions is in favor of an immediate act of God. This is particularly true with regard to the origin of the first human soul. From the standpoint of metaphysics it is difficult, if not impossible, to see how the soul, so superior in its power to any material agent, could have been brought into existence by any activity short of divine causality acting directly. This is the common opinion of theologians which cannot be refuted by any convincing argument although the Church has not defined it as being *de fide*.

(ca. 1935)

# LIGHT TO THE SOUL FROM GOD

ST. THOMAS AQUINAS

ABOVE the intellectual soul of man we must need suppose a superior intellect, from which the soul acquires the power of understanding. For what is such by participation, and what is mobile, and what is imperfect, always requires the pre-existence of something essentially such, immovable and perfect. Now the human soul is called intellectual by reason of a participation in intellectual power; a sign of which is that it is not wholly intellectual but only in part. Moreover, it reaches to the understanding of truth by arguing, with a certain amount of reasoning and movement. Again, it has an imperfect understanding; both because it does not understand everything, and because in those things which it does understand, it passes from potentiality to act. Therefore, there must needs be some higher intellect, by which the soul is helped to understand. . . . But the separate intellect, according to the teaching of our faith, is God Himself, Who is the soul's

Creator, and only beatitude. . . . Wherefore the human soul derives its intellectual light from Him.

(1272)

THOUGH belief in a spiritual soul does not solve the problem of the supernatural, or take us out of the land of mystery, it enables us in some measure to understand how the God on Whom life and movement, intelligence and free-will all depend, has designed to use the mystery of life and spirit in the natural order as a starting-point for a scale of marvelous life whose lower end may be on earth, but the top of which is hidden in the heavens, far out of the sight of men or angels.

THE MOST REV. JOHN HEDLEY (1904)

SINCE the human soul cannot be produced by the transmutation of matter, it cannot but be produced immediately by God.

ST. THOMAS AQUINAS (1272)

## MAN'S USE OF CREATED THINGS
### ST. IGNATIUS LOYOLA

MAN was created to praise, reverence and serve God Our Lord and by this means to save his soul; and the other things on the face of the earth were created for man's sake, and in order to aid him in the prosecution of the end for which he was created. Whence it follows that Man must make use of them in so far as they help him to attain his end, and in the same way he ought to withdraw himself from them in so far as they hinder him from it. It is, therefore, necessary that we should make ourselves indifferent to all created things, in so far as it is left to the liberty of our free will to do so, and is not forbidden; in such sort that we do not for our part wish for health rather than sickness, for wealth rather than poverty, for honor rather than dishonor, for a long life rather than a short one; and so in all things, desiring and choosing only those which most lead us to the end for which we were created.

(1548)

# MAN: THE BRIDGE BETWEEN VISIBLE
## CREATION AND GOD

THE REV. IGNATIUS W. COX, S.J.

MAN was placed in this world as the crown and masterpiece of visible creation. Man summed up in himself all the elements of the universe. He is called by philosophers a microcosm, that is, a miniature universe. He contains in himself the perfections of vegetative, sensitive, rational life. He converts into the substance of his own being the perfections of non-living matter. Through him, in a certain sense, the universe becomes incarnate, becomes humanized, rational and vocal. . . . Through man as its priest and interpreter, the whole universe gives external glory to its creator. . . .

Man is the bridge between all lower forms of being and God. Through man, all other beings can give God formal glory; through man they can become vocal and rational, through him they can adore, praise and love eternal being and eternal love.

But the solidarity of all things with God by a more marvelous manifestation of creative love is in a still more elevated order. By creation man is an image of God; by grace he is in a certain sense deified, participates in the Divine nature, becomes in an incomprehensible sense a son of God. Thus man, the bridge between the visible creation and God, by the supernatural gift of grace, establishes a new solidarity of the universe with God.

But there is still another solidarity we needs must mention. God, in raising Adam to the destiny of the Beatific Vision and giving him sanctifying grace by which he could reach that destiny, in that act raised all humanity to a supernatural state, to a state above and beyond nature. . . .

The physical solidarity of the universe with God, its dependence upon His creative love continued by His conserving power and providential guidance, is an ironclad necessity. Neither God nor man can alter or break the physical dependence of the universe on God. But the moral solidarity of the universe with God, through man as its priest and interpreter, the solidarity which was to arise by man's loving obedience and service, was by the very gift of free will a voluntary solidarity. The genuineness and willingness of man's obedience and subjection to God, imposed by nature, commanded by grace, and advised by all human principles of decency and honor, must be tried out on the anvil of free will. By the law of solidarity, humanity as well as Adam was put to the test in the trial of Adam. . . .

The sin of Adam shattered the supernatural solidarity between man and God. It shattered also the solidarity between man and the universe. Creatures revolted against man, as man had revolted against God. It shattered likewise the solidarity of man with himself. Immortality was lost; concupiscence raised the forces of rebellion within man's nature. And last of all the fraternal solidarity of man with his fellow man was shattered by the sin of Adam.

As the first sin of man was revolt against God, the second sin of man was revolt of brother against brother. Apostasy of man from God led the way to apostasy of man from his brother-man. That has been the history of human kind ever since. With intellect blinded and will weakened by sin, man fell further and further away from God; the disunion of man with man was more and more emphasized. The primitive revelation of God to man became weaker and weaker, save in the one race chosen by God to preserve it. . . . Disorder reigned supreme for sin is supreme disorder. Men lost the very meaning of life. Philosophers died by their own hands face to face with the emptiness of human existence. Unthinking men lived as animals. "Let us eat, drink, and be merry, for tomorrow we die." Man was not an emergent beast but a fallen son of God. And only God could make him rise again.

When it would seem man could sink no lower in the scale of degradation, when the fulness of time was come, God made ready to lift man up through a second Adam in the fulfillment of His purpose "to restore all things in Christ." . . . The Son of God would take upon Himself human nature, would unite human nature to the divine nature in His own person. God-made-man would show His brother-man how to live the God-life by showing how a God-man lived.

(1933)

# ECHOES OF GOD'S VOICE

### ERIC GILL

SIMPLE people, between whom and God there is no barrier of pride, whose minds are not clouded or confused by the innumerable theories and hypotheses of experimental science, who, moreover, are not the possessors of great material wealth or highly organized by subdivision of labor for the production of wealth for others, such people, such souls, are readily attuned to divine wind. For them it seems most natural and most reasonable that all the things of earth should be analogues of the divine reality, echoes of the divine voice, material counterparts of the divine ideas. And if the trees and rocks, the thunder and the sea, the frightful avidity of animal life and the loveliness of flowers are so many hints of God who made them, how much more obviously are the things of humanity analogues of the things of God!

(1934)

THAT man should be able to know and realize his own insignificance; that he, a being of a day, an atom swallowed in immensity, should be capable of thoughts which wander through eternity, of hopes and loves which touch on infinity, is the most indisputable evidence of his heavenly descent and nature; and we are prepared to find that the profoundest minds have the best insight into the essential littleness of human life, the deepest sentiment of its utter vanity, when it is considered merely as a fact of time.

RT. REV. JOHN LANCASTER SPALDING (1903)

## MAN IS MADE FOR GOD

### DÉSIRÉ JOSEPH CARDINAL MERCIER

WE are made for God, for His glory, and not for our own satisfaction. Reflect on all your surroundings, on yourselves; Not a single being that falls within our experience is in possession of what is necessary for its own proper subsistence. Not one is self-sustaining; all have their day of birth, their transitory evolution and their day of destruction.

Hence, one or other of two alternatives: Either *all* beings, without a *single* exception, are marked by this essential contingency, are devoid of a reason within themselves for their existence; in which case we are face to face with an unavoidable contradiction. For, in point of fact each of these things is in actual possession of existence: if he is not himself the source of this existence, he must have received it from some other being: but if all are in the same case all alike must have received it: Consequently no single one of them could have been the first to give it to another: and hence the intrinsic contradiction involved in the actual existence of such a being,—a contradiction which repeats itself to our perplexed intelligence for every single contingent being in the universe around us.

Or else we take the other alternative and affirm that every contingent being that exists owes its existence to some cause exterior to itself; that consequently there exists, outside and independent of contingent beings, a Being that is not contingent; a Being whose nature is *altogether different* from that of contingent beings; a Being who has in Himself the reason of His existence and Himself sustains it, intrinsically and inalienably. Such in a word is the Being we call the *necessary* Being, and it is easy to understand that this Being should have called into existence all contingent beings; all those creatures whose very contingency has served to reveal to us the existence and perfection of their Author. For, by the very necessity of His being, He is necessarily perfect, almighty—as may be seen from a simple analysis of the concept of the "necessity of being," "self-subsistence," or "aseity."

Now it is clear that God, the Creator of all things other than Himself, could not have had any other motive other than Himself in creating them: Himself, His glory, the outward manifestation of His perfections to our intelligence; nor any other intention than that of subordinating our wills to the law of His love and to the duty of respect for His Holy Will. "The Lord hath made all things for himself." This must be the key of our highest intentions and the supreme purpose we must set before our minds; this we must aim at; this we must wish for and love with all our hearts and manfully strive to attain. This alone is what we were made for; nor could there be any other end for the existence of an intelligent creature.

(1912)

## MAN'S HAPPINESS

### ST. THOMAS AQUINAS

IT is impossible for any created good to constitute man's happiness. For happiness is the perfect good, which lulls the appetite altogether; else it would not be the last end, if something yet remain to be desired. Now the object of the will, i.e. of man's appetite, is the universal good; just as the object of the intellect is the universal true. Hence it is evident that naught can lull man's will, save the universal good. This is to be found, not in any creature, but in God alone; because every creature has goodness by participation. Wherefore God alone can satisfy the will of man, according to the words of *Psalms* 102:5: Who satisfieth desire with good things. Therefore God alone constitutes man's happiness.

(1272)

## MAN CAN ONLY SUBSERVE GOD

### ALFRED NOYES

IT is true, of course, that on our own planet, there are certain creatures which do appear to subserve others; but all these creatures are at least conscious of one another's existence, while Man, whose range of observation is incomparably wider, can discover nothing on the entire planet which his incomparably higher development (including his capacity to think or dream of God) can possibly subserve. Further than this, if he looks out through space to distances far beyond the little circle which his physical life or death could possibly affect in any way whatsoever, all the apparatus of his Science is still utterly unable to discover anything, between his own intellect and the Mind of God, which his existence or obliteration could possibly subserve.

(1934)

## MAN'S MORAL PILGRIMAGE

### DÉSIRÉ JOSEPH CARDINAL MERCIER

THERE is within us a mysterious something that impels the soul towards abiding realities; that lifts it above material things to heights from whence we can perceive the invisible and love that which experience cannot grasp. What is this free and immaterial soul of ours, ever seeking after the Infinite,—what but a wanderer, yearning for Him who having launched it on the billows of time, unceasingly attracts it towards Himself?

By right, the moral life of man is a circular movement of the free soul—come out from God and to Him returning. In point of fact, it is the passage from a state of damnation, through a period of free effort, to a state of perfection. . . .

The two great master minds of the ages of faith, the one in the

*Summa Theologica,* the other in the *Divina Comedia,* have described the passing of man through the trial-state of time. . . .

This general conception pervades all ascetic theology; the masters of the spiritual life divide into three stages the moral pilgrimage of the soul towards its end: the *purgative* way, in which the soul is cleansed from the stains of sin; the *illuminative* way, in which it progresses in enlightenment and virtue; the *unitive* way, in which it resolutely clings to God with full conformity to His Will in all things.

(1912)

# EACH MAN HAS A PARTICULAR
# VOCATION

## THE REV. DON LUIGI STURZO

THE idea of vocation is intrinsic to our personality. Each one of us has an inherent finality. Our development, our welfare, the full realization of our ego and of its modes of expansion, constitute this inward finality. Since each has his own particular way of knowing himself, loving himself and seeking the fulfilment of his being, he may well be said to have a particular vocation, a goal towards which an inner voice urges him in the midst of the difficulties in which he finds himself, of his surroundings, of the position he has attained.

The particular end of each man cannot exist outside the orbit of the ends connatural to man, which can be summed up as the quest for the good. The more the particular end of each is conformable to nature, the more it contributes to his good. Under this aspect, a man's personal vocation would be his mode of achieving the good, according to his inclinations, qualities and possibilities. Among the myriad particular ways, each man finds those best fitted to him and makes a choice conditioned by circumstances in varying degrees. He who is best able to overcome cramping or adverse circumstances (which have their uses in promoting the growth of conquering energies) will be best able to decide his own destiny. Others, on the contrary, will submit with more or less resignation to the course of events. . . .

If man were an illimitable and self-creating being, whose "I" was immersed in the universal spirit, the vocation of each man would be only the apparent phenomenon of a single reality. There would indeed not be vocations but determinations, even if these were called, as they are by idealist philosophers, auto-determinations. Man is, on the contrary, a finite, bounded, temporal creature, and he is at the same time an indestructible spiritual entity. On the one hand he realizes himself and is self-realizing; on the other, he is helped to realize himself, to overcome his limitations, to create his own happiness. He is called to this by the creative voice of God; following this voice he achieves his own perfection. . . .

I do not deny that there is a natural vocation, an intermediate end that may become the means for a further end. What I do deny is that this natural vocation is definitive and conclusive. The quest for individual welfare, in the purely natural field, is either subordinated to the ethico-religious conception or else it is an illusion; actually, the way leads from diversion to perversion. . . .

The natural vocation is a call to life, which cannot be ignored, and which impels us to work and to make conquest of ourselves and of the surrounding world. Our personality is formed and characterized by a vocation (the inner voice), which becomes a finality (the good to be attained). It is a necessary premise for the fulfilment in us of the supernatural life to which we are raised. Just as the supernatural life is not realized in the concrete save in man as a living individual, so the supernatural vocation in the concrete renews and subordinates to itself the natural vocation.

The supernatural vocation is as universal as the natural one. We can view the two, under a certain aspect, as a single vocation to the good to be attained by man in the twofold order, natural and supernatural. For the true, sole good, that which can satisfy us, is God alone; all other goods are good only insofar as they partake of the Sovereign Goodness.

(1943)

# MAN'S ETERNAL VOCATION

### THE REV. ANTONIN SERTILLANGES, O.P.

THE paradox of man is entirely summed up in these three statements: matter penetrated by spirit; an earthly life called even in the present to become heavenly; a temporal destiny bound to an eternal vocation. And man being thus constituted, the paradox of our era lies in his only taking account of one part of himself—the lower part—in orienting himself towards matter at the expense of spirit, in organizing a wholly earthly life, and denying or totally neglecting his eternal vocation.

But destiny remains. One cannot change the Creator's plan; one can frustrate it only at the expense of man himself. And that is indeed what is happening. Effort to fill our lives with satisfactions leave us gasping for breath, exasperated by the contest, disgusted, and ungratified. The desire to divert us, in the pleasant sense of that term, throws us into the Pascalian "diversion": to wit, forgetfulness of what we are, folly, and moral, if not actual, suicide. . . .

According to St. Thomas Aquinas, the moral virtues have no other office than that of "properly fulfilling the tendencies of our nature." This is a declaration to astound those who believe in some sort of moral or religious "regimentation." But what is our nature? That is the crux of the matter.

To content ourselves with the lower nature is to belittle ourselves; to yield to it is to be lost. All our deepest cravings go beyond such a truncated concept of life, and beyond it lie all the objects of our aspirations, our true atmosphere; consequently, our end.

If, then, our hopes for the future consist only in being loyal to the best that is in us and to the realities identified with this, I can understand that philosopher who, on being asked what he was dreaming about, answered: "About waking up."

(1950)

# THE HIGHEST GOOD AND
# MAN'S HAPPINESS

## THE REV. J. A. MC WILLIAMS, S.J.

By the very fact of doing a morally good act man attains the highest purpose for which both he and the whole world were created. There is nothing greater than even God can do than what is right and good, and that, whether done by man or God, is what is meant by the glory of God. Every man who does a morally good act (and everybody does thousands of them) attains by such an act the highest level of all good and value. It is to be noted that his own final happiness, however, is not to be identified with those acts, but (if he perseveres) *results* from them.

God could not create a rational being without putting in that being an ineradicable desire for perpetual happiness; that nature and that desire are inseparable. That happiness is therefore the intrinsic purpose of my being, it is to benefit me personally. My extrinsic purpose, as we have just seen, is to perform morally good acts, which are good in themselves, whether I am personally benefitted by them or not. My role is to lead a morally good life, and to this I am so bound that nothing whatever can ever serve as a valid excuse for doing what I know to be wrong. But if my extrinsic purpose is absolutely obligatory, then my intrinsic purpose must be promoted by these same acts; otherwise there would be a contradiction in my nature. I therefore know that God wishes me to be perpetually happy and that he wishes that happiness to result from a morally good life. So inseparable are these two that even if I were capable, which I am not, of renouncing all desire of happiness, it would be wrong so to wish, because that would be going against the will of God implanted in my very nature. Nor should I think that once perpetual beatitude has been granted me I will cease from moral good; quite the contrary, that beatitude will guarantee the continued opportunity to enjoy the highest function of life, the secure exercise and fruition of the highest good. . . .

It seems imperative that we review our concept of what precisely morality is. Philosophers do not, at first thought, seem to differ much in their answers to this question. All agree that the morally good life is the supreme and most lasting good to which human nature can attain. But some philosophers give only an incomplete answer as to what the good is. John Dewey, for instance, leaves the impression that it consists in the agreeable emotions which we experience in co-operating with the world in which we live. That answer is incomplete, for although emotional enjoyment usually attends a virtuous life, it often does so in a very minor role; the virtuous man realizes that there is something *more* at stake than his personal feelings or even the feelings of the whole community. And while he is eager to co-operate with his fellow men he first demands to know what end the co-operation is intended to achieve. The co-operation is not good unless the end is good. If the end is, as Dewey implies, merely the emotional gratification of the group, that is only saying again that agreeable feelings are the highest good man can know. But then every gunman and every tyrant could claim that he is a paragon of perfect morals because he finds his emotional enjoyment in getting co-operation by means of a gun. It is to be feared that there is too much of this kind of "philosophy" in the world today.

Dewey certainly does not intend anything like tyranny or gangster-dom. He believes that if men were relieved of the constraint of meta-physics and religion their natural good-heartedness would flower and no one would enjoy doing anything unless others enjoyed it too. That is putting a good deal of trust in the human animal. For my part I, too, trust human nature. We all do. But we trust it because it *has* a certain amount of metaphysics and religion in its make-up. As a matter of fact and by their very nature men do not always act on the principle that their feelings are the final arbiter of right and wrong, they act on that principle only when they want an *excuse* for acting *against* their metaphysics and their religion. Without a modicum of these latter you could never trust any man. I don't want to say that our feelings are always against our true good. But unfortu-nately they sometimes are. And it is then that we must either ignore them or bring them into line with the higher good. This is only say-ing that in our reflective moments we realize that mere temporal prosperity and enjoyment are not the supreme good, we somehow desire *more* than that, and we are convinced that unless we aim at the more we cannot have the temporal enjoyment with any degree of security. . . .

Let those who complain about the restraint of the moral law re-member that the vast majority of good things that men do they are not compelled to do by any moral obligations. Moral obligations stop at a certain level, the obligation to do right stops at the point where we can say: the opposite would not be wrong.

But though the obligation stops there the moral good goes right on to any height you choose. Thus we say that a citizen who is called by the law to the defense of his country is obliged to go, he does wrong, is a "slacker," if he refuses. But a person who is not called, and never will be called, may still be volunteer; there is no obliga-tion to volunteer, nor is it wrong to decline to volunteer. The volunteer sees that there is good even beyond obligation; and after being sworn into the service, may again volunteer for special tasks. There is no restraint in the moral law except the restraint of avoiding evil. Beyond that it is *ad lib*. And although a man truly gives when he avoids evil, because he is acting freely, yet the truest giving is when he does good without being under the penalty of avoiding evil. Such giving is the joy of living, and most of our lives is made up of that sort of good.

What I am saying is not that the joy of life is in following our impulses—or our "impulsions," as Dewey calls them. Impulses are not free. It is good to have them. Nature supplies many, some come from the physical environment in which we live, some are the result of training, most of them come from the habits we have freely built up within ourselves. But impulses when they come, come unfreely, they wouldn't be impulses if we chose at the moment which ones we should have. The joy of living consists in the fact that after the impulses come we still can choose which ones to give the "go" sign to, and how much energy to put into the "go."

(1942)

## SOUL'S IMMORTALITY GIVES
## MEANING TO LIFE

### DÉSIRÉ JOSEPH CARDINAL MERCIER

As succeeding generations of men are laid to rest in the dust from which they sprang, the souls that for a time breathed life into them escape destruction and go forth laden with their works, good or bad, to take their appointed places in a world that knows no end. If, as materialists argue, the whole of man were only matter, subject consequently to total dissolution, the world with its actual social organization such as we see it, and such as we all wish to maintain it, would be simply meaningless. If there be no power above me, and no hereafter for me, if the few years I spend here in life are all that belong to me, I should be foolish indeed not to make the most of them for my own individual interests! . . .

A French scholar, Monsieur Félix Le Dantec, an *enfant terrible* of the materialist school, candidly acknowledges the logic of our conclusion. But fortunately, he adds, the greater number of materialists shrink from putting into practice these deductions from their own doctrines; fortunately, humanity does not act up to such beliefs. But why "fortunately"? we ask. If materialism be true, if it be dictated by science, why should its failure be desirable?

56

Those who thus rejoice at this want of logic in the human animal, those whose cherished ideal is a solidarity of so-called *superior* interests which they place above what they call (one wonders why), the *baser* appetites of man: those men I maintain are honest men, good men almost in spite of themselves, men who have retained their consciousness of a principle distinct from matter and superior to it, a principle whose aspirations soar above the perishable and rest only in the immutable, only in the absolute. . . .

Each one of us is conscious of a tendency within him, whereby he aspires towards something better, truer, nobler, more beautiful than aught he sees around him. Now, either these urgent, irresistable, universal aspirations are vain—in which case we must conclude that this human machine, this masterpiece of the visible universe, is a wretched failure; and abandon that "belief in order" upon which the certitude of science is based;—or else we must admit that above the realities which come within our experience, and are true, good, or beautiful in a certain degree, there is a Perfection complete, absolute, unshared and self-sufficing, of which the things around us are but faint and short-lived imitations. . . .

The morality of duty implies freedom in the moral agent. Duty performed without any reference to self-interest is the highest ideal to which man can attain. But then what will be the result? Will those heroic souls who have most completely laid aside all self interest be left without reward? That would be incredible. There must, therefore, be a Higher Power to sanction the disinterested accomplishment of duty, and to reward virtue by happiness. And since in the course of our life here below virtue is not duly rewarded, there must be a future life in which a Sovereign Ruler completes His sanction of the moral order by giving to each according to his deserts. . . .

Think on this, our Divine Master used to say to His disciples, take it to heart—*videte,*—your souls are destined for immortal life. On the glow of the flame that will one day consume the generations of men and their works; on the last awful upheaval of the earth and the heavens; on the spectacle of all the great catastrophes recorded in history; on all that let your thoughts be often and deeply fixed. Picture to yourselves the Last Judgment and the final rendering of accounts to Him who will judge both the living and the dead. "Take ye heed, watch and pray."

(1912)

57

# EARTHLY LIFE ORDERED TO
# ETERNAL ENDS

## ETIENNE GILSON

CHRISTIANITY had [in the Middle Ages] put the end of man beyond the limits of this earthly life; it had affirmed at the same time that a creative God allows nothing to fall outside the designs of His providence; it therefore had to admit also that everything, both in the life of individuals and in the life of societies of which individuals form a part, is ordered to this supraterrestrial end. Now the first condition of such ordering is that there should be a regular unfolding of events in time, and first of all, of course, that there should be a time. This time is no abstract framework within which things endure, or, at any rate, it is not only that. Essentially it is a certain mode of existence proper to contingent things, unable to realize themselves all at once in the permanence of a stable present. God is Being, and there is nothing which He can become because there is nothing which He is not; change and duration have therefore no existence for Him. Created things, on the contrary, are finite participations of Being; fragmentary so to speak, always incomplete, they act in order to fulfill their own being, and therefore they change and consequently endure. That is why St. Augustine considers the universe a kind of unfolding, a *distension,* which imitates in its flowing forth the eternal present and total simultaneity of the life of God.

Man's state, indeed, is neither that of God nor that of things. He is not simply carried forward on an ordered stream of becoming like the rest of the physical world; he is aware that he stands in the midst of it and grasps in thought the flux of becoming itself. Successive instants, that would otherwise simply arrive and pass away into the void, are gathered up and held in his memory, which thus constructs a duration, just as the sense of sight gathers up dispersed matter into a framework of space. By the mere fact that he remembers man partially redeems the world from the stream of becoming that sweeps it along, and redeems himself along with it. In thinking the universe, and in thinking ourselves, we give birth to an order of being which is a kind of intermediary between the mere instantaneity of the being of bodies and the eternal permanence of God. But beneath the frail stability of his memory, which would founder into nothingness in its turn did not God support and stabilize it, man himself passes away. Wherefore, far from ignoring the fact that all things change, Christian thought felt almost to anguish the tragic character of the instant. For the instant alone is real; here it is that thought gathers up the debris saved from the shipwreck of the past, herein live all its anticipations of the future; nay, it is here that it simultaneously constructs this past and this future, so that this precarious image of a true permanence that memory extends over the flux of matter, is itself borne on by that flux, and with it all that it would save from collapse into pure nought. Thus the past escapes death only in the instant of a thought that endures, but the in-stans is something that at once stands in the present and presses on toward the future where likewise it will find no resting-place; and at last an abrupt interruption will close a history and fix a destiny for ever.

Thus for all mediaeval thinkers there existed men that pass in view of an end that does not pass. But this was not all. In proclaiming the "good news" the Gospels not only promised the just an individual beatitude, but also pronounced their entry into a Kingdom, that is to say, a society of the righteous, united by the bonds of their common beatitude. The preaching of Christ was early understood as the promise of a perfect social life, and the constitution of this society came to be looked upon as the last end of the Incarnation. Every Christian realized therefore that he was called to enter as a member into a far vaster community than any human one to which he belonged already. A stranger to every nation, but recruiting its members from all nations, the City of God will gradually build itself up while the world lasts, and the world itself has no other reason for lasting than the expectation of its final fulfillment. In this celestial, that is to say invisible and mystical, city, men are the stones, and God is the Architect. Under His direction it grows, towards it tend all the laws of His providence, to assure its advent He made Himself Legislator, expressly promulgating the divine law He had already written on men's hearts, and carrying that law beyond what the due order of a merely human society would require, but which would be an insufficient basis for a society in which man should dwell with God.

(1940)

59

# SELF-KNOWLEDGE THROUGH CONFRONTATION WITH GOD

## DIETRICH VON HILDEBRAND

THE only fruitful self-knowledge, and the only true one, is that which grows out of man's self-confrontation with God. We must first look at God and His immeasurable glory, and then put the question, "Who art Thou, and who am I?" We must speak with St. Augustine: "Could I but know thee, I shouldst know myself." It is only in recognition of our metaphysical situation, only in awareness of our destiny and our vocation that we can become truly cognizant of ourselves. Only the light of God and His challenge to us can open our eyes to all our shortcomings and deficiencies, impressing upon us the discrepancy between what we ought to be and what we are. Contemplation of one's own self in this light is animated by a profound earnestness; it is vastly different from all species of a "neutral" and purely psychological self-analysis. He who seeks for self-knowledge in that true sense of the word regards his own nature, not as an unchangeable datum or a curiosity to be studied without any implication of responsibility, but as a thing which demands to be changed, and for whose qualities and manifestations he is accountable. Self-knowledge in this sense presupposes the readiness to change. We take an interest in what we are *because* we are determined to become "new men" in Christ. Here is no place for idle curiosity, nor for egoistic fixation of oneself as a paramount theme. It is *for the sake of* God that we would become better men; and because we would become so we enquire about our present state and condition. That basic attitude of a solemn confrontation with God—the motif which in a unique way pervades the Liturgy of the Church—is fitted, rather than any other, to make us sensitive to values and to present us with a picture of our defects stripped of any illusions. It is an attitude which we cannot maintain while playing, at the same time, the part of unconcerned spectators. It presupposes a penitent disposition; and in its turn, necessarily gives birth to contrition: in the *Confiteor* it finds its supreme expression.

Self-knowledge thus understood, as contrasted with its false counterpart, is not destructive but fruitful. Because it is founded in our readiness to change, it implies the discovery of any defect of ours to be the first step towards its elimination. However painfully the revelation of the patches of darkness in our souls may affect us, it will always lack the discouraging and depressing effect which in the context of mere natural self-knowledge would attend disagreeable revelations. For, referring all truth to God Who is the prime source and the epitome of Truth as such, we shall derive happiness from the knowledge of any important truth, however painful its content may be, since by the very fact of its possession we progress one step nearer towards God.

(1948)

# III

# Man's Freedom, Duties,
# and Potentialities

*Free will. Man and natural law. God's challenge to man. Man's power and freedom. Man's duty. Man's work in the world. Man's potentialities. Man's duty to live. Religion's help to man.*

OF what use would it be to study the ways of God and of the spirit, if in practice one were to choose the way of perdition and to submit supinely to the god of the flesh? . . .

The root of modern evils and of their baneful consequences is not, as in pre-Christian times or in regions yet pagan, invincible ignorance of the eternal destiny of man and of the principal means of attaining it; rather it is lethargy of the spirit, weakness of the will, and coldness of heart.

PIUS XII, (February 10, 1952)

## MAN'S SELF-MADE SPIRITUAL
## PERFECTION

JOHN HENRY CARDINAL NEWMAN

THOUGH man cannot change what he is born with, he is a being of progress with relation to his perfection and characteristic good. Other beings are complete from their first existence, in that line of excellence which is allotted to them; but man begins with nothing realized (to use the word), and he has to make capital for himself by the exercise of those faculties which are his natural inheritance. Thus he gradually advances to the fullness of his original destiny. Nor is this progress mechanical, nor is it of necessity; it is committed to the personal efforts of each individual of the species; each of us has the prerogative of completing his inchoate and rudimental nature, and of developing his own perfection out of the living elements with which his mind began to be. It is his gift to be the creator of his own sufficiency; and to be emphatically self-made. This is the law of his being, which he cannot escape; and whatever is involved in that law he is bound, or rather he is carried on, to fulfil.

(1870)

# FREE WILL NECESSARY TO
# RATIONAL CREATURES

### ST. THOMAS AQUINAS

MAN has free choice, or otherwise counsels, exhortations, commands, prohibitions, rewards, and punishments would be in vain. In order to make this evident, we must observe that some things act without judgment, as a stone moves downwards; and in like manner all things which lack knowledge. And some act from judgment, but not from a free judgment; as brute animals. For the sheep, seeing the wolf, judges it to be a thing to be shunned, from a natural and not a free judgment; because it judges, not from deliberation, but from natural instinct. And the same thing is to be said of any judgment in brute animals. Now man acts from judgment, because by his apprehensive power he judges that something should be avoided or sought. But because this judgment, in the case of some particular act, is not from a natural instinct, but from some act of comparison in the reason, therefore he acts from free judgment and retains the power of being inclined to various things. For reason in contingent matters may follow opposite courses, as we see in dialectic syllogisms and rhetorical arguments. Now particular operations are contingent, and therefore in such matters the judgment of reason may follow opposite courses, and is not determinate to one. And in that man is rational, it is necessary that he have free choice.

(1272)

# THE NECESSITY TO RECOGNIZE
## MAN'S FREE WILL

### THE REV. J. A. MC WILLIAMS, S.J.

THE overseer, the pilot, the lookout in man is intelligence, a power not possessed by any other creature in the visible world. And there is in man an operator that is its own master, his free will. Everything else in the world is necessitated to do what it does, everything except man is under the doom of antecedent necessity; man alone, in his human acts, is exempt, man alone is free. I do not mean that man finds no obstacles in his path; there are many obstacles and many of them are unjustly put there. Nor do I mean that man is exempt from responsibility for his acts, he is responsible for whatever he does freely, but that is only *because* he acts freely.

Let us be clear about what freedom means. There are three kinds of freedom: freedom from physical restraint, freedom from legal restriction and freedom of will. The first is what the man in prison lacks, he is not physically free to move about as he pleases. And all of us are hindered by certain forces of nature; I am constrained by the force of gravity from walking on the clouds. The second freedom is that of independence, and is what the United States celebrates on the Fourth of July. It means that there is no human sovereignty over us, dictating what we shall do. Not only independent nations enjoy such freedom, but the better governments permit as much of it to the individual citizen as is consonant with the public good. Thus, though the citizen is not free to disregard the traffic laws, he is otherwise free to use the highways, and he may order what he pleases for lunch. Both these freedoms are external, and man has a right to as much of them as the public welfare will permit. But external freedom is not what we mean by freedom of the will.

Freedom of the will is internal. Free will means that man is not, in everything he does, predetermined by his circumstances and antecedents. Everything else in the world *is* predetermined that way, but not man. A man can choose his own objectives, he can make up his own mind, his mind is not already made up for him by his ancestors or by the world about him. In many things he can and does decide for himself what he intends to do.

This unfortunately complicates the task of the social and individual betterment of man. If man were unfree, all you would have to do would be to set him like a clock, and he would go straight thereafter. But any system of social betterment which does not take into account that the individual man is possessed of a free will leaves out the biggest factor in the situation, it is ignoring the master of the revels, it is reckoning without the host, and will sooner or later find itself out in the cold. Man is not a mere shuttle in the loom of "progress"; he wants to weave his own pattern of life and is not content to be hurled about by some machine. Many of us, it is true, could name governments that proceed on the principle that man has no free will, and so, logically enough, deny him the other two freedoms as well. But such governments are inhuman, and they are inhuman because they are based on an inhuman philosophy.

Further, if man has no free will, then all schemes for his individual and social betterment are idle dreams, for in that case neither the ordinary citizen nor the man at the top can do anything except what he is foredoomed to do. To deny free will is to make mankind nothing but driftwood on the inexorable river of fate, and how we jostle one another is beyond our power to help. If we dream of better things, even our dreams are predetermined. If we pretend to experiment, it is only a pretense and we are no more experimenting than flotsam or jetsam tossed by the waves is experimenting on where to go next. We can only watch and see what happens. Thus the edict of materialistic science banishing free will at one fell swoop destroys science itself, and philosophy and all hope of social betterment. In such a scheme of things it is all the same whether I drown a man or rescue him from drowning; either way I had to do what I did. In such a scheme, to let the farmer live by the fruit of his labor is in no way different from taking his harvest away and letting him starve; what I do I cannot help doing, for I was predetermined to do it; there is no right, no wrong; you get what you get, and there never was so much as a possibility of your getting anything else.

The question is simply this: Is man necessitated in everything he does, or are there any acts of his, even though the number be small, in which he is not necessitated? Unprejudiced philosophy answers that there are many acts in which he exercises his own free choice. That answer agrees with the conviction of mankind, even with the conviction of the materialistic philosopher when he is not talking materialistic philosophy. Man has a free will, and all men know it. . . .

The practical application of these truths is that you cannot treat man as a mere machine, or a part of a machine. If you put a part of a machine into place it will act as its connections with other parts determine it to act. Man likes to exercise his free will. Although, as we have seen, free will is not the same thing as freedom from restraint, the one nevertheless clamors for the other, and if you force men into situations that do violence to their human nature, you may well expect that somewhere along the line they will revolt. Some one will decide that he does not care for life under such conditions, some one will raise the cry, "Give me liberty or give me death!"

In our machine age mankind first organized the forces of nature into a machine, then the forces of nature turned around and organized mankind into a machine. But do not blame that on the machine, blame it on the philosophy that has been making the world ring with the doctrine that man *is* a machine, and nothing more, that he has no free will, that he is predetermined in all that he does, that he is altogether the victim of his environment and heredity, that he is pre-doomed to whatever part he plays in this world. In such philosophy there is place for neither justice nor injustice, man is no more than a wheel or a crank-shaft, something to be driven by the industrial or political engine; nay, the very man at the wheel, so we are told, is not driving the engine, but is driven by some larger engine. Such philosophy is inhuman, and it is inhuman because it denies the very things that make men human, make them different from the rest of the world. The only sound philosophical basis of social and economic betterment is the recognition of the individual human being as possessed of intelligence and free will and destined to another life than this. Until there is general recognition of these distinctive factors in the human being, there will be no social uplift but only a deeper degradation of man.

By recognition I mean an intellectual conviction and rational esteem of these truths, I do not mean merely stirring up our emotions about man as merely a more sensitive sort of animal. . . .

By his intelligence and free will and his consequent appreciation of things eternal, man rises superior to the rest of the world. By this he knows the role he is to play, the part for which he is cast. His gifts make him the only moral being in the world. He must therefore control his dealings with the rest of nature, control even the sentiments of his own heart, for his gifts make him master not alone of the outer world but, what is more wonderful still, master of himself and of his own destiny.

(1942)

# MAN AND NATURAL LAW

### JACQUES MARITAIN

WE admit that there is a human nature, and that this human nature is the same in all men. I am taking it for granted that we also admit that man is a being gifted with intelligence, who, as such, acts with an understanding of what he is doing, and therefore with the power to determine for himself the ends which he pursues. On the other hand, possessed of a nature, or an ontologic structure which is a locus of intelligible necessities, man possesses ends which necessarily correspond to his essential constitution and which are the same for all— as all pianos, for instance, whatever their particular type and in whatever spot they may be, have as their end the production of certain attuned sounds. If they do not produce these sounds they must be tuned, or discarded as worthless. But since man is endowed with intelligence and determines his own ends, it is up to him to put himself in tune with the ends necessarily demanded by his nature. This means that there is, by the very virtue of human nature, an order or a disposition which human reason can discover and according to which the human will must act in order to attune itself to the essential and necessary ends of the human being. The unwritten law, or natural law, is nothing more than that. . . .

What I mean is that every being has his own natural law, as well as it has its own essence. Any kind of thing produced by human industry has, like the stringed instrument that I brought up a moment ago, its own natural law, that is, the *normality of its functioning,* the proper way in which, by reason of its specific construction, it demands to be put into action. . . .

Any kind of thing existing in nature, a plant, a dog, a horse, has its own natural law, that is, the *normality of its functioning,* the proper way in which, by reason of its specific structure and specific ends, it *"should"* achieve fulness of being either in its growth or in its behavior. . . .

When I said a moment ago that the natural law of all beings existing in nature is the proper way in which, by reason of their specific nature and specific ends, they *should* achieve fulness of being in their behavior, this very word *should* had only a metaphysical meaning (as we say that a good or normal eye *"should"* be able to read letters on a blackboard from a given distance). The same word *should* starts

67

to have a *moral meaning,* that is, to imply moral obligation, when we pass the threshold of the world of free agents. Natural law for man is *moral* law, because man obeys or disobeys it freely, not necessarily, and because human behavior pertains to a particular, privileged order which is irreducible to the general order of the cosmos and tends to a final end superior to the immanent common good of the cosmos. . . .

In its ontological aspect, natural law is an *ideal order* relating to human actions, a *divide* between the suitable and unsuitable, the proper and the improper, which depends on human nature or essence and the unchangeable necessities rooted in it. . . .

To sum up, let us say that natural law is something both *ontological* and *ideal.* It is something *ideal,* because it is grounded on the human essence and its unchangeable structure and the intelligible necessities it involves. Natural law is something *ontological,* because the human essence is an ontological reality, which moreover does not exist separately, but in every human being, so that by the same token natural law dwells as an ideal order in the very being of all existing men. . . .

Natural law is not a written law. Men know it with greater or less difficulty, and in different degrees, running the risk of error here as elsewhere. The only practical knowledge all men have naturally and infallibly in common as a self-evident principle, intellectually perceived by virtue of the concepts involved, is that we must do good and avoid evil. This is the preamble and the principle of natural law; it is not the law itself. Natural law is the ensemble of things to do and not to do which follow therefrom in *necessary* fashion. That every sort of error and deviation is possible in the determination of these things merely proves that our sight is weak, our nature coarse, and that innumerable accidents can corrupt our judgment. . . .

Natural law is an unwritten law. Man's knowledge of it has increased little by little as man's moral conscience has developed. The latter was at first in a twilight state. . . . The knowledge men have had of the unwritten law has passed through more diverse forms and stages than certain philosophers or theologians have believed. The knowledge which our own moral conscience has of this law is doubtless still imperfect, and very likely it will continue to develop and to become more refined as long as humanity exists. Only when the Gospel has penetrated to the very depth of human substance will natural law appear in its flower and its perfection.

(1951)

# GOD'S CHALLENGE TO MAN

### AUBREY DE VERE

It is the whole vast and manifold being of man—his mind and his heart, his conscience and his practical judgment, his soul and his spirit—the Divine Truth challenges. The sceptic, when proud of his scepticism, insists upon the mighty and manifold problem being presented to his logical faculty alone, and wonders why he can make so little of it. In place of dilating his being to embrace the largest of Truths, he contracts it to a lance's point, and pushes it forth in oppugnancy. He does not perceive that this mental attitude is one that violates not merely the philosophic conditions under which alone the knowledge he seeks could become his, but those under which only it professes to be cognizable. He makes this demand because he insists on gaining his knowledge of things divine in no degree by way of gift, but exclusively as his own discovery: that is, not as a religion but as a science. He assumes that because religion, like nature, *has* its science, it therefore *is* science, and is nothing more. As well might he assume that nature is nothing more than natural philosophy. If he came forth to the threshold of his house, he would be bathed in the sunbeams. He has another way of ascertaining whether a sun exists. He retires to the smallest and darkest chamber in his house, closes the shutter, and peers through a chink.

(1887)

# THE "SELF" WE HAVE AND ITS POWER

### THE REV. MARTIN D'ARCY, S.J.

Man has been called a tool-bearing animal, but he is far more than this: he has a power to mirror himself and to mirror within himself the length and breadth of reality, and he can stand off from his impulses and thoughts and guide them in a direction which he himself chooses. Moreover, one part of himself, and that the most intimate, does not belong to anything, being or power in the world. There he knows himself morally, and not physically, subject to an absolute, a subjection which is first discerned in the duty of keeping his word, saying what is true and choosing what is right. It is on these grounds he claims to be regarded as a moral person with rights and duties, a self in the full and proper sense of the word.

As sharing a body with the animals and possessing mind and a rational will man begins a new order. What is animal will not be destroyed but taken up into the life of the unified self. Freud tends to ignore the new setting in which the instincts and desires are grouped, and even Jung argues as if the spiritual self were only a voyager out of the racial self, who must return to seek health there when he grows impoverished. Taking facts at their surface value they argue that there are several selves, egos and super-egos and ids, but in fact in their very explanation they presuppose a fundamental unity, only they ignore it or misunderstand it. It is true that neither consciousness nor self-consciousness sums up what is meant by being a self and a person; the mind which thinks, the will which is desire in action, are activities of the same self which animates the body. One does not work without the other in this life, and the thoughts which I think, the hopes I have, the memories I cherish, the habits I have grown into, the aches and disappointments, the physical and spiritual scars, are mine in a sense which they can never be to any other. I am their owner, the only being who has suffered them or enjoyed them in the past, who is conscious of that past as being present to me now and to no one else as both past and present; and who now can make them work together to the fulfillment of my personal destiny. . . .

Whatever view we take it is clear that the self is more than mere consciousness or even self-consciousness. The self has the power of thinking and willing; it is real and alive even when it is asleep or robbed by illness or immaturity of thinking; it is independent and unique and has rights and duties. All indeed that is human in us, and that is everything, is of and from and by the self.

(1914)

# THE SOCIAL NECESSITY FOR MAN
# TO WORSHIP GOD

## COMMISSION ON AMERICAN CITIZENSHIP,

### OF CATHOLIC UNIVERSITY OF AMERICA

A MAN becomes less a man if he refuses to acknowledge the fact of his creaturehood and sets himself apart from God. When he lives and acts as though he belongs to himself, he shrinks in human stature. The consequent distortion of his own personality brings about a distortion in his relations with others. They become for him means to his own ends and, even when his life and deeds are cloaked in the semblance of humanitarianism and he makes a great gesture at being social minded, he is worshiping at the shrine of his own importance and ministering to his own ego. He does not really love his neighbors; he loves only himself, and towards all others his attitude is calculating.

A social order which puts a premium on self-interest and self-gratification, which facilitates forgetfulness of the Divine Law, which makes it difficult for men and women to practice virtue, is a bad social order. A social order which is founded on the acceptance of the fact of creation with all that is therein implied of creaturehood, which is imbued with the consciousness that man is destined not for the things of earth but for union with God, which facilitates noble and virtuous living, is a good social order. The test of any institution, of any group, of any government, is its potentiality for bringing men closer to God and thus increasing their human stature.

The human personality is sacred because it came forth from God, and is destined to return to God. If it is to fulfill its destiny, its life must not be artificially limited nor its liberty unreasonably circumscribed. It must not be impeded in its striving for that true happiness which is the fruit of virtuous living. These are the truths that are implied in our faith in democracy; our task is to make them explicit in our daily living.

(1943)

# FREEDOM AND A HIGHER LIFE

## DIETRICH VON HILDEBRAND

By "true freedom" we mean that ultimate and blissful freedom which Christ—and He alone—can give us, if we give ourselves to Him without reserve. Negatively speaking, it consists in the dissolution of all spasms of egotism; in getting rid of all inhibitions. . . . We are now concerned with that freedom which one cannot possess except as an element of Christian perfection: in other words, which constitutes a goal which is reached in our transformation in Christ.

71

Possessing this freedom, we participate in a higher life. We are lifted by Christ above our nature, including all factors that tend to weigh us down. We no longer live, as it were, on the natural plane but in the perspective of Christ, released, in a sense, from all the weight of our nature. In this freedom we experience the truth of St. Paul's words: "Who then shall separate us from the love of Christ?" (Rom. 8:35). Nothing but a complete and unreserved surrender to Christ—meaning that we fling ourselves in His arms without any thought of a natural security or stronghold, that we "burn the boats" behind us, that we answer the call *sequere me* unconditionally—can give us this freedom of the children of God.

(1948)

# MAN MUST CHOOSE

### CHRISTOPHER DAWSON

THUS, in Marx, the cult of equality and social justice led to the sacrifice of human freedom and spiritual creativeness to an inhuman economic whole. He condemned the whole humanistic morality and culture as bourgeois, and accepted the machine, not only as the basis of economic activity, but as the explanation of the mystery of life itself. The mechanical processes of economic life are the ultimate realities of history and human life. All other things—religion, art, philosophy, spiritual life—stand on a lower plane of reality; they are a dream world of shadows cast on the sleeping mind by the physical processes of the real world of matter and mechanism. Hence Marxism may be seen as the culminating point of the modern tendency to explain that which is specifically human in terms of something else. For the Marxian interpretation of history is in fact nothing but an explaining away of history. It professes to guide us to the heart of the problem, and it merely unveils a void. And thus, according to Berdyaev, the essential importance of Marxism is to be found not in its constructive proposals, but in its negations, its sweeping away of the semi-ideological constructions of nineteenth-century thought. For the optimistic rationalism of the nineteenth-century tended to hide the true significance of the conflict between materialism and spiritualism. Just as behind all religion and all spiritual philosophy there is a metaphysical assent—the affirmation of Being—so behind materialism and the materialist explaining away of history there is a metaphysical ne-

72

gation—the denial of Being—which is the ultimate and quasi-mystical ground of the materialistic position. In Berdyaev's words, "Man must either incorporate himself in this mystery of Not-being, and sink in the abyss of Not-being, or he must return to the inner mystery of human destiny and unite himself once again with the sacred traditions" that are the true basis of the historical process.

(1931)

## MEN MUST ACT

### PETER WUST

WE may ask, should not God raise up among ourselves . . . some great figure, like, for instance, St. Francis or St. Dominic, who through the miracle and grace of his character would bring about at one blow the great reaction, which the weakness of our hands and the poverty of our souls make it impossible to effect by the natural way of isolated actions? It would surely be a mistake if we men of little faith denied the possibility of such an amazing intervention of Providence. But it would be equally mistaken to sit still and placidly await such a miracle of grace in order thereby to get rid of all personal responsibility. That would be disastrous fatalism. . . . It is true, *spiritus ubi vult spirat;* we can never force the Spirit's miracle of grace; we must hope for it, wait for it, beg for it. But we must never make such a hope the pretext for sinking into a mystic lethargy, for shirking personal effort. We ourselves must begin to take action, and only then may we justly expect that God will act with us. We must ourselves try to prepare for the new outpouring of the Spirit.

(1931)

## LIVING THE COMPLETE LIFE

### RUDOLPH ALLERS

AT bottom, there is only one ideal—"doing one's job in life"—involving self-surrender and service; in the same way there is really only one virtue—humble, volitional conformity to the will of God—and only one sin—defiance of God's will. . . .

Man should win to the constant awareness of his own inalienable,

73

individual value and the absolute oneness of his person, combined with the knowledge that he has that value only if he knows and feels himself to be a member of totalities greater than himself.

This paradox and antithesis, which is, however, scarcely greater than other antinomous influences in human life, is expressed or exemplified by the fact that Christ continues to live in the Church, regarded as the Community of Saints, but can also live within the individual human breast: "Not I live, but Christ liveth in me."

Thus, the character-ideal that can alone fully satisfy the conditions of man's being must—however much it may vary from case to case in accordance with individual, cultural, national, and situational exigencies—reconcile and synthetize the conflicting claims of the individual and the community, of the value of the individual and the value-giving totality, of the finiteness of the creature and the call to participation in the divine life. . . . Catholic life, based on Catholic principles, can reconcile the antitheses of our being and bring about a resolution of tension. To live . . . according to the whole, should be a possibility, not only for the Church, which does so live, but for each of her members.

(1943)

## DOING THE WORK AT HAND

### ST. TERESA OF AVILA

THE devil sometimes puts ambitious desires into our hearts, so that, instead of setting our hand to the work which lies nearest to us, and thus serving Our Lord in ways within our power, we may rest content with having desired the impossible. Apart from praying for people, by which you can do a great deal for them, do not try to help everybody, but limit yourselves to your own companions; your work will then be all the more effective because you have the greater obligation to do it. Do you imagine it is a small advantage that you should have so much humility and mortification, and should be the servants of all and show such great charity towards all, and such fervent love for the Lord that it resembles a fire kindling all their souls, while you constantly awaken their zeal by your other virtues? This would be indeed a great service to the Lord and one very pleasing to Him. By your doing things which you really can do, His Majesty will know that you would like to do many more, and thus He will reward you exactly as if you had won many souls for Him.

(ca. 1560)

# SUPERNATURAL HEROISM

### GEORGES BERNANOS

I BELIEVE, in fact I am certain, that many men never give out the whole of themselves, their deepest truth. They live on the surface, and yet, so rich is the soil of humanity that even this thin outer layer is able to yield a kind of meagre harvest which gives the illusion of real living. I've heard that during the last war timid little clerks would turn out to be real leaders; without knowing it, they had in them the passion to command. There is, to be sure, no resemblance there with what we mean when we use the beautiful word "conversion"—but still it had sufficed that these poor creatures should experience the most primitive sort of heroism, heroism devoid of all purity. How many men will never have the least idea of what is meant by supernatural heroism, without which there can be no inner life! Yet by that very same inner life shall they be judged: after a little thought the thing becomes certain, quite obvious. Therefore? . . . Therefore when death has bereft them of all the artificial props with which society provides people, they will find themselves as they really are, as they were without even knowing it—horribly undeveloped monsters, the stumps of men.

Fashioned thus, what can they say of sin? What do they know about it? The cancer which is eating into them is painless—like so many tumors. Probably at some period in their lives most of them felt only a vague discomfort, and it soon passed off. It is rare for a child not to have known any inner life, as Christianity understands it, however embryonic the form. One day or another all young lives are stirred by an urge which seems to compel; every pure young breast has depths which are raised to heroism. Not very urgently perhaps, but just strongly enough to show the little creature a glimpse which sometimes half-consciously he accepts, of the huge risk that salvation entails, and gives to human life all of its divinity. He has sensed something of good and evil, has seen them both in their pristine essence

75

unalloyed by notions of social discipline and habit. But of course his reactions are those of a child, and of such a decisive solemn moment the grown-up man will keep no more than the memory of something rather childishly dramatic, something mischievously quaint, whose true meaning he will never realize, yet of which he may talk to the end of his days with a soft, rather too soft a smile, the almost lewd smile of old men. . . .

It is hard to measure the depths of puerility of those the world describes as "serious men"! An inexplicable, truly supernatural puerility! Although I am only a young priest, I can't help smiling sometimes. . . . And how kind, how indulgent they are to us! An Arras solicitor to whom I ministered on his death-bed, a man of considerable standing, a former senator, said to me once—apparently by way of some apology for the touch of a quite benevolent scepticism with which he received my exhortations:

"Yes, yes, father, I quite understand. I used to feel just as you do yourself. I was very pious. Why, when I was a lad of eleven nothing on earth would have persuaded me to go to sleep without having said my three 'Hail Marys'—and I even made myself say them all in one breath. Otherwise it might have been unlucky. That's how I felt about it."

He supposed that was the point at which I had stuck, that we poor priests all stick at eleven years old. Finally, on the day before he died, I heard his confession. What could be said of it? Nothing much. A "solicitor's life" could most times be expressed in very few words. . . .

The sin against hope—the deadliest sin and perhaps also the most cherished, the most indulged. It takes a long time to become aware of it, and the sadness which precedes and herald its advent is so delicious! The richest of all the devil's elixers, his ambrosia.

(1938)

## GRACE AND MAN'S POTENTIALITIES

### RUDOLPH ALLERS

I DECLARE that it is fundamentally false to maintain that the potentialities of anyone, including our own, are exhausted. Such an attitude leaves out of account the fact that by the influence of grace something unexpected may emerge from a human being. It is true that it is likely that grace works on something that is already there—but it is also conceivable that it creates something new. Therefore, this argument in itself cannot be of very considerable weight.

Individual life, like the historical life of mankind—but this begins, be it well understood, with the Fall!—is nothing more than the *successive realization of all values inherent as potentialities*. The transformation of potentiality into act, to employ the terminology of scholasticism, is the essence and meaning of human life. I am convinced that the tension between what has been realized and what remains to be realized—granting the possibility of a storehouse of values in the core of the person—that this "gradient of values," as I call it, provides the real motor power, the actual driving-force, by which the movement of life is maintained. When a man has ceaselessly realized all that there was of value-potentialities in the depth of his being, his life must come to a standstill; he must die. That is, I think, why so many saints die young. If we consider the life of a St. Aloysius Gonzaga, a St. John Berchmans, a St. Theresa of the Child Jesus, or her uncanonized but very saintly companion in the same Order, Maria of the Most Holy Trinity, or Angelica of Jesus, or many others, do we not get the strong impression that for these people there was nothing left over for them to do on earth, that they had realized everything that it had been in any way possible for them to realize? And further, that so many of these young saints had died in such grievous suffering because the endurance of pain and sickness was the last task for them to accomplish? In German common parlance one says of such people that they were *früh vollendet,* "completed early," a delicate and penetrating phrase. They have completed what was in them to complete; they are complete, because all the value-potentialities they housed have become value-actualities. It is true that we cannot reverse the formula and say that when a man's life comes to an end, he *has* realized all his value-potentialities. Most people's lives decline without their having done so; but as long as a man lives, so long does he incorporate realizable values.

(1943)

# MAN'S STRUGGLE AGAINST
# HIS ANIMAL NATURE

LECOMTE DU NOÜY

LET us read Genesis very carefully.

On the eighth day,[1] God creates another living being having the human form also, and for the first time the sacred text uses a different language. God first breathes in the soul through man's nostrils, and then commands him *not* to eat of the fruit of the tree of knowledge of good and evil, knowing that he will eat it. What does this mysterious language signify?

It signifies that the most important event of evolution has taken place. It signifies the appearance of a new discontinuity in nature, a discontinuity as deep as that which exists between inert matter and organized life. It signifies the birth of conscience, and of the last freedom. . . .

This is precisely indicated by the fact that God "breathed into his nostrils the breath of life; and man became a living soul," which may be taken as signifying that He gave him—and him alone—a conscience, that is to say, the liberty of choice. From then on, God can forbid this creature to obey certain intransgressible orders given to all the others, the physiological orders, the animal instincts. He can do this because this new being is *free,* which signifies that his endocrine bondage can cease *if he wishes.* Man, henceforth, has the choice either of obeying the orders of the flesh and consequently of rejoining his animal ancestors, of regressing; or else, on the contrary, of struggling against these impulsions, these animal instincts, and of affirming the dignity he won when he acquired the last and highest liberty. If he chooses to play the part of Man, at the price of physical suffering and privations, he leaves the animal behind, he progresses as a Man, he continues evolution in the moral plane and is on the road which will eventually lead him to the spiritual plane. . . .

The importance attributed by the sacred text to this event, the fact that it develops it and in reality makes it *the first human event,* the fact that, in spite of his disobedience, this guilty man is chosen as the

[1] The writer is aware of the orthodox exegesis of the two sucessive creations reported in the first and second chapters of Genesis. But the use of a prohibition, instead of a command, is so startling that he felt authorized to submit a new hypothetical interpretation. It seems indeed improbable that the same momentous event could have been reported in two such widely different ways.

founder of the human line, proves the henceforth preponderant importance of the liberty of choice.

In spite of the interdiction, man disobeys and commits the original sin from which humanity must eternally wash itself. This cannot signify an arbitrary punishment imposed on all the descendants of man. It signifies that the actual human being has not yet attained the degree of perfection he must reach. He did not pass the test. He is still dominated by his ancestral instincts and he disobeys God by obeying them. It signifies that *every man will be confronted with same dilemma,* that every man will have to face the same conflict and that he will only triumph by crushing the animal impulses within himself and by consecrating himself to the triumph of the spirit. Thus, he will fulfill his mission as a man, and will contribute to the divine plan which tends to produce a spiritually perfect being. Human progress, therefore no longer depends solely on God, but on the effort made by each man individually. By giving man liberty and conscience God abdicated a part of his omnipotence in favor of his creature, and this represents the spark of God in man ("God is within you"). Liberty is real, for God Himself refused to trammel it. It is necessary, for without it man cannot progress, cannot evolve.

The animal struggle against nature, against the elements, and against the enemy, the "struggle for Life," from which the human form finally emerged after ten million centuries, is transformed into a struggle of Man against the *remains* of the animal within him. But, from now on, because of his conscience, it is the individual alone who counts and no longer the species.

(1947)

## MAN'S DUTY TO PRESERVE
## HIS OWN EXISTENCE

### THE REV. ADOLPH DOMINIC FRENAY, O.P.

Is life worth living? No! the suicide will cry and offer the argument that under the circumstances it was the most reasonable thing to do. . . .

Let me ask you: Have we been born to do away with ourselves? Is our life to be crowned by an act of self-destruction? No, suicide is a most unnatural thing. There is no need for even a single suicide.

79

There is no sufficient reason for any self-willed death. For what can be more unreasonable than an act which is contrary to the laws of nature? There is an undying urge in the heart of every man to preserve his own being. A natural fear of death arises in every bosom at the approach of danger. By a law of nature we hate to see even the approach of sickness because it may lead to death.

No light is glorified in being extinguished. No life rejoices in being annihilated. Light aims to shine, life desires to live. For, says St. Thomas Aquinas: ". . . everything naturally loves itself, the result being that everything naturally keeps itself in *being,* and resists corruptions as far as it can. Wherefore suicide is contrary to the inclination of nature, and to charity whereby every man should love himself. Hence suicide is always a mortal sin, as being contrary to the natural law and to charity."

The advocate of suicide is a poor philosopher. His arguments betray all the evidences of confused thinking. The reasons he gives are fallacies, for one of the first principles of moral philosophy is the maxim that any human being has the right, and the duty, to preserve his own existence. And this law of self-preservation derives its source, as St. Thomas has pointed out, from the natural inclination to resist corruption and the unextinguishable love for one's own being.

Before the light of reason the defender of self-inflicted death is, indeed, a poor, pitiful and ever-losing advocate. And still more miserable becomes his role when he has to face the judgment seat of the omniscient God. Here in the courtroom of eternity his arguments collapse before they are uttered. They vanish by mere self-exhaustion. For the eternal and omnipotent majesty of God will rise and address such a soul, saying: Friend, what are you doing here? I have not called you. Who gave you the right to invade eternity? You hold a self-written death certificate. Your hands are soiled by your own blood. Did I, the Eternal Word, not tell you: "Thou shalt not kill." . . .

Here the suicide will puff up with a feeble effort to justify himself. But here, too, he will be buried under a weight of his own construction. Let us listen to the suicide when he defends his right of self-determination. "Am I not my own lord," he will cry. Yes, we will answer him. You are the lord of your own deeds. But you are not your own ultimate lord. There is one to whom you are responsible for every one of your deeds. To God you owe your body and your soul and to God you will have to give an account of your stewardship . . .

We are not born for this mortal life. We are born for eternity. If we consider our earthly life as the beginning of our eternal destination we possess the values needed to solve the paradoxical problem of suffering. We have at hand all the consolations necessary to endure pain and suffering, distress and agony. It is a merciful God Who makes us realize that we are heading towards an eternal life. It is His grace which visits us. "Sufferings are the money with which one buys heaven," said the blessed Theophane Venard. Sufferings, gauged on the scale of eternity, possess new properties, properties which enable us to unlock the gates of heaven. The world cannot conceive the value of suffering but Christianity does. "How incomprehensible are his judgments, and how unsearchable his ways." . . .

God never abandons us. No matter how heavy the cross, how severe the test, how trying the pain, God always gives us sufficient graces to remain faithful and patient, but we on our part have to co-operate with these His graces. . . .

It is the suicide who dares to rebel against the plans of an all-wise God, who tries, though in vain, to force his way through to escape what he fears, who is blind to the whisperings of the graces of God in his heart and who is materialistic enough to see only the things of the earth, disregarding the things eternal. Hoping to escape some temporal discomforts he plunges himself, head over heels, into the fire of an eternal hell.

(1933)

# RELIGION ENRICHES THE
# INDIVIDUAL LIFE

THE REV. THOMAS VERNER MOORE, O. CART., M.D.

RELIGION as a therapeutic aid in mental difficulties is applicable only to those who have sincere and honest religious convictions. If a patient has no religious convictions he cannot be aided by religious concepts until he sees the truth and honestly adopts them. . . .

Every intelligent being should formulate to the best of his ability a philosophy of life. What is meant by a philosophy of life? An interpretation of life, a view, provisional at least, of the purpose of life and a body of principles to govern conduct in the more or less serious problems and difficulties of life. . . . Every serious philosophy of life involves a positive or negative attitude toward God and religion. So that a philosophy of life may be termed religious when the concept of God holds therein a central and all-important place. . . .

When we conceive of religion as an honestly developed philosophy of life, we can readily see what it does for one to whom this philosophy has become the dominating principle of thought and conduct. It provides what is essential in the life of every man, a *Zielvorstellung,* an end, a purpose, an object in living. . . .

To the religious-minded man God is the Supreme Intelligence in a universe of intelligent beings. And as the Supreme Intelligence in this universe of intelligent beings, He is directing all minds to an end conceived by Himself and worthy of His own transcendent powers. . . . And so we may say that the Supreme Intelligence in this universe of intelligent beings exerts His omnipotent power to bring to its realization an end that in its fulness only Infinite Intelligence can conceive, but in which finite intelligent beings can participate. . . .

One who has really made a religious philosophy of life the great living force in his mental activity can view his own humble lot with patience and contentment. He realizes that in order to live and accomplish something worth while he need not attain to any position of great political importance, nor become a man of great wealth and influence, or even be blessed with good health and freedom from trial and sorrow. But it is necessary to submit his mind to the guidance of the Supreme Intelligence and devote his energy day by day to accomplishing in the most perfect manner possible the duties that each day imposes.

And so the religious philosophy of life leads to fruitful production, to patient persistence in one's plan of life in spite of difficulties and discouragement. There have been thousands and thousands of individuals who have failed in life, not because they lacked ability or were unfortunate in finding opportunities, but because they had no *Zielvorstellung,* no purpose in life, no sense of value, no ideal of doing something worth while in the great scheme of things. They wavered for the very lack of an ideal and changed from one thing to another, following whims, seeking personal satisfaction, unwilling to endure with patient self-denial the hardships, disappointments, and monotony that one must suffer to the end that a life's work may be finished and an unselfish contribution made to the welfare of humanity and to that eternal order which the Supreme Intelligence is establishing in a world of intelligent beings. . . .

There is much more poetry and idealism in the lives of plain, ordinary people than the pessimism of some can possibly imagine. . . . The privileged few in our days sometimes think that they alone can relish the higher things in life; but in factories and offices, in tenements and hovels, thousands know and appreciate truths of which even the better classes have little or no understanding. . . .

And so it is with the honest everyday life of the honest everyday man. The idealism is there. He does not see it himself, but when he has lived out his life faithful to the end, a poem has been written, a work of religious value has been accomplished, and a contribution made to the divine order that God is bringing out of the chaos of human sorrows and perplexities, wanderings and doubts, labors and strivings that seem, but only seem, to end in failure.

Religion alone can enable the toiling thousands to understand the meaning and value of life's monotonous drudgery and so to endure sorrows that would otherwise be unendurable and to carry burdens that would otherwise be insupportable. It is after all only human to endure gladly when endurance leads to something that is worth while and to collapse under burdens for which there seems to be no "why" or "wherefore" of any kind.

(1944)

# IV

# Man's Relations
# with His Fellowman

*Human rights. Charity. Marriage, love, and sex. Rhythm.
Abortion. Sterilization. Racial Tolerance.*

CHRISTIAN teaching alone, in its majestic integrity, can give full meaning and compelling motive to the demand for human rights and liberties because it alone gives worth and dignity to human personality. In consequence of his conception of the nature and gifts of man, the Catholic is necessarily the champion of true human rights and the defender of true human liberties; it is in the name of God Himself that he cries out against any civic philosophy which would degrade man to the condition of a soulless pawn in a sordid game of power and prestige, or would seek to banish him from membership in the human family.

PIUS XI, (1939)

## HUMAN RIGHTS

### THE REVS. WILFRID PARSONS, S.J.

### AND JOHN M. PAUL, C.S.P.

A HUMAN right may be defined as a moral and inviolable power of having or doing something or of demanding something from others. Thus one can be said to have a right to life, or a right to get married, or a right to receive a living wage. A right is an inviolable power in the sense it may not be interfered with by others. It is a moral power in the sense that it is power conferred on one by the *moral* law, it exists even though the person who has it may not be able to defend it by physical force. Violation of one person's right by another person is violation of the moral law. If human rights were not conferred by the moral law we should be obliged to accept the principle that "might makes right." . . .

If we want to know why we have God-given natural rights we must first know what human life is for, why we are in this world. . . .

What is the purpose of human life? If we examine the nature of man we find that man seeks happiness. Finite goods do not make man completely happy. The greatest combination of goods of this earth will not satisfy. . . . Since perfect happiness cannot be found in this world, it must be found in the next. Since perfect happiness must comprise unlimited good, perfect happiness consists in the possession of God in eternity. And if man is to reach the goal of perfect happiness for which he is destined he must prepare during this life for union with God in eternity. This he does by a right ordering of his free acts here on earth, i.e., of acts which are the result of a decision of his free will. . . .

If we are going to reach the end or goal of human life, which is union with God hereafter . . . , we must have the *means*. Rights are the means for this purpose. Hence it must be a part of the eternal plan of God for the direction of all things to their end, it must be required by the eternal law of God, or by the natural moral law, that we have *rights* to certain things. . . .

Every human being, whether the person be a crippled person in old age, a weak infant, or an unborn babe, has an inalienable God-given right to life and the other fundamental inalienable rights since every human being has an immortal soul, as well as a body, destined for happiness in eternity. . . .

Sometimes there may be an apparent conflict of natural rights. For instance, suppose a person is literally starving to death and the only food he can get is the private property of someone. The starving person has a natural right to the food he needs to preserve his life; the property holder has a natural right to the property. The conflict is solved by the fact that the right of the starving man to preserve his life is a more important, more necessary means for carrying out God's plan than the right of the property holder, who is not starving, to maintain his property. A hierarchy of different rights exists, their relative importance and value depending upon how necessary they are as means to enable people to live in accord with human dignity and prepare for happiness with God. In the case of rights which are on the same plane of necessity, rights which are for the benefit of the community in general take precedence over rights which are for the benefit of the individual. . . .

The most basic or primary rights of the human person would be: the right to *life* and bodily integrity; the right to *liberty*—including right to serve and worship God, perform acts of virtue for fellowmen and societies, and right to education and association and whatever else is necessary for exercise and development of intellect and will and other faculties; the right to *marriage,* if one chooses to marry, or the right to choose and freely maintain a state of life; the right to such *material goods* and satisfactions as are necessary for or contribute to the welfare of the whole person. The right to serve God or fulfill the moral law is the most basic of all rights and includes in it all the other rights. It could also be called the right to the pursuit of happiness. . . .

The human person has the right to *assistance from society, if necessary from the State, in distress of person or family.* This follows from the nature and purpose of society in providing men with advantages they need which they cannot obtain adequately for themselves; and it follows from the State promoting the general welfare in so far as it cannot be adequately provided for by private or subordinate societies. The State has the duty to protect all rights and make adequate provision for the securing of such rights (e.g. economic rights) as otherwise could not be secured.

(1947)

# THE VIRTUE OF JUSTICE

### THE REV. MARTIN J. HEALY

MEN are by nature social beings. They live together and work together for their mutual advantage. This cooperation of men with one another is necessary if men are to achieve real success in human living. . . . The fullness of human living is possible to mankind only through the cooperation of all in the pursuit of the common good of all. Men must live together and work together if each man is to have his chance to lead a full, rich human life. Briefly, men must live in society.

Society succeeds in promoting the common welfare of its members only to the extent that the common life of the members is ruled by order and peace. . . . Without peace and order no society could live long. Without peace and order the life of mankind would be a will-o'-the-wisp tossed about violently by the hurricane winds of brute force.

But the peace and order of society are attained through the practice of the virtue of justice. It is justice which leads the customer to pay the merchant the proper price for his merchandise. It is justice which leads the farmer to respect the fields and crops of his neighbors. It is justice which leads the policeman to enforce the laws without fear or favor. It is justice which prevents a man from stealing the money, the home or the wife of another man. In a word, it is justice which leads each man to give to every other man what is due to him. It is justice which leads men to respect each other's rights. In this way justice gives to society the stability and efficiency which are necessary for successful living.

The virtue of justice is based on the recognition in each man of both rights and obligations. We are all familiar with the notion that men have rights. A man, we say, has a right to his own life. The worker has a right to his wages. The citizen has a right to be protected by the police against thieves or murderers. A right is something that is due to a man, something that he can claim as his own. . . .

The virtue which inclines men to respect the rights of others is the virtue of Justice. Justice is a habit by which a man, by a perpetual and constant will, gives to each one what is due to him. It is a virtue because it makes human acts good. It is a virtue of the will of man because it is concerned not with the knowledge of man or the internal passions of man but with man's external actions in relation to other men. . . .

The virtue of justice is the mortar that binds together the bricks of the house of mankind. It is justice which gives to human life the stability which men need to work without fear or anxiety in the search for happiness. Where justice rules, there men need not fear that their food will be taken from their mouths or their homes burned to the ground by vandals. It is justice which gives men the inspiration to work fruitfully. Where justice rules, there men know that the fruits of their labor are their own. Justice is more excellent than the other moral virtues. It surpasses fortitude and temperance because it is a perfection of the rational will of man, which is a more excellent power than the sensitive appetite, the subject of fortitude and temperance. It is more excellent than prudence, for general justice seeks the common good—which is superior to the private good of the individual— and particular justice is directed also to the good of another.

(1952)

# CHARITY IS A DUTY

### LEO XIII

THEY [those of rank, wealth or superior culture] are not free to choose whether they will take up the cause of the poor or not; it is a matter of simple duty. People in a community do not live each on his own resources alone, but on the resources of the community. . . . What the weight of our obligation is, we may discover from the proportionate superabundance of the good things we have received; the larger it is the stricter must be the account we shall have to render to God, Who gave it to us.

(January 18, 1901)

# MORAL LAW COMMANDS RELIEF
# OF POVERTY

### HENRY CARDINAL MANNING

POLITICAL economy . . . is circumscribed by higher moral laws to which, if it come in collision with them, it must at least for a time give way. If on the sound and strict principles of political economy, poverty and sickness could be remedied by thrift and provident dispensaries, I should rejoice; but knowing, as we all must, that thrift and providence have as yet made but little impression upon the multitudes who are poor, hungry, sick, and dying, we are compelled to relieve human suffering for which no sounder or more disciplined relief as yet exists. The Good Samaritan did not delay to pour oil and wine into the wounds of the man half-dead until he had ascertained whether he was responsible for his own distress. Necessity has no law, nor has present distress, except a claim for prompt relief.

(1886)

# CHARITY BEGETS FELLOWSHIP

### JAMES CARDINAL GIBBONS

As commonly understood, charity is manifested in deeds that tend to the relief of suffering in any of its various forms, or that provide opportunities of advancement for those who have none, or that add somewhat to the scant pleasure of many laborious lives. And these beyond question are deeds that deserve all praise. But it is the source whence they come, in the good will which prompts them, that the essence of charity consists. We may love others from a sense of our common humanity, from sympathy, from natural pity for pain and distress. Yet this benevolence is securely based and immeasureably ennobled when it is quickened with the higher motive of love for God, the heavenly Father. Then the pale form of altruism or humanitarianism is replaced by the divine presence of charity.

By its very nature, charity is a social virtue. Wherever a social group is formed—in the home, the community, the civic association—good will is a necessity. It is charity rather than justice that overcomes selfishness, casts out rancor, forbids hatred, clears away misunderstanding, leads to reconciliation. After justice has rendered impartial decision, it is charity that brings men back to fellowship. And if at times it be fitting that mercy should season justice, the quality of mercy itself is but charity touched by compassion.

(1919)

WHOSOEVER takes up the burden of his neighbor, and wishes to help another who is worse off in those respects in which one is the stronger, and ministers unto those in need out of the abundance of things he has received and keeps out of God's bounty—this man becomes a god to those who receive from him, and this man is an imitator of God.

EPISTLE TO DIOGNETUS (AUTHOR ANONYMOUS)

(CA. A.D. 250)

# THE CHURCH'S PRINCIPLES
## OF CHARITY

MOST REV. BRYAN J. MCENTEGART

THE practice of charity is "focal, not marginal, in the Christian ideal of life." The practice of this virtue is the test and the measure of loyalty to Christ. "By this shall all men know that you are My disciples, if you have love for one another." But love for the neighbor must be more than a kindly sentiment of the heart. As in the life of the Master Himself, it must show itself in spiritual and corporal works of mercy. For the Christian, then, the works of mercy are not optional. They are as truly a matter of obligation as the Ten Commandments. We are not merely advised to assist our neighbor in body and in soul. We are commanded to do so. . . .

Organized charity forms an integral part of the life of the Church. She cannot be satisfied with the mere function of inspiring individuals to a more kindly life. Following the thought of St. Paul, she believes that she is the "Mystical Body of Christ" and as such must give corporate expression to the charity of Christ. In harmony with the system of government given her by her Founder, she lays upon each bishop the care of the poor within the confines of his diocese. From the earliest times, she has called on him to exercise the duties of the true Shepherd in seeking out "that which was lost," reclaiming "that which was driven away," binding up "that which was broken" and strengthening "that which was weak." . . .

Different centuries have presented different conditions and different needs. The agencies and types of service which have served her in one day may reach the end of their usefulness, but her duty remains clear—she must adapt herself to the new needs. She must originate new institutions and works to carry on her mission of charity. . . .

To the Church, the practice of charity is limited only by the boundaries of human need. She does not cramp private charity into any narrow field of experimentation. Since her purpose is not only the alleviation of distress but also the inculcation of unselfishness in the hearts of men and women, she cannot agree with the principle that the routine care and support of the needy and the afflicted is a concern solely of the state and dependent, therefore, entirely on taxes grudgingly given.

This does not mean that the Church at the present time is ready to undertake all the social work of the community. She is limited as to resources, as to workers, and as to powers. The demands for the support of churches, schools and missions are so exacting that they constrain her to leave certain fields which deal almost exclusively with the physical and material welfare of people to other private agencies better equipped with finances, training and experience. Moreover, she recognizes that the far-flung forces of the state and its ability to enforce its policies with legal sanctions and to raise vast sums for maintenance through taxes, fit public agencies to exercise certain functions more effectively and comprehensively.

(1926)

THE charity of Christ directs all of us to take an active interest, not only in those we term our own, but in the welfare of all our brother-citizens who are in need. As Catholics and good Americans, we must be concerned with the social-welfare standards that should prevail in State and city institutions, together with the general well-being of all those residing in them. We should, on the other hand, resist every effort indicative of a trend to a totalitarian state, which would capriciously and arbitrarily undertake to do in welfare what can be done efficiently and constructively by individuals and voluntary associations of free men.

MOST REV. PATRICK A. O'BOYLE (1948)

## PRINCIPLES OF CHRISTIAN MARRIAGE

### LEO XIII

WHAT was decreed and constituted in respect to marriage by the authority of God, has been more fully and more clearly handed down to us, by tradition and the written Word, through the Apostles, those herald of the laws of God. To the Apostles, indeed, as our masters, are to be referred the doctrines which *our holy Fathers, the Councils, and the Tradition of the Universal Church have always taught,* namely, that Christ our Lord raised marriage to the dignity of a sacrament; that to husband and wife, guarded and strengthened by the heavenly grace which His merits gained for them, He gave power to attain holiness in the married state; and that, in a wondrous way, making marriage an example of the mystical union between Himself and His Church, He not only perfected that love which is according to nature, but also made the natural union of one man with one woman far more perfect through the bond of heavenly love. . . .

A law of marriage just to all, and the same for all, was enacted by the abolition of the old distinction between slaves and freeborn men and women; and thus the rights of husbands and wives were made equal; for, as St. Jerome says, "with us that which is unlawful for women is unlawful for men also, and the same restraint is imposed on equal conditions." The self-same rights also were firmly established for reciprocal affection and for the interchange of duties; the dignity of the woman was asserted and assured; and it was forbidden to the man to inflict capital punishment for adultery, or lustfully and shamelessly to violate his plighted troth.

It is also a great blessing that the Church has limited, so far as is needful, the power of fathers of families, so that sons and daughters, wishing to marry, are not in any way deprived of their rightful freedom; that, for the purpose of spreading more widely the supernatural love of husbands and wives, she has decreed all marriages within certain degrees of consanguinity or affinity to be null and void; that she has taken the greatest pains to safeguard marriage, as much as is possible, from error and violence and deceit; that she has always wished to preserve the holy chasteness of the marriage bed, personal rights, the honor of husband and wife, and the security of religion. . . .

In Christian marriage the contract is inseparable from the sacrament; and that, for this reason, the contract cannot be true and legitimate without being a sacrament as well. For Christ our Lord added to marriage the dignity of a sacrament; but marriage is the contract itself, whenever that contract is lawfully concluded. . . .

Among Christians every true marriage is, in itself and by itself, a sacrament; and nothing can be further from the truth than to say that the sacrament is a certain added ornament, or outward endowment, which can be separated from the contract at the caprice of man. . . .

Divorce once being tolerated, there will be no restraint powerful enough to keep it within the bounds marked out or presurmised. Great indeed is the force of example, and even greater still the might of passion. With such incitements it must needs follow that the eagerness for divorce, daily spreading by devious ways, will seize upon the minds of many like a virulent contagious disease, or like a flood of water bursting through every barrier. . . .

As often, indeed, as the supreme Pontiffs have resisted the most powerful among rulers, in their threatening demands that divorces carried out by them should be confirmed by the Church, so often must we account them to have been contending for the safety, not only of religion, but also of the human race. For this reason all generations of men will admire the proofs of unbending courage which are to be found in the decrees of Nicholas I against Lothair; of Urban II and Paschal II against Philip I of France; of Celestine III and Innocent III against Alphonsus of Leon and Philip II of France; of Clement VII and Paul III against Henry VIII; and lastly, of Pius VII, that holy and courageous Pontiff, against Napoleon I, when at the height of his prosperity and in the fulness of his power. . . .

In like manner, all ought to understand clearly that, if there be any union of a man and a woman among the faithful of Christ which is not a sacrament, such union has not the force and nature of a proper marriage; that although contracted in accordance with the laws of the State, it cannot be more than a rite or custom introduced by the civil law.

(February 10, 1880)

## "THE SACRED PARTNERSHIP
## OF TRUE MARRIAGE"

### PIUS XI

EACH individual marriage, inasmuch as it is a conjugal union of a particular man and woman, arises only from the free consent of each of the spouses; and this free act of the will, by which each party hands over and accepts those rights proper to the state of marriage, is so necessary to constitute true marriage, that it cannot be supplied by any human power. . . . But the nature of matrimony is entirely independent of the free will of man, so that if one has once contracted matrimony he is thereby subject to its divinely made laws and its essential properties. . . .

By matrimony . . . the souls of the contracting parties are joined and knit together more directly and more intimately than are their bodies, and that not by any passing affection of sense or spirit, but by a deliberate and firm act of the will; and from this union of souls by God's decree, a sacred and inviolable bond arises. Hence the nature

93

of this contract, which is proper and peculiar to it alone, makes it entirely different both from the union of animals entered into by the blind instinct of nature alone in which neither reason nor free will plays a part, and also from the haphazard unions of men, which are far removed from all true and honorable unions of will and enjoy none of the rights of family life. . . . The sacred partnership of true marriage is constituted both by the will of God and the will of man. . . .

The love, then, of which We are speaking is not that based on the passing lust of the moment nor does it consist in pleasing words only, but in the deep attachment of the heart which is expressed in action, since love is proved by deeds. This outward expression of love in the home demands not only mutual help but must go further; must have as its primary purpose that man and wife help each other day by day in forming and perfecting themselves in the interior life, so that through their partnership in life they may advance ever more and more in virtue, and above all that they may grow in true love towards God and their neighbor, on which indeed "dependeth the whole Law and the Prophets." For all men of every condition, in whatever honorable walk of life they may be, can and ought to imitate that most perfect example of holiness placed before man by God, namely Christ Our Lord. . . .

Domestic society being confirmed, therefore, by this bond of love, there should flourish in it that "order of love," as St. Augustine calls it. This order includes both the primacy of the husband with regard to the wife and children, the ready subjection of the wife and her willing obedience. . . .

This subjection, however, does not deny or take away the liberty which fully belongs to the woman both in view of her dignity as a human person, and in view of her most noble office as wife and mother and companion; nor does it bid her obey her husband's every request if not in harmony with right reason or with the dignity due to wife; nor, in fine, does it imply that the wife should be put on the level with those persons who in law are called minors, to whom it is not customary to allow free exercise of their rights on account of their lack of mature judgment, or of their ignorance of human affairs. But it forbids that exaggerated liberty which cares not for the good of the family. . . . Again, this subjection of wife to husband in its degree and manner may vary according to the different conditions of persons, place and time. In fact, if the husband neglect his duty, it falls to the wife to take his place in directing the family. But the structure of the family and its fundamental law, established and confirmed by God, must always and everywhere be maintained intact.

(December 31, 1930)

# NULLIFICATION OF MARRIAGES

### THE REV. M. J. BROWNE

IF a question be raised whether a particular marriage is valid and binding, the Church must answer that question herself. She cannot hand it over to the State, and at the same time hold that marriage is a sacrament. She is, therefore, bound to provide a tribunal to decide that question fully and formally, according to the written law of Christian marriage. Otherwise she would be false to the divine teaching that the marriage of Christians is a sacrament and false to her duty to Christians.

The decision of matrimonial cases is, therefore, for the Church the discharge of a duty. The only cases which are considered by an ecclesiastical court are cases of nullity, those in which it is contended that the marriage was from the beginning null and void because of the absence of some of the conditions required for marriage; and in which the decision sought is a declaration of that nullity. Thus one of the obvious conditions required for a valid marriage is that each of the contracting parties be sane; lunatics cannot contract marriage. Now if a question be raised about a particular marriage, and if it be proved that one of the parties was insane at the time of the ceremony, the Court will give a declaration of nullity. It does not dissolve a marriage; it merely gives an official recognition of a fact—that there was no marriage there from the beginning. Decisions of nullity do not affect the sanctity or indissolubility of the marriage bond; they do not break, lessen, or weaken that bond; they are not opposed to the doctrine of the indissolubility of marriage, for they are concerned only with the preliminary question whether a valid marriage had been contracted at all.

They are totally distinct in law and in practice from divorce cases. In law a divorce case is one in which the marriage is admitted by both parties to have been valid, but for some reason which has supervened since the marriage, a dissolution or breaking of the bond is sought.

In these cases the Court does not merely recognize a fact; it claims and exercises a power, to make what has been good and binding no longer of any effect. . . .

That there is a world of difference between divorce cases and cases of nullity is quite clear to any person who reflects. The difference is of vast theoretical and practical importance. Divorce in theory is based on a denial of the sacredness of the marriage tie. . . . Cases of nullity . . . do not impugn the binding force of marriage, and they are of their nature so rare and infrequent that they cannot by any stretch of imagination lead to abuse.

(1928)

# THE TRANSFIGURATION OF LOVE

## COVENTRY PATMORE

LOVE is rooted deeper in the earth than any other passion; and for that cause its head, like that of the Tree Igdrasil, soars higher into heaven. The heights demand and justify the depths, as giving them substance and credibility. . . .

The whole of after-life depends very much upon how life's transient transfiguration in youth by love is subsequently regarded. . . . If society is to survive its apparently impending dangers, it must be mainly by guarding and increasing the purity of the sources in which society begins. The world is finding out, as it has often done before, and more or less forgotten, that it cannot do without religion. Love is the first thing to wither under its loss. What love does in transfiguring life, that religion does in transfiguring love: as any one may see who compares one state or time with another. Love is sure to be something less than human if it is not something more; and the so-called extravagances of the youthful heart, which always claims a character for divinity in its emotions, fall necessarily into sordid, if not shameful, reaction, if those claims are not justified to the understanding by the faith which declares man and woman to be priest and priestess to each other of relations inherent in Divinity itself, and proclaimed in the words, "Let us make man in our own image" and "male and female created He them." Nothing can reconcile the intimacies of love to the higher feelings unless the parties to them are conscious—and true lovers always are—that for the season at least, they justify the words "I have said, Ye are gods." Nuptial love bears the clearest marks of being nothing other than the rehearsal of communion of a higher nature. "Its felicity consists in perpetual conversion of phase from desire to sacrifice, and from sacrifice to desire, accompanied by unchangeable complaisance in the delight shining in the beauty of the beloved; and it is agitated in all its changes by fear, without which love cannot long exist as emotion." Such a state, in proportion to its fervor, delicacy, and perfection, is ridiculous unless it is regarded as a "great sacrament." It is the inculcation of this significance which has made love between man and woman what it is now —at least to the idea and aspirations of all good minds. It is time that the sweet doctrine should be enforced more clearly.

(1895)

# THE MYSTERY OF HUMAN LOVE

### THE REV. GERALD VANN, O.P.

THERE is an essential difference between sex in man and sex in animals. Sex in man is all that the biologist says it is; but it is infinitely more, and more precious, than that. For in the union of two bodies, it is the union of two persons that can be achieved. That is why sex is a mystery. If you view sex simply as a biological function or a physical plaything you miss its whole meaning, and the deep human realities it could disclose to you will remain hidden. . . .

. . . The only possible human way in which we can approach human beings is with awe and reverence as towards a mystery, though admittedly the mystery is not without its humour. If we forget the mystery, we are brutish, even though we may not be brutal. It may be the blind animal brutishness that has never known the spirit, or it may be the shallow commercialized brutishness that exploits the body and ignores the mind; in either case it is a destruction of humanity because it cannot adore, it can only grab. . . .

Temperateness is not the absence of passion, it is the transfiguring of passion into wholeness. Without it, you will have the chaos that follows the primal sin: you will have the senses usurping sovereignty and excluding the spirit; you will have them deciding good and evil and excluding God; you will have the destruction of the integrity of the person where you should have an immense enhancement of life. But is not temperateness always trying to tell us what not to

97

do, trying to exclude and deny? No, it excludes only as a sculptor or an etcher excludes, in order to create form; it denies only in order to affirm. It is positive as the temperateness of spring is positive; but it is positive also as art is positive. Look at its opposite, the grasping mauling autonomy of dehumanized passion, if you want to see what it means to destroy. . . .

Think of the immensity of the total love of two human beings. At the height of passion, love produces ecstasy. The word means being outside the self: it means "I live, now not I," it means "It is thyself." A man and a woman are each unique and infinite: "I have said, Ye are gods." Here you have two infinities that are one: not a drab assuagement of tumescence, not a slick exercise of a biological function, not the feckless gathering of rosebuds, but the marriage of gods. Ecstasy means living in another. Here, you are living in the being you love; you are living in the race whose history you summarize, whose function you fulfill, whose life you gather in your hands and pass on to the future ages; you are living (if you have eyes to see) in God, to whose life and love you thus do homage, whose infinite mighty art waits upon you to work with you—you making the body, He the spirit—to fashion another infinity. This is the immensity that sex can open out to you; and will you isolate it and turn it into a toy? For here if anywhere it must be clear that you are not the master of heaven and earth, and that you must go down on your knees to receive a gift greater than yourself. It is the snatcher and the mauler who destroy; the temperate man adores. . . .

How terrible when people are led to believe, or left to believe, that once they are in love they have nothing to do but live happily ever after, they have nothing further to learn. Love is an endless creative process; the oneness of the two is not born but made. Do you think that two people, however much in love, will love each other in exactly the same way? Do you think they will never differ in the way they want to express their love? Do you think that because they are living in love they cease to be individuals, or that the false self is wholly dead? There is always the tension; there is always the temptation to sink back into the separate selfhood, there is always the danger that passion may destroy the unity of the person; it is only by long, patient labour that you can hope to forge the unity of the deep personal will which can govern separate superficial desire.

So, when you make love you must be gentle and humble, because it is to the mystery of a human being that you are making love. Love

98

is an endless creative process; it is also an endless voyage of discovery. . . .

If you degrade love by brutality or selfishness or pride, you destroy it; and you will find its wholeness broken up into two fragments, each of them ugly; you will find passion twisted into lust, and emotion twisted into sentimentality. Both of them are superficial, both of them are unreal, both of them are disruptive; and their fruit is loneliness. When passion breaks away from the deep life of a man it can never enlarge him, it has nothing to say to the heart; it can never be a marriage of gods, only an animal mauling its prey. When emotion breaks away from the deep will of a man it runs away from reality; it makes for itself a fantasy-object which obscures the real; endlessly agitated over the superficial well-being of its object it never goes down to the depths to find the real good and the real evil; there is no meeting, it can never help.

We live a many-levelled life, and real love is a sharing of life on all these levels, but a sharing of them in their integrity, a sharing of the whole being; and that is why the fulness of love is not likely to be given us this side the grave for we are not likely this side the grave to be completely whole. But though the fulness of love is something that must wait upon our wholeness, love itself is precisely what makes us whole; when we have the fulness to say, "It is Thyself," but it is love that makes us begin to say it.

Lust and sentimentality separate, but love unites; and God who is Love Redemptive gives us love with its joys and sorrows to restore our wholeness, to bring us again out of the cold. He gives us love with its joys and especially its sorrows because it can lead us to rebirth. If you skim along the surface of life, you will never know the needs of a Saviour except by hearsay, for you will never know the depths of the human heart. If love were an endless idyll unflecked by sorrow you would be endlessly happy, but you would not know the intensity of happiness as you might, for you would still not know the depths of the human heart. But if you know the love that can lead you near to heartbreak, if you know not only the heights of ecstasy but the depths of pain, then you will know you stand before a mystery and you will be silenced, you will have seen the abyss of the human heart which only infinity can fill, and perhaps you will find yourself forced to look beyond the barriers of the finite for the Love in which all other loves are fulfilled. . . .

Love, like prayer, has its moments of ecstasy; but it is made up not

of these but of the simplicities, the common joys and burdens, of
every day. It is a long and laborious process, though its drudgeries
are suffused with joy. We are led to it because of our incompleteness,
because the heart is a hunger, because we are always seeking for fulfillment of body, mind and will. . . .

You want to be a maker, and you cannot make unless you have
learnt to love; but if you are a lover, then indeed you are inescapably
a maker, for loving is itself making. By their love the two are made
one; the long, laborious process is itself happiness because it is the
making of life; the daily sharing of joys and burdens, of work and
play, of deepening vision and of worship—all this is love-making, and
making of love is the making of life. But love is endlessly self-diffu-
sive; the two are made one most completely in and through their
common making of the family; and the family in its turn, if it is living in love, will not rest in a private, enclosed beatitude, but will shed
its light and warmth in an ever-widening arc of love and service upon
the world.

(1945)

IF we want to know in what relationship we really stand to God we
cannot do better than consider our feelings about other people. This
is peculiarly the case when one person, above all others has touched
our affections. If he is seen to be the source of all our happiness and all
our pain, if our peace of mind depends on him alone, then, let it be
said at once, we are separated as far from God as we can be, short of
having committed mortal sin. Not that love of God condemns us to
aridity in our human friendships, but it does lay on us the duty of seeing that our affection for other human beings shall not be an end in
itself, shall not usurp the place of that utterly complete love which no
one can begin to understand who has not felt it.

FRANCOIS MAURIAC (1941)

# THE USE OF RHYTHM

## PIUS XII

THERE is the serious question today as to whether and how far the
obligation of ready disposition to serve motherhood can be reconciled

with the ever more widely diffused recourse to the periods of natural sterility (the so-called agenetic periods of the woman).

If the carrying out of this theory means nothing more than that the couple can make use of their matrimonial rights on the days of natural sterility too, there is nothing against it, for by so doing they neither hinder nor injure in any way the consummation of the natural act and its further natural consequences. . . . If, however, there is further question—that is, of permitting the conjugal act on those days exclusively—then the conduct of the married couple must be examined more closely.

Here two other hypotheses present themselves to us. If at the time of marriage at least one of the couple intended to restrict the marriage right, not merely its *use,* to the sterile periods, in such a way that at other times the second party would not even have the right to demand the act, this would imply an essential defect in the consent to marriage, which would carry with it invalidity of the marriage itself, because the right deriving from the contract of marriage is a permanent, uninterrupted and not intermittent right of each of the parties, one to the other.

On the other hand, if the act be limited to the sterile periods insofar as the mere use and not the right is concerned, there is no question about the validity of the marriage. Nevertheless, the moral licitness of such conduct on the part of the couple would have to be approved or denied according as to whether or not the intention of observing those periods constantly was based on sufficient and secure moral grounds. The mere fact that the couple do not violate the nature of the act and are prepared to accept and bring up the child which, in spite of their precautions, came into the world would not be sufficient to guarantee the rectitude of intention and the unobjectionable morality of the motives themselves. . . .

To embrace the married state, continuously to make use of the faculty proper to it and lawful to it alone, and, on the other hand, to withdraw always and deliberately with no serious reason from its primary obligation, would be a sin against the very meaning of conjugal life.

There are serious motives, such as those often mentioned in the so-called medical, eugenic, economic and social "indications," that can exempt the positive and obligatory carrying out of the act. From this it follows that observing the non-fertile periods alone can be lawful only under a moral aspect. Under the conditions mentioned it really is so. But if, according to a rational and just judgment, there are no similar grave reasons of a personal nature, or deriving from external circumstances, then the determination to avoid habitually the fecundity of the union, while at the same time to continue fully satisfying their sensuality, can be derived only from a false appreciation of life and from reasons having nothing to do with proper ethical laws.

(October 29, 1951)

# THE "DIRECT KILLING" OF
# AN UNBORN CHILD

### PIUS XII

ANY direct attempt on a human life as a means to an end—in this case to the end of saving another life—is unlawful.

Innocent human life, in whatsoever condition it is found, is withdrawn, from the very first moment of its existence, from any direct deliberate attack. This is a fundamental right of the human person, as valid for the life still hidden within the womb of the mother, as for the life already born and developing outside of her; as much opposed to direct abortion as to the direct killing of the child before, during or after its birth. . . .

This principle holds good both for the life of the child as well as for that of the mother. Never and in no case has the Church taught that the life of the child must be preferred to that of the mother. It is erroneous to put the question with this alternative; either the life of the child or that of the mother. No, neither the life of the mother nor that of the child can be subjected to an act of direct suppression. In the one case as in the other, there can be but one obligation: to make every effort to save the lives of both, of the mother and of the child. . . .

If, notwithstanding all the progress of science, there still remain, and will remain in the future, cases in which one must reckon with the death of the mother, when it is the mother's wish to bring to birth the life that is within her, and not to destroy it in violation of the command of God: Thou shalt not kill!—nothing else remains for the man—who will make every effort right up to the last moment to help and save—but to bow respectfully before the laws of nature and the dispositions of Divine Providence.

But—it is objected—the life of the mother, especially the mother of a large family, is of incomparably greater value than that of a child not yet born. . . . The reply to this harrowing objection is not difficult. The inviolability of the life of an innocent human being does not depend on its greater or lesser value. . . . Who can judge with certainty which of the two lives is in fact the more precious? Who can know what path that child will follow and to what heights of achievement and perfection he may reach? Two greatnesses are being compared here, one of them being an unknown quantity. . . .

On purpose We have always used the expression "direct attempt on the life of an innocent person," "direct killing." Because if, for example, the saving of the life of the future mother, independently of her pregnant state, should urgently require a surgical act or other therapeutic treatment which would have as a necessary consequence, in no way desired or intended but inevitable, the death of the fetus, such an act could no longer be called a direct attempt on an innocent life. Under these conditions the operation can be licit, like other similar medical interventions, granted always that a good of high worth is concerned, such as life, and that it is not possible to postpone the operation until after the birth of the child, nor to have recourse to other efficacious remedies.

(November 26, 1951)

# MORAL ASPECTS OF STERILIZATION

## RT. REV. JOHN A. RYAN

GRAVE mutilation of one's self, without grave reason, is quite as contrary to the constitution of rational nature, in essence though not in degree, as the destruction of one's life. Evidently one is justified in severing a limb from the body to prevent blood poisoning or to make possible an artificial substitute. A part is removed for the sake of the whole. The part has no intrinsic worth; it exists and functions only to serve the person. Sterilization is, therefore, morally lawful when undergone for the preservation of life or the prevention of grave physical or mental disability. The part is sacrificed for the whole.

When, however, it is effected for any less important end than the person's safety or health, it is immoral. Prominent among such lesser ends are the avoidance of the burdens associated with pregnancy and child rearing and prevention of the birth of persons who might be "socially unfit" or "socially inadequate." While a faculty, even the faculty of procreation, may licitly be sacrificed for the safety of the whole person, it may not be destroyed for his mere convenience or for the alleged welfare of society. Sometimes these are legitimate ends but they can and must be attained through other means than the degradation of personality.

This conclusion of reason and natural ethics is confirmed by the teaching of revealed religion. In his encyclical on "Christian Marriage," Pope Pius XI condemned compulsory sterilization, as a violation of individual rights:

"Those who act in this way are at fault in losing sight of the fact that the family is more sacred than the State and that men are begotten not for the earth and for time, but for heaven and eternity. Although often these individuals are to be dissuaded from entering into matrimony, certainly it is wrong to brand men with the stigma of crime because they contract marriage, on the ground that, despite the fact that they are in every respect capable of matrimony, they will give birth only to defective children, even though they use all care and diligence.

Public magistrates have no direct power over the bodies of their subjects; therefore, where no crime has taken place and there is no cause present for grave punishment, they can never directly harm, or tamper with the integrity of the body, either for the reason of eugenics or for any other reason."

As to voluntary sterilization, it is pronounced immoral by all Catholic authorities.

(1944)

# INTOLERANCE TOWARD
# EARLY CHRISTIANS
### TERTULLIAN

MEN cry out that the state is beset, that the Christians are in their fields, in their forts, in their islands. They mourn as for a loss that every sex, condition, and now even rank, is going over to this sect. And yet they do not by this very means advance their minds to the idea of some good therein hidden; they allow not themselves to conjecture more rightly, they choose not to examine more closely. The generality run upon a hatred of this name, with eyes so closed that in bearing favourable testimony to any one they mingle with it the reproach of the name. "A good man Caius Seius, only he is a Christian." So another, "I marvel that that wise man Lucius Titius hath suddenly become a Christian." No one reflecteth whether Caius be not therefore good and Lucius wise because a Christian, or therefore a Christian because wise and good. They praise that which they know, they revile that which they know not. Virtue is not in such account as hatred of the Christians. Now, then, if the hatred be of the name, what guilt is there in names? What charge against words? Unless it be that any word which is a name have a barbarous or ill-omened, or a scurrilous or an immodest sound. If the Tiber cometh up to the walls, if the Nile cometh not up to the fields, if the heaven hath stood still, if the earth hath been moved, if there be any famine, if any pestilence, "The Christians to the lions" is forthwith the word.

(ca. A.D. 197)

WHOEVER exalts race, or the people, or the State, or a particular form of State, or the depositories of power, or any other fundamental value of the human community—however necessary and honorable be their function in worldy things—whoever raises these notions above their standard value and divinizes them to an idolatrous level, distorts and perverts an order of the world planned and created by God: he is far from the true faith in God and from the concept of life which that faith upholds.

PIUS XI (March 14, 1937)

## THE SIN OF "SOCIAL COLOR BLINDNESS"

THE REV. WILLIAM J. SMITH, S.J.

THE brotherhood of man, under the Fatherhood of God, is a fundamental tenet embodied in the Catholic Attitude on the human race.

All men are men and nothing can change the fact or transform their human nature. Essentially, every human being is possessed of a superior dignity worthy of respect and reverence. Because of circumstances or culpable responsibility, few men are near-perfect and the general run of individuals mar the beauty of their own beings by faults, defects and negligences. The conflict between man as he is and man as he should be gives rise to misunderstandings, dislikes, discriminations. Proper education may purify the mind of prejudice; no amount of pleading, persuasion or propaganda can convince a normal human being that he likes what he dislikes.

The Catholic Attitude holds fast to the Divine dictum, "Love thy neighbor," "Do good to them that hate you." At the same time it cannot stultify its sincerity by pretending to be blind to the difficulties of the practical application of even the noblest principle. Men do not live in a vacuum of celestial equanimity. They rub elbows with one another in a hundred different relationships day by day. There, indeed, is the "rub" that creates friction and results all too often in untold miseries. Human nature is tried in the crucible of personal contact and its manifest weaknesses are all to clearly revealed.

The Catholic Attitude elevates a man above the dismal atmosphere of the natural. It bids him soar into the stratosphere of the supernatural. By birth from human parentage he is a natural, human offspring. By Baptism, regenerated through water and the Holy Spirit, he is made an adopted child of God. He participates in some way in the very nature of his Creator. He is made one in a mystical union with Christ the Redeemer of all mankind. He can no longer view things merely as they are seen; the dull-dark veil that shrouds the human senses is penetrated by the piercing light of a Faith born of God. Men are still men in all their human frailties, but glowing out from beneath the sin-covered coating, the man of faith beholds the brilliant beauty of an immortal soul. It is that vision and that alone that can correct the astigmatism of social color-blindness. In the very act of seeing, the cataracts of racial hate drop from the strained eyelids of the short-sighted. It is the miracle of grace in a modern day. . . .

The Catholic Attitude embraces all men and encircles them in the love of a God-man who died that they might live. It directs men's minds to concentrate on the substance and to ignore the shadow. It does not presume that likes and dislikes can be eliminated from human life; they are rooted too firmly in the fallow ground of a fallen nature. It not only presumes but positively prescribes the all-consuming motive of a strong, deep, supernatural love of neighbor as the only sound basis for human relations. That love is not a mere natural passion or emotion. It is a sweeping force within the soul and settled there by God Himself. Divine Love, even as it is shared in the human soul, is not, cannot be blind to the irritations, the annoyances, the multifarious misdeeds that grate upon human sensibilities. But it can and does brush aside dislikes and displeasures that rise to rankle in the human breast. Not always, however, without a struggle. It recognizes realities; it cannot call black, white, or inconvenience, comfort. It takes life as it is. But it steels the soul to mount above the petty tyrannies of sense-reaction and serenely grapples with unpleasantness until it makes man master even of himself. This is the only fool-proof prescription for the malady of racial, class and color intolerance.

The Catholic, the Negro and the Jew are often the special targets of discrimination in America. Surely they should not be antagonistic one to the other. The Jew is the spiritual brother of the Catholic by the very nature of God's Divine Dispensation. Any individual who thinks otherwise is just so much off the beam of the Catholic Attitude. Catholicism is the flowering of the bud of Judaism. The rejection by Jewish leaders of the redemption of mankind through the mediation of Jesus Christ does not change one iota of the historical fact. The misguided adherents of many of the Jewish people to a traditional hope that has long ago ceased to have a meaning for them, does not give to any follower of Christ the right to judge the soul of his neighbor. Racial characteristics that differ among people are not the cause for criticisms among intelligent men. The Jew, as any other human person, is to be judged solely on the merits of his own personal worth or lack of it. He should not expect special privilege or exaggerated sympathy for himself because he happens to be a member of a traditionally persecuted people. Nor should he be blamed and boycotted, as an individual, for faults that some other son of Israel may unfortunately possess. He is a man with all the rights and all the dignity of any other man. Let him be treated with respect or reserve, according to circumstances, like the rest of men.

The Negro is much more sinned against than guilty of sin. Suffice it to say that it is a crime that cries to heaven for vengeance when one of God's creatures must bear the chains of a cruel constraint because of the color of his skin. It is doubly damnable when his inferior social and economic status is the result of inhuman neglect or positive discrimination by fellow-humans who had condemned him to slavery in the first place and kept him in servitude even after he had been released from the bondage of a fraternalistic tyranny. The restoration of the Negro to the plane of equal opportunity is one of the primary obligations on the collective conscience of American society. . . .

As Catholics we can neither be content with the smug assurance that social disturbances will right themselves without effort on our part nor can we allow either the racial idiosyncrasies of a Hitler or the class-conscious poison of a Stalin to have any play in our minds and hearts. Individually we have the obligation to perfect and save our own souls. Socially, we are our brother's keepers. Spiritually we have the protection of an international organization, guaranteed by God Himself to outlast the ravages of time and the resentments of men. We can neither be more Catholic than the Church by rushing to extremes nor must we fall short of the mark by nurturing pet theories that run counter to her teachings.

(1946)


WE regard racism and exaggerated nationalism as barriers raised between man and man, between people and people, between nation and nation. . . . All men are, above all, members of the same great kind. They all belong to the single great family of the living. Humankind is therefore a single, universal, catholic race.

PIUS XI (July 28, 1938)


## THE SOLUTION OF ANTI-SEMITISM

### EDWARD CARDINAL MOONEY

THERE is no solution for the problem of anti-Semitism or any similar problem in the latitudinarian tendency to brush aside as non-essential the religious differences that divide us. Is the latitudinarian Jew for that reason any less the object of anti-Semitic prejudice? Or is the latitudinarian Christian for that reason any less susceptible to the virus of present-day anti-Semitism? Personally, I do not think so. We should never forget that anti-Semitism developed in Germany in direct ratio to the effectiveness of the official repression of Christianity, and that the Nazis, notorious for their atrocious persecution of the

Jew, were branded by Pope Pius XI as the "deniers and destroyers of the Christian as well."

This brings me to the consideration of the positive contribution which Christians can make to the solution of the problem of anti-Semitism. To be consistent with the observation I made a moment ago, I should restrict myself to what I might call the Catholic prophylaxis against anti-Semitism. Briefly I might say that it is to be found in a better understanding of the doctrine the Church teaches and to a better observance of the moral precepts She inculcates. Catholic teaching formally and explicitly condemns anti-Semitism. To cite an instance from the records of our day I quote a Papal decree of March 25, 1928, which reads: "The Apostolic See . . . condemns most emphatically the hatred directed against a people which was once chosen by God, that particular hatred which today commonly goes by the name of anti-Semitism." Catholic teaching directly and by manifold implication emphasizes the dignity of the human person, which anti-Semitism outrages. Catholic teaching exalts the historic religious role of the Jewish people, and glories in the heritage from Judaism which is an essential element in Christianity. . . .

The moral precept which the Catholic Church considers most distinctively Christian is the command of Christ to love our neighbor. Anti-Semitism is diametrically opposed to this virtue of Christian charity.

(1944)


THROUGH Christ and in Christ we are the spiritual descendents of Abraham. No, it is not possible for Christians to participate in anti-Semitism. We acknowledge the right of everyone to defend himself, to take legitimate measures to protect himself against all that menaces his legitimate interests. But anti-Semitism is inadmissable. Spiritually we are Semites.

PIUS XI (September 6, 1938)


## MAN CANNOT JUDGE MAN

### PIUS IX

IT must . . . be held for certain that they who suffer from real ignorance of religion, if they cannot conquer it, are not bound by any fault herein before the eyes of the Lord. And now who will arrogate to himself so much as to think he can define the limits of such ignorance, according to the nature and variety of peoples, places, temperaments, and so many other things? For when we are freed from the captivity of the body and see God as He is, we shall forthwith understand by what close and beautiful bonds are bound together the divine mercy and the divine justice; so long as we live here on earth, weighed down by this mortal flesh, that dulls the soul, let us most firmly hold that according to Catholic doctrine there is one God, one Faith, one Baptism, and to go further [in our inquiry as to the fate of souls] were sin.

(December 9, 1854)

# V

# Man's Role in Society

*Society's need for religion. Secularism. The Church's social mission. The Christian in society. Catholics of the "right" and "left." Property, capital, and labor. Catholic education.*

## GOD IN SOCIETY

### PIUS XII

In the social field the counterfeiting of God's plan has gone to its very roots by deforming the Divine image of man. Instead of his real created nature with origin and destiny in God, there has been substituted the false notion of a man whose conscience is a law unto himself, who is his own legislator brooking no control, who has no responsibility towards his fellows and society, with no destiny beyond the earth and no other purpose than the enjoyment of finite goods, with no rule of life except that of the *fait accompli* and the unbridled satisfaction of his desires. . . .

Only a society illuminated by the dictates of faith, respectful of the rights of God, certain of the account which responsible leaders will have to render to the Supreme Judge in the depths of their conscience and in the presence of the living and the dead—only such a society will be able to interpret correctly your needs and just aspirations to defend and fight for your rights, to guide you with wisdom in the fulfilment of your duties in accordance with the hierarchy of values and the harmony of domestic and civil life that nature has established.

Do not forget that without God material prosperity is for those who do not possess it a tormenting wound, while for those who do, it proves a death trap. Without God intellectual and aesthetic culture is a river cut off from its source and its outlet; it becomes a quagmire filled with sand and mud.

(Christmas, 1949)

## SOCIETY'S NEED FOR RELIGION

### THE CATHOLIC BISHOPS OF THE UNITED STATES

RELIGION makes man a citizen of the Kingdom of God; for it is through religion that man gives his allegiance to his Maker. . . .

As an act, religion is the communion of man with God, the source of all life. It is this that explains the essential importance of religion to man both as an individual and as a member of society, a citizen of a nation. Religion, then, is not only the individual's most precious possession; it is also a nation's most vital asset.

Man, as an individual, needs religion. He needs it for many reasons. He needs it because he is a creature of God, entirely dependent on his Creator, and hence must acknowledge his obligation of adoration and love. He needs it to give meaning to his present existence. . . .

Again, man needs religion to give him that sense of responsibility which prevents human existence from becoming a wilderness of warring passions and aimless strivings. He needs religion because, apart from God, man is lonely and he can never find in himself or in the institutions which bear his image the means to fill up that void of loneliness which is in the human heart.

Man needs religion because he is weak, and in his weakness he must have access to the Source of all strength.

Man needs religion because without the hope that religion alone can give, he cannot rise above that pessimism, that sense of despair, which threatens to engulf the whole of our civilization.

Man needs religion because he has an impelling need to worship, and if he does not worship God he will direct his worship to base objects that will pervert his mind and his heart.

Religion necessary to individual man is necessary also to human society. From the very beginning the family, the primary unit of society, has been intimately dependent on religion, and from it has drawn its unity, its stability and its holiness. . . .

Nor is the civic community less dependent on religion. Men are indeed forced by the conditions of human nature to unite and co-operate in the fulfillment of their common needs. But union and cooperation can continue to exist among free men only when justice and charity, universal in their binding force because imposed by God Himself, are embodied in law. While civic authority may have its immediate source in the consent of the governed, that authority must be recognized as coming ultimately from Him upon whom all men depend. . . .

Nor is religion less important to the complex modern state than to the more primitive social structure. In the measure the State has excluded religion, it has shown a tendency to become an instrument of tyranny. The irreligious state sets itself up in place of God, substituting its own arbitrary dictates for the decrees of eternal Wisdom. It demands an absolute loyalty such as can be claimed only by Truth itself, and it has no effective deterrent from violating its solemn treaties and from waging unjust and aggressive wars. . . .

Religion, then, is of the utmost importance to society in all its stages of development. It is like the rays of the sun, bringing the light of God's wisdom and grace into man's whole social life. It lights up and purifies the City of Man and turns it into the City of God. Without these sustaining influences the City of Man is gradually overrun by a Mayan-like jungle of human passions, in whose rank undergrowth of greed and cruelty and every other vice man lives his life in terror—and in the end perishes. . . .

The imminent threat to our country comes not from religious divisiveness but from irreligious social decay. The truly religious man is certain to be one who treasures all those ideals which religion helped to build into this nation. To the man who is lacking in religious belief, nothing in the end is likely to be sacred, nothing worth preserving. In that direction lies the real danger to our country. . . .

But our best religious traditions are not fulfilled by mere theoretical acknowledgment of religion as a possible aid in solving our problems, or by a perfunctory attendance at Sunday devotions, or even by a stiff bow on the part of government in the general direction of God. If our country is truly religious, the influence of religion will permeate every part of our national life. The State will not merely tolerate religion; it will honor and welcome it as an indispensable aid in building the complete good life of its citizens. . . .

Religion requires that justice, tempered by charity, must prevail in the State's legislation and policy relative to economic groups. It will also inspire and guide the employer in the fulfillment of his duties toward his employees in the spirit of justice and charity. In the workingman's struggle for his rights the religious conscience of the nation was not among the least of the forces that sustained him. Now that those rights have been largely vindicated, religion still insists on his responsibility to his employer and to society in the achievement of a right economic solidarity. . . .

It is true that the founders of this country, in their public utterances, gave as the religious foundation of their work only the truths of the natural order—belief in God as the Omnipotent Creator; belief in man as God's free creature endowed with inalienable rights; belief in the eternal truth and universality of the moral law.

But it is also true that these convictions were part of their Christian tradition. Historically these truths had been received by and elaborated by intellect illumined by faith and guided by revelation. It would be wrong to imagine that these truths are sufficient for the religious life of the individual, or that they can of themselves guarantee the firm foundation of society.

After all, the truths which can be known by reason are but a part of religious truth. It is through supernatural faith alone that man comes to the knowledge of religious truth in its fullness. Man is not free to pick and choose among the truths God has made known either through reason or revelation. His obligation is to accept the whole of God's truth.

Man himself is not merely a creature of the natural order. At the moment of creation he was elevated by God to the supernatural state and destined to an everlasting and supernatural life. To the fall of man from this high estate are traceable all the woes which have marked human history. . . .

All the religious truths, natural and supernatural, are parts of one integral whole. Ultimately in man's mind they must stand or fall together. Subtract one part and you distort the rest; deny one part and in the end you deny the whole.

Nor, in the light of Divine Revelation, can the principles of natural ethics be separated from the principles of Christian morality. Only the life of Christian faith can guarantee to man in his present state the moral life; and the Christian life is lived in its entirety only through the one true Church of Christ.

(November 15, 1952)

# GOD: THE BASIS OF LAW

### THE REV. DANIEL U. HANRAHAN

IN the classical and Christian tradition, reverence for law rests on allegiance to three great verities. First, there is a law above human positive law and beyond man's reach to abrogate or amend. Secondly, by God's will all men are equal. Thirdly, before the courts all men must be treated alike.

Speaking of that law Cicero explains: True law is right reason in agreement with nature. It summons to right actions by its demands and averts from evil-doing by its prohibitions. There is one eternal and unchangeable law, valid for all nations, and all times. God is the author of this law, its promulgator and its enforcing judge.

To this notion of fundamental natural law governing human behavior everywhere and always, Christianity added something—the inviolable sacredness of all men and their complete equality before the law. Its most colorful expression is found in the cherished and unforgettable words of St. Paul: "No more Jew or Gentile, no more slave or freeman, no more male and female; you are all one person in Jesus Christ. And if you belong to Christ, then you are indeed Abraham's children: the promised inheritance is yours."

And these men all equal in God's sight must be treated alike before the law. The pledge of the Magna Carta reads: "To no man will we sell, to no man will we deny, to no man will we delay right and justice." . . .

That democracy has its shortcomings is evident. So many vital national and political decisions result from the mere force of numbers!

Generally speaking, a majority, however small, can make its will prevail. And that majority could inaugurate a tyranny as gruesome as any tyranny sponsored by a dictator.

Is it not evident, then, that our people must have a deep sense of reverence for those principles of right conduct, for the fundamental rights which, as clearly as the commandments were incised on the tablets Moses received on Sinai, have been etched on the hearts of all men, even the uncorrupted primitives?

Would you gentlemen of broad education and legal experience, men of perspective and vision, not be delinquent in duty to the point of betrayal of our beloved land if by callous indifference you allowed our people to lose reverence for the law and the virtues on which it rests and thus they should fall into the error that law is nothing but a proclamation for protection of vested interests, or human fancy temporarily stabilized by legal form?

In a democracy the vote of a patriot who has served his country well counts for no more than the vote of a fifth columnist.

In a democracy the vote of a boob counts as much as the vote of a genius; the vote of a social parasite carries as much force as the vote of the industrious citizen: the vote of a double-dealer and a liar counts as much as the vote of a man who reveres justice and speaks the truth.

It logically follows that since our government counts the votes of all alike, the continuance of this government in any fashion akin to what it has been, requires that our citizens in overwhelming numbers have a deep and abiding reverence for the law.

The indispensable condition for such deep and abiding reverence for the law is reverence for God and the law that came into being with man's creation, that law to which the fathers of our country referred when they spoke of inalienable rights.

Unfortunately, so deep is the neutrality in vast areas of our educational system towards God and man's duties towards Him that the minds of many men are encumbered by the fallacy that disbelief in God is as logical as belief in Him.

And there is a parallel assumption, equally irrational, that, granting God's existence, we need not take Him into account either in the decisions made by society or in decisions of personal behavior.

Long ago, an eminent lawyer, St. Thomas More, observed that the loss of conviction of God's existence and our accountability to Him forces man to debase "the high nature of his soul to the vileness of brute beast bodies."

Loss of reverence for God and His law destroys all permanent values, including the abiding value and validity of all law and all human rights.

As a matter of fact there is a large section of the legal profession which does hold that the value of all law and the validity of all rights are entirely dependent upon the current opinion among experts in the field, who establish and disestablish all legal propositions, merely by yielding to or withdrawing support from them.

When such a concept of laws seeps down from the academic citadels to the common people, shall we be surprised if the people contemptuously break the law, frustrate the courts, and mock its decisions since in the minds of leading legal authorities laws and decisions based upon the law are nothing but passing social prejudices and legal preferences.

It is startling how even some of the greatest humanitarians of the bench have made the struggle for justice not a struggle to defend true and abiding principles, but a struggle in a world of make-believe.

I quote from a letter written by one of the most eminent justices who ever graced the American bench:

"Our personality is a cosmic ganglion. I suspect that all my ultimates have the mark of the finite upon them, but as they are the best I know, I give them practical respect, love, etc., but inwardly doubt whether they have any importance . . . It makes me enormously happy when I am encouraged to believe that I have done something of what I should have liked to do, but in the subterranean misgivings I think, I believe I think sincerely, that it does not matter much."

Reflect, gentlemen, upon the sacrifices many citizens of this generation have been called upon to make in defense of democracy and what we are pleased to call our way of life.

Think of the parents whose sons lie in graves in the South Pacific and on the Normandy coast. Think of the battle-maimed men in our military hospitals.

If they should learn from the leaders of your profession, that our God-given rights are but a legal fiction, a bit of verbal hocus-pocus in a game of make-believe, would you blame them if they mock the law and the government which imposed such sacrifices upon them?

If all laws are based on expediency, who can blame the citizen if he lives by expediency? Or that he offers bribes, commits perjury, exploits the greed, the gluttony, the lust and all the other weaknesses of his fellow man when he finds it expedient.

Where such an attitude would lead us can be seen, of course, in some European lands where democracy has become a byword for corruption and the term politician a synonym for knave.

There is hardly a class of men who can do more good or more harm than lawyers. In that they are like priests.

What preserves the priest as a minister of spiritual life is reverence for God's ways and God's law.

And the same reverence makes the lawyer a defender of the abiding values in civil society.

So we end as we began, reiterating God's admonition: "Hearken to me you that know what is just, my people who have my law in your heart; fear ye not the reproach of men, and be not afraid of their blasphemies."

(1951)

# SECULARISM,
## PRODUCT OF ABNORMALITY

### THE REV. JOHN LA FARGE, S.J.

THE ancient pagans spoke with horror of the "anarchic" or the godless man; and early Christianity warned against the worldly man, the *anthropos kosmikos*. But secularism, in the peculiar sense we understand it, would doubtless have been strange to the ancient Hebrew, Greek, Roman or even medieval Christian, as Dr. Ernest Johnson remarks in the recent symposium, *Religion and the World Order*. "What is implied by secularism," writes Dr. Johnson, "is that man's religious life is conceived as an inner and private affair, having no necessary relevance to his business or political activities and incapable of furnishing him with sanctions to guide his organized social relationships."

There is no reason to improve on this excellent definition. To put the same idea in a more pungent manner:

"There is the man whose short hair bristles at the interference of the Church in Politics, Business, Social Life, Pocketbook, Legal Practice, Medical Practice and who just can't see why Church Property should not be taxed. They are the ones who just don't want the Church to intrude. And I rather sympathize with them, beause I can understand selfishness, and an intruding Church is a very disturbing thing. If you let them intrude it gets right into the home and into yourself and it upsets your whole microcosm; it devastates you." [1]

For the real understanding of secularism in any of its relationships, it is especially important to emphasize that it is not a *natural* nor a *normal* attitude for men to take. Secularism—the deliberate exclusion

[1] John Louis Bonn: *America*, April 15, 1944.

of religion from interference in human relationship—is not a rever-
sion to something elementary, simple and primitive in human affairs.
The more we know of primitive man, the less secularistic we find
him. . . .

Secularism is not normal, because it is the product of an abnormal
condition, the disruption of the spiritual unity of Christianity. Other
beliefs, such as the syncretic pagan religions of the East, or the religious philosophizings of the ancient world, could tolerate disunity.
But Christianity is essentially a religion of unity. Christ our Lord
placed unity above all attributes of the supernatural society which he
founded: when individual Christian people, or when large bodies of
Christian people, or Christian nations as a whole, embrace disunity,
they suffer a wound in their very souls, and secularism, historically,
is an expression of that very disturbance. Even a Protestant, says Dr.
F. E. Johnson, "should see that a concomitant of the fragmentizing of
Christendom was the divorcement of large areas of life from effective
religious and moral sanctions—in other words, the rise of secularism.
When the economic life of the Western world acquired a moral autonomy of its own the way was open to all the ills of unrestrained *laissez
faire*. With the decline of the spiritual authority of the Church in national affairs, however badly that authority may have been exercised,
the way was open to the rise of nationalism as a false and pernicious
religion. Can it be coincidence that the divorce of faith and reason,
the dualistic conception of human nature and the rise of mechanistic
natural science and psychology date from the time when the spiritual
unity of the Western world was dissolving away."

Once that religious individualism had been accepted as a proper
thing by the dissident elements in the Western nations, the trend to
secularism grew through the subsequent centuries since the Reformation. . . .

The trend to secularism was further reinforced by the economic and
social individualism that has penetrated our religious as well as our
social philosophy. . . .

The moral vacuum which secularism has created will not perma-
nently remain empty. The vacuum must be filled, and if not filled
by the principle of order and unity will be replenished with the
principle of disorder and disunity, in the form of the totalitarian
ideologies.

(1945)

119

# THE CHURCH'S SOCIAL MISSION

COMMISSION ON AMERICAN CITIZENSHIP

OF CATHOLIC UNIVERSITY OF AMERICA

THE sphere of the Church's competence and activity is not limited to those things which are purely spiritual. Union with God demands union with our fellow man, and the Commandment to love God above all things is obeyed in the degree that we love our neighbor as ourselves. Religion embraces everything in life, and nothing is outside its orbit. . . .

We go to Church on Sunday in order to obtain the light and strength that we need to make the church go with us during the week—go with us into our homes and communities, into the marts of trade and commerce, into the fields, the factories, and the mines, into our world of relaxation and recreation. Wherever men have need of truth and love and moral strength, which is everywhere, Christ expects us to take Him. We bear His Name in vain if we deny Him access to any phase or aspect of our daily existence.

This being so, it follows that the Church has the right to maintain and to direct all the instrumentalities that are required for her social mission. Among these are schools and the means of education, youth organizations, facilities for the care of the sick and the needy, provisions for salutary recreation. To the extent that she is impeded and restricted in any of these and similar fields of endeavor, she is deprived of the rights that belong to her by virtue of her supernatural nature and divine mission.

(1943)

# THE LIMITS OF RELIGIOUS
# SOCIAL ACTION

THE REV. JOHN LA FARGE, S.J.

THE strength of religious social action lies precisely in its being religious, with the limitations and the powers that such a sphere implies. I do not believe it is the function of the Church to engage in the purely technical field; to convey, for instance, all the answers to our economic problems, especially when the professional economists so notably disagree, as is only proper that they should. . . .

Catholics, it is true, differ among themselves on a number of very vital points. We are not agreed, for instance, as to the exact nature of social justice; or as to the moral obligation of certain types of public legislation; or as to the Christian position on the functioning of vocational groups in the industrial order. . . .

Though religion is not adapted to speak outside of its own field, it is all the more called to speak a prophetic word in the area which is properly its own; to designate clearly as moral matters those things which are moral in their nature, and to be utterly fearless in so doing.

The Church has not the function of telling people how to run their business; but it has the right and duty to tell businessmen what is right and wrong in the conduct of business; to speak on industrial morality for employers, trustees, managers, union officials, and so on. This truth alone is revolutionary to many an American mind.

The Church, likewise, cannot tell an employer whom to hire or fire. But it can tell him, as an elementary principle of ordinary morality, that he is violating the moral code and injuring the institution of the family if he lets his hiring practices be guided not by a man's intrinsic worth and acquired skill but by purely racial, religious or national considerations.

(1952)


# SOCIAL REFORM BEGINS IN HEARTS
## RT. REV. WILLIAM J. KERBY

THE Church conceives her mission to be primarily spiritual and supernatural. She holds that she is divinely commissioned as teacher and sanctifier, that her constitution is divine, and that she alone is its qualified interpreter. She sees life, truth, action in their organic unity, drawing inspiration and law for present life from life to come. She sees spiritual in relation to material, temporal in relation to eternal, and social in relation to individual. Hence the Church's judgment of social processes, institutions, problems, and reforms is part of a comprehensive spiritual view of life.

Within the content of the Church's normal teaching are views on human rights and personality, justice, property, family; on social relations, the constitution of society, the sanction and function of authority, of law, of virtue, derived from revelation and from her understanding of natural law. Social questions present themselves to the Church's mind primarily in the form of error or sin, to be met and conquered by truth and virtue. Hence her first impulse to social reform directs her, not so much to social institutions as to correction of minds by true teaching and by reforming hearts by instilling virtue.

(1908)

## "A CITIZEN OF ANOTHER CITY"
### ROSALIND MURRAY

WE do not suggest that it is impossible to serve both God and Man; to serve our fellow men may be, and often is, an excellent form of service to Our Maker; but the end we have in view is all-important, and the relation in which we see our service. There cannot, in the very nature of things, be equal balance between Man and God, to imagine such equality is in itself denial of the whole idea of God.

The "difference" of God is no new idea; it has been fundamental from the beginning in the religious attitude to life, but it is as persistently ignored or contradicted in all the varying forms of non-belief. The old assertion that there is no God is less common in the contemporary world than the almost as misleading compromise of proposing this or that as "God-substitutes": service to Man, to the State, to Science, to abstract Knowledge, are offered to us as equivalent to God. . . .

The Good Pagan and the Christian may often act in the same way, make the same moral judgments; they may both be virtuous, honourable and just, they may both be charitable and unselfish, they may be equally so, but the Pagan is satisfied, the Christian, not at all. The Pagan has attained his aim of the "good life," he is a man of honour, a good citizen, a good human being, he knows it and is content.

The Christian, on the other hand, measures himself by quite another standard, not in human excellence, but in relation to God. He is a citizen of another city. The idea of God becomes, to him, more real, more absorbing, in proportion as he himself draws nearer to Him. He is living his life as if it were in a new dimension, in which the goodness he has attained seems negligible, non-existent, in comparison to the goodness he apprehends.

(1939)

### JACQUES MARITAIN

THE Christian is *part* of history, he is *in* history; since he is to witness there to a supra-historic world *to which he belongs,* he wishes only to use good means: thus we have good means employed in a context where evil means predominate, and running the risk of being themselves mixed up in such a context. . . .

This man, if he fears God, should only employ means that are good in themselves; and he should in any case envisage the context also, so that this may have the possibility of being evil in the least possible degree. After that, let him be at peace. The rest belongs to God.

The fear of soiling ourselves in entering into the context of history is a pharisaical one. We cannot touch human flesh and blood without staining our fingers. To stain our fingers is not to stain our hearts. The Catholic Church has never feared to lose its purity in touching our impurity. If, instead of dwelling in the heart, purity mounts to our heads, the result is sectaries and heresies. Some seem to think that to put our hands to the real, to this concrete universe of human things and human relations where sin exists and circulates, is in itself to contract sin, as if sin were contracted from without, not from within. Hence they claim to interdict the use of all means not evil in themselves to which men have given an impure context (the writer must not publish, for modern publicity is impure; citizens must not vote, for Parliament is impure); they insist that men should not cooperate in a common aim when impure means are mingled in it by accident (as always happens); the crusaders should not set out for the Holy Land for rapine and cruelty have had their part in the crusades. This is pharisaical purism: it is not the doctrine of the purification of the means.

(1936)

# CHRISTIAN RESIGNATION IS NOT
# NON-RESISTANCE TO EVIL

### PAUL CLAUDEL

FOR a hundred years the assertion of professors that Christianity is an oriental doctrine in the manner of Buddhism and Islamism, a school of resignation, fatalism and death, has been rubbed into us *ad nauseam*. It is unfortunate for them that the history of the Church from its origin down to our own days, shows us on the contrary a spectacle of intense energy, of universal enterprise, moral and material activity against evil and error which has never known decline, and which ceases as soon as heresy and schism have spread over a great part of her domain their death-dealing influence. . . .

When they ask Our Lord: "What is the Great Commandment?" He replies with the Scripture: "Thou shalt love the Lord Thy God with thy whole heart, with thy whole soul and with thy whole mind. And the second is like to this: Thou shalt love thy neighbor as thyself."

Since these faculties in us serve to love God and carry out His Will, therefore is it: firstly, that none of them is evil, that none of them is superfluous; that all the strength of our soul and of our body, of our nature and of our sensitiveness, is holy, precious, excellent, inasmuch as it allows us to do our essential duty; and thus it is: secondly, that not only must we utilise them all, but even not leave any particle unused, not the least thought, not the least word, for we shall have to render account of all—stretch them out to the last extremity like the body of Jesus Christ upon the Cross, to the extreme end of our powers, and beyond. On this condition do we realise in very truth, each in his own way, the state of goodwill: *as thy strength so be thy daring.* . . .

It is false therefore to pretend that at any moment Christianity preached non-resistance to evil. He who would allow injury or wrong to be done before his eyes to one of his brethren to whom he is bound, without using every means, every strength available, to aid him, would fail the fundamental precept of our Faith. So too, with him who by the deed of an aggressor shall see diminished and impaired in his own person the God whose image he is and the neighbors whose resource he is.

(1933)

THE Catholic thinker sees everything in relation to eternity. For him applied sociology is not an end in itself but a means to a higher end— the salvation of human souls. For this reason the philosophical approach, taking account as it does of moral value, will always be exceedingly important in the eyes of the Catholic.

THE REV. PAUL HANLY FURFEY (1929)

# CATHOLICS OF THE
# "RIGHT" AND "LEFT"

THE REV. ALFRED F. HORRIGAN

UNDER the pressure of historical circumstances, too involved to review here, there has emerged among Catholics a rather large number of opinions and points of view which can be grouped according to the "right" and "left" classification. The following necessarily oversimplified examples may serve as illustrations.

The Catholic "right" often tends to identify itself with the *status quo*. It usually is sympathetic towards retaining in unchanged form the economic and political institutions under which the Church has operated in the past. It is suspicious of what appears novel or "radical" because it fears that too much concern with new applications may threaten the purity of fundamental rights and truth.

It is quick to defend anything or anybody associated in any way with the Church. It is not eager to emphasize the distinctions between the accidental and the essential, the changeable and the unchangeable, the divine and the human, in Catholic life and practice.

The Catholic "left," while yielding nothing to the "right" in its devotion to essentials, tends to feature the "reforming" character of Christ's teaching.

It is usually insistent upon preventing an identification of the Church with any particular social or political institution. Making the necessary distinctions between the accidental and the essential, it has no hesitancy in indulging in self-criticism.

From these generalizations, the strength, as well as the potential dangers, in the Philosophy of the Catholic "right" and "left" will be apparent.

Descending to greater detail, there are a number of rather identifiable questions concerning which the lines of "right" and "left" are applicable in our country today.

Catholics on the "right," for example, usually have more to say about the rights of private property than they do about the obligations of private property. They call particular attention to the necessity of caution and prudence in solving the problems of racial and social justice.

They are much more conscious of the threats to the Christian and democratic way of life offered by Communism than they are of the dangers to this same way of life offered by an ill-advised curtailment of civil rights. They usually consider it necessary to defend as best they can the head of a Catholic nation, such as Franco, since they feel there is some degree of identification between him and the Church.

American Catholics who incline to the "left" of center can usually be identified according to the shifting of the emphasis described in the above examples.

Needless to say, this matter of "right" and "left" does not fit into any simple black-and-white pattern. There are as many shades of emphasis as there are newspapers or people. Often a newspaper or individual will appear to favor the "left" on one problem and the "right" on the other.

We believe that everyone knows the Church is against Communism; we are not at all sure that there is a sufficient understanding of the Church's teaching on civil rights.

There is little need to proclaim that the Church is not promoting social upheaval; there is an almost inexpressibly great need to make clear to everyone that the present practices of racial and social injustice are completely incompatible with Catholic teaching.

Practically every informed person knows that the Church claims to be infallible in matters of faith and morals; too few people are aware that the political systems of Catholic countries, or the actions of prominent Catholic statesmen and leaders, need not in the least be considered and defended as applications of Catholic truth.

Space does not permit prolonging the discussion further. We should like to end it by recalling the observation of Chesterton that a "heresy is a truth which has gone mad through loneliness."

(1952)

# THE STATE'S DUTIES
## TO THE POOR AND HELPLESS

### LEO XIII

To the State the interests of all are equal whether high or low. The poor are members of the national community equally with the rich; they are real component parts; living parts, which make up, through the family, the living body; and it need hardly be said that they are by far the majority. . . .

Justice, therefore, demands that the interests of the poorer population be carefully watched over by the Administration, so that they who contribute so largely to the advantage of the community may themselves share in the benefits they create—that being housed, clothed, and enabled to support life, they may find their existence less hard and more endurable. It follows that whatever shall appear to be conducive to the well-being of those who work, should receive favorable consideration. Let it not be feared that solicitude of this kind will injure any interest; on the contrary, it will be to the advantage of all; for it cannot but be good for the commonwealth to secure from misery those on whom it so largely depends. . . .

Rights must be religiously respected wherever they are found; and it is the duty of the public authority to prevent and punish injury, and to protect each one in the possession of his own. Still, when there is question of protecting the rights of individuals, the poor and helpless have a claim to special consideration. The richer population have many ways of protecting themselves, and stand less in need of help from the State; those who are badly off have no resources of their own to fall back upon, and must chiefly rely upon the assistance of the State. And it is for this reason that wage-earners, who are, undoubtedly, among the weak and necessitous, should be specially cared for and protected by the commonwealth.

(May 15, 1891)


In human affairs there is the common good, the well-being of the state or nation; there is also a human good which does not lie in the community, but is personal to each man in himself; not, however, that it is privately profitable to the exclusion of others.

ST. THOMAS AQUINAS (1261)


# THE RIGHTS AND OBLIGATIONS
# OF PROPERTY

### PIUS XI

If the social and public aspect of ownership be denied or minimized, the logical consequence is Individualism, as it is called; on the other

127

hand, the rejection or diminution of its private and individual character necessarily leads to some form of Collectivism. . . .

The right of property must be distinguished from its use. It belongs to what is called commutative justice faithfully to respect the possessions of others, not encroaching on the rights of another and thus exceeding the rights of ownership. . . .

It follows from the twofold character of ownership, which We have termed individual and social, that men must take into account in this matter not only their own advantage but also the common good. To define in detail these duties, when the need occurs and when the natural law does not do so, is the function of the government. Provided that the natural and divine law be observed, the public authority, in view of the common good, may specify more accurately what is licit and what is illicit for property owners in the use of their possessions. . . .

When civil authority adjusts ownership to meet the needs of the public good it acts not as an enemy, but as the friend of private owners; for thus it effectively prevents the possession of private property, intended by Nature's Author in His Wisdom for the sustaining of human life, from creating intolerable burdens and so rushing to its own destruction. It does not therefore abolish, but protects private ownership, and, far from weakening the right of private property, it gives it new strength.

At the same time a man's superfluous income is not left entirely to his own discretion. We speak of that portion of his income which he does not need in order to live as becomes his station. On the contrary, the grave obligations of charity, beneficence and liberality which rest upon the wealthy are constantly insisted upon in telling words by Holy Scripture and the Fathers of the Church.

However, the investment of superfluous income in searching favorable opportunities for employment, provided the labor employed produces results which are really useful is to be considered, according to the teaching of the Angelic Doctor an act of real liberality particularly appropriate to the needs of our time. . . .

Now, not every kind of distribution of wealth and property amongst men is such that it can at all, and still less can adequately, attain the end intended by God. Wealth, therefore, which is constantly being augmented by social and economic progress, must be so distributed amongst the various individuals and classes of society that the common good of all, of which Leo XIII spoke, be thereby promoted. In other words, the good of the whole community must be safeguarded. By these principles of social justice one class is forbidden to exclude the other from a share in the profits. . . . Each class, then, must receive its due share, and the distribution of created goods must be brought into conformity with the demands of the common good and social justice, for every sincere observer is conscious that the vast differences between the few who hold excessive wealth and the many who live in destitution constitute a grave evil in modern society. . . .

Every effort, therefore, must be made that at least in future a just share only of the fruits of production be permitted to accumulate in the hands of the wealthy, and that an ample sufficiency be supplied to the workingmen. The purpose is not that these become slack at their work, for man is born to labor as the bird to fly, but that by thrift they may increase their possessions and by the prudent management of the same may be enabled to bear the family burden with greater ease and security, being freed from that hand-to-mouth uncertainty which is the lot of the proletarian. Thus they will not only be in a position to support life's changing fortunes, but will also have the reassuring confidence that when their lives are ended, some little provision will remain for those whom they leave behind them. . . .

In the present state of human society, however, We deem it advisable that the wage contract should, when possible, be modified somewhat by a contract of partnership, as is already being tried in various ways to the no small gain both of the wage-earners and of the employers. In this way wage-earners are made sharers in some sort in the ownership, or the management, or the profits. . . .

Every effort must therefore be made that fathers of families receive a wage sufficient to meet adequately ordinary domestic needs. If in the present state of society this is not always feasible, social justice demands that reforms be introduced without delay which will guarantee every adult workingman just such a wage. . . .

The condition of any particular business and of its owner must also come into question in settling the scale of wages; for it is unjust to demand wages so high that an employer cannot pay them without ruin, and without consequent distress amongst the working people themselves. If the business make smaller profit on account of bad management, want of enterprise or out-of-date methods, that is not a just reason for reducing the workingman's wages. If, however, the business does not make enough money to pay the workman a just wage, either because it is overwhelmed with unjust burdens, or because it is compelled to sell its products at an unjustly low price, those who thus injure it are guilty of grievous wrong; for it is they who deprive the workingmen of the just wage, and force them to accept lower terms.

(May 15, 1931)

THE art of acquiring money is subordinate to the art of using money, not so much by way of providing material for it as by way of providing tools for it. For money and every kind of wealth are merely economic tools.

ST. THOMAS AQUINAS (ca. 1270)

ONLY too often it happens that economic life and the employment of capital are no longer ruled by human needs in the order of their natural and real importance. On the contrary, what needs are to be satisfied, and to what extent, is decided in the interests of capital and its profits. In consequence, it is not man's labor for the general welfare that attracts and uses capital, but capital which moves labor about like a pawn in a game of chess. . . . In the divinely willed order of nature, man would be the master of things by his labor; he would not be dominated by them.

PIUS XII (November 1946)

# THE ACCUMULATION OF
# ECONOMIC POWER

### PIUS XI

IT is patent that in our days not alone is wealth accumulated, but immense power and despotic economic domination is concentrated in the hands of a few, and that those few are frequently not the owners, but only the trustees and directors of invested funds, who administer them at their good pleasure.

This power becomes particularly irresistable when exercised by those who, because they hold and control money, are able also to govern credit and determine its allotment, for that reason supplying so to speak, the life-blood to the entire economic body, and grasping, as it were, in their hands, the very soul of production, so that no one dare breathe against their will. . . .

This concentration of power has led to a threefold struggle for domination. First, there is the struggle for dictatorship in the economic sphere itself; then, the fierce battle to acquire control of the state, so that its resources and authority may be abused in the economic struggles. Finally, the clash between states themselves. . . .

Unbridled ambition for domination has succeeded the desire for gain; the whole economic life has become hard, cruel and relentless in a ghastly measure. Furthermore, the intermingling and scandalous confusing of the duties and offices of civil authority and of economics has produced crying evils and have gone so far as to degrade the majesty of the state. The state which should be the supreme arbiter, ruling in kingly fashion far above all party contention, intent only upon justice and the common good, has become instead a slave, bound over to the service of human passion and greed. . . .

Since the present economic régime is based mainly upon capital and labor, it follows that the principles of right reason and Christian social philosophy regarding capital, labor and their mutual cooperation must be accepted in theory and reduced to practice. In the first place, due consideration must be had for the double character, individual and social, of capital and labor, in order that the dangers of Individualism and of Collectivism be avoided. The mutual relations between capital and labor must be determined according to the laws of the strictest justice, called commutative justice, supported however by Christian charity. Free competition and still more economic domination must be kept within just and definite limits, and must be brought under the effective control of the public authority, in matters appertaining to this latter's competence. The public institutions of the nations must be such as to make the whole of human society conform to the common good, *i.e.,* to the standard of social justice. If this is done, the economic system, that most important branch of social life, will necessarily be restored to sanity and right order.

(May 15, 1931)

THE good life does not consist in renouncing wealth, though that is one method of finding it. Easier for a camel to go through the eye of a needle than for a rich man to enter heaven—the impossibility is not alleged but the rarity is emphasized.

ST. THOMAS AQUINAS (ca. 1270)

# STRIKES

### LEO XIII

WHEN work-people have recourse to a strike, it is frequently because the hours of labor are too long, or the work too hard, or because they consider their wages insufficient. The grave inconvenience of this not uncommon occurrence should be obviated by public remedial measures; for such paralysis of labor not only affects the masters and their work-people, but is extremely injurious to trade, and to the general interests of the public; moreover, on such occasions, violence and disorder are generally not far off, and thus it frequently happens that the public peace is threatened. The laws should be beforehand, and prevent these troubles from arising; they should lend their influence and authority to the removal in good time of the causes which lead to conflicts between masters and those whom they employ.

But if the owners of property must be made secure, the workman, too, has property and possessions in which he must be protected; and, first of all, there are his spiritual and mental interests. . . . It is the soul which is made after the image and likeness of God; it is in the soul that sovereignty resides. . . . In this respect all men are equal; there is no difference between rich and poor, master and servant, ruler and ruled, "for the same is Lord over all." No man may outrage with impunity that human dignity which God Himself treats with reverence, nor stand in the way of that higher life which is the preparation for the eternal life of Heaven. Nay, more; a man has here no power over himself. To consent to any treatment which is calculated to defeat the end and purpose of his being is beyond his right; he cannot give up his soul to servitude; for it is not man's own rights which are here in question, but the rights of God, most sacred and inviolable.

(May 15, 1891)

# THE DUTIES OF EMPLOYEE
## AND EMPLOYER

### LEO XIII

THE great mistake . . . is to possess oneself of the idea that class is naturally hostile to class; that rich and poor are intended by nature to live at war with one another. So irrational and so false is this view, that the exact contrary is the truth. Just as the symmetry of the human body is the result of the disposition of the members of the body, so in a State it is ordained by nature that these two classes should exist in harmony and agreement, and should, as it were, fit into one another, so as to maintain that equilibrium of the body politic. Each requires the other; capital cannot do without labor, nor labor without capital. Mutual agreement results in pleasantness and good order; perpetual conflict necessarily produces confusion and outrage. . . . Religion teaches the laboring man and the workman to carry out honestly and well all equitable agreements freely made, never to injure capital, nor to outrage the person of an employer; never to employ violence in representing his own cause, nor to engage in riot and disorder; and to have nothing to do with men of evil principles, who work upon the people with artful promises, and raise foolish hopes which usually end in disaster and in repentance when too late. Religion teaches the rich man and the employer that their work people are not their slaves; that they must respect in every man his dignity as a man and as a Christian; that labor is nothing to be ashamed of, if we listen to right reason and to Christian philosophy, but it is an honorable employment, enabling a man to sustain his life in an upright and creditable way, and that it is shameful and inhuman to treat men like chattels to make money by, or to look upon them merely as so much muscle or physical power. . . . The employer must never tax his work-people beyond their strength, nor employ them in work unsuited to their age or sex. His great and principal obligation is to give to every one that which is just. Doubtless before we can decide whether wages are adequate many things have to be considered; but rich men and masters should remember this—that to exercise pressure for the sake of gain, upon the indigent and destitute, and to make one's profit out of the need of another, is condemned by all laws, human and divine. To defraud any one of wages that are his due is a crime that cries to the avenging anger of Heaven. . . . The rich must religiously refrain from cutting down the workingman's earnings, either by force, fraud or by usurious dealing; and with more reason because the poor man is weak and unprotected, and because his slender means should be sacred in proportion to their scantiness.

(May 15, 1891)

IF all may justly strive to better their condition, yet neither justice nor the common good allows anyone to seize that which belongs to another, or, under the pretext of futile and ridiculous equality, to lay hands on other people's fortunes. It is most true that by far the larger part of the people who work prefer to improve themselves by honest labor rather than by doing wrong to others. But there are not a few who are imbued with bad principles and are anxious for revolutionary change, and whose great purpose is to stir up tumult and bring about a policy of violence. The authority of the State should intervene to put restraint upon these disturbers, to save the workmen from their seditious acts, and to protect lawful owners from spoliation.

LEO XIII (May 15, 1891)

## RIGHTS AND DUTIES OF
## LABOR UNIONS

### MOST REV. FRANCIS J. HAAS

THE Church has consistently held that workers have the right to form unions and, with due regard for the public interest, to manage them as they deem best for their own interests. The reasoning back of this position is not hard to follow. It starts from the basic premise that in Catholic teaching all are children of God, in and through Jesus Christ, brothers and sisters to one another, owing one another the duties and good offices of justice and charity. But the Church observes that in modern industry a wide chasm stands between the individual worker and the employer—usually a corporation—and that the distance between them frustrates the equality of brotherhood. On the other hand, it observes that collective bargaining through freely chosen representatives of both sides is the only procedure thus far devised that bridges the chasm and brings both parties together on a basis approaching equality. Consequently autonomous unions are necessary.

But it is to be noted that autonomy does not mean license. The Encyclicals recognize this vital distinction and lay down the rule that unions, like other voluntary associations, are, with respect to internal policy, subject to certain restrictions. Accordingly they forbid Catholic wage and salary workers to enroll in unions which disregard the just and equitable claims of other classes or which interfere with the freedom of conscience of their Catholic member in matters of faith and worship. They further provide that while Catholic wage and salary workers may and in fact should join unions free from the indefensible policies just indicated, they are at the same time to take an active part in study club organizations devoted to a wider diffusion of the encyclical programs on the moral phases of industry and business. To be sure, such study club organizations are in no sense to be regarded as substitutes for labor unions.

(1939)

THE laborer's right to a decent livelihood is the first moral charge upon industry. The employer has a right to get a reasonable living out of his business, but he has no right to interest on his investment until his employees have obtained at least living wages. This is the human and Christian, in contrast to the purely commercial and pagan, ethics of industry.

CATHOLIC BISHOPS OF THE UNITED STATES,
(January, 1919)

## THE PRIESTHOOD AND THE WORKERS

### THE REV. BENJAMIN L. MASSE, S.J.

IT is quite possible that there are some priests who are not sympathetic to organized labor; who look at its faults with a magnifying glass and see its virtues through smoked spectacles; who have so far forgotten the Divine Model whom they are supposed to imitate—the Divine Model who spent most of His adult life at a carpenter's bench in Nazareth—that they tend to identify the interest of the Church with the interests of the rich.

Such priests are not the Church, nor are they in any way typical of the priesthood. . . . The priesthood of the Church is largely recruited from the poor, from people who are not afraid to have families or to give their sons and daughters to the service of Almighty God. The Church in the United States has been accused of a good many crimes and misdemeanors; but she has never, thank God, been called a "fashionable" church. She is identified with the masses of the people, not with high society, and in this she glories. The rich and the poor, the ignorant and learned, the workingman and his employer cannot always in this country meet on a level of equality. One of the few places where they can so meet is a Catholic church.

(1949)

THE object of gain is that by its means man may provide for himself and others according to their state. The object of providing for himself and others is that they may be able to live virtuously. The object of a virtuous life is the attainment of everlasting glory.

ST. ANTONINO (ca. 1457)

## CATHOLICISM NOT COMMITTED TO CAPITALISM

### THE REV. JAMES M. GILLIS, C.S.P.

I AM always puzzled or angered when I hear an orator, Catholic or other, declaring that the Catholic Church is "the one great bulwark against Socialism or Communism." In fact she is, but I fear lest indiscriminating listeners may misunderstand. The Catholic Church is a bulwark against Communism, but she is decidedly *not* a bulwark *for* Capitalism. She does not stand or fall with Capitalism. She was here a long time before Capitalism was created and she intends to be—and will be—here when Capitalism is gone. We Catholics must never again make a mistake like that of those who thought monarchy essential to Catholicism. We know better now. Kings come and go (mostly of late they go) but the Church continues. The number of thrones diminishes but the number of altars is multiplied. As with Monarchism, so with Capitalism. We are not wedded to it. We owe it no special loyalty. We make no bombastic protestation, "Live or Die, Sink or Swim, Survive or Perish, Catholicism and Capitalism are one!" God forbid! If Capitalism reforms, we shall give it another trial. But the reform must be radical. . . . If Capitalism cannot or will not reform altogether, we shall have to take upon our lips words . . . from Sacred Scripture, "Why cumbereth it the ground? Cut it down and cast it into the fire!" That will be no small fire, but a conflagration and a holocaust. But the Church will not be consumed in it. Doubtless she will suffer somewhat; the smell of the fire will for some time cling to her garments, but even though it were hell fire, it shall not prevail against her.

(1933)

# THE "DEPERSONALIZATION" OF MODERN MAN

### PIUS XII

MODERN industry has unquestionably had beneficial results, but the problem which arises today is this: Will a world in which the only economic form to find acceptance is a vast productive system be equally fitted to exert a happy influence upon society in general and upon the three fundamental institutions of society in particular? We must answer that the impersonal character of such a world is contrary to the fundamentally personal nature of those institutions which the Creator has given to human society.

In fact, marriage and the family, the state and private property tend of their very nature to form man as a person. The creative wisdom of God is therefore alien to that system of impersonal unity which strikes at the human person, who is the origin and the end of society and in the depths of his being the image of his God.

This sad reality is already with us. Wherever the demon of organization invades and tyrannizes the human spirit, there at once is revealed the signs of a false and abnormal orientation of society. In some countries the modern state is becoming a gigantic administrative machine. It extends its influence over almost every phase of life; it would bring under its administration the entire gamut of political, economic, social and intellectual life from birth to death.

No wonder then if in this impersonal atmosphere, which tends to penetrate and pervade all human life, respect for the common good becomes dormant in the conscience of individuals and the state loses more and more its primary character of a community of morally responsible citizens.

Here may be recognized the origin and source of that phenomenon which is submerging modern man under its tide of anguish; his "depersonalization." In large measure his identity and name have been taken from him.

One must no longer consider the standard of living and the employment of labor as purely quantitative factors, but rather as human values in the full sense of the world.

Whoever therefore would furnish assistance to the needs of individuals and people cannot rely upon the security of an impersonal system of men and matter, no matter how vigorously developed in its technical aspects.

Every plan or program must be inspired by the principle that man, as subject, guardian and promoter of human values, is more important than mere things.

It is upon the basis of this solidarity and not upon worthless and unstable systems that we call upon men to build the social fabric. Solidarity demands that outrageous and provoking inequalities in living standards among different groups in a nation be eliminated. To achieve this urgent end the efficacious voice of conscience is preferable to external compulsion. . . .

Human society is not a machine, and it must not be made such; not even in the economic field. Rather one must always work with the native endowment of the human person and the individuating characteristics of nations as the natural and basic point of departure in striving to attain the end of the economic order, which is to ensure a stable sufficiency of goods and material services, directed in their turn at improving moral, cultural, and religious conditions.

Indeed, modern society, which wishes to plan and organize all things, comes into conflict, since it is conceived as a machine, with that which is living, and which therefore cannot be subjected to quantitative calculations. . . .

Consciences are today afflicted by other burdens. For example, against the wills and convictions of parents, teachers are prescribed for children. Again access to employment or places of labor is made to depend on registration in certain parties or in organizations which deal with the distribution of employment. Such discrimination is indicative of an inexact concept of the proper function of labor unions and their proper purpose, which is the protection of the interests of the salaried worker within modern society, which is becoming more anonymous and collectivist. In fact is not the essential purpose of unions the practical affirmation that man is the subject and not the object of social relations? Is it not to protect the individual against collective irresponsibility of anonymous proprietors? Is it not to represent the person of the worker against those who are inclined to consider him merely a productive agent with a certain price value?

How, therefore, can it be considered normal that the protection of the personal rights of the workers be more and more in the hands of an anonymous group working through the agency of immense organizations which are of their very nature monopolies? Whoever would find our solicitude for true liberty to be without foundation when we speak as we do to that part of the world which is generally known as the "free world" should consider that even there, first the real war and then the "cold war," forcibly drove social relations toward an inevitable curtailment of liberty itself, while in another part of the world this tendency has reached the ultimate consequence of its development.

(Christmas, 1952)

HUMAN society has no use for the imaginary "economic man" of our political economists, but needs the human being in the full reality of the divine breath of life that animates him; it needs the man of the family of Adam . . . invested with all the sympathies, all the dignities of our human race. . . .

We have been strangled. We have been strangled by an exaggerated form of Individualism. But the coming century will show that human society is grander and nobler than anything merely individual. . . . The future will call forth into the light of reason the social state of the world of labor. We shall then see upon what laws the Christian society of humanity rests.

HENRY CARDINAL MANNING (1886)

# THE "DISAPPEARANCE" OF SIN

ETIENNE GILSON

THE very idea that there is an objective distinction between good and evil, and that man, by consulting his reason, can tell with certitude what is right and what is wrong, is today publicly discussed, subjected to a sharp critique and, as often as not, rejected as wholly deprived of rational justification.

This is something entirely different from, and much more serious than, any temporary relaxation or loosening of moral laws themselves. This is the denial of the very existence of such laws. The real trouble with our times is not the multiplication of sinners, it is the disappearance of sin.

There are reasons for this tremendous change in attitude. First of all, one must cite the openly-stated denial that there is a God—the decision, made by certain men, and even by certain States, to proclaim the non-existence of God as a scientifically established dogma, and not only to profess it, but to teach it in the schools, in colleges, and in universities.

Nor is this all. For indeed, if it is true that there is no God, then the whole of human life, both private and public, has to be reorganized on the basis of this new truth. For centuries and centuries, men have been taught to believe that there is a God, and even today, millions of them still believe that there is one. . . . For the first time since the beginning of the world, mankind, is approaching the day when it will have to live alone, left to its own decisions and to its own resources, without the guidance of God and, consequently, of any religion.

This is the most tremendous revolution that ever took place in world history. . . .

For indeed, if there is no God, who but man himself can teach man the distinction between what is right and what is wrong? This is perfectly logical.

However, there is still one more question to be answered. What do we mean by man? Man in general does not exist; there are individual men only, and who among them will have authority to teach the distinction between good and evil? Thus far, no one. And this is what I call the true breakdown of morals, not indeed the all too-frequent breaking of the moral code, but the new fact that today there is no moral code to break. . . .

The only reason why a State may not want children to be educated in view of God is that it wants them educated in view of itself. Totalitarian education does nothing more than go the whole way along the same line. The result is what we know; political, economic, intellectual and spiritual slavery.

140

Our own liberal States, on the one hand, refuse to mistake themselves for the God of their citizens; yet on the other hand, while professing that they are not the ultimate end of man, they refuse to say what the ultimate end actually is. In other words, while acknowledging the fact that the temporal welfare of the State presupposes the recognition, by its citizens, of an order of ends and means set above the State, our liberal societies persist in considering as "separate" the only schools which can provide them with the very type of citizens they need, namely, Christian schools. . . .

If we do not care to awaken some morning on the wrong side of the Iron Curtain, then we ought all to be interested in not letting the liberal State believe that it can indefinitely persist in educating children in view of nothing. Either the liberal State will recognize that there is no education without religion, or it will cease to be liberal by turning itself into a god, and civil service into a religious service. Our only choice is not between religion and no religion, but between true religion and false religion.

To sum up, the breakdown of morals is a matter of life and death for the liberal State. After heedlessly squandering the Christian heritage on which it has lived so long a time, the day is now come when it has to make a choice: either to draw openly from all the sources of religious life and thus to survive, or else let them dry up and thus itself to perish.

(1952)

SINCE the Church of God, like a good mother, is bound to provide so that the poor who can get no help from the wealth of parents should not be deprived of the opportunity of learning and making progress in letters, let a complete benefice be assigned in every cathedral church to a schoolmaster, who will teach clerics and poor scholars for nothing.

DECREE, THIRD LATERAN COUNCIL (1179)

# PRINCIPLES OF CATHOLIC EDUCATION

THE REV. WILLIAM J. MC GUCKEN, S.J.

THIS fact of facts, the existence of a personal God, is of supreme importance for any program of education. For education deals with the formation of the whole man, body and soul, intellect and will. In the area of character education, for example, the Catholic would hold that any character-training program that left God out of consideration would be not merely inadequate but utterly false. . . .

A great deal of our philosophy of education depends upon our view of the person taught, in other words, upon the nature of man. Obviously, those who hold that the child is composed of a material body and an immortal soul will differ *toto coelo* from those who hold that the educand is merely a machine or a physico-chemical combination, or a bundle of S-R bonds or a product of the cosmic evolutionary process. That is the reason why we have *philosophies* of education, not a philosophy of education. . . .

The key of the Catholic system is the supernatural. Not only Catholic theology, but Catholic practice, the Catholic attitude toward life, and most of all, Catholic education are insoluble mysteries if we exclude an understanding of the supernatural. The Church holds that she is divinely commissioned by Christ to carry on His Work, to do what He did. "I am come that you may have life, that you may have it more abundantly." The Church continues that work, bringing this supernatural life to men who have not yet received it, surrounding it with safeguards that it may not be lost, restoring it once more to those who perversely cast it aside. The same is true of her educational system. Her primary purpose in establishing schools, kindergartens or universities is not merely to teach fractions or logarithms, biology or seismology, grammar or astronomy—these subjects are subordinate to her main purpose to inculcate the "eminent knowledge and love of Jesus Christ our Lord," a knowledge so intimate, a love so strong, that it will lead necessarily to a closer following of Christ. Otherworldly? Yes, if you will. . . .

The ultimate objective of Catholic education can be stated very simply. In the words of Pius XI:

"The proper and immediate end of Christian education is to cooperate with divine grace in forming the true and perfect Christian, that is, to form Christ Himself in those regenerated by Baptism. . . .

For precisely this reason, Christian education takes in the whole aggregate of human life, physical and spiritual, intellectual and moral, individual, domestic, and social, not with a view of reducing it in any way, but in order to elevate, regulate, and perfect it, in accordance with the example and teaching of Christ.

Hence the true Christian, product of Christian education, is the supernatural man who thinks, judges, and acts constantly and consistently in accordance with right reason illumined by the supernatural light of the example and teaching of Christ; in other words, to use the current term, the true and finished man of character. For, it is not every kind of consistency and firmness of conduct based on subjective principles that makes true character, but only constancy in following the eternal principles of justice.

. . . The true Christian does not renounce the activities of this life, he does not stunt his natural faculties; but he develops and perfects them, by coordinating them with the supernatural. He thus ennobles what is merely natural in life and secures for it new strength in the material and temporal order, no less than in the spiritual and eternal."

With this ultimate aim of Catholic education, there never has been, there can be no change. Given the Church's teaching about man's nature, and supernature, and man's supernatural destiny, it is impossible to see how there could be any change. Into this ultimate aim every type of Catholic educational institution must fit from kindergarten to graduate school; otherwise it has no right to be called a Catholic school. . . .

Classical culture, Christian culture, the medieval synthesis of Thomas Aquinas, and modern science and modern thought—these are the strands that the Catholic believes must be combined somehow into unity to provide a liberal education for the youth of our day, to place him in contact with truth, and beauty, and goodness. How can integration be secured for these divergent and sometimes clashing forces? The metaphysics that President Hutchins speaks of is a partial solution; it is not a complete solution. The Catholic believes humbly and sincerely that the answer to this problem of integration is one word, a monosyllable, Christ. Christianity *is* Christ. Christianity is not the history of one nation or race or people; it is universal history, the history of the human race, the most human thing in the world. The humanism of Christ, who is also God, as the Catholic confidently believes, this is Christian humanism, integral humanism that will make a marvelous synthesis of old and new. In this framework the classical theory of a liberal education remains not a relic, however glorious, of a golden past, not something static, but a dynamic force, transformed and vivified by all that is of permanent value in past and present, providing the world with a liberal education in the truest and finest sense of the word.

(1948)

143

# IN DEFENSE OF PAROCHIAL SCHOOLS
# IN AMERICA

MOST REV. RICHARD J. CUSHING

SECULARISM has put to work the genius of skillful propaganda in a flood of books, magazine articles and forum lectures which have accomplished much toward persuading the rank and file of the American public that secularism has been the religious philosophy of America from the beginning; that separation of Church and State means segregation of civic concerns from spiritual values and even hostility between those who are charged with temporal matters and those who bear witness to the eternal, especially in the field of education. . . .

President Conant [of Harvard University] does not say, as some others have said, that he merely objects to tax help for children who attend independent schools like parochial schools. He does not even suggest that his objection is to the standards maintained in such schools.

He . . . announces without qualification that his objection is to the parochial and private school as such.

He sets forth clearly his conviction that those who believe in "democracy" or in "American principle" should not argue about tax support or about standards, but should take the position that the independent school, whether it pays for itself or not, whether it meets standards or not, is an offense against "democracy," a violation of "American principle," as Dr. Conant and his associates now define "democracy" and "American principle."

Independent schools like the parochial school, we are told, offend against democracy because they bring what Dr. Conant calls "a divisive attitude" into American society, and they do so because they are not State monopoly schools.

We have said that such a statement from such a source is astonishing, coming as it does from the president of Harvard University, in the Commonwealth of Massachusetts, in this late year of grace.

A person familiar with the history of education in Massachusetts must have difficulty believing his own ears when he is told that the concept of aid to children in religious schools is some new phenomenon, and when he is told that private schools, and particularly private schools operating on a religious basis, have recently brought "cleavages" and "divisive attitudes" into American society, particularly in the last 20 years. . . .

Throughout the colonial period, Cubberly writes, there was never a time when Massachusetts did not apply the principle that it was a function of the state to promote religion and when the majority did not believe that taxation for religious purposes was justified. . . .

Furthermore, in all the schools, whether tax-supported or not, and in Harvard College, which received many grants from the state, the teaching of religious subjects and the training of a religious spirit were considered fundamentally important.

During this period toleration had been established for all except Roman Catholics, though all taxpapers had to support the religious worship approved by the majority of each town, except that Episcopalians might have their tax transferred to their own minister, and Quakers and Baptists, if members of a regular church society, were exempted out of respect for their conscientious scruples.

True, this attitude was considerably modified later, though it was not entirely changed until very much later.

No one of us would wish a return to the relations between Church and State which then existed in Massachusetts, or to the control of civil authority over pulpit and school or the control of the pulpit over civil authority which existed in our state when it was still a Protestant Puritan Commonwealth. No one, Catholic, Protestant, or other, would wish such a turning back of the clock of history.

But against the background of this history, a history with which his own institution has been so intimately identified, it is a little astonishing to be told by the eminent speaker that "in *recent* years" "divisive attitudes" have been brought into the community by *our* schools—by *independent* schools, built and supported by ourselves, with neither State grants nor other State aid except that which the State gives for the general defense against fire, disease and like hurt to all citizens and institutions within its confines. . . .

Less subtle minds than that of Dr. Conant may wonder how it was once sound Americanism and good Puritan democracy to seek, require and accept tax support for religious schools, though it is now impossible even to raise such a question in behalf of the schools of another religion, and is bad Americanism to *maintain* such schools, even without state support! . . .

One wonders if "American principle" means not so much *whether*

State grants, tax aid, or cooperation are given, but *when* and to *whom* such things are given. In other words, it is sometimes a question of whose ox is being gored.

When the president of Harvard announces in 1952 that independent schools operated for religious reasons have introduced "divisive attitudes" and "stratification" into the American community while making not so much as a passing reference to the past 300 years of educational history in Massachusetts with its "numerous clauses" in colleges, its admission restrictions of a completely non-academic character and its ingrained caste system, then he is either indulging in high humor or in something considerably less attractive.

It took a long long time—the time required for the poor finally to build their own private schools—before a university president was heard to announce that private religious schools are inconsistent with American democracy!

Some of those who heard that announcement must have come from cities within the United States where Catholic nuns have long been teaching colored children who, until very recently, were prevented by "divisive attitudes" in their communities from receiving any chance for education proportionate to their ability or dignity.

The Roman Catholic Sisters received them in independent parochial schools operated on a religious basis in accordance with "an American principle" older and more valid than Dr. Conant's principle of the "single public school system for all children."

It would have been interesting to hear the comments of the educators from such States, States into which no parent, priest, or teacher of *our* tradition introduced the idea of "divisive attitudes" and "stratification," but into which our schools brought the best opportunity children of embarrassing color, regardless of their creed, have had to receive an education.

I hope that sometime a speaker at a National Education Association convention will find it in his heart to refer to this kind of work when he is talking about "democracy" and "American principle." . . .

President Conant tells us that "the greater the proportion of our young who attend independent schools, the greater the threat to our democratic unity." He tells us that private high schools operated along economic or religious lines endanger "the American principle of a single public school system for all youth."

One wonders why a principle allegedly so basic only holds good with respect to primary and secondary schools.

146

Can it be that President Conant intends to recommend that his own university and like universities be turned over to the Commonwealth of Massachusetts or to the Federal Government so that they become "citizens" colleges to be operated in accordance with this newly-found "American principle of a single school system for all youth?" . . .

By such a procedure "divisive attitudes" might be eliminated from American society and the so-called "dualism" in the field of education would certainly give way to a strictly monolithic educational system under state monopoly—but much more would also be lost which scholarship, civilization and "democracy" prefer to keep.

I do not believe that Dr. Conant would make such a proposal. . . . He would probably protest that such regimentation, when applied to a university, is Fascism—and in this he would be quite right. It is strict totalitarianism—"everything in the State, nothing outside the State"—which is why Fascism of every stripe opposes private and parochial schools and always demands a single state school system without independent competition, challenge, or rival of any kind.

But just as the things which constituted "Americanism" in the 17th, 18th or 19th Century are also somehow "American" in the 20th, so Fascism in the 12th grade is Fascism in the eighth, and what would be Fascism on the university level is Fascism if required down through the rest of the school system.

Perhaps the most important political contribution that the private school, operated for religious or other reasons, makes here in America at the moment is the witness it bears to the independence of the mind and soul of a *person* in the face of the omnipotent modern state.

We build our schools out of the desire to include the knowledge of God in the minds of our children together with their knowledge of all things else. We declare war on no one's schools.

On the contrary, to the extent that any school provides that sound education which is a pre-requisite of political freedom and of spiritual growth, we wish it well.

But we reserve the right, both as Christians and as Americans, to promote the common good and to seek the salvation of our children through our own schools whenever and wherever these may be needed. . . .

Unless we who live by the Faith of the Risen Christ, the Christ who rose from the dead and dieth now no more, are vigilant against every aggression against the institution by which the Faith is preached and

147

preserved, we stand in danger of seeing American and Western Civilization go by default to the secularists.

In an age of state socialism, the threat to independent schools is a powerful part of the total threat to freedom of every kind—and when those schools are also religious schools, it is a part of the threat to the Faith.

(1952)

## THE BLASPHEMY OF SECULARISM

### THE REV. JOHN J. CAVANAUGH, C.S.C.

AFTER World War II the victorious powers, including America, decided to come together in a gigantic, unheard-of undertaking, to set up a world organization that would one day function as a world government and bring law and order and peace to all the peoples of the earth. Numerous conferences were held in San Francisco, London, Paris, and New York; and throughout all these conferences in which the courageous, victorious leaders set forth their hopes and plans for peace, there was talk of areas of influence, of races and colors, of economic affairs, of tariffs and military controls and disarmament, of almost everything in the world, but there was sensitive exclusion of God. Was this merely a concession, an appeasement, to Russia? Or was it not an expression of peoples convinced themselves that although one might argue this way or that about God's existence, God's presence and God's part mattered little in the practical affairs of life?

These great leaders of the world seemed convinced that although a sparrow cannot fall to the ground without God's providence, they in the might of their scientific minds and with the riches of atomic energy at their command could erect a workable world order without God's aid. To me this is one of the most indicative and striking facts in history—this studied attempt to keep quiet on God's active presence and influence in the world at such a turning point in history. It is the sign of something, a symptom of the blasphemous thing which I am trying to describe.

There are, of course, many other signs and symptoms. One reads constantly "learned" articles on juvenile delinquency, on crime and divorce and birth control and euthanasia, on sex-perversion and sex-

148

excesses, thoroughly important human problems, I should say, that at least in some instances are caused by the free will of man; problems with definite moral and religious implications; but the new paganism deals with them as being exclusively scientific, psychological effects of heredity and environment that should be referred for solution—not to the moralist—but to the psychiatrist or the hospital. . . .

I have been suggesting by examples the secularistic theory and way of life out of which in Russia emerged communism, in Germany nazism, and in Italy fascism; I have been suggesting that in this country this new atheistic secularism is everywhere and if it is not checked, some other variant, equally terrifying, of totalitarianism, is bound to come about even in America. . . . Like modernism in theology, secularism is a synthesis of many particular views and attitudes. Sometimes it is called naturalism, or the new paganism, or agnosticism, or scientism, or atheism (both theoretical and practical), or more recently, existentialism. Among the adherents and supporters of secularism, you will find many who say they believe in God but think that education, business, the practice of medicine and of law can go on just as well or better without any relationship whatsoever to the spiritual and the moral. I have even known nominal Catholics who subscribe to this dogma of excluding God from the practical thought and action of their lives, although they think He is wonderful to invoke during misfortune, sickness and thunderstorms. . . .

If man is nothing but a high-grade materialistic machine, if he is not a child of God and need not one day account for his actions to that God, then the nazis and fascists and communists are perfectly logical in considering him as an individual subordinate to the State. After all, the good of many millions is much greater than the good of a single individual, if all are material things. Government is no longer a servant of the individual, but the individual is an instrument, a thing of the State. The State has a right to dictate his education, his moral principles, his entire way of life. And this is the essence of totalitarianism. Thus, without too much elaboration, we may say that secularism, by nature, is totalitarian, and that under any form of secularistic government order must be established by force and fear. No doubt this is the reason why we already find so much subversive thinking in our secularistic schools.

It is idle to say that boys and girls, young men and women can study the arts and sciences all day in an arid atmosphere of Godlessness and, at night for five minutes at their mother's knee, make religion the moral influence, the living, dominating force in their lives. Young people have questions to ask about the complex relationship of religion to the affairs of life. God's presence is everywhere in the field of knowledge. His influence is in the heart of the atom as it is in the heart of morality and in laws of economics and the science of government. God is all or nothing at all to the one who teaches as well as to one who learns. I am with Him or against Him as I write, and you are with Him or against Him as you read. There is simply no neutral middle-ground that God can occupy in the field of education or in life. Religion cannot, therefore, be confined to psalm singing, emotional experiences. It is the substance, the framework for all thought and action, or it is nothing.

(1950)

## "CATHOLIC SCHOOL CHILDREN ARE AMERICAN CITIZENS"

### THE REV. ROBERT C. HARTNETT, S.J.

In the cross-fire of emotionalism which marks the debate over the extension of tax-supported public-welfare services to Catholic school children, one essential fact seems to be overlooked: it is that Catholic school children are American citizens entitled in every way to the "equal protection of the laws" with all other American school children.

When a Catholic child is sent by his parents to a parochial school, he is carrying out a duty of American citizenship. He has no choice about going to school. The Catholic Church cannot attach any legal penalties to the failure of Catholic parents to send their children to school. It is the State which requires school attendance. When a Catholic child boards a bus to go to a distant school, he is therefore fulfilling a civic obligation. To enable children living great distances from schools to fulfill this civic obligation without imposing extraordinary costs of transportation on their parents, many States appropriate public funds to cover the bus fare. As everyone considers adequate schooling of young citizens to be essential to an enlightened electorate, this policy seems very well conceived. It is the only way of relieving some parents of an extraordinary expense involved in fulfilling the compulsory education laws, which oblige all parents.

The purpose of such laws is social: it is not to insure that the next generation will possess the equipment necessary to pursue purely private satisfactions, but to insure that the grown-up citizens of the America of tomorrow will have the training they must have to be a credit and not a burden to the community. They must be able to make a living, to increase the total prosperity of the nation, to found a home and raise a family, to understand and conform to American ideals of living, to cooperate with others in community enterprises, and to vote and help form a sound public opinion. . . .

One of the reasons why the United States has become the strongest and most productive and resourceful nation in the world is that we as a people have understood for over a hundred years the connection between national prosperity and an educated citizenry. Our task has been heavier than that of any other nation because we have absorbed into our population tens of millions of immigrants, many of them from countries where they had no chance to go to school.

Our school system, the most extensive and expensive in the world, has succeeded in moulding our people into a great national unity despite the circumstances that they have come here from all over the globe. The public-school system has carried the burden with remarkable success on this score. But it has not carried the burden alone. The Catholic parochial-school system has educated millions and millions of American citizens. Does anyone pretend that products of parochial schools have not shown themselves just as much a credit to the nation as the products of the public schools?

The Catholic schools have performed this notable public service under a great handicap. Catholic parents as American citizens have to pay the same taxes as all American citizens. From these taxes the public-school system receives its lavish support. But as Catholics want their children to be instructed in religion along with instruction in secular subjects, they have to dig into their pockets again, after paying taxes to support public schools, in order to make the voluntary contributions on which Catholic schools operate. . . .

Our Catholic schools are fulfilling a civic function, and the circumstance of their also fulfilling a religious function is no solid reason for penalizing American citizens who are exercising their constitutional right to have their children educated in religion in conjunction with their education in secular subjects.

The only reasonable basis for denying to children attending nongovernmental schools the public-welfare benefits afforded children in governmental schools would be the failure of non-governmental schools to provide the civic training in view of which governmental schools are thought to deserve public support.

No one has been bold enough to try to prove that parochial schools fail to teach children secular subjects just as well as do public schools. Do children in parochial schools learn less American history? Do they fail to learn arithmetic, spelling, English composition, geography, civics just as well as children in public schools? In competitions they frequently gain victories over public-school children. The graduates of parochial schools are at least as prompt as any others in enlisting in the armed services of their country in time of war. If there is any score on which Catholic-school children fail to measure up to public-school children, we would like to know what precisely that score is.

(1948)

# THE FUNCTION
# OF THE CATHOLIC COLLEGE

THE REV. GEORGE BULL, S.J.

THE function of the Catholic College is not merely to teach the formulas of the Catholic religion, but to impart in a thousand ways, which defy formularization, the Catholic attitude towards life as a whole. It is not merely to graduate students who have, what I may call the Catholic's ready answer in all the fields of knowledge, but students who are so steeped in the Catholic mood, that it colors their every activity, and not their religious activity alone. In a word, the function of the Catholic College is not merely to send forth men and women who can repeat, however intelligently, the Catholic formula, in religion, in philosophy, or science, or the arts; but students who are stamped with certain traits which come into play and govern their approach to life in every sphere; students, therefore, who realize that Catholicism is not merely a creed, but a culture. . . .

There is one trait of the Catholic culture to which I should like to draw special attention. I mention it, not because you do not know it, but because it is peculiarly related to the function of the Catholic College I am discussing; and because it shows with peculiar force how Catholicism as a *culture* is at grips with the modern world, and not merely as a religion. That trait is totality of view regarding life: the habit of looking at life as a whole, and not as a series of departments. . . .

If that unity and totality have passed from the civilization in which we now live, they have not passed from Catholic thinking on the fundamentals of existence. Catholics still believe that every sphere of human life is related essentially to every other; and that in the conscious and deliberate activity of man, there is no action that can be evaluated as an absolute entity—isolated, that is, from the central fact of man's relation to the Universe. And because this reference of all human activity to the whole, under which for Catholics life is organized, is nearly always implicit and spontaneous, a habit of totality of view is set up, which sets the Catholic at odds with the whole modern outlook on life. . . .

The Catholic College must fit its graduate not only to give a reason for the Faith within him, but to catch the whole implications of the life around him. And if the Catholic College has brought him to realize that, his whole attitude towards the modern world will be more secure. He will see that world in that only unity which (as St. Augustine tells us) it has—namely, its oneness in opposing the whole Catholic point of view! He will see in its institutions a challenge, not to this or that article of his Faith, but an implicit challenge to everything he takes for granted, no matter what activity he may be engaged in—whether it be discussing religion, selling stock, interpreting an Oscar Wilde, or a Noel Coward, going to Church, or attending the opera. Any formula he may have learned is pregnant now with a new power. He can use it as it was intended to be used, merely as the ready answer. He is made independent of it in the sense that he knows what it implies, and not merely what it says. It is no longer an isolated proposition; something external to the habits of his life and thought. He comes to look first to the substance, which is Catholicism, and only afterwards to the terms, in which, minds however great have sought to give it expression. He is no longer harried by a merely defensive psychology. He is alert, he is serene, he is enthusiastic, as only he can be who not only knows abstractly his Catholicism, but realizes its divine totality even in the spontaneous activity of his daily life.

This, then, is the function of the Catholic College. . . . It is not its only function. It is merely one which is sometimes overlooked. To say that the Catholic College exists merely to teach the formal Catholic religion is, to my mind, to express only part of its purpose. Catholicism is a culture, not merely a creed; an attitude, a whole complexus of things taken for granted, in every activity of life and not in the sphere of the strictly religious alone. And it is the business of Catholic education to impart that culture, just as it is the business of all other systems to communicate the culture which is theirs.

(1933)

## ACADEMIC FREEDOM

### MOST REV. KARL J. ALTER

IF the religious and academic world would once clearly grasp the fact that the infallibility of the Church is concerned only with the message of Divine Revelation and not with science, art, or culture, then it would find no difficulty in reconciling infallibility with intellectual freedom. . . .

The Church confines her teaching to matters of faith and morals. She surrounds her pronouncements with such formalities and such strict safeguards that there can be no question in any honest mind as to the limited nature of her claims.

We readily grant that, as a matter of historical fact, there have been some over-zealous churchmen, just as there have been careless and irresponsible scientists who have made pronouncements outside the field of their own competence or far beyond the legitimate conclusion of demonstrated facts. . . .

A Church-affiliated institution of higher learning enjoys as much freedom in the search for knowledge and the unrestricted right to teach the truth as any other institution, whether private or public, religious or secular. . . .

In its true sense, academic freedom merely implies that no instructor or professor should be restrained in teaching truth or in his search for knowledge, as long as he follows the discipline and methods of his own particular science or art or form of culture.

But this does not mean that a professor has the right to substitute his own theories for facts. To do so would be an abuse of freedom.

In a word, every professor must hold rigorously to the logic of demonstrated facts and not exaggerate the validity of his findings beyond the weight of his evidence. The classroom is a privileged forum.

If the term academic freedom is used in the sense that the professor has a right to use this privileged forum of the classroom for purposes of propaganda, then we say that it is an abuse of freedom.

If, for instance, a professor wishes to explain Communism as a theory, surely there can be no objection, as long as he does so in any objective scientific fashion.

Should the same professor, however, advocate and defend Communism as a system to be imposed on us, then we say that he is abusing his academic freedom. He should be charged with taking public money under false pretenses.

(1953)

## FREEDOM FOR CATHOLIC EDUCATION

MOST REV. JOHN T. MC NICHOLAS

In the United States atheists, agnostics, communists, certain fraternal organizations, indifferentists, and secularists are opposing freedom of education and consequently taking a stronger position against church schools. These several groups make the claims—clandestinely, semi-publicly, boldly—that the only American system of education is the tax-supported school. The strategy of these opponents would depreciate the values of schools conducted by religious bodies; would make it more difficult for these schools to continue to function. Many in the secular school profession would have the general public think that religious schools teach only religion, that they are foreign in character, and that they should be relegated to a second-class status and merely tolerated. This attack on freedom of education is only the initial move. The attack is really directed against the unchangeable principles of Christianity. . . .

The Catholic Church is not opposed to tax-supported schools. On the contrary, she heartily endorses our compulsory system of education in America; she sincerely commends the traditional freedom of American education, and also the generous spirit of America to make adequate provision for education. . . . At the same time, the Catholic Church, as the wisest and most patient mother, recognizes the fundamental injustice to which religious schools are subjected. She also knows that her schools are rendering an unsurpassed public service. She knows that her school is a school, not a church. The Catholic school is not failing to do anything that any properly standardized American school should do. Catholic schools will stand any test to which tax-supported schools will submit. . . .

The State has very definite rights in education. The State arises from the very nature of organized society. Its origin, therefore, goes back to God, from whom its authority is derived. The State is supreme in its sphere. It governs the material order and is responsible for the physical well-being of its citizens. It is the custodian of the common good, of an orderly society, affording due protection and security. The State should be a help, not an impediment, to the moral well-being of its citizens. The State that undermines the authority of God and rejects the supremacy of the moral order is thereby destroying the strongest supports of its own authority and is on the way to ruin. . . .

As the custodian of the common welfare, our country wisely insists on compulsory education, remaining in theory at least the protector of parents, and guaranteeing to fathers and mothers freedom of education, setting standards of education and supporting in large measure the schools of our country. . . . When the State assumes parental obligation, when it establishes State or local schools, as it must do in a modern world in order to assure suitable education for a country blessed as ours is, it can not endow itself with arbitrary powers. If it does so, it becomes a Fascist State in education. Usurped totalitarian powers in education, if not checked by freedom of education, will inevitably lead to a Fascist State in all functions. . . .

In general, we must be happy about the partnership of family, Church, and State in our country, regarding the development of tax-supported schools, and about freedom of education in schools conducted under the auspices of religion. Our complaint is not so much against government, as it is against high-pressure groups of the school profession that attempt to foist on the American public the pseudo-religion of public education as if it were the only true American education. These same groups are becoming more insistent on the complete secularization of American education; they are presenting separation of Church and State in a wrong light; they are increasing the economic burdens of parents who wish their children trained in religious schools; they are striving, unwittingly perhaps, to make our government a dictator in education. They do not seem to realize that freedom of education is a perfecting power and that monopoly of education is a tyrannous or degrading power. Perhaps without grasping its implications, they are promoting Fascism in education. They are promoting a false theory of democracy by condemning the divisive influence of religious schools, and by making a false application of majority rule.

(1947)

# THE CHILD: CITIZEN OF TWO WORLDS

## CATHOLIC BISHOPS OF THE UNITED STATES

THE child must be seen whole and entire. He must be seen as a citizen of two worlds. He belongs to this world surely, but his first and highest allegiance is to the kingdom of God. From his earliest years he must be taught that his chief significance comes from the fact that he is created by God and is destined for life with God in Eternity.

The child's prospects for fulfilling this great hope which God has reposed in him must be viewed realistically. He will come to maturity in a society where social, moral, intellectual and spiritual values are everywhere disintegrating. In such a society, he will urgently need the integrating force of religion as taught by Christ. Such a force will give him a complete and rational meaning for his existence. . . .

The child is not complete in himself. He will find his completion only in life with God; and that life must begin here upon earth. Parents, therefore, should make early provision for their child's growth in God. This is not something to be postponed for nurture by school authorities. It must begin in the home through simple and prayerful practices. . . .

Only two courses are open to the child—either he will be God-centered or self-centered. He is made and destined for God, but he bears in his nature the lingering effects of original sin which incline him to seek the satisfaction of every selfish whim. To correct this bend in his will so that God, rather than self, will occupy the center of his life is one of the most challenging tasks facing parents. . . .

The child must *know* God. There is a vast difference between "knowing about God" and "knowing God." The difference is made by personal experience. It is not enough that the child be given the necessary truths about God. They ought to be given in such a way that he will assimilate them and make them a part of himself. . . .

In learning the valuable lesson that he is accountable to God for the use of his time and talents the child will acquire not only a sense of responsibility, but a sense of mission as well. For this religious training will remind him that his future happiness lies not in the indulgence of selfish desires, but in the complete dedication of his whole personality to God's service. "I am come to do the will of Him who sent me." This must be the keynote of the child's mission in this world. For him the Will of God must come to be more important than any other personal consideration. Only when he masters this truth will he be given to see how all things, even disappointments and setbacks, can be turned to good account in the service of God.

Since everyone is not called to serve God in the same way, great care should be exercised in the child's vocational guidance. Otherwise, aimlessness in his training will leave him without permanent direction for his talents and aptitudes. Parents and teachers must help him to choose and to follow a calling for which he is fitted and in which he can best serve God. A deeper awareness in the child of his mission in life will do much to reduce the shocking waste of time and energy which in so many instances characterize his formative years today, and later prevents him from taking his full place in civic life.

(1950)

158

# VI

# Man as a Citizen
# of the World

*Man's quest for peace. Essence of Catholic internationalism.
The reality of international society. World strife and natural
law. Isolationism. The totalitarian menace. War. World
moral revolution. Christ in human history.*

## MAN'S QUEST OF PEACE

### ST. AUGUSTINE

WHOEVER gives even moderate attention to human affairs and to our
common nature, will recognise that if there is no man who does not
wish to be joyful, neither is there any one who does not wish to have
peace. For even they who make war desire nothing but victory—
desire, that is to say, to attain to peace with glory. For what else is
victory than the conquest of those who resist us? and when this is
done there is peace. It is therefore with the desire for peace that wars
are waged, even by those who take pleasure in exercising their warlike nature in command and battle. And hence it is obvious that peace
is the end sought for by war. For every man seeks peace by waging
war, but no man seeks war by making peace. For even they who in-
tentionally interrupt the peace in which they are living have no hatred
of peace, but only wish it changed into a peace that suits them better.
They do not, therefore, wish to have no peace, but only one more to
their mind. . . .

Even wicked men wage war to maintain the peace of their own

circle, and wish that, if possible, all men belonged to them, that all men and things might serve but one head, and might, either through love or fear, yield themselves to peace with him! It is thus that pride in its perversity apes God. It abhors equality with other men under Him; but, instead, of His rule, it seeks to impose a rule of its own upon its equals. It abhors, that is to say, the just peace of God, and loves its own unjust peace; but it cannot help loving peace of one kind or other. For there is no vice so clean contrary to nature that it obliterates even the faintest trace of nature.

He, then, who prefers what is right to what is wrong, and what is well-ordered to what is perverted, sees that the peace of unjust men is not worthy to be called peace in comparison with the peace of the just. And yet even what is perverted must of necessity be in harmony with, and in dependence on, and in some part of the order of things, for otherwise it would have no existence at all. . . .

But, as man has a rational soul, he subordinates all this which he has in common with the beasts to the peace of his rational soul, that his intellect may have free play and may regulate his actions, and that he may thus enjoy the well-ordered harmony of knowledge and action which constitutes, as we have said, the peace of the rational soul. And for this purpose, he must desire to be neither molested by pain, nor disturbed by desire, nor extinguished by death, that he may arrive at some useful knowledge by which he may regulate his life and manners. But, owing to the liability of the human mind to fall into mistakes, this very pursuit of knowledge may be a snare to him unless he has a divine Master, whom he may obey without misgiving, and who may at the same time give him such help as to preserve his own freedom. And because, so long as he is in this mortal body, he is a stranger to God, he walks by faith, not by sight; and he therefore refers all peace, bodily or spiritual or both, to that peace which mortal man has with the immortal God, so that he exhibits the well-ordered obedience of faith to eternal law. But as this divine Master inculcates two precepts—the love of God and the love of our neighbour—and as in these precepts a man finds three things he has to love—God, himself, and his neighbour—and that he who loves God loves himself thereby, it follows that he must endeavour to get his neighbour to love God, since he is ordered to love his neighbour as himself. He ought to make this endeavour in behalf of his wife, his children, his household, all within his reach, even as he would wish his neighbour to do the same for him if he needed it; and consequently he will be at peace, or in well-ordered concord, with all man, as far as in him lies. And this is the order of this concord, that a man, in the first place, injure no one, and, in the second, do good to every one he can reach. Primarily, therefore, his own household are his care, for the law of nature and of society gives him readier access to them and greater opportunity of serving them.

(A.D. 426)

# THE ESSENCE OF CATHOLIC INTERNATIONALISM

### PIUS XII

THE Church . . . cannot and does not think of deprecating or disdaining the particular characteristics which each people, with jealous and intelligible pride, cherishes and retains as a precious heritage. Her aim is a supernatural union in all-embracing love, deeply felt and practiced, and not the unity which is exclusively external and superficial and by that very fact weak.

The Church hails with joy and follows with her maternal blessing every method of guidance and care which aims at a wise and orderly evolution of particular forces and tendencies having their origin in the individual character of each race, provided that they are not opposed to the duties incumbent on men from their unity of origin and common destiny. . . .

Nor is there any fear lest the consciousness of universal brotherhood aroused by the teaching of Christianity, and the spirit which it inspires, be in contrast with love of traditions or the glories of one's fatherland, or impede the progress of prosperity or legitimate interests. For that same Christianity teaches that in the exercise of charity we must follow a God-given order, yielding the place of honor in our affections and good works to those who are bound to us by special ties. . . . But legitimate and well-ordered love of our native country should not make us close our eyes to the all-embracing nature of Christian charity, which calls for consideration of others and of their interests in the pacifying light of love.

(October 20, 1939)

# THE REALITY AND NECESSITY
# OF INTERNATIONAL SOCIETY

## THE REVS. WM. L. LUCEY, S.J., AND
## PAUL W. FACEY, S.J.

THE society of nations does not have to be created. It exists. It is as natural as the family. It is as natural as the state. The Catholic Bishops of this country late in 1944 said in clear and unmistakable words:

"There is an international community of nations. God Himself has made the nations interdependent for their full life and growth. It is not a question of creating an international community, but of organizing it." International society is a fact beyond controversy. . . .

There is a society of nations because the human race is one. All men are one in origin, all have the same essential nature, all have the same divine destiny. They may differ in language, in customs, even in color; but all these differences are trifling compared to their oneness. . . .

The human race being one race, human individuals are not isolated units, but as Pius XII has reminded us, they are "united by the very force of their nature and by their eternal destiny into an organic, harmonious mutual relationship which varies with the changing of the times." Although there are national differences among men, nations are designed, not to break the unity of the human race, but to enrich it by a sharing and reciprocal interchange of their own peculiar gifts and goods. . . .

It is the insufficiency of the individual states and the resulting interdependence of all nations that compel states to associate together in a society of nations.

This insufficiency is not a defect of the state. States are not supposed to be all-sufficient, capable of doing alone all that is necessary for their citizens. It is obvious that states have never been all-sufficient and are not so today. This inevitable insufficiency needs to be remedied by mutual aid and assistance within the society of nations. . . .

When we consider the need of security against military attack, we see that nations are even more interdependent. Small nations do not possess the military means to protect their interests abroad and to guarantee their national independence and territorial security. They are at the mercy of strong neighbors. Even the strong nations have continually to enter into alliances to ensure their mutual self-protection—alliances like the Atlantic Pact today.

International society, then, is not the fancy of utopian dreamers. It is real; it is a necessity. The unity and the solidarity of the human race are at its roots. The insufficiency and interdependence of every nation demonstrate its needs. . . .

The primary function of organized international society is peace with justice among the nations. Its objective is not merely the absence of war, but a sound international order based on peace with justice in which every state is secure in its legitimate independence and free to enjoy its rights and free to fulfill its duties to its own citizens and to the other states of the world.

Despite the alarms of nationalists, organized international society is not a substitute for states and does not absorb the member states. It exists for the good of the states, just as the state itself is for the good of its citizens. Hence it must not only respect the legitimate authority of the states, but it must also protect and guarantee their independence. On the other hand, the states are not free to assume an air of indifference to the international society. Its organization is for their own good and they have responsibilities to it. Unless they recognize and fulfill these responsibilities, the perils of perpetual disorganization face them.

What shape and form the organization of international society is to take is something that must be slowly hammered out in the free discussion of the nations. In the formation of the attitude of tomorrow's citizens, stress must be laid on the one point that it must have *authority* to achieve its ends.

(1950)

# AGAINST ISOLATIONISM

## PIUS XII

A CONVINCED Christian cannot confine himself within an easy and egoistical "isolationism," when he witnesses the needs and the misery of his brothers; when pleas for help come to him from these in economic distress; when he knows the aspirations of the working classes for more normal and just conditions of life; when he is aware of the

163

abuses of an economic system which puts money above social obligations; when he is not ignorant of the aberrations of an intransigent nationalism which denies or spurns the common bonds linking the separate nations together, and imposing on each one of them many and varied duties toward the great family of nations.

The Catholic doctrine on the state and civil society has always been based on the principle that, in keeping with the will of God, the nations form together a community with a common aim and common duties. Even when the proclamation of this principle and its practical consequences gave rise to violent reactions, the Church denied her assent to the erroneous concept of an absolutely autonomous sovereignty divested of all social obligations.

The Catholic Christian, persuaded that every man is his neighbor and that every nation is a member, with equal rights, of the family of nations, cooperates wholeheartedly in those generous efforts whose beginnings might be meagre and which frequently encounter strong opposition and obstacles, but which aim at saving individual States from the narrowness of a self-centred mentality. This latter attitude of mind has been largely responsible for the conflicts of the past, and unless finally overcome or at least held in check, could lead to new conflagrations that might mean death to human civilization.

(Christmas, 1948)

## THE TOTALITARIAN MENACE

### PIUS XII

THE fabric of peace would rest on a tottering and ever threatening base, if an end were not put to such totalitarianism, which lowers man to the state of a mere pawn in the game of politics, a mere cipher in economic calculations. With a stroke of the pen it changes the frontiers of states; by a peremptory decision it deprives a people's economy—always part of its life as a nation—of its natural outlets; with ill-concealed cruelty it too drives millions of men, hundreds of families, in the most squalid misery, from their homes and lands, tears them out by the roots and wrenches them from a civilization and culture which they had striven for generations to develop. . . .

And yet, by Divine Right it is not the will or the power of fortuitous and unstable vested interests, but man in the framework of the family and of society, who by his labor is lord of the world.

Consequently, this totalitarianism fails by what is the only measure of progress, namely the progressive creation of ever more ample and better conditions in public life to ensure that the family can evolve as an economic, juridic, moral and religious unit.

Within the confines of each particular nation as much as in the whole family of peoples, state totalitarianism is incompatible with a true and healthy democracy. Like a dangerous germ it infects the community of nations and renders it incapable of guaranteeing the security of individual peoples. It constitutes a continual menace of war.

The future peace structure aims at outlawing from the world every aggressive use of force, every war of aggression. Who could not greet such an intention enthusiastically, especially in its effective realization?

But if this is to be something more than a beautiful gesture, all oppression and all arbitrary action from within must be banned.

In the face of this accepted state of affairs, there remains but one solution: a return to God and to the order established by Him.

The more the veil is lifted from the origin and increase of those forces which brought about the war, the clearer it becomes that they were the heirs, the bearers and continuers of errors of which the essential element was the neglect, overthrow, denial and contempt of Christian thought and principles.

(Christmas, 1945)

# MAN'S DUTY TO OPPOSE
## UNJUST AGGRESSION

### PIUS XII

A PEOPLE threatened with an unjust aggression, or already its victim, may not remain passively indifferent, if it would think and act as befits Christians. All the more does the solidarity of the family of nations forbid others to behave as mere spectators, in an attitude of apathetic neutrality. . . .

Neither the sole consideration of the sorrows and evils resulting from war, nor the most careful weighing of the act against the advantage, avail to determine finally, whether it is morally licit, or even in certain concrete circumstances obligatory (provided always there be solid probability of success) to repel an aggressor by force of arms.

One thing, however, is certain: the commandment of peace is a matter of Divine law. Its purpose is the protection of the goods of humanity, inasmuch as they are the gifts of the Creator. Among these goods some are of such importance for society, that it is perfectly lawful to defend them against unjust aggression. Their defense is even an obligation for the nations as a whole who have a duty not to abandon a nation that is attacked.

The certainty that this duty will not go unfulfilled will serve to discourage the aggressor and thus war will be avoided or, if the worst should come, its sufferings will at least be lessened.

(Christmas, 1948)

## "THE AGE OF AMERICA'S SOUL"

THE REV. LAURENCE J. MC GINLEY, S.J.

THE international responsibilities of our maturing power have become such that the age on whose threshold we now stand must be, for our own salvation, the age of America's soul. This then is the challenge of our future, our new and great American adventure; to seek out and make our own that strength of the spirit which is wisdom.

Among the sources of this wisdom is first and above all worship of God. We face a fanatical foe who has become the high priest of a new religion. No middle-class virtue of respectability can steel us to this crisis. Only the strong God of religion, the real God, God personal to me, God intelligently believed in, prayed to and adored on bended knee, can give us wisdom commensurate with our strength. "Unless the Lord build the house, they labor in vain who build it."

In our search for wisdom we must return to law, to law of man and the law of our own being. A trying, agonizing cold war stretches before us over the years. It will make demands on patience and skill and the solid heroism of endurance; it will be aggravated by the constant nagging of our own rich opportunities for ease and heedless pleasure. Yet we must persevere to the end or be lost—and this demands of us that mature fidelity which can come alone from the abiding moral integrity of personal conscience.

The mature wisdom of America in the age now dawning must

come from our increased love, one for another. Without the sense of a true community, of mutual support, we shall be, for all our physical power, weak indeed. The strength of this love will be drawn from our understanding of the lessons of the past: shared purposes in attaining our common destiny as sons and daughters of the one same God, sympathetic understanding of the varied paths each man walks to reach that destiny in the inviolability of his own personal dignity.

(1952)

# THE NECESSITY FOR A WORLD
## *MORAL* REVOLUTION

### THE REV. ROBERT C. HARTNETT, S.J.

THE present struggle between East and West, between tyranny and freedom, between atheism and at least religious liberty, is unparalleled in human annals. It involves every people on the face of the earth. This is the first show-down contest in recorded history in which every nation on every continent will sooner or later have to take one side or the other. . . .

In this clash of basic philosophies of life, the stakes are entire civilizations. World War II, we can now see, was really only a *prelude* to this planet-wide show-down.

Even if we succeed in averting World War III, as we all hope and pray and labor and even *fight* to avert it, the upheaval is already upon us. It consists of political, economic and, imbedded in these, moral and religious transformations of such a magnitude that we hardly know to what we can compare them. They are on the same scale as the geological changes that occurred when whole continents, like North America, rose up from the continental seas that covered them and became dry land, fit for human habitation. . . .

Make no mistake about it: this earth of ours is in the throes of a revolution on a planet-encircling scale. Hardly a single people is in a state of political, social and economic repose. . . .

Some evil more deeply rooted in mankind than the Communist Revolution is causing these recurring disorders among the peoples of this earth. In the light of history, I am afraid that if we destroyed Russian Communism, we would find this basic evil rising from the rubble—maybe not immediately, but after a decade or two—and again sucking the world into the jaws of some new revolutionary beast.

What is this deep-seated evil which raises its head in new forms and under new banners after every war? Call it materialism, call it nationalism, call it greed, call it hate, call it injustice—the evil stalking the modern world is a deadly epidemic of all these *moral disorders*. Essentially, that's what it is: not merely economic dislocations or political revolutions but a *deep-seated moral disorder throughout the whole wide world*.

At root, the trouble is this: *men are not living human life as God intended it to be lived*. That may sound terribly vague. What I mean is that whole peoples, under misguided or malicious leaders, are plainly pursuing purposes at odds with those God had in putting human beings on this planet. . . .

A generous Creator has endowed this planet with enough natural wealth to satisfy the legitimate wants of all the human children with whom He has peopled it. But we, the peoples of the world—including the American people—have by far too large an extent thought only of ourselves.

As a result the whole earth is now like a single nation in which practically no measures, or wholly inadequate measures, have been taken to meet the essential needs of all classes of society within that nation. Such a condition of scandalous neglect of depressed classes almost always leads to a revolution within a nation. Today I think we are witnessing, and participating in, this kind of almost unmanageable upheaval on a world scale, not *within* nations, merely, but *among* nations.

The depressed peoples, especially of Asia, have been, until our day, like the depressed classes within a national society that is ripe for revolution. This revolution, no longer contained within the boundaries of national states, or even within limited areas of the earth's surface, has now been merged into one global revolution, with backward peoples everywhere acting in the role of social outcasts whose claims to a decent life must at long last be met by the new international society now emerging.

It seems to me that there is only one possible long-range solution to this global revolution of our times.

What we need—all of us—is a *moral* revolution. That is the only real answer to social and political upheavals. And the moral revolution we need is shockingly simple: we simply have to look upon all the peoples of the world as God looks upon them.

We know how He looks upon them—as His children forming one immense human family. In God's eyes, a Chinese coolie, a beragged East Indian sharecropper, a sweating and illiterate black native miner in South Africa and a yellow flunky on a rubber plantation in Burma are *just as human, as precious, as you or I.*

To the limit of our financial and other abilities we must help them to live in the decency and dignity befitting children of God. The teeming, impoverished peoples of Asia, Africa, the Middle East, Central and South America are in a state of revolution. Whether we like it or not, they want the better life to which they have every right. The era in which the democratic and capitalist countries of the West, including ourselves, could exploit them and the rich natural resources of their lands is over—abruptly, finally over.

If, in the course of several years, we of the West put back a few billion dollars into the lands from which we have taken that much and far more in oil, tin, rubber and other resources, we will only be evening the score. The score is going to be evened eventually. Nothing is surer than that. The only question is whether we have the spiritual vision and the moral character to even it out of a sense of justice and charity, or are going to stumble into a war which will only postpone the task and make it immeasurably harder and more expensive to accomplish. . . .

What we must do, I think, and what we are trying to do, is to build up a wall of military defense around the yet unconquered peoples of the world. Why? So that behind that wall we can safely and securely co-operate in substituting large-scale and long-range reform for the short-term, deceptive methods of violent revolution.

The danger and deception that we ourselves must avoid lies in believing that our towering military might will somehow frighten the world into peace. It will not. At best, all that military power can do is insure to us the time and the opportunity to apply really effectual remedies. Now, when our military preparations are beginning to erect a formidable wall of military protection, a defensive shield, between the free world and Communist aggressors, *now,* I say, is the time for us to decide what we are going to do behind that protective wall. Do we mean to take advantage of the last chance we may have to help pacify the world by diverting the world revolution into constructive paths? Much of the world needs to be reorganized before it can ever know stability and genuine social and political order. Do we realize that? Do we realize that leadership in this process of diverting the forces of world revolution has in God's Providence fallen at our doorstep?

The only plan for peace I know is God's plan. We cannot expect God's plan for peace to work unless we take it whole and entire. That will call for almost as big a revolution in our thinking as the profound social and political revolution we are trying to channel. . . .

Judgments may differ about the best ways to carry out our responsibilities, about the allocation of aid to other peoples, about means to make it most effective and about the limits of our own abilities. Such questions belong to the field of policy, not religious principle.

But about the *attitude* a religious person should take there can be no debate. This must be an attitude of eagerness to help, within the limits of our abilities. Almighty God has made His divine purposes in human living perfectly clear. Those divine purposes establish the standards on which we shall be finally judged. They are the standards of justice and love towards all mankind.

(1952)

# CHRIST IN THE HEART OF
# HUMAN HISTORY

### JACQUES MARITAIN

It is obvious that Christianity and Christian faith can neither be made subservient to democracy as a philosophy of human and political life nor to any political form whatsoever. That is a result of the fundamental distinction introduced by Christ between the things that are Caesar's and the things that are God's, a distinction which has been unfolding throughout our history in the midst of accidents of all kinds, and which frees religion from all temporal enslavement. . . .

But the important thing for the political life of the world and for the solution of the crisis of civilization is by no means to pretend that Christian faith compels every believer to be a democrat; it is to affirm that democracy is linked to Christianity and that the democratic impulse has arisen in human history as a temporal manifestation of the inspiration of the Gospel. The question does not deal here with Christianity as a religious creed and road to eternal life, but rather with Christianity as leaven in the social and political life of nations and as bearer of the temporal hope of mankind; it does not deal with Christianity as a treasure of divine truth sustained and propagated by the Church, but with Christianity as historical energy at work in the world. It is not in the heights of theology, it is in the depths of the secular conscience and secular existence that Christianity works in this fashion, while sometimes even assuming heretical forms or forms of revolt where it seems to be denying itself, as though the broken bits of the key to paradise, falling into destitute lives and combining with the metals of the earth, were more effective in activating the history of this world than the pure essence of the celestial metal. . . .

Christ sent the word to the heart of human history. The human race will emerge from the era of great sufferings only when the activity of hidden stimulation, by means of which the Christian spirit moves along and toils at bloody cost in the night of earthly history, will have joined with the activity of illumination, by means of which the Christian spirit sets souls up in the truth and life of the kingdom of God. It is not at the end of the present war that this goal will be reached. But the present war reveals to us, as by an apocalyptic sign, the direction in which we must move; and peace, if peace is won, will denote that the creative forces in motion within human history are decidedly set in this direction.

The Christian spirit is threatened today in its very existence by implacable enemies, fanatics of race and blood, of pride, domination and hate. At the core of the horrible ordeal, everything indicates that in the depths of human conscience a powerful religious renewal is in preparation, which concerns and which will restore to their vital sources all the persecuted, all the believers of the great Judeo-Christian family, not only the faithful of the Catholic Church and those of the Protestant Churches, but also those of Judaism. . . . This spiritual renewal, whatever be the irreducible division that it involves on the dogmatic and religious plane, will exercise a common action and will bring forth common fruits.

Democracy, too, is threatened in its very existence, and by the same enemies. Although its roots are evangelical, although it springs from that process of hidden stimulation mentioned above, and by means of which Christianity dimly activates earthly history, it is nonetheless by aligning itself with erroneous ideologies and with aberrant tendencies that it manifested itself in the world. Neither Locke nor Jean-Jacques Rousseau nor the Encyclopedists can pass as thinkers faithful to the integrity of the Christian trust. Here too everything indicates that a great renewal of the spirit is taking place which tends to restore democracy to its true essence and purify its principles. The re-examination of values and the heroic effort which might have saved the democracies from war, if they had been attempted in time, are taking place and will take place in the midst of the ruins.

Thus in the fearful historical upheaval, on which the Pagan Empire is staking its all to liquidate at the same stroke Christianity and democracy, the chances of religion, conscience and civilization coincide with those of freedom; freedom's chances coincide with those of the evangelical message.

(1944)

# VII

# The Church's Credentials, Universality, and Continuity

*Its divine origin. Apostolic succession. Tradition. Dogmatism in the early Church. History supports the Church's claims. Comparative religion and Christian truth. Durable and adaptable because universal. The Church in history.*

## THE DIVINE SOURCE

### ST. CLEMENT, BISHOP OF ROME

THE Apostles for our sakes received the gospel from the Lord Jesus Christ; Jesus Christ was sent from God. Christ then is from God, and the Apostles from Christ. Both therefore came in due order from the will of God. Having therefore received his instructions and being fully assured through the Resurrection of our Lord Jesus Christ, they went forth with confidence in the word of God and with full assurance of the Holy Spirit, preaching the gospel that the Kingdom of God was about to come. And so, as they preached in the country and in the towns, they appointed their first-fruits (having proved them by the Spirit) to be bishops and deacons (overseers and ministers) of them that should believe. And this was no novelty, for of old it had been written concerning bishops and deacons; for the Scripture says in one place, 'I will set up their bishops in righteousness, and their deacons in faith' (Is.lx.17).

Our Apostles knew also, through our Lord Jesus Christ, that there would be strife over the dignity of the bishop's office. For this reason therefore, having received complete foreknowledge, they appointed the aforesaid, and after a time made provision that on their death other approved men should succeed to their ministry.

(ca. A.D. 200)

THE greatest Church, the most ancient, the most conspicuous, and founded and established by Peter and Paul. To this Church, every Church, that is, the faithful from every side must report, or must agree with it, *propter potiorem principalitatem.*

ST. IRENAEUS (ca. A.D. 175)

## APOSTOLIC SUCCESSION

### ST. IRENAEUS

THE Church, scattereth abroad throughout the whole world, hath received this doctrine and this faith . . . and doth guard it diligently, as though she dwelt in one house, and likewise believeth it, as though she had one heart and one soul, and doth proclaim and teach and convey the same with one voice as though she had but a single mouth. For although there are many diverse tongues spoken in the world, yet the force of the doctrine conveyed is one and the same. . . .

Whoever would know the truth, may see the tradition of the Apostles . . . manifest in all the Churches. We can follow the line of those who were appointed bishops by the Apostles and their successors to our own day. . . . But because it would be very tedious in a book such as this to enumerate the succession of Bishops in every Church, we confute all who assemble together unlawfully . . . by pointing out to them the tradition received from the Apostles, and preached to men, and handed down by the succession of Bishops to our own day, in that Church, the greatest, the most ancient, and known to everyone, founded and established at Rome by the two most glorious Apostles Peter and Paul. For by reason of the great pre-eminence of this Church, in which the tradition of the Apostles has been preserved by men of every race, it is necessary that every Church, that is to say the faithful from everywhere, should meet together and be in agreement with it. The blessed Apostles, then, founding and building up this Church, committed the office of Bishop and the ministration of the Church to Linus . . . after him succeeded Anencletus, and then Clement was made Bishop, third from the Apostles. This same Clement had seen the Apostles and had conversed with them, so that he had their preaching still ringing in his ears and their tradition before his eyes. . . . Under Clement also a great dissension arose among the brethren at Corinth, and the Roman Church sent a most powerful letter to the Corinthians, restoring them to peace and unity. . . . Evaristus succeeded Clement, and Alexander . . . Sixtus . . . Telesphorus . . . Hyginus, Pius, Soter and Eleutherus, who now hath the Bishopric, twelfth from the Apostles. In this order, then, and in this succession, the tradition of the Apostles and the true doctrine has come down to us. . . .

The doctrine of the Church changeth not, but is in every place constant, having the testimony of the prophets and Apostles and of every disciple until now. . . . As breath is given unto man, so hath the divine gift of Faith been entrusted unto the Church, that they who receive it may have life. . . . In these things they have no part who sever themselves from the Church.

(ca. A.D. 175)

# AUTHORITY AND TRADITION
## VERSUS HERESY

### ST. VINCENT OF LERINS

I HAVE therefore continually given the greatest pains and diligence to inquiring, from the greatest possible number of men outstanding in holiness and in doctrine, how I can secure a kind of fixed and, as it were, general and guiding principle for distinguishing the true Catholic Faith from the degraded falsehoods of heresy. And the answer that I receive is always to this effect; that if I wish, or indeed if anyone wishes, to detect the deceits of heretics that arise and to avoid their snares and to keep healthy and sound in a healthy faith, we ought, with the Lord's help, to fortify our faith in a twofold manner, firstly, that is, by the authority of God's Law, then by the tradition of the Catholic Church.

Here, it may be, someone will ask, Since the canon of Scripture is complete, and is in itself abundantly sufficient, what need is there to join to it the interpretation of the Church? The answer is that because of the very depth of Scripture all men do not place one identical interpretation upon it. The statements of the same writer are explained by different men in different ways, so much so that it seems almost possible to extract from it as many opinions as there are men. Novatian expounds in one way, Sabellius in another, Donatus in another, Arius, Eunomius and Macedonius in another, Photinus, Apollinaris and Priscillian in another, Jovinian, Pelagius, and Caelestius in another, and latterly Nestorius in another. Therefore, because of the intricacies of error, which is so multiform, there is great need for the laying down of a rule for the exposition of Prophets and Apostles in accordance with the standard of the interpretation of the Church Catholic.

Now in the Catholic Church itself we take the greatest care to hold THAT WHICH HAS BEEN BELIEVED EVERYWHERE, ALWAYS AND BY ALL.

That is truly and properly "Catholic," as is shown by the very force and meaning of the word, which comprehends everything almost universally. We shall hold to this rule if we follow universality (i.e. oecumenicity), antiquity, and consent. We shall follow universality if we acknowledge that one Faith to be true which the whole Church throughout the world confesses; antiquity, if we in no wise depart from those interpretations which it is clear that our ancestors and fathers proclaimed; consent, if in antiquity itself we keep following the definitions and opinions of all, or certainly nearly all, bishops, and doctors alike.

What then will the Catholic Christian do, if a small part of the Church has cut itself off from the communion of the universal Faith. The answer is sure. He will prefer the healthiness of the whole body to the morbid and corrupt limb.

But what if some novel contagion try to infect the whole Church, and not merely a tiny part of it? Then he will take care to cleave to antiquity, which cannot now be led astray by any deceit of novelty.

What if in antiquity itself two or three men, or it may be a city, or even a whole province be detected in error? Then he will take the greatest care to prefer the decrees of the ancient General Councils, if there are such, to the irresponsible ignorance of a few men.

But what if some error arises regarding which nothing of this sort is to be found? Then he must do his best to compare the opinions of the Fathers and inquire their meaning, provided always that, though they belonged to diverse times and places, they yet continued in the faith and communion of the one Catholic Church; and let them be teachers approved and outstanding. And whatever he shall find to have been held, approved and taught, not by one or two only but by all equally and with one consent, openly, frequently, and persistently, let him take this as to be held by him without the slightest hesitation.

(ca. A.D. 430)

# DOGMATISM IN THE EARLY CHURCH

## JOHN HENRY CARDINAL NEWMAN

THERE are writers who refer to the first centuries of the Church as a time when opinion was free, and the conscience exempt from the obligation or temptation to take on trust what it had not proved; and that, apparently on the mere ground that the series of great theological decisions did not commence till the fourth. . . . What can be meant by saying that Christianity had no magistrates in the earliest ages?—but, any how, in statements such as these the distinction is not properly recognized between a principle and its exhibitions and instances, even if the fact were as is represented. The principle indeed of Dogmatism develops into Councils in the course of time; but it was active, nay sovereign from the first, in every part of Christendom. A conviction that truth was one; that it was a gift from without, a sacred trust, an inestimable blessing; that it was to be reverenced, guarded, defended, transmitted; that its absence was a grievous want, and its loss an unutterable calamity and again, the stern words and acts of St. John, of Polycarp, Ignatius, Irenaeus, Clement, Tertullian, and Origen;—all this is quite consistent with perplexity or mistake as to what was truth in particular cases, in what way doubtful questions were to be decided, or what were the limits of Revelation. Councils and Popes are the guardians and instruments of the dogmatic principle; they are not that principle themselves; they presuppose the principle; they are summoned into action at the call of the principle; and the principle might act even before they had their legitimate place, and exercised a recognized power, in the movements of the Christian body. . . .

What Conscience is in the history of an individual mind, such was the dogmatic principle in the history of Christianity. Both in the one case and the other, there is the gradual formation of a directing power out of a principle. The natural voice of Conscience is far more imperative in testifying and enforcing a rule of duty, than successful in determining that duty in particular cases. It acts as a messenger from above, and says that there is a right and a wrong, and that the right must be followed; but it is variously, and therefore erroneously, trained in the instance of various persons. It mistakes error for truth; and yet we believe that on the whole, and even in those cases where it is ill-instructed, if its voice be diligently obeyed, it will gradually be cleared, simplified, and perfected, so that minds, starting differently will, if honest, in course of time converge to one and the same truth. I do not hereby imply that there is indistinctness so great as this in the theology of the first centuries; but so far is plain, that the early Church and Fathers exercised far more a ruler's than a doctor's office; it was the age of Martyrs, of acting not of thinking. Doctors succeeded Martyrs, as light and peace of conscience follow upon obedience to it; yet, even before the Church had grown into the full measure of its doctrines, it was rooted in its principles.

(1878)

# THE EVIDENCE THAT THE CHURCH
# IS TRUE TO ITS ORIGIN

### HILAIRE BELLOC

FOUR men will be sitting as guests of a fifth in a private house in Carthage in the year 225. They are all men of culture; all possessed of the two languages, Greek and Latin, well-read and interested in the problems and half-solutions of their skeptical time. One will profess himself Materialist, and will find another to agree with him; there is no personal God, certain moral duties must be recognized by men for such and such utilitarian reasons, and so forth. He finds support.

The host is not of that opinion; he has been profoundly influenced by certain "mysteries" into which he has been "initiated": That is, symbolic plays showing the fate of the soul and performed in high seclusion before members of a society sworn to secrecy. He has come to feel a spiritual life as the natural life round him. He has curiously followed, and often paid at high expense, the services of necromancers; he believes that in an "initiation" which he experienced in his youth, and during the most secret and most vivid drama or "mystery" in which he then took part, he actually came in contact with the spiritual world. Such men were not uncommon. The declining society of the time was already turning to influences of that type.

The host's conviction, his awed and reticent attitude towards such things, impress his guests. One of the guests, however, a simple, solid kind of man, not drawn to such vagaries, says that he has been reading with great interest the literature of the Christians. He is in admiration of the traditional figure of the Founder of their Church. He quotes certain phrases, especially from the four orthodox Gospels. They move him to eloquence, and their poignancy and illuminative power have an effect upon his friends. He ends by saying: "For my part, I have come to make it a sort of rule to act as this man Christ would have had me act. He seems to me to have led the most perfect life I ever read of, and the practical maxims which are attached to His Name seem to me a sufficient guide to life. That," he will conclude simply, "is the groove into which I have fallen, and I do not think I shall ever leave it."

Let us call this man who has so spoken, Ferreolus. Would Ferreolus have been a *Christian?* Would the officials of the Roman Empire have called him a *Christian?* Would he have been in danger of unpopularity where *Christians* were unpopular? Would *Christians* have received him among themselves as part of their strict and still somewhat secret society? Would he have counted with any single man of the whole Empire as one of the *Christian* body?

The answer is most emphatically *No.*

No Christian in the first three centuries would have held such a man as coming within his view. No imperial officer in the most violent crisis of one of those spasmodic persecutions which the Church had to undergo would have troubled him with a single question. No Christian congregation would have regarded him as in any way connected with their body. Opinion of that sort, "Christism," had no relation to the Church. How far it existed we cannot tell, for it was unimportant. In so far as it existed it would have been on all fours with any one of the vague opinions which floated about the cultured Roman world.

Now it is evident that the term "Christianity" used as a point of view, as a mere mental attitude, would include such a man, and it is equally evident that we have only to imagine him to see that he had nothing to do with the Christian *religion* of that day. For the Christian religion (then as now) was a thing, not a theory. It was expressed in what I have called an organism, and that organism was the Catholic Church. . . .

Let me briefly set down what we know, as a matter of historical and documentary evidence, the Church of this period to have held. . . .

Let us take such a writer as Tertullian and set down what was certainly true of his time.

Tertullian was a man of about forty years in the year 200. The Church then taught an unbroken tradition that a Man who had been put to death about 170 years before in Palestine—only 130 years before Tertullian's birth—had risen again on the third day. This Man was a known and real person with whom numbers had conversed. In Tertullian's childhood men still lived who had met eye witnesses of the thing asserted.

This Man (the Church said) was also the supreme Creator God. There you have an apparent contradiction in terms, at any rate a mystery, fruitful in opportunities for theory, and as a fact destined to lead to three centuries of more and more particular definition.

This Man, Who also was God Himself, had, through chosen companions called Apostles, founded a strict and disciplined society called the Church. The doctrines the Church taught professed to be His doctrines. They included the immortality of the human soul, its redemption, its alternative of salvation and damnation.

Initiation into the Church was by way of baptism with water in the name of The Trinity: Father, Son and Holy Ghost.

Before His death this Man Who was also God had instituted a certain rite and *Mystery* called the Eucharist. He took bread and wine and changed them into His Body and Blood. He ordered this rite to be continued. The central act of worship of the Christian Church was therefore a consecration of bread and wine by priests in the presence of the initiated and baptized Christian body of the locality. The bread and wine so consecrated were certainly called (universally) the Body of the Lord.

The faithful also certainly communicated, that is, ate the Bread and drank the Wine thus changed in the *Mystery*.

It was the central rite of the Church thus to take the Body of the Lord.

There was certainly at the head of each Christian community a bishop: regarded as directly the successor of the Apostles, the chief agent of the ritual and the guardian of the doctrine.

The whole increasing body of local communities kept in touch through their bishops, held one doctrine and practiced what was substantially one ritual.

All this is plain history.

The numerical proportion of the Church in the city of Carthage, where Tertullian wrote, was certainly large enough for its general suppression to be impossible. One might argue from one of his phrases that it was a tenth of the population. Equally certain did the unity of the Christian Church and its bishops teach the institution of the Eucharist, the Resurrection, the authority of the Apostles, and their power of tradition through the bishops. A very large number of converts were to be noted and (to go back to Tertullian) the majority of his time, by his testimony, were recruited by conversion, and were not born Christians.

Such is known to have been, in a very brief outline, the manner of the Catholic Church in these early years of the third century. Such was the undisputed manner of the Church, as a Christian or an inquiring pagan would have been acquainted with it in the years 160–200 and onwards.

I have purposely chosen this moment, because it is the moment in which Christian evidence first emerges upon any considerable scale. Many of the points I have set down are, of course, *demonstrably* anterior to the third century. I mean by "demonstrably" anterior, proved in earlier documentary testimony. That ritual and doctrine firmly fixed are long anterior to the time in which you find them rooted is obvious to common sense. But there are documents as well.

Thus, we have Justin Martyr. He was no less than sixty years older than Tertullian. He was as near to the Crucifixion as my generation is to the Reform Bill—and he gave us a full description of the Mass.

We have the letters of St. Ignatius. He was a much older man than St. Justin—perhaps forty or fifty years older. He stood to the generations contemporary with Our Lord as I stand to the generation of Gladstone, Bismarck, and, early as he is, he testifies fully to the organization of the Church with its Bishops, the Eucharistic Doctrine, and the Primacy in it of the Roman See.

The literature remaining to us from the early first century and a half after the Crucifixion is very scanty. The writings of what are called "Apostolic" times—that is, documents proceeding immediately from men who could remember the time of Our Lord, form not only in their quantity (and that is sufficiently remarkable), but in their quality, too, a far superior body of evidence to what we possess from the next generation. We have more in the New Testament than we have in the writings of these men who came just after the death of the Apostles. But what does remain is quite convincing. There arose from the date of Our Lord's Ascension into heaven, from, say A.D. 30 or so, before the death of Tiberius and a long lifetime after the Roman organization of Gaul, a definite, strictly ruled and highly individual *Society,* with fixed doctrines, special mysteries, and a strong discipline of its own. With a most vivid and distinct personality, unmistakable. And this Society was, and is, called "The Church." . . .

Whether the Church told the truth is for philosophy to discuss: What the Church in fact *was* is plain history. The Church may have taught nonsense. Its organization may have been a clumsy human thing. That would not affect the historical facts.

By the year 200 the Church was—everywhere, manifestly and in ample evidence throughout the Roman world—what I have described, and taught the doctrines I have just enumerated: but it stretches back one hundred and seventy years before that date and it has evidence to its title throughout that era of youth.

To see that the state of affairs everywhere widely apparent in A.D. 200 was rooted in the very origins of the institution one hundred and seventy years before, to see that all this mass of ritual, doctrine and discipline starts with the first third of the first century, and the Church was from its birth the Church, the reader must consider the dates.

We know that we have in the body of documents contained in the "canon" which the Church has authorized as the "New Testament," documents proceeding from men who were contemporaries with the origin of the Christian religion. Even modern scholarship with all its love of phantasy is now clear upon so obvious a point. The authors of the Gospels, the Acts, and the Epistles, Clement also, and Ignatius also (who had conversed with the Apostles) may have been deceived, they may have been deceiving. I am not here concerned with that point. The discussion of it belongs to another province of argument altogether. But they were *contemporaries* of the things they said they were contemporaries of. In other words, their writings are what is called "authentic." . . .

It is all-important for the reader who desires a true historical picture to seize the *sequence of the dates with which we are dealing,* their relation to the length of human life and therefore to the society to which they relate.

It is all-important because the false history which has had its own way for so many years is based upon two false suggestions of the first magnitude. The first is the suggestion that the period between the Crucifixion and the full Church of the third century was one in which vast changes could proceed unobserved, and vast perversions of its original ideas be rapidly developed; the second is that the space of time during which those changes are supposed to have taken place was sufficient to account for them.

It is only because those days are remote from ours that such suggestions can be made. If we put ourselves by an effort of the imagination into the surroundings of that period, we can soon discover how false the suggestions are.

The period was not one favourable to the interruption of record. It was one of a very high culture. The proportion of curious, intellectual, and skeptical men which that society contained was perhaps greater than in any other period with which we are acquainted. It was certainly greater than it is today. Those times were certainly less susceptible to mere novel assertion than are the crowds of our great cities under the influence of the modern press. It was a period astonishingly alive. Lethargy and decay had not yet touched the world of the Empire. It built, read, traveled, and, above all, *criticized,* with an enormous energy.

In general, it was no period during which alien fashions could rise within such a community as the Church without their opponents being immediately able to combat them by an appeal to the evidence of the immediate past. The world in which the Church arose was one; and that world was intensely vivid. Any one in that world who saw such an institution as Episcopacy (for instance) or such a doctrine as the Divinity of Christ to be a novel corruption of originals could have, and would have, protested at once. It was a world of ample record and continual communication. . . .

That there should have been discussion as to the definition and meaning of doctrines is natural, and fits in both with the dates and with the atmosphere of the period and with the character of the subject. But that a whole scheme of Christian government and doctrine should have developed in contradiction of Christian origins and yet without protest in a period so brilliantly living, full of such rapid intercommunication, and, *above all, so brief,* is quite impossible.

(1920)

# HISTORY VINDICATES CHRISTIANITY'S TEACHING

### DOUGLAS JERROLD

PRECISELY as archeology has verified, in the most minute detail, the historical portion of the Old Testament narrative, so the historical method applied to the facts of archeology has vindicated the Christian, Moral and Political philosophy. They show that artistic achievement precedes the organization of society for wealth, and that the period of maximum wealth is a prelude to decline, an historical vindication of the Christian esthetic, which teaches that creative art is the process of informing matter with spirit. They show us also that, with the decay of spirituality and the growth of materialism, societies fall by their own weight, an historical vindication of the doctrine of original sin. They teach us that the decline of society is invariably preceded by a departure from traditional moral standards, particularly in regard to sexual morality, an historical vindication of the Christian teaching that the family is antecedent to the State and that society has no rights against the family. Again, we learn that the age of criticism, introspection and imitation of old arts through which we are passing today is a familiar experience of civilizations, and that it carries with it always the same Nemesis; the scepticism which man turns first on his rulers and then on his gods, he turns ultimately on himself; an historical vindication of the cardinal doctrine of Christianity, that man is not sufficient for his own salvation.

(1938)

# CATHOLIC CONSERVATISM

### DIETRICH VON HILDEBRAND

THE true Christian is of necessity unconventional. The mere fact that something "has always been done that way," that it is part of a public tradition, is no motive force with him. He accepts unconditionally only what has been willed by God and is pleasing to God. Great and glorious is the tradition of the Church, without doubt; but that tradition is merely a fruit of her continuity, by virtue of which she preserves through all the whirlpools of the times all that is of true value and of divine origin. It is not, by any means, the automatic product of pure conservatism.

(1948)

# COMPARATIVE RELIGION AND
# CHRISTIAN TRUTH

CHRISTOPHER HOLLIS

It is the argument of those who use the weapons of comparative religion to criticize Christianity that every one of the important Christian claims is but a copy and an echo of claims of numerous other older religions. There is not novelty, we are told, in the notion of the God-man: Greek thought never insisted on a rigid distinction between the God and the great man, and the Eastern habit of flattering the King by calling him a God was a common one which had but lately before the beginning of our era transferred itself to the West with the establishment of the custom of deifying Caesar. As little novelty is there in the notion of a God, who is slain and who rises again. The reverence for consecrated virginity was no invention of Christianity, nor was the notion of the possibility that one person could take upon himself the sins of others, nor again the strange notion that people could under certain defined conditions eat their God and derive benefit therefrom. Fathers had sacrificed their sons before. The religion of Osiris and the mysteries of Eleusis had already given to man Christianity's comfort of immortality.

There is too the contention, certainly true but of a less general importance, that Christianity has annexed the dates of old pagan festivals for the dates of its great feasts. . . .

No student of religion can possibly deny, or can possibly wish to deny, the existence of what may at least be called *a priori* similarity between other religions and Christianity. The question is not whether there is such a similarity, but what it proves. One thing we can clearly say. Even if our inquiry should demonstrate that there is not one word of originality in Christianity, it would not be sufficient to say that Christianity was an imitation of the religions among whom it

185

grew. For the similarities between Christianity and the religions of the Mediterranean are hardly more striking than the similarities between Christianity and the religions of Mexico and of the American world, of which the Christians had no breath of knowledge in the days when they were shaping their creed. The conclusion then would be not that Christianity was an imitation of other religions, but rather that all religions were essentially the same, that men in every clime and continent had always the same beliefs about the nature of the universe, and that they differed only in the details of the names of the myths in which they dressed up their beliefs. But is this the conclusion to which the facts lead us?

That many of the beliefs of other religions have a similarity to those of Christianity is certainly true. But are they the same?

First, there is the notion of the God-man. It is true enough that there were claimants to the title of God-man before Christ, and have been claimants to that title since. But what sort of claimants? If we turn to Sir James Frazer's chapter on Incarnate Human Gods, we find that he gives examples of people who were supposed to incarnate God, first, from various savage tribes of Africa and Polynesia. These Gods were usually, though not always, either kings or priests. He then gives us the example from Ancient Egypt, of the God Anubis, of Empedocles from Sicily, of Demetrius Policretes from Athens of the fourth Century B.C. He adds many more examples from many parts of the world of people who saw and see divinity in their rulers. He then details Christian heretics, who have claimed divinity—Montanus and Elipandus of Toledo, the Albigensians, the Brethern and Sisters of the Free Spirit, a nineteenth century Kentucky lunatic. He turns our attention to Thibet and the Grand Lama, and then concludes his chapter with some interesting examples of God-Kings in Babylon, in Egypt, Peru, and elsewhere.

All these instances are intensely interesting, and it is fascinating to inquire what exactly the believers in such God-men meant by their beliefs. But whatever they meant, it is surely clear that they meant something very different from what the Christian means when he affirms his belief in the divinity of Christ. One and all, these believers in the Gods are polytheists. God is incarnate in this king or priest to-day, but he will die and God will then return to the earth to inhabit his successor. The Christian heretics saw divinity in every man. But the Christian does not believe that God was incarnate in Jesus Christ and will some other day become incarnate in somebody else. Christ is to the Christian a unique figure, as were none of the other God-men to their believers. For the Christian alone believes at one and the same time in Incarnate God and in One God. Christ to him is not a God; He is God. The most abject believer in the divinity of Caesar did not believe that Caesar alone had created the universe, nor did the maddest nor the proudest Caesar ever claim to have done so. If there be any other than Christ who made the claim, it is in the padded cell that we must look for him, and it is hard to resist the con-clusion that such a claim must certainly be a claim of insanity, if we cannot admit the awful possibility that it is the claim of truth.

Then again the notion of resurrection. Man did not need to wait till the Christian revelation, we are told, to be familiar with the no-tion of resurrection of the slain God. Almost every culture symbolizes the reaping and rebirth of the crops by a story of death and resurrec-tion. In Russia, there survived, right through Christian times, the old ceremonies of the resurrection of the mythological Kostrubouko. Syria gave us the story of Attis, Egypt of Osiris, the Greeks of Dio-nysus and of Persephone. In many countries in Europe, Asia and dis-tant Mexico we find customs of slaying the man in whom God is incarnate, when his first vigour begins to flag, in order that the god may transfer himself to a more nearly perfect physical frame. It is this notion that Sir James Frazer finds the key to the mystery of Nemi, of

> The priest who slays the slayer
> And shall himself be slain,

which set him out on his long search.

Again, there is nothing to be said save that such beliefs are pro-foundly interesting and at the same time profoundly different from those of Christianity. In the first place, Attis and Osiris, Dionysus and Persephone were creatures of myth. A story is told of how they rose again in order to symbolize the great truth that, if winter comes, spring cannot be far behind. But Christ lived at a certain date in place and time and faces us with a historical claim that He did rise again. The myth symbolizes a process of nature which completes itself every year. It was the essence of Christ's claim that His Resurrec-tion was a unique event, accomplished once and by that once achiev-ing its purpose. If it be true that the purpose of the Resurrection myths of the mythological religions was to teach their devotees of the proc-esses of the seasons on earth, the purpose of Christ's Resurrection was certainly something entirely different, to teach His disciples of the conquest of death and to demonstrate that the ultimate reality was not to be found on this earth at all. . . .

Of all the great pagan religions the one that most closely resembles Christianity was certainly that of Osiris. Osiris was the son of the earth-God, Seb, and the sky-Goddess, Nut. At his birth a voice rang out proclaiming that the Lord of All had come down to dwell among men. He reigned as a King over the Egyptians, reclaimed them from their savagery and taught them civilization and true religion. Committing the Government of Egypt to his wife, Isis, he then travelled over the world conferring similar benefits on the other nations. But on his return to Egypt he was murdered by his wicked and jealous brother, Set. Set afterwards cut his dead brother's body into fourteen pieces, which he distributed in fourteen different places throughout Egypt. But Isis collected these fourteen pieces together, and she and her sister, Nephthys, then lamented the murdered God. Their laments were not in vain. Ra, the sun-god, heard them, and sent down Anubis, by whom Osiris was brought back to life, and reigns ever afterwards as Lord of the Underworld.

It is clear that there are remarkable similarities between this story and that of Christianity. But also that there are differences no less striking, and the great difference is that there is no pretence of evidence that the story of Osiris ever happened. The Christian claims meet the world with an historical challenge. So, too, there is this enormous difference, whatever may be the alleged similarities, between Christianity and Mithraism which was a dangerous rival of Christianity in the early Roman Empire, but about which we know but little.

No contention could therefore be less scholarly than one, which maintained that Christianity was in any way the same as earlier religions. There had been indeed great ethical teaching before Christianity—teaching, which bore similarity to that which Christ was afterwards to give to the world—but it came not from the pagan religions, but, as we have shown, from philosophers and poets, who were forced into self-expression, simply because they were in search of a religion greater than that with which their age provided them. . . .

That there were similarities is indeed true, and some of those similarities are surprising to those nurtured in the traditions of the nineteenth-century secularism. What do these similarities prove? Do they prove Christianity false? Or do they show man from the first haunted with dim inkling that truth was found down strange roads, where what prides itself as common-sense might hesitate to journey, unable to see clearly what the truth was, muddling it, perverting it, lacking the courage to proclaim it in all its goodness?

> So the all-great were the all-loving, too—
> The madman saith he said so—it is strange.

If man from the first has felt that there is in some strange way, incomprehensible, a possibility of vicarious atonement, a mystery in sex, a conquest over death, a mystery of the sacraments, a mystery of the trinity, if he has had some obstinate feeling that his own human nature was linked, or destined to be linked, in one body with a nature that is more than human, does this prove Christianity false? Should not the very strangeness of the notions, when combined with their universality, cause us rather to pause? May not the explanation be that God who created the world was a God of Three Persons and that in the years before the Incarnation He was already leading man stumblingly up to ask for his own Redemption? And may not the faults of misunderstanding be due to a secularist humanitarianism that has been so anxious to be secular that it has forgotten to be humane?

(1941)

# A CHURCH WITH GOD-GIVEN VITALITY

### THE REV. ROBERT HOWARD LORD

THE Catholic Church is universal, as is no other Christian society. In the past she has shown a striking ability to adapt herself to all races, to all kinds and conditions of men, and to all changes in civilization. And today, still showing that same power, she is everywhere. She has always been by far the largest of Christian societies; more than half the Christians in the world are her children (over 300,000,000); and no other body of Christians is so uniformly extended in every part of the globe and among all the races of men.

She has a matchless unity. Wherever the Catholic goes, he finds the same teaching, the same worship, the same institutions with which he is familiar at home: from Canada to Cape Town, from Hongkong to Buenos Aires. And the present-day Catholic would have just about this same sense of familiarity, of perfect unity with those around him, could he be wafted back in time and be present with St. Francis in the church at Assisi in the 13th century, with St. Ambrose or St. Augustine in the 4th century, or at the Mass celebrated by St. Peter among the first Christians at Rome.

Of all the influences that have moulded European civilization, the Church is incontestably the greatest. Indeed, she made "Europe." For what do we mean by "Europe" i.e., the nations of European civilization, except that group of peoples who were converted, civilized, and brought into a permanent cultural unity by the Catholic Church? "There is no aspect of our modern life"—government, law, education, literature, art, science—"which has not at some period passed through the mould of the Catholic Church" (Arnold Lunn). Nearly all the great cathedrals were built by Catholics. Nearly all Christian art is Catholic. So is most of the best religious music. John Ruskin discovered that "all beautiful prayers were Catholic, and all wise interpretations of the Bible." What other body of Christians has a system of theological and moral teachings so complete, coherent, and scientific as that of the Catholic Church? What other religious body has ever drawn forth from its adherents on so large a scale and through so long a period of time the passionate loyalty, the self-sacrifice, the limitless devotion that the Catholic Church evokes from her children? What other religious body has such a roll of illustrious thinkers, great mystics, saints, martyrs, heroes and heroines of the spiritual life?

But there are two points about the Catholic Church, above all, which excite the attention of all outside observers.

The first of them is her absolute self-confidence, her unshakable faith in her own authority and the truth of her teachings. She speaks with a calm assurance such as no other religious body possesses, and she receives from her children an unfaltering trust and obedience such as no other religious body elicits. And that is because she makes a claim that no other religious society in all history has ever made: the claim to infallibility, *i.e.,* the claim that when she speaks authoritatively upon a question of religion or morals, she is divinely safe-guarded from error. . . .

The second point about the Church that most arrests the attention of outside observers is her mysterious and almost uncanny strength and vitality. She is the oldest institution in the world today, and yet as young in spirit, as active and alert, as if created only yesterday. In her long history she has faced every kind of formidable opposition—the power of imperial Rome, the barbarians, the Mohammedans, the Hohenstaufen, the religious rebels of the 16th century, the French Revolution, Napoleon, Bismarck. She has never been vanquished. Over and over again she has faced crises so severe that her enemies have celebrated her inevitable demise and thanked whatever deities they had that she at last was done for. Chesterton has an essay on "The Five Deaths of the Faith." But in every crisis the Church has pulled herself together, renewed her strength, and come forth rejuvenated and reinvigorated from what ought, humanly speaking, to have killed her. The tremendous political and intellectual revolutions of the past century and a half, the fierce onslaughts directed upon her by modern "Liberalism," Anticlericalism, rationalism, and infidelity have only demonstrated anew that storms and perils galvanize the Church into new life. Today, when almost everything around her is quaking, tottering, or collapsing, she stands firm. . . .

To Catholics there seems to be only one explanation commensurate with the facts. It is that the Catholic Church is something absolutely *sui generis* in her nature, her claims, her strength, her vitality, because she is the only society on earth that has had God for its founder and because He has granted to her an authority and an unfailing guidance and support that were never promised to any other institution. It is because, though not unmixed with human elements and human imperfections, the Church is essentially a divine society, the "kingdom of God" on earth. To Catholics the Church is, above all, in St. Paul's phrase, the mystical "Body of Christ," in which and through which through all the centuries since His Ascension He has lived and worked upon earth; when she speaks on the subjects committed to her they recognize in her voice His voice; her cause is His cause, her losses are His losses, and her victories His triumphs.

(1934)


# CATHOLICISM'S UNIVERSALITY

### JUAN DONOSO CORTÈS

CATHOLICISM is a complete system of civilization. It is so complete that in its immensity it includes everything—the science of God, of angels, of the universe, of men. . . . There stand revealed the final causes of all things; the adjustment of human events, the nature of bodies and that of the spirits, by what ways men proceed, the limit of their progression, from whence they come, the mystery of their peregrination, the course of their journey, the enigma of their sorrows, the secret of life and the arcana of death. Children who are nourished at this fruitful source know more today than did Aristotle and Plato, the two luminaries of Athens. . . .

This theology is called Catholic because it is universal; and it is so in every sense, under every aspect, and in all respects. It is universal because it includes the substance of all truth. It is so because in its very nature it is destined to extend everywhere and to last through all time. It is universal in its God and in its dogmas.

(1842)

## CATHOLICISM'S DURABILITY

### THOMAS F. WOODLOCK

THE Thing (it is of course the Catholic Church I am talking about) is in nothing more remarkable than its history, which seems to controvert most of the laws that govern the lives of men and of institutions. For instance:

1. *The Church began in a remote and quite unimportant corner of a great empire with a group of a dozen simple men and a story which can be fairly described as wildly improbable.*

2. *The official annalists of these men, the Evangelists, are at pains to tell us that of the dozen one was a traitor, another a perjurer and a coward, and nine of the remainder were cowards, leaving only one unimpeached (John). All this, moreover, at the very moment of the death of their Leader.*

3. *They started out (after Pentecost) to preach a way of life which challenged every canon of the world around them—choosing for their battle-standard a symbol representing the ultimate of shame and failure, the Cross.*

4. *Notwithstanding this, their gospel, after three centuries of persecution, conquered the Roman Empire just before it fell a victim to its own weakness in face of the barbarian incursions.*

5. *No sooner had the Church done this than she had to meet a storm of heresies among her own people and bitter internal quarrels among*

192

*her own leaders, and again and again it seemed as if she must go down in death. But she did not.*

6. *Instead, after a period of intense struggle around her (fifth to tenth centuries) and despite internal human mismanagement (and worse), she established herself as the center of stability in the Western world and the heart of the Western civilization in the Middle Ages (eleventh to thirteenth centuries).*

Up to here by all the human rules of the game she should have died not only aborning, but many times thereafter. Always she was at strife within herself. Again and again there were scandals in high places, even in the highest. . . .

After the Middle Ages came the Renaissance and the tremendous cleavage in Christendom that we call the Reformation, tearing the Church herself apart and wresting from her influence a great part of the Western world. On top of this came the great current of apostasy from religion itself in the Enlightenment, the Revolution, and the advance of "science," so that by the middle of the nineteenth century the Church seemed (not for the first time) to be to all intents and purposes a dead thing. Her gospels were impeached as entirely unhistorical, science claimed to have destroyed the foundations not only of Christianity but of all religion, and the Aristotelian—Thomist philosophy of the Middle Ages was supposed to have been shown by Kant and his school to be completely illusory. Finally, in 1870, the Church was stripped of the last of her "temporal" possessions and power. To the eyes of the intelligent world of the time she was no longer to be reckoned with as a living force; she was no more than a relic of bygone ignorant and superstitious ages, of interest only to students of history. Yet, it was at that very moment that the Church flung in the world's face her most arrogant challenge (humanly speaking), the dogma of Papal infallibility! That dogma declared it to be a doctrine of the Church that the occupant of the Holy See, when speaking from the Chair of Peter and teaching the whole Church on a matter of faith or morals, was divinely protected from teaching error. In promulgating it the Church put herself upon peril of her very life, for upon the day it should be shown that a single dogma of the Church was untrue the whole edifice would necessarily crumble into dust. . . .

The Church is today seemingly quite alive and, so far as her Pattern is concerned, quite unchanged as compared with what she was many centuries ago. She has unsaid nothing that she ever said in doctrine. She still philosophizes (or rather her doctors do, for philosophy *as such* is not the Church's first business) essentially as her doctors did in the thirteenth century. She preaches the same morals as she did when she was born. Doctrinal polemics within Christendom have, however, largely died down; Catholic and Protestant no longer fight with Scriptural texts as they used to do a century ago. As a matter of fact religious controversy, that is, controversy on points of pure *doctrine,* has almost ceased. Such controversy as remains concerns itself mainly with broader issues, e.g., the truth of religion as such, or issues of a social, economic, or political character. It is, consequently, rather scattering, disorderly (in approach), and, where it occurs in what one might call intellectual circles, mainly tinged with "scientific" considerations and conclusions.

(1942)

## "THE CHURCH IS ETERNAL"

### JOHN HENRY CARDINAL NEWMAN

IT is the peculiarity of the warfare between the Church and the world, that the world seems ever gaining on the Church, yet the Church is really ever gaining on the world. Its enemies are ever triumphing over it as vanquished, and its members ever despairing; yet it abides. It abides, and it sees the ruin of its oppressors and enemies. "O how suddenly do they consume, perish, and come to a fearful end!" Kingdoms rise and fall; nations expand and contract; dynasties begin and end; princes are born and die; confederacies are made and unmade, and parties, and companies, and crafts, and guilds, and establishments, and philosophies, and sects, and heresies. They have their day, but the Church is eternal; yet in their day they seem of much account.

(1843)

## THE "SIGN OF THE PROPHET JONAS"

### RT. REV. MSGR. ROBERT HUGH BENSON

HERE is a religious society which is not only up to the present the one single religious force that can really control and unite the masses, but also the one single religious body with clear dogmatic principles which can attract at any rate a considerable selection of the most advanced and cultivated thinkers of the age. It is the easiest thing in the world to become an Individualist; it is always easy to believe in the practical infallibility of one's self; one only requires the simple equipment of a sufficient resolute contempt of one's neighbor; but it is not very easy to believe in the infallibility of someone else. That requires humility, at least intellectual. The craving for an external authority is not, in spite of a popular and shallow opinion to the contrary, nearly so natural to man as a firm reliance upon his own. Yet here the fact remains of this continuous stream of converts into the most practically and theoretically dogmatic society in the world, of converts who through their education and attainments surely should be tempted, if any were tempted, to remain in the pleasant Paradise of Individualism and Personal Popery. . . .

The future of Catholicism lies in its power of recuperation. Not only is it the sole religion which has arisen in the East and has dominated the West, and now once more is reconquering the East; but it is also the one religion that has been proclaimed as dead, over and over again, and yet somehow has always reappeared. Once "the world groaned to find itself Arian"; now Arius is enshrined in the text-books, and the Creed of Athanasius is repeated by living men. Once Gnosticism trampled on the ancient faith everywhere; now not one man in a hundred could write five lines on what it was that the Gnostics believed. Once the Turks overran Africa and Spain and threatened Christendom itself; now the nations trained by Christianity are wondering how they can best dispose of Constantinople. Nero thought that he had crucified Christianity in Peter; now Peter sits on Nero's seat. Once Elizabeth disemboweled every seminary priest she could lay hands on, and established Protestantism in Ireland. Now Westminster Cathedral draws immeasureably larger congregations than Westminster Abbey, where Elizabeth lies buried; and Catholic Irishmen are dictating in an English Parliament how the children in English schools are to be educated.

At every crisis in the history of Christendom—at the captivity of Avignon, the appearance of Luther, and the capture of Rome in 1870 —it was declared by "modern thinkers" that Catholicism was discredited forever. And yet, somehow or other, the Church is as much alive today as ever she was; and that, in spite of the fact that she is, in her faith, committed to the past and to doctrines formulated centuries before modern science was dreamed of.

Is there any other society in the world, secular or sacred, that has passed through such vicissitudes with such a burden on its shoulders, and survived? For it is a burden which she cannot shift. She cannot, at least, "recast her theology" and drop unpopular or unfashionable dogmas (as can all sects which claim merely human authority), and yet live. Yet who can doubt that she is more of a force today than all the most accommodating denominations around her. She has lived, too, in the tumultuous rush of Western life, not in the patient lethargy of the East. She has struggled, not only with enemies in her gate, but with her own children in her own house. She has been betrayed over and over again by the treachery or wickedness or cowardice of her own rulers; she has been exiled from nearly every country which she had nursed into maturity; she has been stripped in nearly everyone of her lands of all her treasures; she has finally seen her supreme sovereign on earth driven to take refuge in his own house by the children of the men whom she raised to honor. And yet on her secular side she has seen every kingdom of Europe rise and fall and rise again; she has seen a republic give birth to a monarchy or an empire, and an empire yield to a republic; she has seen every dynasty fall except her own; she has seen, in religious affairs, every "modern" sect —whose one claim to efficiency lies in its modernity—fail to keep pace with herself who has the centuries on her shoulders; and she remains today the one single sacred and secular commonwealth which has faced the revolutions and the whirling religions of the West and has survived, with a continuity so unshaken that not one of her enemies can dispute it, and an authority which they can only resent; she reigns even in this day of her "discredit" over more hearts than any other earthly sovereign, and more heads than any philosopher of the schools; she arouses more love and obedience on the one side and more hatred or contempt on the other than the most romantic, brutal, or the most constitutional sovereign, sage, or thinker ever seen.

I called this characteristic of her Recuperation. I call it now Resurrection, for this is the "sign of the Prophet Jonas" to which her Divine Founder appealed. And yet our "modern religious thinkers" are dreaming in their arm-chairs of another "creed!"

(1910)

# THE UNCHANGING CHURCH

## JAMES CARDINAL GIBBONS

AMONG the continual changes in human institutions, the Church is the one institution that never changes. Amid the universal ruins of earthly monuments she is the one monument that stands proudly preeminent. Not a stone in this building falls to the ground. Amid the general destruction of kingdoms her kingdom is never destroyed. Ever ancient and ever new, time writes no wrinkles on her Divine brow.

The Church has seen the birth of every government of Europe, and it is not at all improbable that she shall also witness the death of them all and chant their requiem. She was more than fourteen hundred years old when Columbus discovered our continent, and the foundation of our republic is but as yesterday to her. . . .

Of her we can truly say in the words of the Psalmist: "They shall perish, but thou remainest; and all of them shall grow old as a garment. And as a vesture thou shalt change them, and they shall be changed. But thou art always the self-same, and thy years shall not fail. The children of thy servants shall continue, and their seed shall be directed forever."

God forbid that we should ascribe to any human cause this marvelous survival of the Church. Her indestructibility is not due, as some suppose, to her wonderful organization, or to the far-reaching policy of her Pontiffs, or to the learning and wisdom of her teachers. If she has survived, it is not because of human wisdom, but often in spite of human folly. Her permanence is due not to the arm of the flesh, but to the finger of God.

(1886)

# THE CHURCH IN HISTORY

## CHRISTOPHER DAWSON

IN spite of the Christian opposition between "This World" and "The World to Come," there can be no tampering with the reality and uniqueness of the historical process. . . .

The whole anti-Gnostic apologia of St. Irenaeus is directed to the defense of the value and reality of the historical development. "Since men are real, theirs must be a real establishment. They do not vanish into non-existence, but progress among existent things." "There is one Son who performs the Father's will, and one human race in which the mysteries of God are realised." "God arranged everything from the first with a view to the perfection of man, in order to deify him and reveal His own dispensations, so that goodness may be made manifest, justice made perfect, and the Church may be fashioned after the image of His Son. Thus man may eventually reach maturity, and, being ripened by such privileges, may see and comprehend God."

It was to this consciousness of its unique character and mission that Christianity owes its extraordinary powers of expansion and conquest which revolutionized the whole development of Western civilization. . . .

In the Roman West, in spite of its lower standard of civilization, the conditions were more favourable for the development of an original and creative Christian culture. For here the Church did not become incorporated in a fixed social and political order which it was powerless to modify; it found itself abandoned to its own resources in a world of chaos and destruction. It had to contend, not with the influence of an alien spiritual tradition but with the forces of barbarism and social disorder. But long before the fall of the Empire, Western Catholicism had already acquired the distinctive characteristics that were to mark its future development. The oldest document of Western Christianity—the First Epistle of Clement—already shows the Latin sense of order and its practical ideal of social duty. Even the Western heresies from the days of Novatian and the Donatists to Pelagius and Priscillian are not concerned with speculative theology, but with the concrete matters of Church order or with the problems of moral conduct and moral responsibility.

Moreover the emphasis on the social aspect of the Christian tradition led the Western Church to assume a much more independent attitude to the state than that of the Byzantine Church. Hilary of Poitiers in the reign of Constantine, attacks the interference of the state in religious matters with a vehemence that is hardly surpassed by the champions of the mediaeval Papacy, and St. Ambrose, in his relations with the Christian Emperors, affirms the authority of the spiritual power in the spirit of a mediaeval pontiff rather than a Byzantine prelate. . . .

Hence the new civilization which slowly and painfully began to emerge in the early middle ages was in a very special sense a religious creation, for it was based on an ecclesiastical not a political unity. While in the East, the imperial unity was still all inclusive and the Church was essentially the Church of the Empire, in the West it was the Church that was the universal society and the state that was weak, barbarous and divided. The only true citizenship that remained to the common man was his membership of the Church, and it involved a far deeper and wider loyalty than his allegiance to the secular state. It was the fundamental social relation which overrode all distinctions of class and nationality. The Church was a world in itself, with its own culture, its own organization and its own law. In so far as civilization survived, it was directly dependent on the Church, whether in the great Carolingian monasteries, such as St. Gall or Fulda, which were the chief centres of cultural and economic life, or in the cities which came to depend on the bishops and the ecclesiastical element for their very existence. The state, on the other hand, had become divorced from the city and the civic culture and reverted more and more to the warlike traditions of a barbarous tribal aristocracy.

For mediaeval Europe no longer possessed a homogeneous material culture, such as we find, for example, in China or India. It was a loose federation of the most diverse type of race and culture under the hegemony of a common religious and ecclesiastical tradition. This explains the contradictions and disunity of mediaeval culture—the contrast of its cruelty and its charity, its beauty and squalor, its spiritual vitality and its material barbarism. For the elements of higher culture did not spring naturally from the traditions of the social organism itself, but came in from outside as a spiritual power which had to remould and transform the social material in which it attempted to embody itself.

And so in the 11th and 12th centuries, when the social revival of Western Europe began, the new development was inspired by religious motives, and proceeded directly from the tradition of the spiritual society. . . . Everywhere men became conscious of their common citizenship in the great spiritual commonwealth of Christendom. And this spiritual citizenship was the foundation of a new society. As members of the feudal state, men were separated by the countless divisions of allegiance and jurisdiction. They were parcelled out like sheep with the land, on which they lived, among different lordships. But as members of the Church, they met on a common ground. "Before Christ," writes St. Ivo of Chartres, "there is neither free man nor serf, all who participate in the same sacraments are equal."

And, in fact, a new democratic spirit of brotherhood and social cooperation begins to make itself felt in Europe at this epoch. In every walk of life men leagued themselves together in voluntary associations for social objects under religious auspices. . . .

Thus by the 13th century Christendom had organized itself as a vast international unity founded on an ecclesiastical rather than a political basis. . . .

But it is in the region of thought that the new realization of the reality and value of humanity and the whole order of nature had the more important results. The great intellectual synthesis of the 13th century has often been regarded as the triumph of theological dogmatism. It was in reality the assertion of the rights of the human reasons and the foundation of European science. As Harnack has said, "Scholasticism is nothing else but scientific thought," and its weakness in the sphere of natural science is simply due to the fact that there was as yet no body of observed facts upon which it could exercise itself. . . .

It was the work of the new philosophy, as represented above all by St. Thomas, for the first time to break with the old established tradition of oriental spiritualism and Neoplatonic idealism, and to bring man back into the order of nature. He taught that the human intelligence is not that of a pure spirit, it is consubstantial with matter, and finds its natural activity in the sphere of the sensible and the particular.

Consequently man cannot attain in this life to the direct intuition of truth and spiritual reality. He must build up an intelligible world slowly and painfully from the data of the senses, ordered and systematized by science, until at last the intelligible order which is inherent in created things is disengaged from the envelope of matter and contemplated in its relation to the absolute Being by the light of higher intelligence.

(1938)

# VIII

# The Church
# as an Organism and Teacher

*The vital principle of society. The Mystical Body of Christ. The Church as an organism. The essence of Catholic Christianity. The Church and science. Catholic "exclusiveness." A fixed moral code. The Church in a changing world. Catholic "censorship." Catholic "intolerance." Salvation outside the Church. Restating the Christian tradition.*

## HIS EARTHLY TABERNACLE

### ST. AUGUSTINE

He Who has His house very high in secret place, hath also on earth a tabernacle. His tabernacle on earth is the Church. It is here that He is to be sought, for it is in the tabernacle that is found the way by which we arrive at the house. *For I will go into the place of Thy admirable tabernacle, even into the house of God.* God's tabernacle on earth is the Faithful. . . . Yet when I come to *the house of God,* I am even struck dumb with astonishment. It is there, in the sanctuary of God, in the house of God, is the fountain of understanding.

(ca. A.D. 415)

# "THE VITAL PRINCIPLE
# OF HUMAN SOCIETY"

## PIUS XII

THE unity and completeness of the Church made clear by the manifestation of her supranational character is of great importance for the foundation of life in society. This does not mean that it is the office of the Church to include and somehow embrace, as in a gigantic world empire all human society. Such a concept of the Church as an earthly empire and a world domination is fundamentally false. . . .

The Church—while fulfilling the mandate of her Divine Founder of spreading the gospel everywhere and of winning over to the gospel every creature—is not an empire, especially in the imperialistic sense, such as is now meant by the word. Her progress and expansion are marked by a trend contrary to that of modern imperialism. Her development is before all else in depth, then in length and breadth. She seeks out above all man as such. Her study is to form man, to model and perfect in him the Divine Image. Her work is done in the depth of each man's heart, but has its effects, extending throughout his life, in all his activities. Through men thus formed the Church prepares for human society a basis on which it can rest securely.

Modern imperialism, on the contrary, goes in just the opposite direction. It does not seek out man as such but the material things and forces to which it subjects man. . . .

The Church cannot cut herself off, inert in the privacy of her churches, and thus desert her divinely providential mission of forming the complete man, and thereby collaborating without rest in the construction of the solid foundations of society. This mission is for her essential. Considered from this angle, the Church may be called the assembly of those who, under the supernatural influences of grace, in the perfection of their personal dignity as sons of God and in the harmonious development of all human inclinations and energies, build the powerful structure of human intercourse.

Under this aspect, Venerable Brethren, the faithful, and more precisely, the laity, are in the front line of the Church's life; for them the Church is the vital principle of human society. Accordingly they—especially they—must have an ever-clearer sense not only of belonging to the Church, but of being the Church, the community of the faithful on earth under the guidance of the common head, the Pope, and of the Bishops in communion with Him. They are the Church. . . .

Thus the principal meaning of the supranational character of the Church is to give lasting shape and form to the foundations of human society, above all differences, beyond the limits of space and time. . . .

Let us be ourselves the stable foundation of society; may it become, in effect, the "una gens," of which the great Bishop of Hippo speaks, one nation, "because one faith, one hope, one charity, one expectation;" that, then, all those whom the grace of Our Lord has called to His Church, "out of every tribe and tongue, and people and nation," may be conscious in this grave hour of their sacred duty to irradiate from their lively and active faith the spirit and love of Christ in human society; that, in turn, all peoples and men—near the Church or still far from it—may recognize that she is the salvation of God even to the farthest parts of the earth.

(February 20, 1946)

THE object in preaching the faith is the Catholic doctrine, that is to say, the revelation with all the truths which it contains, with all foundations and ideas it presupposes, with all the consequences it carries for the moral conduct of man in domestic, social, public, and even political life. Religion and morality in their close union compose an indivisible whole; the moral order and God's commandments have a force equally in all fields of human activity, without a single exception; wherever they reach, the mission of the Church reaches and therefore also the word of the priest, his teaching, his warnings, his counsels to the faithful entrusted to his care. The Catholic Church will never allow herself to be confined within the four walls of the temple.

PIUS XII (March 17, 1946)

## THE MYSTICAL BODY OF CHRIST

### PIUS XII

THE doctrine of the Mystical Body of Christ, which is the Church, was first taught by the Redeemer Himself. . . . This doctrine by its sublime dignity invites all those who are drawn by the Holy Spirit to study it, and gives them, in the truths of which it proposes to the mind, a strong incentive to the performance of such good works as are conformable to its teachings. . . .

One [must not] imagine that the Body of the Church, just because it bears the name of Christ, is made up during the days of its earthly pilgrimage only of members conspicuous for their holiness, or that it consists only of those whom God has predestined to eternal happiness. It is owing to the Saviour's infinite mercy that place is allowed in His Mystical Body here below for those whom, of old, He did not exclude from the banquet. For not every sin, however grave it may be, is such as of its own nature to sever a man from the Body of the Church, as does schism or heresy or apostasy. Men may lose charity and divine grace through sin, thus becoming incapable of supernatural merit, and yet not be deprived of all life if they hold fast to faith and Christian hope, and if, illumined from above, they are spurred on by the interior promptings of the Holy Spirit to salutary fear and are moved to prayer and penance for their sins. . . .

If anyone unhappily falls and his obstinacy has not made him unworthy of communion with the faithful, let him be received with great love, and let eager charity see in him a weak member of Jesus Christ. . . .

Just as at the first moment of the Incarnation the Son of the Eternal Father adorned with the fulness of the Holy Spirit the human nature which was substantially united to Him, . . . so at the hour of His precious death He willed that His Church should be enriched with the abundant gifts of the Paraclete in order that in dispensing the divine fruits of the Redemption she might be . . . a powerful instrument that would never fail. . . .

Although the juridical principles, on which the Church rests and is established, derive from the divine constitution given to it by Christ and contribute to the attaining of its supernatural end, nevertheless that which lifts the Society of Christians far above the whole natural order is the Spirit of our Redeemer who penetrates and fills every part of the Church's being and is active within it until the end of time as the source of every grace and every gift and every miraculous power. . . .

We deplore and condemn the pernicious error of those who dream of an imaginary Church, a kind of society that finds its origin and growth in charity, to which, somewhat contemptuously, they oppose another, which they call juridical. But this distinction which they introduce is false: for they fail to understand that the reason which led our Divine Redeemer to give to the community of men He founded the constitution of a Society, perfect of its kind and containing all the juridical and social elements,—namely, that He might perpetuate on earth the saving work of Redemption—was also the reason why He willed it to be enriched with the heavenly gifts of the Paraclete. The Eternal Father indeed willed it to be the "Kingdom of the Son of his predilection"; but it was to be a real kingdom, in which all believers should make Him the entire offering of their intellect and will, and humbly and obediently model themselves on Him, Who for our sake "was made obedient unto death." There can, then, be no real objection or conflict between the invisible mission of the Holy Spirit and the juridical commission of Ruler and Teacher received from Christ, since they mutually complement and perfect each other—as do the body and soul in man. . . .

The unbroken tradition of the Fathers from the earliest times teaches that the Divine Redeemer and the Society which is His Body form but one mystical person, that is to say, to quote Augustine, the whole Christ. . . .

Our union in and with Christ is first evident from the fact that, since Christ wills His Christian community to be a Body which is a perfect Society, its members must be united because they all work together towards a single end. The nobler the end towards which they strive, and the more divine the motive which actuates this collaboration, the higher, no doubt, will be the union.

(June 29, 1943)


THE Church is holy because her *Author* is holy and the very source of holiness; because her object is the *sanctification* of men; because the means which she uses, her dogmas, her moral doctrine, her Sacraments are holy in themselves and lead to holiness; because at all times *many of her members* have been distinguished for their sanctity, some of them—those who have fully followed her directions—have even become distinguished by *eminent* sanctity; finally, because all true miracles have been performed to manifest and confirm this sanctity.

THE REV. W. DEVIVIER, S.J. (1924)

# THE ROLE OF PAPAL ENCYCLICALS

## PIUS XII

WHAT is expounded in the Encyclical Letters of the Roman Pontiffs concerning the nature and constitution of the Church, is deliberately and habitually neglected by some with the idea of giving force to a certain vague notion which they profess to have found in the ancient Fathers, especially the Greeks. The Popes, they assert, do not wish to pass judgment on what is a matter of dispute among theologians, so recourse must be had to the early sources, and the recent constitutions and decrees of the Teaching Church must be explained from the writings of the ancients.

Although these things seem well said, still they are not free from error. It is true that Popes generally leave theologians free in those matters which are disputed in various ways by men of very high authority in this field; but history teaches that many matters that formerly were open to discussion, no longer now admit of discussion.

Nor must it be thought that what is expounded in Encyclical Letters does not of itself demand consent, since in writing such Letters the Popes do not exercise the supreme power of their Teaching Authority. For these matters are taught with the ordinary teaching authority, of which it is true to say: "He who heareth you, heareth me" (Luke X, 16); and generally what is expounded and inculcated in Encyclical Letters already for other reasons appertains to Catholic doctrine. But if the Supreme Pontiffs in their official documents purposely pass judgment on a matter up to that time under dispute, it is obvious that that matter, according to the mind and will of the same Pontiffs, cannot be any longer considered a question open to discussion among theologians.

(August 12, 1950)

## "THE CHURCH IS AN ORGANISM"

### MOST REV. JOHN J. WRIGHT

THE Church is more than an organization. The Church is also an organism.

Joan of Arc expressed it perfectly five centuries ago before her judges when she cried, "I make no difference between Christ and His Church. It is all one."

The same Christ who 2,000 years ago in His physical body went about preaching to one race and one nation the eternal will of God, today and in every age still goes about in His Mystical Body, which is His Church, preaching to every race and to every nation the same eternal will of God.

The same Christ who 2,000 years ago in His physical body went about in Judea and Palestine, as the Gospel tells us, doing good, healing the sick, restoring hope to the disconsolate, loosing the spiritually captive—that same Christ today and in every age goes about in His Mystical Body, which is the Holy Catholic Church, doing the same good, healing the sick, loosing the spiritually captive, restoring vision and hope to the disconsolate and the defeated.

The same Christ who 2,000 years ago in His physical body was hailed before Pilate, Herod, Annas and Caiphas, who was falsely accused and sent to prison and to death—that same Christ in His Mystical Body, which is the Church, in this and every century—there is no exception—is still hailed before other Pilates and other Herods, other Annases and Caiphases in the persons of Mindszenty, Stepinac, Beran today, in the persons of Thomas More, John Fisher and Blessed Plunkett in other days.

"I make no difference between Christ and His Church," said St. Joan of Arc. "It is all one." And she was right!

To whom, then, does the Church belong? The Church does not belong to the hierarchy. The hierarchy are called to do a specific work; they are ordained, consecrated, deputed officially to fulfill specific functions. They do their work, they fulfill their functions individually, they die, they are absorbed into history and are forgotten. But the work of the Church goes on.

The Church does not belong to the clergy; neither does it belong to the people.

The Church belongs totally and exclusively to Jesus Christ. In this sense, and this sense only, the Church is totalitarian; it belongs totally to Christ. It belongs to Him as my body belongs to me. It is identified with Him utterly as my personality is identified with me. "I make no difference between Christ and His Church. It is all one." . . .

Yet this is the criticism you hear on all sides: "The Catholic Church is not democratic. It is alien to the spirit of democracy. It is ill at ease in a democratic nation because it is not a democracy. It is not a democracy because it does not elect its leadership; it does not debate its dogma; it doesn't submit its moral or canonical code to revision, to parliamentary debate and discussion, to democratic processes. For all these reasons the Catholic Church is not a democracy."

The criticism is perfectly true, but completely irrelevant. The Catholic Church is *not* a democracy and democratic terms of reference are totally out of point in discussing her because the Catholic Church is not a political organization in the sense these critics imply. It is not a human society. Above all, it is not a debating forum or a religious or philosophical parliament.

"I make no difference between Christ and His Church. It is all one." It is therefore as pointless to talk of the true Church in terms of democracy or socialism or fascism or any other "ism" as it would be to talk of Jesus Christ in these terms.

Christ did not come as the result of a plebiscite. He did not come as a result of a counting of heads. He did not come as the result of resolutions adopted by men. The Incarnation and Redemption were not accomplished by democratic processes.

Christ came by the sovereign mandate of His Father. We have the sad witness of the Gospel to remind us that, if it had depended on a counting of heads, on a majority, the Incarnation and Redemption would never have taken place. "He came unto His own and His own received Him not." There is always a substantial majority against Jesus Christ. "I make no difference between Christ and His Church. It is all one."

Now just as Christ came by the sovereign mandate of His Father to do His Father's work without reference to the numbers for Him or against Him, so the Church, the permanent, living, personal, dynamic presence of the Mystical Jesus in history, also does His work and is totally His. The Church is not the property of princes, nor the property of prelates, nor the property of the people. The Church belongs totally to Jesus Christ. In that sense, and in that sense only—strictly spiritual—the Church is totalitarian.

(1952)

208

### JACQUES MARITAIN

CATHOLICS are not Catholicism. The errors, apathies, shortcomings and slumbers of Catholics do not involve Catholicism. Catholicism is not obliged to provide an alibi for the failures of Catholics. The best apologetic does not consist in justifying Catholics or making excuses for them when they are in the wrong, but on the contrary in emphasising their errors and pointing out that, far from affecting the substance of Catholicism, they serve only the better to display the virtue of a religion which is still a living force in spite of them. The Church is a mystery, her head is hidden in the sky, her visibility does not adequately manifest her nature; if you seek to know what represents, without betraying, her, consider the Pope and the episcopate teaching the faith and morals, consider the saints in Heaven and on earth, avert your eyes from us poor sinners. Or, rather, consider how the Church heals our wounds and leads us hobbling to eternal life. . . . The great glory of the Church is to be holy with sinful members.

(1931)

ONE thing has become increasingly clear to me and it is very important. Accusations against the Church can only be substantiated by Church Doctrine! Do the Christian clergy and laity side with the rich against the poor? Many seem to do so. And is it wrong? You may well think so. But how will you prove it but by recourse to Christian teaching? Is not much of our worship both vain and vain-glorious? And is not vanity reprehensible and vain-glory noxious to the Lord of Hosts? How will you prove these things but from the Holy Writ and the lives of the Saints? And if you are annoyed by the policeman like frame of mind of many of the clergy and their apparent conviction that the spirit killeth but the letter quickeneth (so that you would think getting to heaven was a business of going "by the book") you must still remember that the opposite doctrine is Christian teaching and that it is the authority to which they themselves appeal who is the judge.

ERIC GILL (1941)

# ESSENCE OF CATHOLIC CHRISTIANITY

## ROSALIND MURRAY

THE essence of Catholic Christianity is acceptance of a Supernatural Order, here and now, at every point and turn of daily life, impinging as it were on all we do, breaking through, always at hand, always real; the essence of the Rationalist Good Pagan is denial of such a Supernatural Order, anywhere, altogether. The varieties of intermediate beliefs are all attempts at compromise between them; the numberless different forms of Protestanism are all, if we attempt to analyze them, but bits of Catholic faith taken from their context, mixed up with different proportions of rationalism. . . . We may find corroboration of our assertion in the differing degrees of hostility shown by the avowedly anti-religious towards the different forms of Christian thought; active hostility is reserved almost entirely for the Catholic Christians; the others are neglected as unimportant or in some cases accepted as half-allies. . . .

To be "good" is not the same as to be Christian, although being Christian should include being "good." . . .

One consequence of this loose use of words is a watering-down of the whole force and power of the Christian impact against, or perhaps towards, the Pagan world.

I myself once heard a distinguished Anglican preacher describe Christianity as very easy, simply being a little kinder and more patient to "an aunt you do not like," and so on.

Now we should all agree that a good Christian should be kind to people in general, aunts included, but a view of life which holds such kindness to be the sole, or indeed the chief, character of Christianity is far removed from the totalitarian [word here used in sense of a total Christian] view. True kindness is a valuable virtue, but we may doubt if the high premium set upon that one virtue today is a sign that we should welcome. Very often "kindness" is used when "indifference" would be truer; not to blame, not to condemn, not to "take a strong line about," all this is understood by being kind; how often, in fact, is what is classed as kindness, merely a shirking of responsibility? "Live and let live" is the popular attitude, it is pleasant, and it is easy, but it is not either truly kind, or Christian, nor is any kindness that can be described as easy.

Christianity is not easy, it is difficult; its appeal is not and cannot be to those who demand a comfortable life; it is a challenge, not a soporific.

To present it in such diluted, distorted form can surely lead us nowhere; it means nothing. . . .

This diluted "Christianity without tears" does, it is true, disarm opposition; you cannot feel much hostility to jelly, nor to an eiderdown. It is impossible to have anti-clerical outbreaks against so negative a protagonist, but is to escape notice all we aim at? . . .

Appeal is often made to the early Christians as examples of this "simple kindness" view, but, as Mr. Belloc has pointed out, this vague kindliness would never have provoked the persecution to which the early Christians were subjected. Diocletian and Nero knew what they were about, just as Hitler and Stalin know in our own day. These persecutors are justified from their point of view; they recognize the existence at their doors of an irreconcilable, totalitarian force, whose existence is in itself a challenge to them.

(1939)

## THE CATHOLIC PATTERN

### THOMAS F. WOODLOCK

THE days of my years have covered almost all the discoveries that have transformed the face of the earth, and have come close to the annihilation of time and space for the convenience of man. The world into which I was born was almost as close a prison of time and space as was the world of Julius Caesar. I have seen almost every one of those discoveries turned to the work of destroying the things they had built, and of rebuilding man's prison house, from which we thought, only yesterday, that he had been freed forever. I have seen go bankrupt, one after another, a whole series of "philosophies" which agreed in only one thing, rejection of the Catholic Pattern, all in the space of a man's lifetime. Hardly had we completed what we thought was "The City of Man" when it withered like Klingsor's castle, and we sit today in ruins with a great fear upon us, and wonder what has gone wrong.

If I must choose between answers to that question, each of which must reek with mystery, I must choose one which begins with the beginning and ends with the end. The Beginning and End of all things is God—Alpha and Omega—and the Pattern begins and ends with God, the Triune God. I know of no other "pattern" that contains either beginnings or ends, much less an "account" of either, nor do I know of any other "pattern" that gives a recognizable description of this paradoxical creature, man, with his extraordinary heights and depths that mark him from all other living things on this earth. Extraordinary as is the Pattern in all its parts, is there today anywhere a better explanation of what has happened to us and why? If there is, where is it?

It is not because of that, I remind the reader, that I *believe* the Pattern. But, as a pattern, it seems to me to be in itself, and independently of its Source, the only completely *reasonable* pattern offered to mankind today. The same tremendous question is still posed in the same direct words as it was nineteen centuries ago: "What think ye of Christ? Whose Son is He?" And only in the Catholic Pattern's answer to that will the world find the secret of its own order and its own peace.

(1942)


# HUMAN NATURE VERSUS
# SUPERNATURAL GRACE

### JOHN HENRY CARDINAL NEWMAN

IN truth, the world does not know of the existence of grace; nor is it wonderful, for it is ever contented with itself, and has never turned to account the supernatural aids bestowed upon it. Its highest idea of man lies in the order of nature; its pattern man is the natural man; it thinks it wrong to be anything else than a natural man. It sees that nature has a number of tendencies, inclinations, and passions; and because these are natural, it thinks that each of them may be indulged for its own sake, so far as it does no harm to others, or to a person's bodily, mental, and temporal well-being. . . .

Behold here the true origin and fountain-head of the warfare between the Church and the world; here they join issue, and diverge from each other. . . . The corrupt world . . . deifies and worships human nature and its impulses, and denies the power and the grant of grace. This is the source of the hatred which the world bears to the Church; it finds a whole catalogue of sins brought into light and denounced, which it would fain believe to be no sins at all. . . . It finds itself in danger of being humbled to the earth as a rebel, instead of being allowed to indulge in self-dependence and self-complacency. Hence it takes its stand on nature, and denies or rejects divine grace. Like the proud spirit in the beginning, it wishes to find its supreme good in its own itself, and nothing above it; to undertake to be sufficient for its own happiness; it has no desire for the supernatural, and therefore does not believe in it.

(1849)

## CATHOLIC "EXCLUSIVENESS"
## EXPLAINED
### KNIGHTS OF COLUMBUS PAMPHLET

"CATHOLICS tell us to investigate the Catholic religion," some of our friends will complain, "and they invite us to come to church with them. Yet Catholics are not allowed to investigate Protestantism or to attend Protestant services. This is one-sided. Is the Catholic Church afraid that Catholics might lose their faith if they found out about Protestantism?"

This complaint is familiar and—according to Protestant principles—it is quite logical. Catholics, however, act not according to Protestant principles but according to Catholic ones. And it is Catholic principles that rule out religious instruction from Protestantism and participation in Protestant worship.

When we invite Protestants to investigate the Catholic Church, it is only because of what these Protestants themselves believe about their religious duties. . . .

Protestants . . . obviously have as their idea of religion that it is *a search for truth*. If the foundations of religion are constantly to be re-examined, if it is considered that truth is not yet possessed in a definitive form, then they may certainly be invited to look into what the Catholic Church teaches. It is only logical that in the search for truth the teaching of Catholicism should not be ignored.

But this is not the Catholic position on religion. In Catholic belief, the Catholic religion is the truth. The reasonable bases on which the Catholic Faith rests can be shown to the satisfaction of any inquiring

213

person. We do not conceive of religion as a searching for, but as a possession of the truth. *We are not seeking truth—we have it.* Hence we do not investigate what other religions have to offer.

Some may be tempted to dismiss this as prejudice and narrow-mindedness. But we repeat, the reasons for what we say of the Church can be *shown*. A non-Catholic may reply that these reasons are not sufficient to convince him. That is not the point; for us they are sufficient. . . .

Protestants and Catholics mean vastly different things when they speak of "faith" and of "losing faith." They consequently place vastly different values on its possession and loss. Loss of faith to some Protestants is not of major consequence. If it does not matter greatly what a man believes, then it does not matter much more whether he believes at all. Loss of faith can be just as much "the search for truth" as finding faith.

But faith to the Catholic means the acceptance of truths, on God's word, which we must believe if we shall save our souls. This acceptance is a reasonable act. But it is precisely because not every person is capable of demonstrating these reasons that the Church safeguards faith in many ways which seem repressive to the Protestant.

A skilled debater might present to an unlearned Catholic arguments that he could not meet, arguments that might shake his faith. This does not mean that the arguments cannot be answered—they can. But that will do no good for the person in question. Meanwhile, faith is all important, and the Church cannot stand idly by and see faith destroyed in an individual simply because he is a poor hand in an argument. A Catholic who truly believes in the Church will, therefore, heed her command to stay away from non-Catholic religions.

In this sense, then, the Catholic Church is afraid that Catholics—some of them—might lose their faith. Her fear arises merely from her concern as to what might be the eternal consequences of such a loss. . . .

But there is an even more important reason for Catholics to avoid non-Catholic religious services. . . .

The reason is, rather, that worship is an act of religion. Worship is an expression of the faith that prompts it. To a greater or less degree, the worship of any religion is a reflection of the principles according to which that religion exists. Episcopalians worship in one way—according to the creeds and the prayer book of the Episcopalian

Church. Methodists worship in their way, Quakers in theirs, Unitarians in a third way. And Catholics worship according to the faith of the Catholic Church.

Catholics believe in one true Church. They believe that that one Church was set up for a great purpose—to guide mankind through its teaching authority and to safeguard Christ's revelation in its purity, to provide men with the sacraments, the means of heavenly grace, and to offer due worship to God. We believe, therefore, that the worship of the Catholic Church is that which God has commanded of us and that God will be displeased if we attempt to offer Him any other form of worship.

Do not misunderstand us. We do not say that God refuses to hear any sincere prayer. We do not say that persons of other faiths displease God when they worship Him according to their conscience. We know that many good people are outside the Catholic Church and that they are perfectly sincere in their own beliefs. Their worship is likewise sincere. But their worship would not be sincere if offered by us. For we do not believe in it if we are consistent Catholics.

We all worship God. But we worship Him in many ways. And the Catholic who believes in the Catholic Church maintains that he worships God in God's way. If God has revealed a true Church to offer Him true worship, then it is base ingratitude for a member of this Church to attempt worship in any other way.

(1950)

# DETERMINISM VERSUS
## MORAL STANDARDS

### WILLIAM AYLOTT ORTON

To minds and wills so enfeebled, deterministic theories offer a blanket alibi for human failure; especially moral failure. Under the spell of agnostic or atheistic teachings, modern life has become largely a technique for the evasion of moral responsibility: a phenomenon that now characterizes public as well as private life in an amazing degree. It may surely be said that the American people are somewhat uneasy as they contemplate the ruins of Dresden and Hiroshima, or the occupation policies in Europe, or that kind of law that has been improvised at Nuremburg; but they take refuge in the thought that years ago somebody else started a certain historical process, and it has to go on, riding roughshod over our doubts or dreams or wishes, and there is nothing we can do. Least of all can we take any chances or risk looking foolish.

Similarly, in the personal life we welcome an alibi. Deterministic theories, sociological and psychological, are popular because they offer people a plausible excuse to go on fooling themselves and ignoring or denying their own experience. It is a simple fact—and everybody knows it—that when we refuse to fulfill the demands of our higher nature a sense of failure and remorse besets us: we feel and know that we have sinned and come short of the glory of God. Since this feeling is uncomfortable, an age that has made a god of comfort will not admit it: it is barred as far as may be from consciousness, and the word sin is banished from polite usage. Instead, we invent all sorts of elaborate disguises for the fact to which it refers.

A deterministic dogma comes in very handy as an escape from responsibility. Sociology proffers a variety of comfortable excuses for human failure. You can blame, according to the school of your choice, either the "environment" (ignoring the circular argument involved); or the "culture"—that commodious *ding-an-sich* suspended in a logical vacuum; or your genes, hormones or chromosomes; or that poor old scapegoat, the "subconscious"—you can blame, in short, almost anything except yourself because you have been taught that you really have no self. If there is a quicker way to weaken the moral fibre of a democracy, it has yet to be discovered; for in all these subterfuges the root-impulse is to escape the more exacting aspects of human responsibility, individual and collective.

The loss of a lively sense of responsibility to absolute moral standards has rather conspicuous results. One is the feeling that nothing matters very much; that however regrettable conditions here or there may be, there is no point in our getting too concerned about them—even when we are directly involved. Thus the normal human impulses of pity, sympathy, compassion, brotherhood, are frustrated and atrophied for lack of hope and an outlet; and the false expediency of power politics becomes a shoddy substitute for constructive action.

(1946)

# THE CHURCH IN A CHANGING WORLD

CHRISTOPHER DAWSON

WE have no right to expect that Christian principles will work in practice in the simple way that a political system may work. The Christian order is a supernatural order. It has its own principles and its own laws which are not those of the visible world and which may often seem to contradict them. Its victories may be found in apparent defeat and its defeats in material success.

The new situation with which the Church is faced today is not merely a question of the victory of materialism over religion and the triumph of brute force over right. . . . Human nature needs a holy community, and though this need finds satisfaction in a true Christian order, it does not find it in the sect and the chapel, which was all the nineteenth century offered to fill the void left by the secular State.

But the Church also has to take the difficult way of the Cross, to incur the penalties and humiliations of earthly failure without any compensating hope of temporal success. She is not an alternative and a rival to the State, and her teaching does not take the place of political needs and ideologies; yet she cannot disinterest herself in the corporate life of the community and confine her attentions to the individual soul. The Church is no human society, but she is the channel by which divine life flows into human society, and her essential task is the sanctification of humanity as a whole in its corporate as well as in its individual activities.

Human society today is in a state of rapid change. The life is going out of the old political and juridical forms and a new community is being created whose appearance marks a new epoch in history. It is not the Church's business to stop this great social change, and she could not if she would; but neither can she abdicate her essential mission, which remains the same in the new circumstances as of old. The new social form offers new opportunities—new openings for the action of grace.

(1934)

# THE CHURCH AND SCIENCE

## SIR BERTRAM C. A. WINDLE

AMONG the numerous taunts which are cast at the Catholic Church there is none more frequently employed, nor, may it be added, more generally believed, nor more injurious to her reputation amongst outsiders—even with her own less instructed children at times—than the allegation which declares that where the Church has full sway, science cannot flourish, can scarcely in fact exist, and that the Church will only permit men of science to study and to teach as and while she permits. . . .

Those who give credit to the allegation must of course ignore certain very patent facts which are, it will be allowed, a little difficult to get over. They must commence by ignoring the historical fact that the greater number—almost all indeed—of the older Universities, places specially intended to foster and increase knowledge and research, owe their origin to Papal bulls. They must ignore the fact that vast numbers of scientific researches, often of fundamental importance, especially perhaps in the subjects of anatomy and physiology, emanated from learned men attached to seats of learning in Rome, and this during the Middle Ages, and that the learned men who were their authors quite frequently held official positions in the Papal Court. They must finally ignore the fact that a large number of the most scientific workers and discoverers in the past were also devout children of the Catholic Church. Stensen, "the Father of Geology" and a great anatomical discoverer as well, was a bishop; Mendel, whose name is so often heard nowadays in biological controversies, was an abbot. And what about Galvani, Volta, Pasteur, Schwann (the originator of the Cell Theory), van Beneden, Johannes Müller, admitted by Huxley to be "the greatest anatomist and physiologist among my contemporaries"? What about Kircher, Spallanzani, Secchi, de Lapparent, to take the names of persons of different historical periods, and connected with different subjects, yet all united in the bond of faith? To point to these men—and a host of other names might be cited—is to overthrow at once and finally the edifice of falsehood reared by the enemies of the Church. . . .

What the Church does—and surely it must be clear that from her standpoint she could do no less—is to instruct Catholic men of science not to proclaim as proved facts such modern theories—and there are

218

many of them—as still remain wholly unproved, when these theories seem to conflict with the teachings of the Church. This is very far from saying that Catholics are forbidden to study such theories.

On the contrary, they are encouraged to do so, and that, need it be said, with the one idea of ascertaining the truth? Men of science, Catholic and otherwise, have, as a matter of fact, been time and again encouraged by Popes and other ecclesiastical authorities to go on searching for the truth, never, however, neglecting the wise maxim that all things must be proved. So long as a theory is unproved, it must be candidly admitted that it is a crime against science to proclaim it to be incontrovertible truth, yet this crime is being committed every day. It is really against it that the *magisterium* of the Church is exercised.

(1915)

CATHOLICISM makes its appeal not to those who demand the latest intellectual novelty nor to those who always want to be on the winning side, but to those who seek spiritual reality. Our advantage lies not in the excellence of our brains, but in the strength of our principles. Like the proverbial conies, we may be a feeble folk but we make our dwelling in the rocks. Our thought is not "free" in the sense that it is at liberty to create its own principles and to make gods in its own image. But it is just this "freedom" which is the cause of the discredit and anarchy into which modern thought has fallen.

CHRISTOPHER DAWSON (1931)

## THE CHURCH'S COMMISSION

### THE REV. PETER FINLAY, S.J.

TELL men what they must believe concerning God and His attitude towards them, concerning life's present purpose and future destiny, the moral law, Christ's work and personality, the means of grace He instituted, the precepts He imposed, the Kingdom He established. Lay before them the Divine message in its entirety, adding nothing, changing nothing and then guide them into the fulfillment of all things.

(1928)

# CATHOLIC "CENSORSHIP"

### JAMES M. O'NEILL

THE Catholic Church is a teacher—a teacher speaking with effect *to those who accept its teaching*. The effectiveness of the Church in the area that is inaccurately called "censorship" depends wholly upon the *voluntary* acceptance of the Church's guidance by those who read or listen. The same thing is true of the effectiveness of the leadership of any religious, political, or economic group.

Anyone would have difficulty in making a clear and rational distinction between the activity of a Catholic agency which adversely criticizes or condemns a book or a movie and the activity of a secular magazine or newspaper which does the same thing. It may be claimed that the Catholic agency will be listened to, and the expressed opinions from these sources will be acted upon, by more people than will act upon the book reviews, the editorials and the dramatic criticisms of the *New York Times, The New Yorker,* the *Herald Tribune,* and *The Saturday Review of Literature.* Such a remark, whether true or false, is irrelevant. . . .

When anyone says that the Catholic who goes to a movie, or a play, or reads a book so condemned will have a feeling of guilt, a "sense of sin," the answer is that that is the individual's private concern and is not a matter for public consideration or a threat to American freedom. Clearly there is no such thing as *punishment* that any agency or arm of the Church can inflict upon him. . . .

If one wishes to reply that "the hierarchy" or the Church claims to *punish in the next world* those who go against Catholic teaching, the answer is easy. Without going into the long, elaborate, *theological* answer that would perhaps in other circumstances be best, it should be enough for a layman who is not a theologian to say here that the threat of such punishment would be no threat at all to those who do not accept the Church as a true and responsible guide. If some Americans wish to be guided by the teachings of the Catholic Church, rather than by the teachings of Protestantism, Judaism, or some secular organization, others should accept that situation without rancor. They will have to accept it so long as they consent to live in the United States and the United States continues to maintain elementary personal freedom.

It may be argued that so many Catholics will follow the advice or direction of individuals or organizations in the Church that the condemned play or movie will be withdrawn, and the book will be hard to get, and that this interferes with the freedom of non-Catholics. This again, is in essence in no way different from the situation we have when a play or movie is so roundly berated by the dramatic critics in a few New York publications that its career on the professional stage is ended for all time. Such are the hazards of living in a free country.

Anyone in a free society who expresses an opinion in public has to run the risk that a good many people may agree with him and act upon his advice. This horrible thought, however, seems not greatly to impede editors, dramatic critics, and book reviewers.

(1952)

## "DOGMATIC INTOLERANCE"

### THE REV. MAX PRIBILLA, S.J.

THIS dogmatic intolerance, which the Church by her very nature must maintain, has often been made a subject of reproach against her. But in fact every Church which takes itself seriously must assert dogmatic intolerance. Recent Protestant theologians have borne witness to this. Hans Liermann, for example, Professor of Canon Law at Erlangen, writes: "You cannot expect dogmatic tolerance from any Church, because each Church believes she possesses a treasure of truth in her dogma which cannot be surrendered. If she yields on this point, she throws in her hand. Henceforth she can only claim to possess a relative truth, and this is not sufficient basis for a Church. A Church which suffers from this dogmatic softening of the bones must sooner or later perish, because she is disloyal to her real and highest end. Consequently it is a fact which has to be recognized, that every Church must be dogmatically intolerant." . . . Dogmatic intolerance belongs to the sphere of knowledge and, since it merely recognizes the primacy of truth and logic, injures no one's rights.

There remains the objection that guaranteeing religious freedom gives the same rights to error as to truth, and thereby dogmatic intolerance is surrendered. The answer to this is that freedom of religion does not mean the protection of error . . . but protection of the erring man, who should not be hindered from serving God according

221

to his conscience. Even an erroneous conscience imposes duties and confers corresponding rights. The protection granted to a man in error in the exercise of his duty is something good. . . . Hence the establishment of religious freedom does not mean that true and false beliefs are put on the same level. But as long as men differ as to what constitutes the true faith, they must respect one another's opinions and exercise toleration.

(1950)

# CATHOLICISM CANNOT BE
# FORCED ON PEOPLE

### PIUS XII

THOUGH We desire . . . that all the straying sheep may hasten to enter the one fold of Jesus Christ, yet We recognize that this must be done of their own free will; for no one believes unless he wills to believe. Hence they are most certainly not genuine Christians who against their belief are forced to go into a church, to approach the altar and to receive the Sacraments; for the "faith without which it is impossible to please God" is an entirely free "submission of intellect and will." Therefore whenever it happens, despite the constant teaching of this Apostolic See, that anyone is compelled to embrace the Catholic faith against his will, Our sense of duty demands that We condemn the act. For men must be effectively drawn to the truth by the Father of light through the Spirit of His Beloved Son, because, endowed as they are with free will, they can misuse their freedom under the impulse of mental agitation and base desires.

(June 29, 1943)

# SALVATION OUTSIDE THE CHURCH

### KNIGHTS OF COLUMBUS PAMPHLET

OF all the statements made by the Catholic Church, possibly none falls harsher on non-Catholic ears than the traditional and ancient teaching: *"Outside the Church there is no salvation."* . . .

This doctrine must be carefully considered in relation to other teachings no less important. First and foremost of these is that God gives to all men sufficient grace to save their souls—and that He will deny salvation only to those who forfeit it through their own fault. The bare words, "outside the Church there is no salvation," apply therefore only in the case of those who recognize the Church as Christ's agent of salvation and yet—for whatever guilty reason—refuse to become members of this Church. Such persons do indeed, reject salvation. . . .

Certainly there is no salvation outside the Church. This is merely saying that the Church is necessary for salvation . . . that Christianity was a necessary revelation . . . that Christ taught and suffered and died for a necessary purpose—not merely as a pastime. If there is salvation outside the Church—if man can pick and choose from any variety of ways in which he will please to save his own soul, including the will to do precisely what pleases him—then the Church is utterly unnecessary . . . then mankind could get along quite as well without it . . . then Christ's life and teaching can be dispensed with, and there is certainly no obligation or reason for anyone to be a Christian. . . .

Either it is necessary to be a Christian, or it is not. If not, then there is utterly no sense in being one. If it is, then the Church is necessary for salvation . . . and man is not morally at liberty to disregard the Church if he values the salvation of his soul.

(1949)

It must be regarded as true that he who does not know the true religion is guiltless in the sight of God so far as his ignorance is invincible. Who would presume to fix the limits of such ignorance, and the infinite variety and difference of peoples, countries and mentalities, and amid so many other circumstances. When we are free from the limitations of the body and see God as He is, then we shall see how closely and beautifully God's mercy and justice are conjoined.

PIUS IX (December 9, 1854)

# DIVERSITY OF OPINION
# WITHIN THE CHURCH

## JACQUES MARITAIN

THE diversity of opinion in human affairs is far greater in the Catholic Church than is generally realized by those not in it. I know that the teaching of the Church can deal with every matter connected with faith; but in being integrally mindful of this teaching I can still disagree most sharply with other Catholics about political or social matters: democracy, trade unionism, the late war in Spain, or the second World War, as well as about philosophical or historical questions. This is because it is only to the purity and integrity of the Word of God that the faithful are bound as such; the teaching authority of the Church intends of itself only to safeguard this living deposit of truth, just as the disciplinary authority of the Church has no other object than to enable the faithful to live by that truth. It is to the First Truth in person, speaking to my heart, that I adhere by means of the statements of dogma that bring the revelation to all. As a Catholic and by my Catholic Faith, I am bound in conscience to no human, theological or philosophical opinion, however well founded it may be, and still less to any judgments on contingent or worldly matters, or to any temporal power. Nor am I bound to any particular form of culture or civilization, and still less of race or blood. I am bound uniquely to what is universality itself and superuniversality: to the Divine, to the words and precepts of Him who said, *I am the Truth, I who speak to you.*

That in brief is how the Catholic outlook appears to me. Catholic theology teaches that it is upon our love, as Saint John of the Cross says, that we shall be judged; in other words, that salvation and eternal life depend on charity. It teaches us that charity presupposes faith and has its roots in faith, in other words, in truth divinely revealed. It teaches that *explicit* faith in Christ, illuminating the human mind regarding the inmost secrets of divine truth and life, is not only the requisite means for souls to attain the highest degree of conformity with God and divine union, and a prerequisite for peoples to achieve a firm position of general morality and perfectly human civilization, but that that faith is also the response or reverence justly due to God's gift, inclining His glory toward us.

(1941)

# THE NEED TO RESTATE THE CHRISTIAN
# TRADITION TO THE MODERN AGE

### EMMET JOHN HUGHES

INHERENT in an institutional structure so elaborate as the Church is a slowness to translate will into action, a tenacious clinging to inherited habits of thought. Yet more serious, no matter how profound be the ideal contradiction between the principles of such an institution and those of the world around it, it is from the existing economy, whatever be its form, that financial strength must be drawn—a fact which does not reinforce the vigor of the Church's revolt from the Liberal Society or its capitalistic ordering of economic life. There follows quickly from this a too frequently apathetic view of the social issues involved in the uncritical perpetuation of Liberal economics: an over-anxious tendency to sharpen the spiritual sword when Marxism is attacked, an often perceptible softening of the blows when Liberalism is the issue.

Not only has much of the institutional strength of the Church thus been subject to atrophy, but also much of its intellectual resources have been wasted in an empty effort to inspire mankind to rally to the banner of medievalism. With regard to the persistence of religious or ethical precepts, this effort is intelligent and obligatory for any institution which does not admit the refashioning of moral standards according to the capricious prescriptions of any given historical moment. But, profound as were many of the central truths of the medieval social gospel, it is grossly unrealistic to assume that these truths need no recasting to govern new social and economic realities. To ignore the past five centuries because so much of them has been sheer heresy, because so much of the whole period has been pharisaical in its social gospel and pagan in its morality—to do this is to forget that five hundred years of human experience cannot be removed from man's legacy by pronouncement of a papal encyclical: to disregard the fact that any modern synthesis comparable to the work of Aquinas must embrace, not seek to repudiate, the material triumphs of science. What the Church faces, in short, is the task of succeeding in the twentieth century in that which it failed to achieve in the sixteenth and eighteenth centuries: to restate the Christian tradition to the modern age—in Archbishop Ireland's words—in terms of things that it feels and in language that it understands.

Men of the Church must have the moral and intellectual strength to face these issues with clear vision. They must be unwilling to accept the cheap solution that the problems do not exist. They must be willing themselves to pay the penance for the historical misjudgments and institutional sins of the Church by acknowledging their existence and laboring for their expiation.

While thus working to fortify the Church in its articulation of the democratic tradition, they in turn will find strength in this knowledge: that it is the only historic force which can be looked to for that articulation. It stands as the most virile moral authority in the contemporary world. It has been the only historic institution defiantly insistent on the social applicability of Christian ethics. It has never compromised with the Liberal Society nor allowed doctrines of the Liberal faith to insinuate themselves into the body of Church philosophy. It has never welcomed the fact of sovereign national states and itself stood forth as the only supra-national power when war struck the Western world in 1939. Its popular base is the laboring masses, and its celibate hierarchy constantly draws its blood and strength from the people.

Intellectual or political association with a landed aristocracy has become an historical impossibility. Between the ethic, the world-perspective, of the bourgeoisie and that of the Church, there has never been, nor can there be, compromise. There is but one historical conclusion, clear and inescapable—perceived and expressed in these words by a man of the Church [Fulton J. Sheen]: "When a culture begins to disintegrate, it is important to realize that some things are not worth saving. The status quo cannot be maintained. When the visitation came from Jerusalem, God did not say, "Fight! Defend!" but "Flee, and go not back for thy coat. Let it perish."

"Our hope rises from below, from those whose wants are too many, whose rights too few, those whom Edmund Burke contemptuously called 'the great unwashed.'"

(1944)

(See page 291 for Mr. Hughes' analysis of Liberalism.)

# IX

# The Church
# as an Organization

*The name of the Church. Authority, tradition, and the Bible.
Need of Church government. Papal infallibility. The powers
of bishops. The priesthood. The priesthood of the laity. Catholic Action.*

THE Church is a society *divine* in its origin, *supernatural* in its ends
and in the means proximately adapted to the attainment of that end;
but it is a *human* community inasmuch as it is composed of men.

LEO XIII (June 20, 1896)

## THE CHURCH'S NAME

### KNIGHTS OF COLUMBUS PAMPHLET

THE full name of our Church is "the Holy Catholic Apostolic Roman
Church." "Roman" is added not to restrict the meaning of "Catholic"
but simply to mark the visible center of unity; and since it must have
a center of unity somewhere, it is obvious that "Roman," far from
neutralizing the meaning of the word "Catholic," serves rather to
confirm it and to make the catholicity of the Church more striking
and unmistakable. . . .

The name "Catholic" has come down to us from earliest Christian
times. Ignatius, who died for his Faith in 107 A.D., appears to have
been the first to have recorded the title: "Where Christ is," he wrote,

"there is the Catholic Church." (Ad Symrn. n.8, P.G.). Some time later, the martyrdom of Polycarp (167 A.D.) was recorded and he was called the "bishop of the Catholic Church in Smyrna." (Ad Eph. n.3). In the same century, referring to a certain Marcion and Valentinus, Tertullian wrote: "It is agreed that they lived not so long ago, generally speaking, in the reign of Antoninus, and that they first believed in the doctrine of the Catholic Church in the Church of Rome. . . ." (De Praescrip. n.30).

Most explicit is Augustine: "The Christian religion is to be held by us," he wrote, "and the communion of that Church which is Catholic, and is called Catholic, not only by its own members, but also by its adversaries. For in spite of themselves . . . when speaking not with their fellows, but with strangers, they call the catholic Church nothing else but the Catholic Church. They cannot be understood unless they distinguish her by that name by which she is designated by the whole world." (De Ver. Relig. n. 12).

(1951)

## AUTHORITY OPENS THE DOOR

### ST. AUGUSTINE

To those desiring to learn the great and hidden good it is authority which opens the door. And whoever enters by it and, leaving doubt behind, follows the precepts for a truly good life, and has been made receptive to teaching by them, will at length learn how pre-eminently possessed of reason those things are which he pursued before he saw their reason. . . .

Now the authority . . . which is true, firm, supreme is that which is called divine. . . . That authority is to be called divine which not only transcends all human capability, but, taking on the actual form of man, shows man to what depth it has condescended for man's sake; and enjoins him not to be bound by the senses, through which those miracles are seen, but to ascend from them to the intellect. . . . Its office is to teach its power by works, its clemency by humility, and its nature by the commandments it gives. And all these things by the holy rites in which we are initiated, are bestowed on us the more secretly and enduringly. And in these the life of good men is cleansed, not by vague disputations, but by the authority of the holy mysteries.

(ca. A.D. 415)

# SCRIPTURE AND TRADITION

### THE REV. E. R. HULL, S.J.

FOLLOWING the career of the Apostles as they carry out their work, we find . . . there occurs no mention of any scheme for producing a written code to dispense with the authority of apostolic preaching. The Apostles show no signs of regarding it as a duty to leave behind them a full written legacy of their teaching. They write to meet incidental occasions and local needs. The Evangelists seem to think it an important matter to leave us, in outline, their recollections of Christ's life and character, but they make no pretense of giving us a complete scheme of His dogmatic teaching. St. John himself declares the impossibility of writing anything like an exhaustive account of all that Christ did. There appears nowhere in the New Testament a consciousness that its writers were thereby supplying Christendom with the one sole and adequate Rule of Faith, which should supersede the need of appeal to their oral teachings. . . .

On the other hand, we find many allusions to Christian doctrine as derived from oral teaching. The Thessalonians are told to "hold fast the traditions which they had been taught, whether by word or by epistle." Timothy, who had been ordained Bishop of Ephesus by St. Paul, is instructed to "hold fast the form of sound words which he has heard from his teacher among many witnesses"; "to continue in the things learnt" (*viz.,* "the gospel which was committed to his trust"), "knowing from whom he had learnt them," "and to commit the same to faithful men who shall be able to teach others."—all of which certainly stands in favor of the Catholic idea of apostolic authority transmitted to a line of successors, and against the Protestant idea of substituting the Bible as the sole and adequate rule of faith.

Still following the course of history, the Catholic view receives yet further confirmation. The various parts which now make up the New Testament were carefully treasured and read in the local churches where they had been received, and it was only by degrees that copies were spread to other places, and the whole series came to be circulated throughout Christendom. Though held in the highest authority, we find no signs of the Scriptures being substituted for traditional teaching as a sole Rule of Faith. The bishops were regarded as the authoritative successors of the Apostles, responsible for the preservation of Christian doctrine, and the people looked to them for the true interpretation of Scripture. Belief did not follow interpretation of Scripture, but interpretation of Scripture followed belief. . . . The general impression given by the history of the third and fourth centuries shows us still in operation the idea of an apostolic teaching body, authorized and guaranteed by Jesus Christ, to provide the rule of Faith; while Scripture is still regarded as a witness to the correctness of the Church's teaching, but not as a sole and adequate Rule of Faith to be put in its place.

Moreover, during the first four centuries of the Church, it remained an unsettled question what belonged to the sacred Scripture and what did not. There were many Gospels current besides the four we now acknowledge, and a few other works, like the Epistles of Clement and Barnabas and the Pastor of Hermas. Of these, several were regarded by certain of the Fathers as parts of Scripture, and were publicly read in local churches; on the other hand, the Epistles to the Hebrews, Revelation, James, Jude, 2nd Peter, 2nd and 3rd John, were called in question in some parts of the Church. It required much discussion to arrive at a final conclusion. But when in the Synods of Hippos and Carthage, about A.D. 393–397, a list of authentic books was agreed upon, and Pope Innocent I, and afterwards Pope Gelasius (A.D. 494) confirmed this list, the discussion was closed; and for the first time the New Testament was capable of being bound up into one book as we have it now.

But how was this question settled after so long a discussion? Purely and simply by an appeal to the traditions existing in local churches where each document had been preserved, and by the authoritative edict of the Church judging according to those traditions; other historic evidence deciding the question in all its details, we do not possess. So that Protestants, in accepting the New Testament as it stands, are implicitly reposing the highest confidence in the authority of the Catholic Church in the fifth century; and some of them have candidly acknowledged this (cf. preface to Revised Version). These facts seem fatal to the idea that Scripture was intended by Christ and His Apostles to be the sole and adequate Rule of Faith; since our very assurance as to what the New Testament contains rests historically on the teaching authority of the bishops of the fifth century, the successors of the Apostles commissioned and guaranteed by Christ.

Passing on through the ages, we find the same system at work. Down to the sixteenth century there existed in Christendom no other than this idea. The Bishops were looked upon as successors of the Apostles, and their unanimous teaching was regarded as absolutely trustworthy —as truly representing the doctrine of Christ. The Church as a whole could not possibly fall into error—this was guaranteed by the promises of Christ; and those who claimed Scripture in support of their new doctrines, and against the prevailing doctrines of the Church, were regarded as heretics and rebels against Christ, and against His authority delegated to the Church.

It was not till the sixteenth century that this state of things received a rude shock. The radical principle of the Protestant Reformation lay in the rejection of the living authority of the Catholic Church, and the substitution of the Bible, interpreted by each individual, in its place. It runs counter to the unanimous conviction of Christendom for fifteen hundred years.

(1925)

You cannot make your way into the holy Scriptures without having someone go before you and show you the road. . . . The science of the Scriptures is the only one which all persons indiscriminately claim as their own! This science the babbling old woman, the doting old man, the wordy sophist, take upon themselves; they tear it to tatters and teach before they themselves have learned. . . . Coming by chance to the study of the Scriptures . . . they fancy what they utter is the law of God, not deigning to learn what the prophets and the Apostles taught. Rather they accommodate to their interpretation the most incongruous passages, as if this were something great instead of a most faulty method of teaching, distorting sentences and forcing the reluctant Scriptures to their own whims.

ST. JEROME (A.D. 340)

You who believe what you like of the gospels and believe not what you like, believe yourselves rather than the gospels.

ST. AUGUSTINE (ca. A.D. 400)

IN the city Rome, on Peter first hath an Episcopal See been conferred, in which Peter sat, the head of all the Apostles, . . . in which one See unity might be preserved by all, lest the other Apostles should support their respective Sees; in order that he might be at once a schismatic and a sinner, who against that one See placed a second. Therefore that one See, which is the first of the Church's prerogatives, Peter filled first; to whom succeeded Linus; to Linus, Clement; to Clement, &c, &c . . . to Damasus, Siricius, who at this day is associated with us, together with whom the whole world is in accordance with us, in the one bond of communion, by the intercourse of letters of peace.

ST. OPTATUS (ca. A.D. 375)

BLESSED Peter hath not deserted the helm of the Church which he had assumed . . . His power lives and his authority is pre-eminent in his See. . . . That immoveableness, which, from the Rock Christ he, when he made a rock, received, has been communicated also to his heirs.

POPE, ST. LEO (A.D. 440)

# THE DOCTRINE OF PAPAL
# INFALLIBILITY
## THE VATICAN COUNCIL

FAITHFULLY adhering to the tradition handed down from the beginning of the Christian Faith, for the glory of God, our Savior, the exaltation of the Catholic religion, and the salvation of Christian peoples, with the approval of the Holy Council, we teach and define it to be a Divinely revealed dogma, that the Roman Pontiff when he speaks *ex cathedra,* that is, when in discharge of his office as Pastor and teacher of all Christians, he defines in virtue of his supreme Apostolic authority a doctrine concerning Faith or Morals to be held by the Universal Church, is through the Divine assistance, promised to him in Blessed Peter, possessed of that infallibility with which the Divine Redeemer willed His Church to be endowed, in defining doctrines concerning Faith and Morals; and that therefore such definitions of the Roman Pontiff are of themselves, and not through the consent of the Church, irreformable.

(1870)

# THE NECESSITY FOR INFALLIBILITY

### THE REV. LESLIE RUMBLE, M.S.C.

IF at one time I felt rather appalled by the arrogant claim to infallibility, today I would be appalled did the true Church not make such a claim. A fine sort of guide to our eternal destiny would have been given us by God if that guide had to admit that she was not sure of the way herself! As has so often been pointed out, the Church was endowed by Christ with the essential notes of unity, holiness, catholicity, and apostolicity. The One, Holy, Catholic, Apostolic Church is an expression familiar to all. Yet not one of these characteristics could perservere were not the Church infallible. Unity would soon go if the Church could teach erroneous doctrine; the sin of heresy would deprive her of her essential holiness as an institution; the separation of groups would destroy utterly the catholicity of one single Church; and the self-same faith and authority derived from the Apostles would be lost. Anyway, Christ included the gift of infallibility in the charter of His Church. His promise that the gates of hell, or the forces of evil, would never prevail against His Church can only mean that His Church will last just as He established it, even retaining the faith He committed to her care. His promise of the perpetual presence of the Holy Spirit, and that He Himself would be with her "all days even till the end of the world" suppose also infallibility, or inability to teach a doctrine which is not identical with principles laid down by Himself. Above all it is inconceivable that Christ would send a church to teach all nations, putting an obligation upon all nations to be taught by her, and even making eternal salvation dependent upon one's submission to His Church, saying, "He who does not believe will be condemned," if that Church could possibly teach doctrine in conflict with His!

(1934)

# THE REASONABLENESS OF
# INFALLIBILITY

### THE REV. MARTIN J. SCOTT, S.J.

CHRIST was an infallible teacher. In establishing a Church which was to teach His doctrine, and which He commanded His followers to hear as they would hear Himself, He instituted an infallible teaching body. He would not have commanded the faithful to follow a teacher if that teacher could mislead. . . .

Since Christ's doctrine was intended for all generations of mankind to the end of the world, it is evident that He took measures to secure its preservation and transmission. If it was important enough to be revealed to mankind, it was important enough to be revealed intact to succeeding generations. From the nature of the case, it is, therefore, altogether reasonable that some means should have been created for the infallible transmission of the Desposit of Faith. We should, therefore, expect that there should be some institution or society established which would be immune from error in teaching revealed truth. It is only reasonable to presume that Christ the infallible Teacher provided an infallible teaching authority in order to transmit His teaching. What is thus seen to be reasonable, and in conformity with the nature of Revelation, Christ actually effected by instituting a society which He called His Church and which He endowed with immunity from error in teaching the truths He had deposited with her. . . .

No Church can be the Church of Christ which does not profess to be an infallible representative of the Infallible Founder of Christianity. Christ did not establish Christianity in order to have it either perish or mislead. He might better never have instituted a religion if it were to mislead mankind, or if it were to fail after He had guaranteed its perpetuity. . . .

There are those who assert that, while it is evident that the true Church of Christ must be an infallible teacher of Revelation, it is against all reason that the Pope individually should be infallible. It is affirmed that the Pope is a man, like the rest of mankind, and that he has accordingly a fallible judgment and free will. As long as his will is free and his mind limited, it is impossible for him, it is asserted, not to be liable to error. However, without interfering with free will, the Son of God can so guide and arrange matters that neither His Church nor His Vicar, the Pope, will teach error. What Christ could do, He has actually done, by guaranteeing not only His Church, but also its official head, against error. . . .

Christ in establishing His Church endowed her with an infallible voice which should define the truths of Revelation with Divine certainty when occasion should require it. This infallible voice does not proclaim a new Revelation, but only states definitely what has been

Divinely revealed. In so defining Revelation, the Pope is not inspired, as were the prophets of old, nor does he announce new doctrines, but simply declares the true sense of the Revelation which has been made once for all. In doing this, he has the guarantee of Jesus Christ that he will be assisted from on high, so that what he defines will be what God intended by the Revelation in question when it was given to mankind.

Not every teaching of the Pope has the guarantee of infallibility, but only those pronouncements which are made in his capacity as teacher of the Universal Church, and what he intends to be accepted by all the faithful as part of the Deposit of Faith. The technical term which is employed for such infallible pronouncements is *ex cathedra*. This is the Latin for proclamations *from the throne*. Unless the Pope speaks *ex cathedra,* his statements are entitled to only such assent as his learning, integrity and lofty position justify. On matters not intimately associated with faith and morals, his views carry the weight of their own worth only.

(1941)

# THE EXERCISE OF INFALLIBILITY

## JOHN HENRY CARDINAL NEWMAN

EVERY exercise of Infallibility is brought out into act by an intense and varied operation of the Reason, both as its ally and as its opponent, and provokes again, when it has done its work, a reaction of Reason against it; and, as in a civil polity the State exists and endures by means of the rivalry and collision, the encroachments and defeats of its constituent parts, so in like manner Catholic Christendom is no simple exhibition of religious absolutism, but presents a continuous picture of Authority and Private Judgment alternately advancing and retreating as the ebb and flow of the tide;—it is a vast assemblage of human beings with wilful intellects and wild passions, brought together into one by the beauty and the Majesty of a Superhuman Power,—into what may be called a large reformatory or training-school, not as if into a hospital or into a prison, not in order to be sent to bed, not to be buried alive, but (if I may change my metaphor) brought together as if into some moral factory, for the melting, refining, and moulding, by an incessant, noisy process, of the raw mate-

235

rial of human nature, so excellent, so dangerous, so capable of divine purposes. . . .

The Catholic Church claims, not only to judge infallibly on religious questions, but to animadvert on opinions in secular matters which bear upon religion, on matters of philosophy, of science, of literature, of history, and it demands our submission to her claim. It claims to censure books, to silence authors, and to forbid discussions. In this province, taken as a whole, it does not so much speak doctrinally, as enforce measures of discipline. It must of course be obeyed without a word, and perhaps in process of time it will tacitly recede from its own injunctions. In such cases the question of faith does not come in at all; for what is matter of faith is true for all times, and never can be unsaid. Nor does it all follow, because there is a gift of infallibility in the Catholic Church, that therefore the parties who are in possession of it are in all their proceedings infallible. . . . To make such admission is no more than saying that the divine treasure, in the words of the Apostle, is "in earthen vessels"; nor does it follow that the substance of the acts of the ruling power is not right and expedient, because its manner may have been faulty. Such high authorities act by means of instruments; we know how such instruments claim for themselves the name of their principals, who thus get the credits of faults which really are not theirs.

(1864)

## ON DISOBEYING THE POPE

JOHN HENRY CARDINAL NEWMAN

A POPE is not infallible in his laws, nor in his commands, nor in his acts of state, nor in his administration, nor in his public policy. . . .

Suppose, for instance, an Act was passed in Parliament, bidding Catholics to attend Protestant service every week, and the Pope distinctly told us not to do so, for it was to violate our duty to our faith:—I should obey the Pope and not the Law. It will be said . . . that such a case is impossible. I know it is; but why ask me for what I should do in extreme and utterly improbable cases such as this, if my answer cannot help bearing the character of an axiom? It is not my fault that I must deal in truisms . . .

But now, on the other hand, could the case ever occur, in which

I should act with the Civil Power, and not with the Pope? Now, here again, when I begin to imagine instances, Catholics will cry out . . . that the instances never can occur. I know they cannot; I know the Pope can never do what I am going to suppose; but then, since it cannot possibly happen in fact, there is no harm in just saying what I should (hypothetically) do, if it did happen. I say then in certain (impossible) cases I should side, not with the Pope, but with the Civil Power . . .

Were I actually a soldier or sailor in her Majesty's service, and sent to take part in a war which I could not in my conscience see to be unjust, and should the Pope suddenly bid all Catholic soldiers and sailors to retire from the service, here again, taking the advice of others, as best I could, I should not obey him . . .

Cardinal Turrecremata says, "Although it clearly follows from the circumstances that the Pope can err at times, and command things which must not be done, that we are not to be simply obedient to him in all things, that does not show that he must not be obeyed by all when his commands are good. To know in what cases he is to be obeyed and in what not . . . it is said in the Acts of the Apostles, 'one ought to obey God rather than man': therefore, were the Pope to command anything against Holy Scripture, or the articles of faith, or the truth of the Sacraments, or the commands of the natural or divine law, *he ought not to be obeyed,* but in such commands is to be passed over."

Bellarmine, speaking of resisting the Pope, says, "In order to resist and defend oneself no authority is required. . . . Therefore, as it is lawful to resist the Pope, if he assaulted a man's person, so it is lawful to resist him, if he assaulted souls, or troubled the state, and much more if he strove to destroy the Church. It is lawful, I say, to resist him, by not doing what he commands, and hindering the execution of his will."

When, then, Mr. Gladstone asks Catholics how they can obey the Queen and yet obey the Pope, since it may happen that the commands of the two authorities may clash, I answer, that it is my *rule,* both to obey the one and to obey the other, but that there is no rule in this world without exception, and if either the Pope or the Queen demanded of me an "Absolute Obedience," he or she would be transgressing the laws of human society. I give an absolute obedience to neither.

(1874)

How can one possibly be in agreement with another if he is in disagreement with the body of the Church and with the universal brotherhood? How can two or three be gathered together in Christ's name if they are manifestly separated from Christ and from His Gospel? For we did not go out from them, but they from us. As heresies and schisms have a later rise, when men set up separate assemblies for themselves, they have left the fountainhead and origin of truth.

ST. CYPRIAN (ca. A.D. 248)

## HIERARCHY IN THE EARLY CHURCH

### ST. IGNATIUS OF ANTIOCH

AVOID divisions as the beginning of evils. All of you follow the bishop as Jesus Christ followed the Father, and follow the presbytery as the Apostles; and respect the deacons as the commandment of God. Let no man perform anything pertaining to the church without the bishop. Let that be considered a valid Eucharist over which the bishop presides, or one to whom he commits it. Wherever the bishop appears, there let the people be, just as, wheresoever Christ Jesus is, there is the Catholic Church. It is not permitted either to baptize or hold a love-feast [i.e. an agape] apart from the bishop. But whatever he may approve, that is well-pleasing to God, that everything which you do may be sound and valid.

(ca. A.D. 107)

## THE EPISCOPAL ORDER

### LEO XIII

SINCE the successor of Peter is one, and those of the apostles are many, it is necessary to examine into the relationship which exists between him and them according to the divine constitution of the Church. Above all things the need of union between the bishops and the successors of Peter is clear and undeniable. This bond once broken, Christians would be separated and scattered, and would in no wise form one body and one flock. . . . Nothing was conferred on the apostles apart from Peter, but . . . several things were conferred upon

Peter apart from the apostles. . . . He alone was designated as the foundation of the Church. To him He gave the power of *binding* and *loosing;* to him alone was given the power of *feeding.* On the other hand, whatever authority and office the apostles received, they received in conjunction with Peter. . . .

Bishops are deprived of the right and power of ruling, if they deliberately secede from Peter and his successors; because, by this secession, they are separated from the foundation on which the whole edifice must rest. They are therefore outside the *edifice* itself; and for this very reason they are separated from the *fold,* whose leader is the Chief Pastor; they are exiled from the *Kingdom,* the keys of which were given by Christ to Peter alone. . . .

The Episcopal order is rightly judged to be in communion with Peter, as Christ commanded, if it be subject to and obeys Peter; otherwise it necessarily becomes a lawless and disorderly crowd. It is not sufficient for the due preservation of the unity of the faith that the head should merely have been charged with the office of superintendent, or should have been invested solely with a power of direction. But it is absolutely necessary that he should have received a real and sovereign authority which the whole community is bound to obey. . . .

It is opposed to the truth, and in evident contradiction with the divine constitution of the Church, to hold that while each bishop is *individually* bound to obey the authority of the Roman Pontiffs, taken *collectively* the bishops are not so bound. For it is the nature and object of a foundation to support the unity of the whole edifice and to give stability to it, rather than to *each component part;* and in the present case this is much more applicable, since Christ the Lord wished that by the strength and solidity of the foundation the gates of hell should be prevented from prevailing against the Church. . . . Jurisdiction and authority belong to him in whose power have been placed the keys of the kingdom of heaven, not alone in all provinces taken singly, but in all taken collectively. . . .

This power over the Episcopal College to which we refer, and which is clearly set forth in holy writ, has ever been acknowledged and attested by the Church, as is clear from the teaching of the General Councils. "We read that the Roman Pontiff has pronounced judgments on the prelates of all the churches; we do not read that anybody has pronounced sentence on him." (Hadrianus ii, Allocution iii.)

(June 20, 1896)

# THE POWERS OF THE BISHOPS
## AND THE POPE

THE REV. E. R. HULL, S.J.

CATHOLIC bishops are no mere "ornamental heads of churches," as Mr. Jacob Primmer called them, but the responsible guardians of the deposit of faith. They are the successors of the Apostles, endowed with their authority and power to teach and govern the Church. Taken singly, they do not inherit the personal endowments of the Apostles; they have neither the gift of inspiration nor of miracles, nor of personal infallibility, nor of universal jurisdiction. They receive no new revelations, nor repetitions of old ones; and yet they are infallible in the sense that they cannot collectively be guilty of false teaching, and so lead the whole Church astray. It is possible for individual bishops to desert their duty and fall into heresy, as some have done in times past; but such are quickly cut off from the Church, and lose their position in the teaching body. For a bishop can retain his office only by remaining in communion with his fellow-bishops and with the Pope; separated from this communion, he ceases to be a member of the teaching Church. It is in this collective body of bishops in communion with each other and with the Pope, that the teaching Church properly consists. Hence it is to this collective body that the promises of Christ apply. Consequently it is believed that any doctrine unanimously taught by this collective body, as part of the deposit of faith, must be infallibly correct; since otherwise the whole Church, clergy and laity (whose belief is simply a reflection of the teaching of the bishops), would be committed to a false doctrine, and so the gates of hell would have prevailed against the Church. . . .

As supreme ruler, the Pope has power to make disciplinary laws binding on the whole Church. As supreme teacher, he possesses authority to settle disputed points of faith and morals. It is with the last-named prerogative that we are now chiefly concerned. Under favorable circumstances, when the teaching of the bishops is unanimous and the belief of the people undisturbed, no ulterior guarantee is needed beyond this fact. But when a heresy arises, and the unanimity of the bishops is disputed; or when the traditional doctrine has been imperfectly transmitted in some part of the Church, and a dispute arises on this or any other account, an authoritative declaration may be needed to close the question in a manner which admits of no evasion. It is then that the decision of the supreme teacher is called for. Now Catholics believe that in these decisions, and in these alone, the Pope is infallible. For it is of the nature of these decisions to bind the whole Church, and commit it irrevocably to teaching and to believing as part of Christ's revelation the doctrine proclaimed by them. Hence, unless the pope were absolutely reliable in such decisions, the faith of the Church might be corrupted by an error, and so the gates of hell would have prevailed against it. . . .

In his private acts as a Christian, in his official acts as a bishop, in his official acts in the government of the Church, he might make a mistake or fail in prudence, and no great harm would be done. But if he made an error in committing the whole Church to a point of faith or morals, the damage would be irreparable; the teaching of Christ's revelation would be adulterated, and the Church would cease to be the guaranteed delegate of Christ. Hence in these acts only is it necessary for the Pope to be infallible, according to Christ's promise that the gates of hell shall not prevail against the Church.

(1925)

## PIUS XI EXTOLLS AND COUNSELS
## THE PRIESTHOOD

THE enemies of the Church themselves well know the vital importance of the priesthood; for against the priesthood in particular . . . they direct the point of their attacks. It is the priesthood they desire to be rid of; that they may clear the way for that destruction of the Church, which has been so often attempted yet never achieved. . . .

The priest, according to the magnificent definition given by St. Paul is indeed a man "taken from amongst men" yet "ordained for men in the things that appertain to God"; his office is not for human beings, and things that pass away, however lofty and valuable these may seem; but for things divine and enduring. . . .

The priest is the minister of Christ, an instrument, that is to say, in the hands of the Divine Redeemer. He continues the work of the redemption in all its world-embracing universality and divine efficacy, that work that wrought so marvellous a transformation in the world. . . .

A priest is the appointed "dispenser of the mysteries of God," for the benefit of the members of the mystical body of Christ; since he is the ordinary minister of nearly all the Sacraments, those channels through which the grace of the Saviour flows for the good of humanity. The Christian, at almost every important stage of his mortal career, finds at his side the priest with the power received from God, in the act of communicating or increasing the grace which is the supernatural life of his soul. . . . From the cradle to the grave the priest is ever beside the faithful, a solace, a minister of salvation and dispenser of grace and blessing. . . .

The Catholic priest is minister of Christ and dispenser of the mysteries of God in another way, that is, by words. "The ministry of the word." . . . The Church exercises her "ministry of the word" through her priests of every grade of the hierarchy, in which each has his wisely allotted place. These she sends everywhere as unwearied heralds of the good tidings which alone can save and advance true civilization and culture, or help them to rise again. The word of the priest enters the soul and brings light and power; the voice of the priest rises calmly above the storms of passion, fearlessly to proclaim the truth, and exhort to the good; that truth which elucidates and solves the gravest problems of human life; that good which no misfortune can take from us, which death but secures and renders immortal. . . .

The priest is public and official intercessor of humanity before God; he has the duty and commission of offering to God in the name of the Church, over and above sacrifice strictly so-called, the "sacrifice of praise," in public and official prayer; for several times each day, with psalms, prayers and hymns taken in great part from the inspired books, he pays to God this dutiful tribute of adoration and thus performs his necessary office of interceding for humanity. And never did humanity, in its afflictions, stand more in need of intercession and of the divine help which it brings. . . .

The dignity of the Catholic priesthood does but reinforce its obligation of singular holiness; for as the Angelic Doctor teaches: "To fulfil the duties of holy Orders, common goodness does not suffice; but excelling goodness is required; and they who receive Orders and are thereby higher in rank than the people, may also be higher in holiness. . . . The priest must preach the law of the Gospel; but for that preaching to be effective, the most obvious and, by the Grace of God, the most persuasive argument is to see the actual practice of the law in him who preaches it. . . .

It is impossible to treat of the piety of a Catholic priest without being drawn on to speak too of another most precious treasure of the Catholic priesthood, that is, of chastity. . . . A certain connection between this virtue and the sacerdotal ministry can even be seen by the light of reason alone; since "God is a Spirit," it is only fitting that he who dedicates and consecrates himself to God's service should in some way "divest himself of the body." . . .

Not less than by his chastity, the Catholic priest ought to be distinguished by his detachment. Surrounded by the corruptions of a world in which everything can be bought and sold, he must pass through them utterly free of selfishness. He must holily spurn all vile greed of earthly gains, since he is in search of souls, not of money, of the glory of God, not his own. He is no mercenary working for a temporal recompense, nor yet an employee who, whilst attending conscientiously to duties of his office, at the same time is looking to his career and personal promotion; he is the "good soldier of Christ" who "entangleth not himself with secular business; that he may please him to whom he hath engaged himself." The minister of God is a father of souls; and he knows that his toils and his cares cannot adequately be repaid with wealth and honors of earth. He is not indeed forbidden to receive fitting sustenance. . . . But once "called to the inheritance of the Lord," as his very title "cleric" declares, a priest must expect no other recompense than that promised by Christ to His Apostles: "Your reward is very great in Heaven." Woe to the priest who, forgetful of these divine promises should become "greedy of filthy lucre." Woe if he join the number of the worldly over whom the Church like the Apostle grieves; "All seek the things that are their own; not the things that are Jesus Christ's." Such a priest, besides failing in his vocation, would earn the contempt of his own people. . . .

By sincere disinterestedness the priest can hope to win the hearts of all. For detachment from earthly goods, if inspired by lively faith, is always accompanied by tender compassion towards the unfortunate of every kind. Thus the priest becomes a veritable father of the poor. . . . Thus the Catholic priest is freed from the bonds of a family and of self-interest,—the two chief bonds which could bind him too closely to earth. . . .

The Catholic priesthood must have the spirit of discipline, or, to use a more deeply Christian word, obedience. It is obedience which binds together all ranks into the harmony of the Church's Hierarchy.

. . . Let obedience temper excessive zeal on the one hand, and put the spur to weakness and slackness on the other. Let it assign to each his place and station. These each should accept without resistance; for otherwise the magnificent work of the Church in the world would be sadly hindered. . . .

But the portrait of the Catholic priest which We intend to exhibit to the world would be unfinished were We to omit another important feature,—learning. This the Church requires of him. . . . The priest should have full grasp of the Catholic teaching on faith and morals; he should know to present it to others; and he should be able to give the reason for the dogmas, laws and observances of the Church of which he is minister. Profane sciences have indeed made much progress; but in religious questions there is much ignorance still darkening the mind of our contemporaries. This ignorance the priest must dispel. Never was more pointed than today the warning of Tertullian "This alone truth sometimes craves, that it be not condemned unheard." It is the priest's task to clear away from men's minds the mass of prejudices and misunderstandings which hostile adversaries have piled up; the modern mind is eager for the truth, and the priest should be able to point it out with serene frankness; there are souls still hesitating, distressed by doubts, and the priest should inspire courage and trust, and guide them with calm security to the safe port of faith, faith accepted by both head and heart; error makes its onslaughts, arrogant and persistent, and the priest should know how to meet them with a defense vigorous and active, yet solid and unruffled. . . .

The dignity of the office he holds, and the maintenance of a becoming respect and esteem among people, which helps so much in his pastoral work, demand more than purely ecclesiastical learning. The priest must be graced by no less knowledge and culture than is usual among well-bred and well-educated people of his day. This to say that he must be healthily modern, as is the Church, which is at home in all times and all places, and adapts itself to all; which blesses and furthers all healthy initiative and has no fear of the progress, even the most daring progress, of science, if only it be true science. . . .

Wise encouragement and help should be given to those members of the clergy, who, by taste and special gifts, feel a call to devote themselves to study and research, in this or that branch of science, in this or that art; they do not thereby deny their clerical profession; for all this, undertaken within just limits and under the guidance of the Church, redounds to the good estate of the Church and to the glory of her divine Head, Jesus Christ. And among the rest of the clergy, none should remain content with a standard of learning and culture which sufficed, perhaps, in other times; they must try to attain—or, rather, they must actually attain—a higher standard of general education and of learning. It must be broader and more complete; and it must correspond to the generally higher level and wider scope of modern education as compared with the past.

Sometimes, it is true, and even in modern times, our Lord makes the world, as it were, His plaything; for He has been pleased to elect to the priestly state men almost devoid of that learning of which We have been speaking; and through them He has worked wonders. But He did this that all might learn, if there be a choice, to prize holiness more than learning; not to place more trust in human than divine means.

(December 20, 1935)

To live in the midst of the world without wishing its pleasures; to be a member of each family, yet belonging to none; to share all sufferings; to penetrate all secrets; to heal all wounds; to go from men to God and offer Him their prayers; to return from God to men to bring pardon and hope; to have a heart of fire for charity and a heart of bronze for chastity; to teach and to pardon, console and bless always, My God, what a life! And it is yours, O Priest of Jesus Christ!

JEAN BAPTISTE LACORDAIRE (ca. 1850)

# DIFFICULTIES OF THE PRIESTHOOD

## DÉSIRÉ JOSEPH CARDINAL MERCIER

ALL defects in the soul of a priest are indeed sincerely to be deplored; still, it must be remembered that the priest himself is a child of Adam, and therefore not immune from those tendencies to evil which, as St. John tells us, drag the whole human race downwards: "The whole world is seated in wickedness"; He receives more grace than the layman, it is true, but is he not at the same time vowed to a higher life, to a discipline incomparably more austere? The layman may legitimately engross himself with secular affairs, reciprocate human affection, dispose freely of his time, and order his own manner of living.

The priest, on the contrary, is bound to a life of disinterested self-sacrifice; he bears about his loins the girdle of chastity and on his arm the maniple of suffering; he has submitted his will to that of his bishop and has taken the vow of obedience to him.

The pious faithful, who see us only through clouds of incense, clothed with the sacred vestments, in all the solemnity of religious ceremonial, sometimes look upon us in much the same light as the superstitious pagans of Lycaonia regarded St. Paul, when, having seen him work a miracle, they would fain raise him and his companion Barnabas to the altars and offer victims to them. "The gods, they cried, "are come down to us in the likeness of men." But Paul and Barnabas, shocked at such sacrilege, rent their garments and "leaped out among the people crying, and saying: Ye men, why do ye do these things? We also are mortals, men like unto you, preaching to you to be converted from these vain things, to the living God." Yes, we all know it too well. We know it by the struggles we have to endure to let grace, which happily never fails us, triumph in our souls. Yes, we have the same passions as our fellow-mortals; and sanctity of soul, with us as with them, can be won only by sustained effort and as a reward of valiant co-operation with grace.

And oh! what perils beset us along the path of our ministry! How often the laity are, in their own families, with the best intentions our greatest stumbling-blocks. As Cardinal Manning observes: "People are very hospitable, and pity a priest's loneliness, and like to have him at their tables. Sometimes the best of people are the least circumspect and most kindly importunate in their invitations. How shall a young and inexperienced mind hold out against these facilities and allurements to relaxation, unpunctuality, self-indulgence, and dissipation?" Thus, little by little, he grows accustomed to what is a life of greater ease and affluence than he ever knew in his own home; and often he loses in this worldly atmosphere of well-being and comfort, perhaps even of tenderness, the virility of character and holy independence which are indispensable to the progress of the priest's soul in piety and charity. Very innocently the world may ensnare you; it invites you to share in its festivities, protesting that these will be kept—nay that your very presence will keep them—within the bounds of the strictest propriety. You yield to its pressing solicitations; then it wonders to see you resemble itself so closely and is secretly scandalized to find that in the many ordinary acts of your daily life you do not show forth in any striking manner yourself the high ideal you profess to hold up to it for its imitation. . . .

Even the very functions of your sacred ministry strew dangers in your path; your schools and sodalities, your clubs and societies for the working classes, your visits to the sick, your work in the confessional, are continually placing you in circumstances that demand the greatest prudence to safeguard the purity of your consciences and the integrity of your virtues. St. Paul would have you sympathize with your flock and share in their joys and sorrows; but sympathy awakens gratitude; gratitude evokes warmth of feeling and expression, wherein it is not always easy for the priest to preserve a proper spirit of detachment and indifference.

The priest's life is full of dangers; and I have always noticed that the harsher the judgments of self-indulgent worldings for the priest who may have momentarily forgotten his obligations, the more compassionate and merciful are the judgments of the saints. For my own part, I do not think I could ever have the melancholy courage to deal harshly with an erring brother acknowledging his fault. When the sinner has washed away his sin in tears of repentance charity no longer considers the malice of the sin, but only the humiliation and the sorrow of him who committed it. The spirit of Christianity inclines us to gentleness and humility, and he who has to do with the culprit need only look into his own heart to behold there the temptation that constantly threatens himself. . . .

On the one hand the weakness of human nature, which belongs to us as to the most abject of our brothers, and the dangers to which we are constantly exposed by our mission among men, are such that, *naturally* speaking, not one of us is capable of remaining for a long time the chaste, detached, submissive, hard-working, self-sacrificing man that the true priest ought to be. Oh! I can fully understand the distrust and incredulity entertained about the priest's life by those who have not had the happiness to possess the Faith. How can they be expected to believe in that of which they have never had the remotest experience? In their own lives passion conquers at its first assault. They yield without a struggle. The novel and theatre have taught them to divide their fellow-men into two classes: those who yield without resistance to every impulse of sensual love; and those who either foolishly or cleverly simulate virtue.

But, on the other hand, that which is not possible to nature alone

247

is being actually and constantly achieved, day after day, through the whole course of their lifetime, under the influence of divine grace, in the hearts of Christians who pray and struggle and mortify themselves for the honour and service of God. . . . .

"God does not demand what is impossible," says the Council of Trent, in words borrowed from Saint Augustine, "but when He lays His commands upon you He warns you to do all in your power, and to appeal to Him for what is beyond your power; and He will then help you to do what of yourself you had not the power to do."

(1912)

# INSTRUCTIONS TO MISSIONARIES

## PIUS XII

LET him [the missionary] not seek any advantage for his own country or religious Institute, but rather what may help towards the salvation of souls. Certainly he should dearly love his fatherland and his Order, but the Church should be loved with a still more ardent devotion. And let him remember that nothing will be to the advantage of his own Order that is detrimental to the good of the Church. . . .

The object of missionary activity, as all know, is to bring the light of the Gospel to new races and to form new Christians. However, the ultimate goal of missionary endeavor, which should never be lost sight of, is to establish the Church on sound foundations among non-Christian peoples, and place it under its own native Hierarchy.

In a letter we wrote on August 9 last year . . . We mentioned the following points among others: "The Church's aim is not the domination of peoples or the gaining of temporal dominions; she is eager only to bring the supernatural light of faith to all peoples, and to promote the interests of civilization and culture, and fraternal concord among nations." . . .

Let religious orders and congregations take legitimate pride in the foreign missions entrusted to them, as well as in the harvest of souls so far won for Christ's Kingdom. But let them remember that they have not received their portion of the Lord's Vineyard by a kind of private title in perpetuity. Rather they hold it at the will of the Holy See, whose right and responsibility is to see that it is fully developed. The Roman Pontiff does not fulfill his apostolic duty merely by portioning out larger or smaller mission territories among different religious institutes. What is more important, he must make it his continuous and anxious care that these institutes send into the territories entrusted to them missionaries sufficient in numbers and especially in apostolic quality to preach the Gospel successfully throughout the whole territory. . . .

The Church from the beginning down to our own time has always followed this wise practice: let not the Gospel on being introduced in any new land destroy or extinguish whatever its people possess that is naturally good, just or beautiful. For the Church, when she calls people to a higher culture and a better way of life, under the inspiration of the Christian religion, does not act like one who recklessly cuts down and uproots a thriving forest. No, she grafts a good scion upon the wild stock that it may bear a crop of more delicious fruit.

Human nature, though owing to Adam's fall, it is tainted with original sin, has in itself something that is naturally Christian; and this, if illumined by divine light and nourished by God's grace, can eventually be changed into true and supernatural virtue.

This is the reason why the Catholic Church has never scorned nor rejected the pagan philosophies. Instead, after freeing them from error and all contamination she has perfected and completed them by Christian revelation. So likewise the Church has graciously made her own the native art and culture which in some countries is so highly developed. She has carefully encouraged them and has brought them to a point of aesthetic perfection that of themselves they probably would never have attained. By no means has she repressed native customs and traditions but she has given them a certain religious significance; she has even transformed their feast days and made them serve to commemorate the martyrs and to celebrate mysteries of the faith.

(June 2, 1951)

# THE PRIESTHOOD OF THE LAITY

### THE REV. KARL ADAM

EVERY baptism is a consecration to the priesthood of Christ, for baptism removes the man from the profane world, appropriates him to Christ and sanctifies him for the performance of those more general acts of worship which belong to the vocation of the child of God. And the sacramental character of Confirmation intensifies this priesthood, since it fits the Christian to take an active share in the building of the temple of God, and equips him for the apostolate and for its "evidences of the spirit and of power." Therefore the Catholic conception of the priesthood of the laity is very far from being a making void of the original doctrine of the priesthood of all Christians. . . .

This priestly conjunction of all with the high-priesthood of Christ, an utterly sacred conjunction, is the source whence springs the close fellowship of all in their prayer and faith and love. . . .

The Catholic fellowship in faith does not mean merely that all the members of the Church loyally profess one and the same faith, presented to them by apostolic authority, that they share the same luminous ideal, the same effective rule and the same fruitful sources of spiritual life. It means more than that. It means that there is a solidarity and partnership of the faith, a reciprocal interaction and fruitful influence, which by intimate and pervasive action makes their external union an inward communion in the faith, a communion which out of the depths of the common experience of the faith is ever expressing itself anew in a single "credo" of the mystical Christ.

(1929)


IF there is one thing written so plainly across the pages of history that no man call fail to read, it is this: that the momentum of a group of men, like that of a physical object hurled through space, is the product of the mass multiplied by the velocity. The gods of Greece and Rome, the Pagan Gods at Ephesus, must have laughed to scorn the humble band of illiterate Galilean peasants who set out to evangelize the world and overthrow them from their pedestals.

And yet, laying aside the Divine foundation and guidance of the Church, viewed solely in terms of human psychology it may be said that the triumph of the Church in this and every age, that Christian civilization itself, is the triumph of zeal.

BEN W. PALMER (1939)

# A CALL TO THE LAITY FOR
## CATHOLIC ACTION

### PIUS XII

THE lay co-operation which we today call Catholic Action has existed since the foundation of the Church. Indeed the Apostles and other preachers of the Gospel received no little help from it and the Christian religion thereby made great advances. . . .

The Gospel followed the great Roman roads and was spread not only by the Bishops and priests but also by public officials, soldiers and private citizens. Thousands of Christian neophytes, whose names today are unknown, were fired with zeal to promote the new religion they had embraced and endeavored to prepare the way for the coming of the Gospel. That explains why after about 100 years Christianity had penetrated into all the chief cities of the Roman Empire. . . .

In every age, thanks to the tireless labors of the clergy and to the co-operation of the laity, the Catholic Church has not only advanced its spiritual kingdom, but has also led nations to increased social prosperity. . . . By their holy lives and zealous labors they brought about improvement in the different classes of society by instituting reforms, by spreading the true Faith everywhere, by valiantly defending the Church and above all by their personal example. . . .

The same conditions which prevailed in the early days of the Church are still to be found in many areas which have been evangelized by missionaries; or at least their peoples suffer disadvantages which had to be left to a future generation to face and remedy. For that reason it is imperative that the laity should in great numbers enter the serried ranks of Catholic Action, and thus co-operate generously, earnestly and diligently with the Hierarchy in promoting the apostolate. . . .

We therefore desire that there be everywhere erected, as far as is possible, associations of Catholic men and women, and also of students, of workers, of artists, of athletes, and other clubs and sodalities, which can be considered the auxiliaries of the missionaries. In the erection and constitution of these organizations let character, virtue and zeal be preferred to numbers. . . .

Although it is clear that Catholic Action should exercise its influence primarily in promoting the works of the apostolate, its members are not prevented from joining other organizations whose purpose is to reform social and political life according to the principles and teaching of the Gospel; in fact, their participation not only as citizens, but as Catholics also, is a right which they possess and a duty to which they are bound.

(June 1951)

# AGAINST THE CULT OF ANTIQUITY

### THE REV. JAMES M. GILLIS, C.S.P.

MY own opinion is that Catholics do the Church a doubtful service when they prate of the glories of the past. . . .

To my mind it were better to concentrate the attention of the world upon our contemporary vigor rather than upon our medieval or ancient glory. If we cannot build cathedrals in the old world, we are building them in the new. If they are not so beautiful, they are more useful. It is sometimes said—to shame us—that we Catholics are still in the "brick and mortar" period here in America. The taunt is really a compliment. So long as we keep putting bricks and mortar together, it must be evident that we are increasing. It is better to see a brick wall going up than a stone wall tumbling down. The smell of fresh mortar is pleasanter (at least to some nostrils) than the musty odor of old churches and sacristies and *schatzkammern* that are never opened until some curious seeker comes along and hands a fee to an ancient and moribund caretaker.

It is odd that certain sentimentalists amongst us seem to associate beauty only with decrepitude. Real beauty is life, and life is beauty. Some of our modern American churches may be architectural monstrosities, but when they are crowded for ten masses on Sunday they take on a supernatural glory—for those who have eyes to see. As far as Catholic apologetics is concerned, I think we might better point to our congregations bursting the doors of the churches, crowding the steps and the approaches, and, as we say facetiously, hanging on to the chandeliers while Mass is going on, than to call attention to a magnificent medieval cathedral that is to all intents and purposes little more than a museum of art and a monument of fine architecture.

(1928)

# X

# The Church
# and the State

*Origin of political power. Christian democracy. God in government. Standards for democracy. Supremacy of the natural law. Church and state. The Catholic citizen. Catholicism and Americanism. Liberalism. Totalitarianism.*

## GOD IS THE AUTHOR OF
## POLITICAL POWER

### LEO XIII

THOSE by whose authority the State is administered must be able so to compel the citizens to obedience that it is clearly a sin in the latter not to obey. But no man has in himself or of himself the power of constraining the free will of others by fetters of authority of this kind. The power resides solely in God, the Creator and Legislator of all things; and it is necessary that those who exercise it should do it as having received it from God. . . .

If the will of rulers is opposed to the will and laws of God, they themselves exceed the bounds of their own power and pervert justice; nor can their authority then be valid, which, when there is no justice, is null. . . .

Theories of the body politic invented by late writers have already produced great ills amongst men, and it is to be feared that they will cause the very greatest disasters to posterity. For an unwillingness to

253

attribute the right of ruling to God, as its author, is no less than a willingness to blot out the greatest splendor of political power and to destroy its force. And they who say that this power depends on the will of the people err in opinion first of all; then they place authority on too weak and unstable a foundation. For the popular passions, incited and goaded on by these opinions, will break out more insolently; and, with great harm to the common weal.

(June 29, 1881)

# SECULAR INTERFERENCE WITH PAPAL JUDGMENTS DENOUNCED

### POPE NICHOLAS I

SINCE according to the Canons the judgments of lesser tribunals must be referred to a tribunal having greater authority, that is, for their reversal or confirmation; it is immediately clear that the judgments of the Apostolic See, than which there is no greater authority, cannot be handled by any other tribunal, nor is it permissible for any to sit in judgment upon its decisions. Appeals are to be made to that See from any part of the world. Such is the meaning of the Canons. But no appeal is allowed from that See. . . . We do not say that the decision of the said See cannot be amended; some of the facts may have been withheld, or the See may have made a decree of a dispensatory nature in view of the circumstances of the time or of some serious and compelling reasons. . . .

But, we beg you, do not make any claim to the prejudice of God's Church; for that Church does nothing to the prejudice of your dominion, since it rather offers supplication to the eternal Godhead for the stability of your Empire and with constant devotion prays for your safety and your eternal salvation. Do not usurp the things that are her own; do not seek to take from her the things which have been entrusted to her alone, knowing that everyone that has the administration of the affairs of this world ought to be kept away from sacred matters, to just the same extent as it is fitting that no member of the ranks of the clergy and the warriors of God should be immersed in any secular business. In fact we are utterly at a loss to understand how those who have been given the right to preside only over human, and not over divine, affairs, may presume to sit in judgment on those through whom divine affairs are administered.

(A.D. 865)

# THE NATURE OF *CHRISTIAN DEMOCRACY*

## LEO XIII

*Christian Democracy* by the fact that it is Christian, is built . . . on the basic principles of divine faith, and provides for the betterment of the masses, with the ulterior object of availing itself of the occasion to fashion their minds for things which are everlasting. Hence, for *Christian Democracy* justice is sacred; it must maintain that the right of acquiring and possessing property cannot be impugned, and it must safeguard the various distinctions and degrees which are indispensable in every well-ordered commonwealth. . . . There is nothing in common between *Social* and *Christian Democracy*. They differ from each other as much as the sect of Socialism differs from the profession of Christianity.

Moreover, it would be a crime to distort this name of *Christian Democracy* to politics, for although democracy, both in its philological and philosophical significations, implies popular government, yet in its present application it is so to be employed that, removing from it all political significance, it is to mean nothing else than a benevolent and Christian movement in behalf of the people. For the laws of nature and of the Gospel . . . are necessarily independent of all modifications of civil government, while at the same time they are in concord with everything that is not repugnant to morality and justice. They are, therefore, and they must remain absolutely free from political parties, and have nothing to do with the various changes of administration which may occur in a nation. . . .

From *Christian Democracy* We must remove another possible subject of reproach, namely: that while looking after the advantage of the working people they should act in such a manner as to forget the upper classes of society; for they also are of the greatest use in preserving and perfecting the commonwealth.

(January 18, 1901)

It is not forbidden to prefer temperate, popular forms of government, without prejudice, however, to Catholic teaching on the origin and use of authority. . . . The Church does not disapprove of any of the various forms of government, provided they be per se capable of securing the good of the citizens.

LEO XIII, (June 20, 1888)

## NATURAL LAW AND
## HUMAN LIBERTY

### LEO XIII

WHEN . . . it is established that man's soul is immortal and endowed with reason and not bound up with things material, the foundation of natural liberty is at once most firmly laid. . . .

Liberty . . . belongs only to those who have the gift of reason or intelligence. Considered as to its nature, it is the faculty of choosing means fitted for the end proposed; for he is master of his actions who can choose one thing out of many. . . . But the will cannot proceed to act until it is enlightened by the knowledge possessed by the intellect. . . .

Such then being the condition of human liberty, it necessarily stands in need of light and strength to direct its actions to good and to restrain them from evil. Without this the freedom of our will would be our ruin. First of all there must be *law;* that is, a fixed rule of teaching what is to be done and what is to be left undone. . . . The reason prescribes to the will what it should seek after or shun, in order to the eventual attainment of man's last end, for the sake of which all his actions ought to be performed. This ordination of *reason* is called law. . . .

Foremost in this office comes the *natural law,* which is written and engraved in the mind of every man; and this is nothing but our reason, commanding us to do right and forbidding sin. . . .

The law of nature is the same thing as the *eternal law,* implanted in rational creatures, and inclining them *to their right action and end;* and can be nothing else but the eternal reason of God, the Creator and Ruler of all the world. . . .

From this it is manifest that the eternal law of God is the sole standard and rule of human liberty, not only in each individual man, but also in the community and civil society which men constitute when united. Therefore, the true liberty of human society does not consist in every man doing what he pleases, for this would simply end in turmoil and confusion, and bring on the overthrow of the State; but rather in this, that through the injunctions of the civil law all may more easily conform to the prescriptions of the eternal law. . . . The binding force of human laws is in this, that they are to be regarded as applications of the eternal law, and incapable of sanctioning anything which is not contained in the eternal law, as in the principle of all law. . . .

Therefore, the nature of human liberty, however it be considered, whether in individuals or in society, whether in those who command or in those who obey, supposes the necessity of obedience to some supreme and eternal law, which is no other than the authority of God, commanding good and forbidding evil. And so far from this most just authority of God over men diminishing, or even destroying their liberty, it protects and perfects it, for the real perfection of all creatures is found in the prosecution and attainment of their respective ends; but the supreme end to which human liberty must aspire is God. . . .

Where a law is enacted contrary to reason, or to the eternal law, or to some ordinance of God, obedience is unlawful, lest, while obeying man, we become disobedient to God. . . .

Once man is firmly persuaded he is subject to no one, it follows that the efficient cause of the unity of civil society is not to be sought in any principle external to man, or superior to him, but simply in the free will of individuals; that the authority in the State comes from the people only; and that, just as every man's individual reason is his only rule of life, so the collective reason of the community should be the supreme guide in the management of all public affairs. Hence the doctrine of the supremacy of the greater number, and that all right and all duty reside in the majority. But . . . this is in contradiction to reason. To refuse any bond of union between man and civil society, on the one hand, and God the Creator and consequently the supreme law-giver, on the other, is plainly repugnant to the nature, not only of man, but of all created things. . . .

A doctrine of such character is most hurtful both to individuals and to the State. For, once ascribe to human reason the only authority to decide what is true and what is good, and the real distinction between good and evil is destroyed; honor and dishonor differ not in their nature, but in the opinion and judgment of each one. . . . This is simply a road leading straight to tyranny. The empire of God over man and civil society once repudiated, it follows that religion, as a public institution, can have no claim to exist, and that everything that belongs to religion will be treated with complete indifference. Furthermore, with ambitious designs on sovereignty, tumult and sedition will be common amongst the people; and when duty and conscience cease to appeal to them, there will be nothing to hold them back but force, which of itself alone is powerless to keep their covetousness in check. . . .

To reject the supreme authority of God, and to cast off all obedience to Him in public matters, or even in private and domestic affairs, is the greatest perversion of liberty and the worst kind of *Liberalism;* and what We have said must be understood to apply to this alone in its fullest sense.

(June 20, 1888)

THE light of natural reason whereby we discern what is good and what is evil, which is the function of the natural law, is nothing else than an imprint on us of the Divine Light. It is therefore evident that the natural law is nothing else than the rational creature's participation of the eternal law.

ST. THOMAS AQUINAS (1272)

## THE SUPREMACY OF THE NATURAL LAW

### PIUS XII

THE radical and ultimate cause of the evils which We deplore in modern society is the denial and rejection of a universal norm of morality as well for individual and social life as for international relations; We mean the disregard, so common nowadays, and the forgetfulness of the natural law itself, which has its foundation in God. . . .

Once the authority of God and the sway of His law are denied in this way, the civil authority as an inevitable result tends to attribute to itself that absolute autonomy which belongs exclusively to the Supreme Maker. It puts itself in the place of the Almighty and elevates the State or group into the last end of life, the supreme criterion of the moral and juridical order, and therefore forbids every appeal to the principles of natural reason and of the Christian conscience. . . .

No one of good will and vision will think of refusing the State, in the exceptional conditions of the world of today, correspondingly wider and exceptional rights to meet the popular needs. But even in such emergencies, the moral law, established by God, demands that the lawfulness of each such measure and its real necessity be scrutinized with the greatest rigor according to the standards of the common good.

In any case, the more burdensome the material sacrifices demanded of the individual and the family by the State, the more must the rights of conscience be to it sacred and inviolable. Goods, blood it can demand; but the soul redeemed by God, never. The charge laid by God on parents to provide for the material and spiritual good of their offspring and to procure for them a suitable training saturated with the true spirit of religion, cannot be wrested from them without grave violation of their rights. . . .

The idea which credits the State with unlimited authority is not simply an error harmful to the internal life of nations, to their prosperity, and to the larger and well-ordered increase in their well-being, but likewise it injures the relations between peoples, for it breaks the unity of supra-national society, robs the law of nations of its foundation and vigor, leads to violation of others' rights and impedes agreement and peaceful intercourse.

A disposition, in fact, of the divinely-sanctioned natural order divides the human race into social groups, nations or States, which are mutually independent in organization and in the direction of their internal life. But for all that, the human race is bound together by recriprocal ties, moral and juridical, into a great commonwealth directed to the good of all nations and ruled by special laws which protect its unity and promote its prosperity. Now no one can fail to see how the claim to absolute autonomy for the State stands in open opposition to this natural way that is inherent in man—nay, denies it utterly—and therefore leaves the stability of international relations at the mercy of the will of rulers, while it destroys the possibility of true union and fruitful collaboration directed to the general good. . . .

To tear the law of nations from its anchor in Divine law, to base it on the autonomous will of States, is to dethrone that very law and deprive it of its noblest and strongest qualities. Thus it would stand abandoned to the fatal drive of private interest and collective selfishness exclusively intent on the assertion of its own rights and ignoring those of others. . . .

Safety does not come to people from external means, from the sword, which can impose conditions of peace but does not create peace. Forces that are to renew the face of the earth should proceed from within, from the spirit.

Once the bitterness and cruel strifes of the present have ceased, the new order of the world, of national and international life, must rest no longer on the quicksands of changeable and ephemeral standards that depend only on the selfish interests of groups and individuals. No, they must rest on the unshakeable foundation, on the solid rock of natural law and of Divine Revelation.

(October 20, 1939)

## CHURCH AND STATE

### LEO XIII

As no society can hold together unless some one be over all, directing all to strive earnestly for the common good; every civilized community must have a ruling authority, and this authority no less than society itself, has its source in nature, and has, consequently, God for its author. Hence it follows that all public power must proceed from God. For God alone is the true and supreme Lord of the world. . . . Whosoever holds the right to govern, holds it from one sole and single source, namely, God, the Sovereign Ruler of all. *"There is no power but from God."* . . .

If those who are in authority rule unjustly, if they govern overbearingly or arrogantly, and if their measures prove hurtful to the people, they must remember that the Almighty will one day bring them to account, the more strictly in proportion to the sacredness of their office and pre-eminence of their dignity. *The mighty shall be mightily tormented.* . . .

As a consequence, the State, constituted as it is, is clearly bound to act up to the manifold and weighty duties linking it to God, by the public profession of religion. Nature and reason, which command every individual devoutly to worship God in holiness, because we belong to Him and must return to Him since from Him we came, bind also the civil community by a like law. For men living together in society are under the power of God no less than individuals are, and society, not less than individuals, owes gratitude to God. . . . Care must especially be taken to preserve unharmed and unimpeded the religion whereof the practice is the link connecting man with God. . . .

The Almighty, therefore, has given charge of the human race to two powers, the ecclesiastical and the civil, the one being set over divine, and the other over human things. Each in its kind is supreme, each has fixed limits within which it is contained, limits which are defined by the nature and special object of the province of each, so that there is, we may say, an orbit traced out within which the action of each is brought into play by its own native right. But inasmuch as each of these two powers has authority over the same subjects, and as it might come to pass that one and the same thing—related differently, but still remaining one and the same thing—might belong to the jurisdiction and determination of both, therefore God, Who foresees all things, and Who is the author of these two powers, has marked out the course of each in right correlation to the other. *For the powers that are, are ordained of God.* Were this not so, deplorable contentions and conflicts would often arise, and not infrequently men, like travelers at the meeting of two roads, would hesitate in anxiety and doubt, not knowing what course to follow. Two powers would be commanding contrary things, and it would be a dereliction of duty to disobey either of the two. . . .

There must, accordingly, exist, between these two powers, a certain orderly connection, which may be compared to the union of the soul and body in man. The nature and scope of that connection can be determined only, as We have laid down, by having regard to the nature of each power, and by taking account of the relative excellence and nobleness of their purpose. One of the two has for its proximate and chief object the well-being of this mortal life; the other the everlasting joys of heaven. Whatever, therefore, in things human is of a sacred character, whatever belongs either of its own nature or by reason of the end to which it is referred, to the salvation of souls, or to the worship of God, is subject to the power and judgment of the Church. Whatever is to be ranged under the civil and political order is rightly subject to the civil authority. Jesus Christ has Himself given command that what is Caesar's is to be rendered to Caesar, and that what belongs to God is to be rendered to God. . . .

Whatever, therefore, is opposed to virtue and truth, may not rightly be brought temptingly before the eye of man, much less sanctioned by the favor and protection of law. A well-spent life is the only passport to heaven, whither all are bound, and on this account the State is acting against the laws and dictates of nature whenever it permits the license of opinion and of action to lead minds astray from truth and souls away from the practice of virtue. To exclude the Church, founded by God Himself, from the business of life, from the power of making laws, from the training of youth, from domestic society, is a grave and fatal error. A State from which religion is banished can never be well regulated; and already perhaps more than is desirable is known of the nature and tendency of the so-called *civil* philosophy of life and morals. . . .

The Church, indeed, deems it unlawful to place the various forms of divine worship on the same footing as the true religion, but does not, on that account, condemn those rulers who, for the sake of securing some great good or of hindering some great evil, allows patiently custom or usage to be a kind of sanction for each kind of religion having its place in the State. And in fact the Church is wont to take earnest heed that no one shall be forced to embrace the Catholic faith against his will, for, as St. Augustine wisely reminds us, "Man cannot believe otherwise than by his own free will."

In the same way the Church cannot approve of that liberty which begets a contempt of the most sacred laws of God, and casts off the obedience due to lawful authority, for this is not liberty so much as license, and is most correctly styled by St. Augustine the "liberty of self-ruin," and by the apostle St. Paul the *cloak of malice.* . . .

Whatever in the State is of chief avail for the common welfare; whatever has been usefully established to curb the license of rulers who are opposed to the true interests of the people, or to keep in check the leading authorities from unwarrantably interfering in municipal or family affairs;—whatever tends to uphold the honor, manhood, and equal rights of individual citizens;—of all these things, as the monuments of past ages bear witness, the Catholic Church has always been the originator, the promoter, or the guardian. Ever therefore consistent with herself, while on the one hand she rejects that exorbitant liberty which in individuals and nations ends in license or in thraldom, on the other hand, she willingly and most gladly welcomes whatever improvements the age brings forth, if these really secure the prosperity of life here below, which is as it were a stage in the journey to the life that will know no ending.

(November 1, 1885)

# THE CHURCH'S RIGHT TO
# DEFEND ITSELF

### LEO XIII

THEY who are engaged in framing constitutions and in enacting laws should bear in mind the moral and religious nature of man, and take care to help him, but in a right and orderly way, to gain perfection, neither enjoining nor forbidding anything save what is reasonably consistent with civil law as well as with religious requirements. On this very account the Church cannot stand by, indifferent as to the import and significance of laws enacted by the State; not in so far indeed as they refer to the State, but in so far as, passing beyond their due limits, they trench upon the rights of the Church. . . .

Inasmuch as the destiny of the State depends mainly on the disposition of those who are at the head of affairs, it follows that the Church cannot give countenance or favor to those whom she knows to be imbued with a spirit of hostility to her; who refuse openly to respect her rights; who make it their aim and purpose to tear asunder the alliance that should, by the very nature of things, connect the interests of religion with those of the State. . . .

Where the Church does not forbid taking part in public affairs, it is fit and proper to give support to men of acknowledged worth, and who pledge themselves to deserve well in the Catholic cause, and on no account may it be allowed to prefer to them any such individuals as are hostile to religion.

(January 10, 1890)

# THE CHURCH DESIRES HARMONY
# WITH ALL GOVERNMENT

### JACQUES MARITAIN

THE Church is in the world but is not of the world. If she invites men to be faithful to social institutions that have been tested by time this does not mean that she is tied to one or other of these institutions; it signifies her recognition that the stability of law is an important element in the welfare of mankind. The Church has constantly shown in the course of history that political and social changes have no terrors for her and that she has a sense singularly free from illusion of the contingent character of human institutions. She teaches obedience to temporal authority and to just laws since all legitimate rule of man over man comes from God; but (saving the case of a temporal power having a ministerial rule in regard to the spiritual authority, as happened with the Empire in the Middle Ages) the Church does not institute the temporal authority, she sanctions the rule of him who is in office—without forbidding efforts to effect a change of government, and without forbidding resistance, by force is need be, to tyrannical rule. With a view to the advancement of her work for the salvation of souls, and so that States also shall respect the ends that are proper to the spiritual nature of man, the Church seeks to act in harmony with the secular power. But she is not unaware that at most times—since the world which turns away from God is subject to a Prince who is not God (*totus in maligno positus est mundus*)— to deal with the temporal power is a little like dealing with the devil. And on the whole one devil is as good as another. A new ruler who establishes his authority cancels out the rights of his predecessor. In truth the Catholic Church took a long time to adjust itself to the bourgeois regime, perhaps because the medieval order which was framed under her protection continued to occupy a place in her memory as it had so long occupied her guardian care.

(1935)

# POPULAR GOVERNMENT'S
## DEBT TO THE CHURCH

### ALFRED O'RAHILLY

THE great Church Councils for over eight centuries slowly trained Europe in the theory and practice of self-government, finally eventuating in commune, cortes, parliament and states-general. The organization of the Church—the representation of cathedral and collegiate chapters, the appointment of proctors, above all the democracy of the friars—showed the way to secular States. The discussions concerning the structure of the Church formed for nearly three centuries the great polemic of the West and thus inaugurated and habituated in men's minds those categories of political thought whose inheritors we are today. And all the while there flowed that stream of deep, patient thinkers who, from Thomas of Aquino, Nicholas d'Oresme, Antonius of Florence, down to Almain, Major, Bellarmine and Suarez, upheld the ideal of popular rights and government by consent. It was the ideas of these men to which the Catholics of the Ligue made their appeal; and notwithstanding their vehemence and passion, their ideals were sound. It was to this same treasure house of the past that the French Calvinists turned in their first and short-lived alliance with democracy. And it was back once more to the rock whence they were hewn that the Covenanters and Presbyterians turned when the day of reckoning came for the Stuarts. From the annals of the past, from Bracton and Fortescue, from forgotten canonists, legists and schoolmen, from the great conciliar controversialists, were dragged forth principles which shattered forever the Reformation tenet of Divine Right and traversing the ocean founded the American Republic, principles whose dynamic possibilities and farreaching consequences are not yet exhausted.

(1919)

SECULAR or civil power is instituted by men; it is in the people unless they bestow it on a prince. This power is immediately in the whole multitude as in the subject of it. For this power is in the Divine Law, but the Divine Law hath given this power to no particular man; if the positive law is taken away, there is left no reason why amongst a multitude (who are equal) one rather than another should bear rule over the rest. Power is given by the multitude to one man or to more by the same law of nature; for the commonwealth cannot exercise this power, therefore it is bound to bestow it upon some one man or some few. It depends upon the consent of the multitude to ordain over themselves a king or counsel or other magistrates. And if there be a lawful cause, the multitude may change the kingdom into an aristocracy or democracy.

ROBERT CARDINAL BELLARMINE, S.J. (ca. 1600)

# STANDARDS FOR DEMOCRACY

## PIUS XII

*Characteristics Proper to Citizens in a Democratic Regime:* To express his own views of the duties and sacrifices that are imposed on him; not compelled to obey without being heard—these are the two rights of the citizen which find in democracy, as its name implies, their expression.

From the solidity, the harmony and good results produced by this between the citizens and the Government, one may decide which democracy is really healthy and well balanced, and what is its life energy and power of expansion.

If then, we consider the extent and nature of the sacrifices demanded of all the citizens, especially in our day when the activity of the state is so vast and decisive, the democratic form of government appears to many as a postulate of nature imposed by reason itself.

When, however, people call for "democracy and better democracy," such a demand cannot have any other meaning than to place the citizen ever more in the position to hold his own personal opinion, to express it and to make it prevail in a fashion conducive to the common good.

Hence follows a first conclusion with its practical consequences, the state does not contain in itself and does not mechanically bring together in a given territory a shapeless mass of individuals.

It is, and should in practice be, the organic and organizing unity of a real people. The people, and a shapeless multitude (as it is called, "the masses") are two distinct concepts.

The people lives and moves by its own life energy; the masses are inert of themselves and can only be moved from outside. The people lives by the fulness of life in the men that compose it, each of whom—at his proper place and in his own way—is a person conscious of his own responsibility and of his own views.

The masses, on the contrary, wait for the impulse from outside, an easy plaything in the hands of anyone who exploits their instincts and impressions; ready to follow in turn, today this flag, tomorrow another. . . .

The masses—as we have just defined them—are the capital enemy of true democracy and of its ideal of liberty and equality.

In a people worthy of the name, the citizen feels within him the

266

consciousness of his personality, of his duties and rights, of his own freedom joined to respect for the freedom and dignity of others.

In a people worthy of the name all inequalities based not on whim but on the nature of things, inequalities of culture, possessions, social standing—without, of course, prejudice to justice and mutual charity —do not constitute any obstacle to the existence and prevalence of a true spirit of union and brotherhood.

On the contrary, so far from impairing civil equality in any way, they give it its true meaning: namely, that, before the state, everyone has the right to live honorably his own personal life in the place and under the conditions in which the designs and dispositions of Providence have placed him.

As against this picture of the democratic ideal of liberty and equality in a people's government by honest and far-seeing men, what a spectacle is that of a democratic state left to the whims of the masses:

Liberty, from being a moral duty of the individual becomes a tyrannous claim to give free rein to a man's impulses and appetites to the detriment of others.

Equality degenerates to a mechanical level, a colorless uniformity: the sense of true honor, of personal activity, of respect for tradition, of dignity—in a word all that gives life its worth—gradually fades away and disappears.

And the only survivors are, on the one hand, the victims deluded by the specious mirage of democracy, naively taken for the genuine spirit of democracy, with its liberty and equality; and on the other, the more or less numerous exploiters, who have known how to use the power of money and of organization, in order to secure a privileged position above the others, and have gained power.

The democratic state, whether monarchical or republican, should, like any other form of government, be entrusted with the power to command with real and effective authority. . . .

If men, using their personal liberty, were to deny all dependence on a superior Authority possessing coercive power, they could by this very fact cut the ground from under their own dignity and liberty— by violating, that is, the absolute order of beings and purposes.

As they are established in this same foundation, the person, the state, the government, with their respective rights, are so bound together that they stand or fall together.

And since the absolute order, in the light of right reason, and in particular of the Christian Faith, cannot have any other origin than in a personal God, our Creator, it follows that the dignity of man is the dignity of the moral community willed by God, the dignity of political authority is the dignity deriving from its sharing in the authority of God.

No form of state can avoid taking cognizance of this intimate and indissoluble connection—least of all in a democracy. Accordingly, if those in power do not see it, or more or less discount it, their own authority is shaken, as is social morality, and that specious appearance of a purely formal democracy may often serve as a mark for all that is in reality least democratic.

Only a clear appreciation of the purposes assigned by God to every human society, can put those in power in a position to fulfill their own obligations in the legislative, judicial and executive order with that objectivity, impartiality, loyalty, generosity, and integrity without which a democratic government would find it hard to command the respect and the support of the better section of the people. . . .

To secure effective action, to win esteem and trust, every legislative body should—as experience shows beyond doubt—gather within it a group of select men, spiritually eminent and of strong character, who shall look upon themselves as the representatives of the entire people and not the mandatories of a mob, whose interests are often unfortunately made to prevail over the true needs of the common good—a select group of men not restricted to any profession or social standing but reflecting every phase of the people's life; men chosen for their solid Christian convictions, straight and steady judgment, with a sense of the practical and equitable, true to themselves in all circumstances; men of clear and sound principles, with sound and clear-cut proposals to make; men above all capable, in virtue of the authority that emanates from their untarnished consciences and radiates widely from them, to be leaders and heads especially in times when the pressing needs of the moment excite the people's impressionability unduly, and render it more liable to be led astray and get lost: men who—in periods of transition, generally stormy and disturbed by passion, by divergent opinions and opposing programs—feel themselves doubly under the obligation to send circulating through the veins of the people and of the state, burning with a thousand fevers, the spiritual antidote of clear views, kindly interest, a justice equally sympathetic to all, and a bias towards national unity and concord in a sincere spirit of brotherhood. . . .

Where such men are lacking, others come to take their places in order to make politics serve their ambition, and be a quick road to profit for themselves, their caste and their class, while the race after private interests makes them lose sight of and completely jeopardize the true common good.

A sound democracy, based on the immutable principles of the natural law and revealed truth, will resolutely turn its back on such corruption as gives to the state legislature an unchecked and unlimited power, and moreover, makes of the democratic regime, notwithstanding an outward show to the contrary, purely and simply a form of absolutism. . . .

If the future is to belong to democracy, an essential part in its achievement will have to belong to the religion of Christ and to the Church, the messenger of our Redeemer's word which is to continue His mission of saving men. For she teaches and defends supernatural truths and communicates the supernatural helps of grace in order to actuate the divinely-established order of beings and ends which is the ultimate foundation and directive norm of every democracy. . . .

The Church has the mission to announce to the world, which is looking for better and more perfect forms of democracy, the highest and most needed message that there can be: the dignity of man, the call to be sons of God.

(December 24, 1944)

# COUNSEL TO CATHOLICS
## IN PUBLIC LIFE

### LEO XIII

As to those who mean to take part in public affairs they should avoid with the very utmost care two criminal excesses: so-called prudence and false courage. Some there are, indeed, who maintain that it is not opportune boldly to attack evil-doing in its might and when in the ascendant, lest, as they say, opposition should exasperate minds already hostile. . . .

The prudence of men of this cast is of that kind which is termed by the Apostle Paul *wisdom of the flesh* and *death* of the soul, *because it is not subject to the law of God, neither can it be*. Nothing is less calculated to amend such ills than prudence of this kind. For the enemies of the Church have for their object—and they hesitate not to

269

proclaim it, and many among them boast of it—to destroy outright, if possible, the Catholic religion. . . .

On the other hand, not a few, impelled by a false zeal, or—what is more blameworthy still—affecting sentiments which their conduct belies, take upon themselves to act a part which does not belong to them. They would fain see the Church's mode of action influenced by their ideas and their judgment to such an extent that everything done otherwise they take ill or accept with repugnance. Some, yet again, expend their energies in fruitless contention, being worthy of blame equally with the former. To act in such a manner is not to follow lawful authority but to forestall it, and unauthorized, assume the duties of the spiritual rulers, to the great detriment of the order which God established in His Church. . . .

Honor, then, to those who shrink not from entering the arena as often as need calls, believing and being convinced that the violence of injustice will be brought to an end and finally give way to the sanctity of right and religion! . . . We greatly desire to fix deep in the minds of each one that which Paul calls the *wisdom of the spirit,* for in controlling human actions this wisdom follows the excellent rule of moderation, with the happy result that no one either timidly despairs through lack of courage or presumes over-much from want of prudence.

(January 10, 1890)


# POLITICAL DUTIES OF WOMEN

### PIUS XII

WHEN it is a question of the fundamental morals of the family and the state, of the rights of God and of the Church, all men and women, of whatever class and station, are strictly obliged to make use of their political rights in the service of a good cause.

Every woman has then, mark it well, the obligation, the strict obligation in conscience, not to absent herself but to go into action in a manner and way suitable to the status of each so as to hold back those currents which threaten the home, so as to oppose those doctrines which undermine its foundations, so as to prepare, organize and achieve its restoration. . . .

The electoral ballot in the hands of the Catholic woman is an important means towards the fulfillment of her strict duty in conscience, especially at the present time.

(August and October, 1945)

# THE LIMITS OF CATHOLIC OBEDIENCE

### THE MOST REV. JOHN ENGLAND

IF this infallible tribunal, which you profess yourselves bound to obey, should command you to overturn our government, and tell you that it is the will of God to have it new modelled, will you be bound to obey it? and how then can we consider those men to be good citizens, who profess to owe obedience to a foreign authority,—to an authority not recognised in our constitution,—to an authority which has excommunicated and deposed sovereigns, and which has absolved subjects and citizens from their bond of allegiance.

Our answer to this is extremely simple and very plain; it is, that we would not be bound to obey it,—that we recognise no such authority. I would not allow to the Pope, or to any bishop of our church, outside this Union, the smallest interference with the humblest vote at our most insignificant balloting-box. He has no rights to such interference. You must, from the view which I have taken, see the plain distinction between spiritual authority and a right to interfere in the regulation of human government or civil concerns. You have in your constitution wisely kept them distinct and separate. It will be wisdom, and prudence, and safety to continue the separation.

You have no power to interfere with my religious rights; the tribunal of the church has no power to interfere with my civil rights. It is a duty which every good man ought to discharge for his own, and for the public benefit, to resist any encroachment upon either. It must hence be apparent, that any idea of the Roman Catholics of these republics being in any way under the influence of any foreign ecclesiastical power, or indeed of any church authority in the exercise of their civil rights, is a serious mistake.

(1826)

# AMERICA'S NEED FOR GOD

COMMISSION ON AMERICAN CITIZENSHIP OF

THE CATHOLIC UNIVERSITY OF AMERICA

WHAT America professes to stand for, what America strives for, what America is fighting for, what America dreams, has neither reality nor substance apart from belief in God. We talk of the brotherhood of man, but men are brothers only because there is a common Father in heaven. We dilate on the sacredness of the human personality; but human beings are sacred, not because we say so, but because they are creatures whom God has fashioned according to His image and likeness, redeemed by the precious blood of His Son, and destined for eternal union with Him. We make strong pronouncements in favor of religious freedom; but some of us are so befuddled in our thinking, so obtuse to the dictates of right reason, that we justify on this score the freedom of government to attempt to destroy religion. We would break asunder the shackles that tyranny has forged to enslave mankind; but we fail to take due cognizance of the fact that human liberty can be guaranteed only on the condition that we recognize the authority of God and submit our wills to the yoke of His Commandments. A nation that is forgetful of God, that pays Him but occasional lip service, could easily enough become a nation that is godless, and godlessness never created anything of lasting value. It is a deadly virus that enervates, debilitates, and eventually devastates all that is fine and decent and noble and sacred. . . .

We must rediscover the America that our fathers founded and in which their hopes were vested, the America of faith in God, the America of churches and churchgoing people, the America of men and women and children who pray and walk in the Divine Presence, the America that feeds its intellect on Heavenly Wisdom and not on the husks served up by shallow-minded teachers and writers who lack the education and the mental stamina to understand the American soul and to cling to the American tradition.

The peace that the world can give is at the very best an armistice; lasting peace can be achieved only under the banner of the Prince of Peace. In Him alone will God gather up the things that are scattered. In Him alone can all things be restored. America can become an effective instrument for this Eternal purpose only in the degree that she accepts His leadership and lives and moves and has her being in His Grace. . . .

Our faith is for us the key to the riddle of life and living. It enables us to glimpse the unity that underlies all variety and to understand the meaning of what would otherwise be meaningless. Our faith is the yoke that emancipates our minds from the thralldom of ignorance and error and doubt. We are not as children tossed about by every wind of doctrine. We are rooted and founded in reality—the reality of the supernatural.

Our mission is to make the power of the supernatural felt and insistently felt in whatever we are doing. We will have failed in the degree that we conform ourselves to the spirit of this world. It is our duty, not only our religious duty but our patriotic duty, to translate our education into a quality of living worthy of the vocation into which we may be called. The diplomas of our schools are not just bits of parchment; they are marching orders from the Prince of Peace. Essentially, every Christian is another Christ going about doing good and bringing salvation to his fellow man.

(1943)

## DUTIES OF THE CATHOLIC CITIZEN

### RT. REV. JOHN A. RYAN

ACCORDING to his abilities and opportunities, every Catholic must promote the welfare of the Church as a society in all its relations. All other members of the Church are his brothers in Christ. They are all organically united—members of a living body of which Christ is the Head. Therefore, the individual Catholic is obliged not merely to love his fellow Catholics as individuals but to further the welfare of the Christian brotherhood as such, as the supernatural body from which all derive their unity and spiritual goods and benefits. . . .

Every citizen has both the right and the duty to bring about the repeal of unjust legislation. A Catholic citizen would have the right and the duty to oppose any unjust laws aimed at the rights of the Church or of individual Catholics. Catholic citizens may properly appeal to legislators and to candidates for office, may threaten to vote against and actually vote against candidates who support legislation

273

of this kind; but they do not need to organize themselves into a Catholic political party. Neither the Church as such nor the Catholic body as such should identify itself with or give its constant support to any partisan organization of a political character. This kind of political action the Holy Father has forbidden to Catholic Action. Nor should local Catholic bodies, such as a parish or a group of parishes, commit themselves to the general support of one political party rather than another. While such a course may sometimes seem to be beneficial, in the long run the advantages are more than offset by the disadvantages. . . .

The Catholic citizen . . . is morally bound to make use of the electoral franchise. From the performance of this duty he can be excused only by a correspondingly grave inconvenience. Since public officials possess great power either to harm or to benefit the community, those who select them are charged with grave responsibility.

The Catholic citizen is also obligated to vote intelligently and honestly. He does wrong when he casts his ballot for incompetent or corrupt candidates on the lazy assumption that their opponents are just as bad, or because he desires to put a friend or a fellow Catholic into office. Legal justice obliges the voter to exercise the franchise always for the common good, not for private advantage.

Finally, the Catholic citizen is morally bound to acquaint himself, so far as he reasonably can, with the merits of candidates and with the public policies which promote the common good. He should vote only for those candidates who understand and advocate the right policies in the halls of the legislature. Lawmakers need to possess something more than elementary honesty. They must know the measures that are best for the common welfare and must have the ability to advocate and the courage to fight for them. Therefore, the voter is under obligation to pay specific attention to these qualifications in making his choice among legislative candidates.

(1941)

THE man to be elected should be the best man for the task, not necessarily the person with the finest character, or the most full of charity.

ST. THOMAS AQUINAS (ca. 1270)

# CHRISTIAN HEROISM
## AND THE CHRISTIAN CITIZEN

### JACQUES MARITAIN

WHILE the Church itself, above all anxious not to become an adjunct of any one particular system, has been more and more freed, not from the necessity of judging things from above, but of administering and directing the temporal things of this world, the individual Christian finds himself more and more engaged in exactly these things, not so much as a member of the Church, but as a citizen of the earthly city, i.e. as a *Christian citizen,* conscious of the task incumbent upon him of working for the inauguration of a new secular order. . . .

Since it is clear that social Christianity is inseparable from spiritual Christianity, it is impossible that a vitally Christian transformation of the temporal order can take place in the same way or by the same means as other temporal transformations and revolutions. If this is to be it will be a fruit of Christian heroism.

"The social revolution will be moral or it will be nothing." This famous saying of Charles Péguy can be entirely misunderstood. "It does not mean that before a reform of the social order can be made effective all men must first be converted to virtuous living. Interpreted in that way, the saying would be merely a pharisaical pretext for avoiding any effort at social reform. Revolutions are the work of comparatively small groups of men who devote all their energies to the task: it is to these men that the words of Péguy are addressed. His meaning is: you can only transform the social order of the modern world by effecting at the same time and first of all within your own soul a renewal of moral and spiritual life: by digging down to the moral and spiritual foundations of human existence, and reviving the moral ideas that govern the life of the social body as such; and by awakening a new impulse in the secret sources of its being. . . .

"But has the true and perfect heroism, the heroism of love, no lesson to offer? Once the Christian conscience comes to realize the essential character of social life, with its distinctive being and reality and technique, will not Christian sanctity have to enter and labor in the field in which the Hammer and Sickle and the Fasces and the Swastika are severally pursuing their heroic task? Is it not high time that sanctity should descend from the heaven of cloistered life that four centuries of the baroque spirit had reserved for it, descend to the world of secular culture and labor in social and political affairs with a view to the reform of the temporal order of mankind? Yes, indeed; on condition that it retains its sanctity and does not lose its character on the way. There is the rub.

"The Christian body has at such a time as ours two opposite dangers that it needs avoid: the danger of seeking sanctity only in the desert, and the danger of forgetting the need of the desert for sanctity; the danger of enclosing in the cloister of the interior life and of private virtue the heroism it ought to share among mankind, and the danger of conceiving this heroism, when it overflows into social life and endeavors to transform it, in the same manner as its materialist opponents: according to a purely external standard; which is to pervert and dissipate it. Christian heroism has not the same sources as heroism of other kinds. It has its sources in the heart of a God scourged and turned to scorn and crucified outside the city gate.

"It is time for Christian sanctity again as in the centuries of the Middle Ages to put its hand to the things of earth but with the consciousness that its strength and majesty are from elsewhere and of another order." [1]

A vitally Christian social renewal will thus be a work of sanctity or it will be nothing: a sanctity, that is, which has turned its energies on the things of time, of this world, of secular culture. Has the world not known heretofore leaders of the people who were saints? If a new Christendom is to arise in history it will be the work of such leaders and such sanctity.

(1936)

# AMERICAN CATHOLICS

## THE CATHOLIC BISHOPS
### OF THE UNITED STATES

WE repudiate . . . the assertion that we need to lay aside any of our devotedness to our Church to be true Americans, and the insinuation that we need to abate any of our love for our country's principles and institutions, to be faithful Catholics. To argue that the Catholic

[1] *Freedom in the Modern World*, pp. 142, 144, 145, by Jacques Maritain.

Church is hostile to our great Republic, because she teaches that "there is no power but from God" (Rom. xiii, 1); because, therefore, back of the events which led to the formation of the Republic, she sees the Providence of God leading to that issue, and back of our country's laws the authority of God as their sanction,—this is evidently so illogical and contradictory an accusation, that we are astonished to hear it advanced by persons of ordinary intelligence. We believe that *our country's heroes were the instruments of the God of nations* in establishing this home of freedom; to both the Almighty and to His instruments in the work we look with grateful reverence; and to maintain the inheritance of freedom which they left us, should it ever—which God forbid—be imperiled, our Catholic citizens will be found to stand forward as one man, ready to pledge anew "their lives, their fortunes, and their sacred honor."

No less illogical would be the notion, that there is aught in the *free spirit of our American institutions,* incompatible with perfect docility to the Church of Christ. The spirit of American freedom is not one of anarchy or of license. It essentially involves love of order, respect for rightful authority, and obedience to just laws. There is nothing in the character of the most liberty-loving American, which could hinder his reverential submission to the Divine Authority of Our Lord, or to the like authority delegated by Him to His Apostles and His Church. . . .

Narrow, insular, national views and jealousies concerning ecclesiastical authority and Church organization, may have sprung naturally enough from the selfish policy of certain rulers and nations in by-gone times; but they find no sympathy in the spirit of the true American Catholic. His natural instincts, no less than his religious training, would forbid him to submit in matters of Faith to the dictation of the State or to any merely human authority whatsoever. He accepts the religion and the Church that are from God, and he knows well that these are universal, not national or local,—destined for all the children of men and not for any special tribe or tongue.

We glory that we are, and with God's blessing, shall continue to be, not the American Church, nor the Church of the United States, nor a Church in any other sense exclusive or limited, but an integral part of the one, holy, Catholic and Apostolic Church of Jesus Christ, which is the Body of Christ, in which there is no distinction of classes and nationalities—in which all are one in Jesus Christ (Gal.iii,28).

(1884)

# ALFRED E. SMITH DEFENDS HIS
# RECORD AND HIS FAITH

## CHARLES C. MARSHALL, ESQ.

Dear Sir:

In your open letter to me in the April *Atlantic Monthly* you "impute" to American Catholics views which, if held by them, would leave open to question the loyalty and devotion to this country and its Constitution of more than twenty million American Catholic citizens. I am grateful to you for defining this issue in the open and for your courteous expression of the satisfaction it will bring to my fellow citizens for me to give "a disclaimer of the convictions" thus imputed. Without mental reservation I can and do make that disclaimer. These convictions are held neither by me nor by any other American Catholic, as far as I know. . . .

My first thought was to answer you with just the faith that is in me. But I knew instinctively that your conclusions could be logically proved false. It seemed right, therefore, to take counsel with someone schooled in the Church law, from whom I learned whatever is hereafter set forth in definite answer to the theological questions you raise. I selected one whose patriotism neither you nor any other man will question. He wears upon his breast the Distinguished Service Medal, the Ribbon of the Legion of Honor, and the Croix de Guerre with Palm of the French Republic. He was the Catholic Chaplain of the almost wholly Catholic 165th Regiment in the World War— Father Francis P. Duffy, now in the military service of my own State.

Taking your letter as a whole and reducing it to commonplace English, you imply that there is conflict between religious loyalty to the Catholic faith and patriotic loyalty to the United States. Everything that has actually happened to me during my long public career leads me to know that no such thing as that is true. I have taken an oath of office in this State nineteen times. Each time I swore to defend and maintain the Constitution of the United States. All of this represents a period of public service in elective office almost continuous since 1903. I have never known any conflict between my official duties and my religious belief. No such conflict could exist. Certainly the people of this State recognize no such conflict. They have testified to my devotion to public duty by electing me to the highest office within their gift four times. You yourself do me the honor, in addressing me, to refer to "your fidelity to the morality you have advocated in public and private life and to the religion you have revered; your great record of public trusts successfully and honestly discharged." During the years I have discharged these trusts I have been a communicant of the Roman Catholic Church. If there were conflict, I, of all men, could not have escaped it, because I have not been a silent man, but a battler for social and political reform. These battles would in their very nature disclose this conflict if there were any. . . .

I did not struggle for these things for any single element, but in the interest of all the eleven million people who make up the State. In all of this work I had the support of the churches of all denominations. I probably know as many ecclesiastics of my Church as any other layman. During my long and active public career I never received from any of them anything except cooperation and encouragement in the full and complete discharge of my duty to the State. Moreover, I am unable to understand how anything that I was taught to believe as a Catholic could possibly be in conflict with what is good citizenship. The essence of my faith is built upon the Commandments of God. The law of the land is built upon the Commandments of God. There can be no conflict between them. . . .

I know your imputations are false when I recall the long list of other public servants of my faith who have loyally served the State. You as a lawyer will probably agree that the office of Chief Justice of the United States is second not even to that of the President in its influence on the national development and policy. That court by its interpretation of the Federal Constitution is a check not only upon the President himself but upon Congress as well. During one-fourth of its history it has been presided over by two Catholics, Roger Brooke Taney and Edward Douglas White. No one has suggested that the official conduct of either of these men was affected by an unwarranted religious influence or that religion played with them any part other than it should play in the life of every God-fearing man.

And I know your imputations are false when I recall the tens of thousands of young Catholics who have risked and sacrificed their lives in defense of our country. These fundamentals of life could not be true unless your imputations are false.

But wishing to meet you on your own ground, I address myself to your definite questions, against which I have thus far made only general statements. I must first call attention to the fact that you often divorce sentences from their context in such a way as to give them something other than their real meaning. I will specify. You refer to the Apostolic Letter of Pope Leo XIII as "declaring to the world that orders of the Church of England were void, her priests not priests," and so forth. You say that this was the "strange fruit" of the toleration of England to the Catholics. You imply that the Pope gratuitously issued an affront to the Anglican Church. In fact, this Apostolic Letter was an answer to a request made at the instance of priests of the Anglican Church for recognition by the Roman Catholic Church of the validity of their priestly orders. The request was based on the ground that they had been ordained in succession from the Roman Catholic priests who became the first priests of the Anglican Church. The Apostolic Letter was a mere adverse answer to this request, ruling that Anglican priests were not Roman Catholic priests, and was in no sense the gratuitous insult which you suggest it to be. It was not directed against England or citizens of that Empire.

Again, you quote from the *Catholic Encyclopedia* that my Church "regards dogmatic intolerance, not alone as her incontestable right, but as her sacred duty." And you say that these words show that Catholics are taught to be politically, socially, and intellectually intolerant of all other people. If you had read the whole of that article in the *Catholic Encyclopedia*, you would know that the real meaning of these words is that for Catholics alone the Church recognizes no deviation from complete acceptance of its dogma. These words are used in a chapter dealing with that subject only. The very same article in another chapter dealing with toleration toward non-Catholics contains these words: "The intolerant man is avoided as much as possible by every high-minded person. . . . The man who is tolerant in every emergency is alone lovable." The phrase "dogmatic intolerance" does not mean that Catholics are to be dogmatically intolerant of other people, but merely that inside the Catholic Church they are to be intolerant of any variance from the dogma of the Church.

Similar criticism can be made of many of your quotations. But, beyond this, by what right do you ask me to assume responsibility for every statement that may be made in any encyclical letter? As you will find in the *Catholic Encyclopedia* (vol. V, p. 414), these encyclicals are not articles of our faith. The Syllabus of Pope Pius IX, which you quote on the possible conflict between Church and State, is declared by Cardinal Newman to have "no dogmatic force." You seem to think that Catholics must be all alike in mind and in heart, as though they had been poured into and taken out of the same mold. You have no more right to ask me to defend as part of my faith every statement coming from a prelate than I should have to ask you to accept as an article of your religious faith every statement of an Episcopal bishop, or of your political faith every statement of a President of the United States. So little are these matters of the essence of my faith that I, a devout Catholic since childhood, never heard of them until I read your letter. Nor can you quote from the canons of our faith a syllable that would make us less good citizens than non-Catholics. In fact and in truth, I have been taught the spirit of tolerance, and when you, Mr. Marshall, as a Protestant Episcopalian, join with me in saying the Lord's Prayer, we both pray, not to "My Father," but to "Our Father." . . .

You claim that the Roman Catholic Church holds that, if conflict arises, the Church should prevail over the State. You write as though there were some Catholic authority or tribunal to decide with respect to such conflict. Of course there is no such thing. As Dr. Ryan writes: "The Catholic doctrine concedes, nay, maintains, that the State is co-ordinate with the Church and equally independent and supreme in its own distinct sphere."

What is the Protestant position? The Articles of Religion of your Protestant Episcopal Church (XXXVII) declare: "The Power of the Civil Magistrate extendeth to all men, as well Clergy as Laity, in all things temporal; but hath no authority in things purely spiritual."

Your Church, just as mine, is voicing the injunction of our common Saviour to render unto Caesar the things that are Caesar's, and unto God the things that are God's. . . .

Our Supreme Court has marked out the spheres of influence of Church and State in a case from which you quote copiously, *Watson v. Jones*, Wall. 729; but you refrain from quoting this statement:

"The right to organize voluntary religious associations, to assist in the expression and dissemination of any religious doctrine, and to create tribunals for the decision of controverted questions of faith within the association, and for the ecclesiastical government of all of the individual members, the congregation and officers within the general association, is unquestioned. . . . It is of the essence of these religious unions and of their right to establish tribunals for the decision of questions arising among themselves that those decisions could be binding in all cases of ecclesiastical cognizance, subject only to such appeal as the organism itself provides for."

281

That is the State's attitude toward the Church. Archbishop Ireland thus puts the Church's attitude toward the State:

"To the Catholic obedience to law is a religious obligation, binding in God's name the conscience of the citizen. . . . Both Americanism and Catholicism bow to the sway of personal conscience." . . .

I next come to education. You admit that the Supreme Court guaranteed to Catholics the right to maintain their parochial schools; and you ask me whether they would have so ruled if it had been shown that children in parochial schools were taught that the State should show discrimination between religions, that Protestants should be recognized only as a matter of favor, that they should be intolerant to non-Catholics, and that the laws of the State could be flouted on the ground of the imaginary conflict. My summary answer is: I and all my children went to a parochial school. I never heard of any such stuff being taught or of anybody who claimed that it was. That any group of Catholics would teach it is unthinkable.

You next challenge the action of the Rota in annulling the Marlborough marriage. You suggest that the Rota by annulling the marriage (where the civil courts recognized it, but granted only a divorce) is interfering with the civil jurisdiction. That might be so if anybody claimed that the decree of the Rota had any effect under the laws of America, or any other nation of the world. But you must know that it has no such effect and that nobody claims it has. The decree merely defined the status of the parties as communicants of the Church. Your Church refuses to recognize the ecclesiastical validity of divorces granted by the civil tribunals. Your Church has its tribunals to administer its laws for the government of its members as communicants of your Church. But their decrees have no bearing upon the status of your members as citizens of the United States. There is no difference in that respect between your tribunals and the Rota. . . .

I summarize my creed as an American Catholic. I believe in the worship of God according to the faith and practice of the Roman Catholic Church. I recognize no power in the institutions of my Church to interfere with the operations of the Constitution of the United States or the enforcement of the law of the land. I believe in absolute freedom of conscience for all men and in equality of all churches, all sects, and all beliefs before the law as a matter of right and not as a matter of favor. I believe in the absolute separation of Church and State and in the strict enforcement of the provisions of the Constitution that Congress shall make no law respecting an establishment of religion or prohibiting the free exercise thereof. I believe that no tribunal of any church has any power to make any decree of any force in the law of the land, other than to establish the status of its own communicants within its own church. I believe in the support of the public school as one of the corner stones of American liberty. I believe in the right of every parent to choose whether his child shall be educated in the public school or in a religious school supported by those of his own faith. I believe in the principle of noninterference by this country in the internal affairs of other nations and that we should stand steadfastly against any such interference by whomsoever it may be urged. And I believe in the common brotherhood of man under the common fatherhood of God.

In this spirit I join with my fellow Americans of all creeds in a fervent prayer that never again in this land will any public servant be challenged because of the faith in which he has tried to walk humbly with his God.

Very truly yours,

ALFRED E. SMITH

(1927)

OUR Constitution is the charter of all that is distinctively American in our national spirit. That document was written in a period as pagan as the Christian centuries had up to that time known. Yet, providentially, that charter of ordered liberty was not written in the pagan spirit of that day.

EDWARD CARDINAL MOONEY (1938)

## AMERICAN CREDO

### FRANCIS CARDINAL SPELLMAN

I BELIEVE in America.
In her high destiny under God to stand before the people of the earth as a shining example of unselfish devotion to the ideals that have, under God, made us a great nation; the Christian ideal of liberty in harmonious unity; builded of respect for God's image in man and every man's right to life, liberty, and happiness.

I believe in America.
For the blood in the veins of America, our heart's blood comes from

the wounds of many peoples, chaliced in humanity's name upon the altar of liberty.

I believe in America.

Not because of the tremendous resources of her fields and mountains, rivers and lakes, valleys and plains, but rather because America has been and must ever continue to be, under God, the Beacon of Liberty, the Hope of the Oppressed, the Refuge of the Weak, the Pledge and the Proof that humanity can live in mutual respect based on the law of God, voiced through the conscience of man, and in mutual esteem, based on the responsibility of democratic life.

Lastly, I believe in America.

Because I believe in God and God's Providence that has been over us from the earliest days of our beginning. Believing in God, I am confident both of His merciful forgiveness of our national sins and His awareness of our national virtues. Believing in God's Providence, I am confident of our high resolve that this fair land, the visible setting of the vast, immaterial soul of the American nation, shall never lose its initial consecration to the common Fatherhood of God, so that we and our children's children shall live in peace and harmony among ourselves and with our neighbors. In this America, I believe; for this America, I live; for this America, I and millions of others would stand ready to die.

(1943)

## CATHOLICS AND AMERICANISM

### JAMES CARDINAL GIBBONS

SIXTEEN millions of Catholics live their lives in our land with undisturbed belief in the perfect harmony existing between their religion and their duties as American citizens. . . .

The separation of Church and State in this country seems to me the natural, inevitable, and best conceivable plan, that one that would work best among us, both for the good of religion and of the State. Any change in their relations they [American Catholics] would contemplate with dread. . . .

Of this body of American Citizens living such a life and imbued with such sentiments (of which there are almost as many proofs as there are Catholics) two synods of Protestant ministers have deemed it just and wise to proclaim to the country that Catholics cannot be trusted with political office; that they cannot sincerely subscribe to the Federal Constitution; that their loyalty is illogical, being contrary to the teaching of the Church; that their religion is opposed to American liberties; and that they themselves, kept in the dark by their religious guides, are ignorant of the true nature of their Church's doctrines. In sounding forth these charges to American Catholics, and to the country in general, they declare themselves inspired, not by religious antagonism or the desire to profit by a good opportunity, but solely by patriotic solicitude for the permanence of American institutions.

The Catholic religion, as they understand it, is in conflict with the Federal Constitution, and with the object of our institutions; Catholics, then, ought not to be trusted with political office. . . . It would logically be desirable to deny the Catholics the right to vote, and with men in the frame of mind their attitude suggests, the realization of this desire in the statute books, and of their complete program, would only be a matter of their possessing sufficient power and judging the act politically expedient. . . .

The distinction between the civil and ecclesiastical powers is very firmly established in Catholic teaching. "The Almighty," says Pope Leo XIII, "has appointed the charge of the human race between two powers, the ecclesiastical and the civil; the one being set over divine, the other over human things. Each in its kind is supreme, each has fixed limits which are defined by the nature and special object of the province of each."

Pius XI approved a pastoral of the Swiss Bishops which teaches the same doctrine, that civil magistrates are "invested in their own domain with a full sovereignty," and that to them "we owe obedience and respect in all things morally permitted and belonging to the domain of civil society." This is but common Catholic doctrine. . . .

This distinction of the two spheres or zones of authority, as I may call them, lying in the very nature of their object, remains even if all the members of the State be Catholics. Cardinal Tarquini, a Jesuit writer of authority, states this clearly. "Civil society," he says, "even though every member of it be a Catholic, is not subject to the Church, but plainly independent in temporal things which regard its temporal end. . . . This is proved by reason. For, whatsoever is done in temporal matters, having in view a temporal end, is outside the domain of the Church. Now, it is a general rule that no society has power beyond its own scope. . . . Hence it follows that the State, although it be composed of Catholics, yet in temporal matters, is by no means subordinate to the Church, but quite independent of her."

The establishment and maintenance of this distinction is one of the greatest contributions of the Catholic Church to civilization. . . . To the long struggle of the Papacy during the Middle Ages it is due that Christianity has not sunk into Byzantine servitude. Guizot, the Protestant historian and statesman, gives to the Popes the credit for having "proclaimed and maintained the difference between Church and State, the distinction of the two societies of the two powers, of their respective domains and rights." . . .

When the Reformers rejected the authority of the Church, the distinction between the two powers was lost to them. . . . Lutheranism, so bold in its first outburst, became the creature of the civil powers before Luther's death; it remains so to this day. Zwingli handed over religion to the care of the civil powers. Calvin went to the other extreme. He attempted a theocracy, failed, and his religion was likewise admitted to the keeping of the State. Every National Protestant Church has been the creature of the State, subject to it in doctrine, ritual, discipline, and government. . . .

The history of the Schismatical Churches of the East repeats the same story. The Patriarchate of Constantinople was first the creature of the Byzantine Emperors, and then of the Mohammedan Sultan. The Church of Russia was the servant of the Tsar. The churches of the Balkan states, each in turn, broke away from the Patriarchs of Constantinople with the cry, "No head but Christ," only to fall under the despotism of the State.

If history points a lesson, then, it shows that the subjection of the religious to the secular authority has ever followed separation from the Church of Rome. Now it will be objected that if Protestantism leans too much towards subservience to the State, the Catholic Church, on the other hand, has too often acted strongly against the State, especially in the Middle Ages. I grant it, but I hold it was justified by the consent of nations, and the public law of that day. . . .

"It is impossible," says the Anglican Dean Milman, "to conceive what had been the confusion, the lawlessness, the chaotic state of the Middle Ages without the Medieval Papacy." . . .

But is there not a twilight zone over which both Church and State put forth claims? True; and I grant that here a collision of authorities comes more within the horizon of possibility. But the American concept of government and of liberty puts this hypothesis outside the range of practical affairs. That concept, as I understand it, is that the Government should leave as large a liberty as possible to individuals and to bodies within the State, only intervening in the interests of morality, justice and the common weal. There are forces at work in this country, I know, that tend to paternalism and Caesarism in government; but true Americanism recognizes that these forces would bring disaster on American liberties. So long as these liberties, under which we have prospered, are preserved in their fullness there is, I assert, no danger of a collision between the State and the Catholic Church. . . .

"But," many Protestants say, "we obey our consciences; you obey the Pope." Yes; we obey the Pope, for our consciences tell us that we ought to obey the spiritual authority of the Pope in everything except what is sinful. "But," they reply, "we do not believe that any human power should come between the human conscience and duty." Neither do we; but while you believe in private judgment, we believe in a religion of authority which our conscience tells us is our lawful guide and teacher in its own sphere. You say that you believe in religious freedom. Do you, however, interpret this freedom to apply only to yourselves; or are you willing to conceive that to others likewise is to be left the freedom to follow their consciences? You can conceive a State passing laws that would violate your conscientious convictions. Would you accept these laws, or would you resist them as your fellow-religionists in England recently resisted an education law of which they did not approve? I think you would not prove false to your religious convictions.

Were the State to compel the Orthodox Jews to accept the Sunday for the Sabbath, or abandon certain Levitical observances which are sacred in their eyes, they would not be worth their salt if they did not resist this encroachment on their rights. Similarly, for example, if the State should forbid us Catholics to continue our parochial schools, we should resist to the uttermost: for we hold that, while the State has the undoubted right to compel her future citizens to receive a certain degree of education, she has no right to deprive them of the daily religious influence which we deem necessary for their spiritual and eternal welfare, as well as for their proper training in the duties of citizenship. In any such essay by the State to establish Caesarism, Catholics would behave precisely as any other conscientious body would behave. They would not think it necessary to await instructions from any source. We believe in the sacredness of and supremacy of conscience; and rulers of the world, from Nero to Clemenceau, have found the Catholic conscience to be a wall of adamant. . . .

American Catholics rejoice in our separation of Church and State; and I can conceive of no combination of circumstances likely to arise which should make such a union desirable either to Church or State. We know the blessings of our present arrangement; it gives us liberty and binds together priests and people in a union far better than that of Church and State. Other countries, other manners; we do not believe our system is adapted to all conditions; we leave it to Church and State in other lands to solve their problems for their best interests. For ourselves, we thank God we live in America, "in this happy land of ours," to quote Mr. Roosevelt, where "religion and liberty are natural allies."

(1909)

## RELIGION AND CITIZENSHIP

### THE CATHOLIC BISHOPS OF THE UNITED STATES

HUMAN life centers in God. The failure to center life in God is secularism . . . the most deadly menace to our Christian and American way of life. . . .

To combat secularism the individual Christian must get the full vision of Christian truth. It is not divisible. One cannot pick and choose from it. Either it is accepted as a whole or it counts for little in real life. . . .

Much of the confusion and chaos about us is attributable more directly to the inaction of the Christian than to the effectiveness of the feverish efforts of the destroyers. . . . The crisis is at hand. Today every Christian must face the full Christian vision and with no thought of compromise must seek vigorously to live it. . . . The reconstruction must start with the individual. He must be vigorously Christian in thought and action—in the home, in the training of his children, in his office or workshop, and in his community. . . .

The inroads of secularism in civil life are a challenge to the Christian citizen—and indeed to every citizen with definite religious convictions. The essential connection between religion and good citizenship is deep in our American tradition. Those who took the lead in establishing our independence and framing our Constitution were firm and explicit in the conviction that religion and morality are the strong supports of national well-being, that national morality can not long prevail in the absence of religious principle, and that impartial encouragement of religious influence on its citizens is a proper and practical function of good government.

(1948)

# THE SPIRIT OF CHARITY IN
# THE TEMPORAL ORDER

## THE REV. JOHN COURTNEY MURRAY, S.J.

THE Church does not and cannot want her own unity, much less the structures that preserve it, to be reflected in the earthly city; the point has recently been emphatically made by Pius XII in a series of discourses to the Roman Rota, begun in 1945. The Church does, however, want the city to have its own proper unity—its own juridical structure wherein the equal rights and freedoms of citizens will be safeguarded, and its own spirit of civic friendship whereby the high values of human living-together will be ensured. And to this end she is urging her children, as citizens, to employ the *mystique* of unity that is inherent in their faith. There is no more effective weapon against the divisive factors within the city: misunderstanding, jealousies, dissensions between classes, clashes of opposed egotisms, the conflicts between ambitions for power—all the many forms that hostility and hate can take.

I suppose, then, that what the Church ultimately wants in the temporal order is to see there reflected, in civic friendship, the spirit of charity that is the primary expression of her faith. She wants this for the sake of the city, as essential to its good; she wants it, too, as the necessary expression of her own faith. . . .

Obviously, the love of God and neighbor is no substitute for political maturity, or for the high technical competence required in organizing the economic life of man. The Church never said it was. What she says is that without the *mystique* of charity the technique of politics and economics will not be able to do more than tinker with the social machine; it cannot make it run. Again, charity is no substitute for social justice; it does not itself regulate the relations between men as possessors—that is the proper work of justice. But unless the relations between men as persons are regulated—and this is the proper function of charity—their relations as possessors will always be snarled. There is no society, national or international, without civic friendship as its soul. And since the time when political liberalism went beyond its premises and committed the course of society to purely secular dynamics, nothing has happened to convince an intelligent man that society can be ensouled by civic friendship unless civic friendship itself have, as its own soul, the virtue of charity that springs from Christian faith.

(1948)

## THE FALSITY OF A "TRIBAL RELIGION"

### THE MOST REV. JOHN IRELAND

To Bishop Doane, Catholicism is "an alien" in America, objectionable to Americans, because its sovereign pontiff is not an American, living in America. Anson Phelps is sure that Catholicism, to satisfy Americans should have been woven in a loom-room even of Anglo-Americanism. In the late June number of the *Atlantic Monthly* a writer heads his article with this caption: "Reasonable Hopes of American Religion," and actually delineates a creed suitable in his judgment to the people of America.

Faith and morals made in America on a design strictly American! Great and good as is America, it must not arrogate to itself the realm of the Almighty God, that of faith and morals. Shall we call the Almighty God a foreigner? Yet, he is not exclusively the God of America. Shall we call the Saviour of Calvary a foreigner? Yet He was neither a native nor a naturalized American: and His message was— "Teach all nations"—instead of teach only America! And now shall we call the Bishop of Rome a foreigner, "an alien," because he stands before the world the universal teacher, the Vicar of Jesus Christ, teacher of all nations, teacher of the whole human family?

Argue that the Almighty God is not the supreme author and norm of an eternal righteousness, that Jesus Christ is not the proven revealer of the thoughts and the love of Almighty God, that the Bishop of

Rome is not the historic successor of Christ's apostolate—then, counsel, perhaps, you may an American-made Church for Americans, an American-made code of faith and morals. But religion is not a product of the mind of an individual man, or of the environment within which he lives: it is not a sheer human growth, changeable as the seasons of the year, fitful and capricious as the likes and dislikes of man and of peoples.

Religion is the mind and the will of God, existing as God exists, objectively outside of men and of peoples, superior to all men, exacting from man the obedience due by the creature to the Creator. The question is never, what is it that suits a man, or a people, but what is it that God has imposed upon men by the eternal laws of his supreme righteousness, or by the teachings of his historic revelations? What Americans require is not an American-made, but a God-made religion. And so, at the bar of American common sense itself, the proposals of the writer of the *Atlantic Monthly* must only be, as he himself despairingly inclines to term them, "dreams that are the shadows of hopes, hopes that are the shadows of dreams."

The Catholic Church is extra-American, supra-national, begotten for all nations, not for America alone; its supreme pontiff is extra-American, supra-national—a foreigner on no spot of earth's surface, everywhere at home, as the spiritual father of all tribes and of all peoples who seek divine truth from a universal God and a universal Saviour.

And this, the beauty; this, the grandeur of the Catholic Church, that it is Catholic, as the eternal God is Catholic, as the salvation given by Jesus Christ is Catholic. Narrowness, provincialism in religion, in faith and morals, on the first face of things, is a perversion of God's eternal law, and of the revelation given to men 1,900 years ago. The days of tribal religions are past; they must not be revived in America.

(1913)

# LIBERALISM VERSUS CATHOLICISM

EMMET JOHN HUGHES

To view Liberalism as an innocuous political attitude to which most educated and civilized people generally subscribe is to stare unknowingly at a shell drained of its substance. The philosophical pillars of

Liberalism constitute a succession of specific postulates, each of which possesses individual and explicit meaning, each of which was erected on the debris of demolished pillars of past ages and past societies. A specialized philosophical technique was utilized in the construction of those pillars, and the social edifice erected upon them was perpetuated by a specialized institutional technique. The completed structure of Liberalism embodies an autonomous, self-sustaining conception of man's relationship to his God, his universe, his society.

In this sense is Liberalism a faith, and by virtue of this fact it has been forced to fight other faiths. It has, in particular, fought the Catholic faith. . . .

From the day when Luther had arraigned a corrupt Church before the bar of an untarnished past, men had moved swiftly to the day when God Himself was summoned before the bar of Reason.

It was an age of dynamic transition, impossible to categorize by fixed stages of development. As Carl Becker has so clearly stated the issue, most men dispensed with any deep fear of God, but maintained a respectful attitude toward an impersonal, mechanical Prime Mover. They disavowed Genesis, but held a faith in a perfectly coordinated universe. They ridiculed the conception of a Garden of Eden, but exalted a similar, though less concrete, state of Nature. They repudiated the authority of both Church and Bible, but avowed a pure and abiding faith in Nature and Reason. They scorned theology and metaphysics, but revered the title of philosopher. They dismantled Heaven until it became something like a Christian Nirvana, but retained a misty faith in the immortality of the soul. They discussed atheism—but not before the servants; they pled for tolerance—but never tolerated priests. They challenged the right of others to derive the assumption of a perfect next-life from an imperfect this-life, but they indulged themselves the faith in a perfect society in the future of man's earthly existence. They scorned miracles, but they believed in the perfectibility of man. . . .

Yet beneath all this intellectual ferment, there came the rising consciousness that it did not suffice to condemn the Christian God—that to build was as imperative as to destroy. To forge a new faith, two instruments already have been uncovered. From the domain of science, men had learned of Nature; the word, the idea, the ideal. And having explored the realm of theology and metaphysics, men emerged with faith in but one thing, Reason: a clean, bright, new instrument which would scatter the hoary hosts of superstition, intolerance and injustice—and would clear the path for all mankind to the solid, true and good world that was to be the future. . . .

The Liberal faith, from the realms of science and metaphysics, had evolved two of its cardinal principles: Nature and Reason. In the construction of its social philosophy, both these precepts were applied and a third added: Humanity. These three—Nature, Reason, and Humanity—became the Trinity of the Liberal's world of ideas. . . .

In retrospect, one can see to what degree the Reformation era had signalized the first militant movement of the forces that were to make the new order. Total assault on a Church which had been the stone and cement of a whole social structure meant, logically and inevitably, the wreckage of that structure. The elaborate medieval synthesis of ideas and values was shattered. Totally and irreparably it was broken by the detachment and isolation of man's conception of his relationship to fellow men. A man's religion became a personalized experience in which there were but two participants, God and the man himself; God distant and omnipotent, man weak and depraved. In this conception of religion, man's role in society could find little or no place: religion became an "internal" matter, the affairs of the world were "external" issues, and between the two was no spiritual bond. In the final analysis, everything in society would instruct and arrange itself, as Luther had said; and if it did not, the poor could still follow Luther's prescription to go and seek their riches in the earth. Thus the Reformation achieved the *sina qua non* of the Liberal Society: emancipation of the problem of man's relationship to man in society from the effective dominion of religion. . . .

The picture of a natural world governed by natural laws and a Divinity whose decrees and very existence stood beyond the reaches of reason—such a combined picture left only a central void, and the traditional religious allegiances of men were not of tough enough fiber to bridge that gulf. In this fashion, these two ideas united in forcing the exile of the Christian God from the realm of the known, rational world. If He existed, at best he was *Deus Emeritus*. . . .

Philosophic individualism and economic individualism were currents that flowed from the same central stream. Both the philosopher and the man of business sought to exploit his own realm on his own terms, and both were supremely confident that the harvest would be almost boundless. Once men had accepted the axiom that the individual was capable of realizing his own spiritual salvation, the next step was already half-taken: the individual was equally competent to

293

attain his own *economic* salvation. Neither religious dogma nor state regulations, neither Church councils nor state boards of trade, could inhibit the individual in the cultivation of his own garden. As it had been stated so succinctly, let there be "freedom of conscience in trade." Hence, in a sense Adam Smith completes an evolution that was continuous from the Reformation. . . .

In its final form the Liberal faith became the rationale of industrial capitalism. It has divested itself of the disorder and contradiction of much of the intellectual legacy of the Enlightenment. It is basically a simple faith. Pragmatism is its hope; fatalism is its apology. On the one hand, through the self-interested and unfettered pursuit of material gain, the good society is promised to come to pass. On the other hand, there is nothing society can do for those who fall and cry out as the human herd rushes over them. They are but the unfortunates who have been caught in the whirling wheels of a machine which no one can control, which no one should control, and whose only sure end is to maintain the dominion of the bourgeoisie. They are, moreover, abnormalities—exceptions proving the rule of the basic harmony of self-interest and social welfare. . . .

The basic ingredient of the Liberal faith of the eighteenth century has turned upon its intellectual sponsors. The Liberal's conception of the universe and the God he derived therefrom; confidence in the positive good implicit in scientific invention; conception of man's rational nature, his essential equality with fellow-man, his inalienable natural rights—all this the changing content of the scientific revelation has ultimately not only failed to sustain, but in many cases has actively attacked. Having climbed skyward on the golden rungs of the ladder of the new science, the Liberal faith came to rest upon a cloud—suddenly to find itself without any means of descending again to the realm of reality.

Consecration of the individual as the supreme judge of truth and the final arbiter of all social issues has left the Liberal Society powerless to defend its own faith. Satisfied with a definition of liberty in terms of emancipation from social or religious disciplines, the Liberal has felt obligated, by the phraseology of his own creed, to accord to others the right and freedom to destroy what he himself maintains to be true.

From men conceived as ever rational and innately good, with the prescriptions of virtue indelibly inscribed upon their hearts—from men such as these there was no just reason for withholding the right to sit as final judges on all social action. There could not exist for them,

294

nor could they be bound by, any superior standard of moral absolutes on any uncontingent code of social ethics. . . .

The political logic of the Liberal creed was as tragically constructed as its economic dialectic. The Liberal was traditionally militant in his opposition to political tyranny, his support of representative government. Having effectively denied the Christian conception of original sin and the concomitant doctrine of man's corruption and fallibility, the Liberal could defend representative government only by his assertion of the virtual infallibility of the individual (and the "common man"). It was by exactly the opposite doctrine that Christian social thought measured and denounced political tyranny—the fallibility of all men, and the consequent necessity of circumscribing the political authority of society's leaders. Besides this, the Liberal doctrine of ubiquitous human infallibility was wistful and wishing. More than that, it was fatal: as the fallacy of insistence on the infallibility of the "common man" became ever more evident, extreme reaction was bound to develop—in the form of Fascism. The terrible, repetitious tragedy of the Liberal faith was enacted here again: not its announced political doctrines, but the philosophical premises on which the Liberal sought to predicate them, proved insubstantial and essentially false.

Working from within the framework of the Liberal Society, these political and economic ideas propelled the process of attrition in three ways. First, the individualism of Liberal economics degenerated into a chaos of competitive greeds; economic inequalities multiplied, avarice became chronic. With freedom converted into a cloak for economic anarchy, the day was fast approaching when men would tear that cloak to shreds—and care little how fine the cloth from which it once was cut might have been. Secondly, with civil liberty accepted as the natural right of all men, uncontingent upon their respect for positive and explicit social ideals, that liberty allowed itself to become the medium by which its own destruction might be assured. Finally, with the individual accepted as the final judge and a majority of individuals acting as the infallible medium by which such judgment was made articulate, the Liberal in effect, welcomed the possibility that a majority expression of opinion through the electoral process might vote the Liberal state out of existence. . . .

In Christian thought, the supreme fact in the life of the individual was death. In the life of the Liberal state, the climactic experience was suicide.

(1944)

295

Liberalism in religion is the doctrine that there is no positive truth in religion, but that one creed is as good as another, and this is the teaching which is gaining substance and force daily. It is inconsistent with any recognition of any religion, *as true*.

JOHN HENRY CARDINAL NEWMAN (1878)

# THE BLEAGUERED "LIBERAL CATHOLIC"

### WILLIAM P. CLANCY

THE antipathy which the Catholic and the liberal have felt for each other is real, and its causes are basic to the philosophy of each. When Pius IX solemnly condemned "Liberalism" and denied that the Church could, or should, reconcile itself with "Progress" he pronounced the Church's judgment, once and for all, on that doctrinaire rationalism, secularism and anti-clericalism which lay at the base of liberalism's spirit in the 19th century. This condemnation was secretly welcomed by many Continental liberals. . . .

As a result of this, the Catholic who associates himself with some of the struggles which are properly identified as "liberal," and who, consequently, gains a reputation as a *liberal* Catholic, is apt to find himself suspect among large numbers of his co-religionists. For them, the idea of a Catholic allying himself in any cause with the traditional enemies of the Church suggests a Catholic whose orthodoxy is at best doubtful, and whose loyalty is obviously weak. Certain Catholic journalists spend a lot of their time damning the "liberals," and when they find a "liberal Catholic," they feel sure that they've found a "so-called" Catholic.

But if a "liberal Catholic" is often viewed with suspicion by some of his fellow Catholics, his lot is even less happy among the liberals. The professional liberal is, of course, glad to find an occasional ally among the orthodox, but he is also surprised—and he is skeptical. To the extent that he trusts the man's liberalism, he tends to doubt his genuine Catholicism. Or, if he is convinced of this, he begins to doubt his liberalism.

The beleaguered "liberal Catholic" thus stands between two worlds which view each other with mutual distrust, and which, according to their proper lights, exclude each other. Those whose theology he shares frequently distrust him because of his politics, and those with whom he feels at home politically may doubt him because of his theology.

The difficulty is partly a semantic one. Probably no Catholic who bears a reputation for "liberalism" welcomes the "liberal Catholic" label. . . . It is essentially a Catholic affirmation of value wherever value is to be found, and an attempt to recover for the Catholic tradition elements which, through default, have been appropriated by movements hostile to the religious spirit. The "liberal Catholic" is a "liberal" only through the accident of liberalism's having struggled for some things which should properly have a Christian name. His efforts are aimed not at compromise but at recovery and redemption.

It is ironic that although many 19th-century liberals actually welcomed the Church's strictures on the modern world, the final victory has belonged to Pius after all. The very things for which he condemned "Liberalism" and "Progress" in the 19th century are also the things which have led to liberalism's bad name in the 20th. Its belief in the inevitability of progress, its overly optimistic estimate of human nature and consequent denial of evil, its dogmatic rationalism—these are ideas turned bitter in the terrible fulfillment of contemporary history. . . .

History has already vindicated the Church's condemnation of "Liberalism" and the vindication may well become increasingly complete. Moral relativism, anti-intellectualism, Rousseauistic optimism, religious indifferentism—all these by-words of historical liberalism have helped to lead us to the precipice on which we now stand. The tragedy of modern history, then, is not the condemnation itself, but rather what so many liberals—and Catholics, have made of the condemnation.

The liberals have taken the condemnation, not only as a rebuke to their philosophy itself, but as a Catholic repudiation of everything for which they have struggled. The Church thus becomes in their eyes not only the enemy of moral relativism, religious indifferentism and dogmatic rationalism; it also becomes the enemy of political liberty, social equality and material progress. It becomes the eternal protector of the status quo, the perpetual tender of inquisitional fires, the vigilant enemy of the city of man. And so the fight for the goals of the city of man—for civil freedom, for social and economic equality, for a pluralistic society—assumes the guise of a struggle against the Church.

The liberals have been assisted toward this interpretation by a good many Catholics who, in their reactions against the philosophical errors condemned by the popes, have tended to identify themselves with reactionary political regimes and social philosophies. Their abhorrence of the anti-religious spirit which poisoned, and unfortunately continues to poison, so much of the liberal outlook has blinded them to the genuinely spiritual and humanitarian value for which liberalism has fought. The result of this double misunderstanding has been the paradox of liberalism's frequently fighting the right battles for the wrong reasons, and Catholics reacting by fighting the wrong battles for the right reasons.

The Church condemned a philosophy of "Liberalism." By extending this to a blanket condemnation of liberals and everything for which they stand, Catholics condemn much that is properly their own, and in reaction espouse things which should be as repugnant to the Christian as they are to the liberal himself.

The outlook frequently described as that of the "liberal Catholic" believes that one of the great hopes for the future lies in the recovery and restoration to a Christian context of all things valuable and true. This does not imply any compromise of the Faith, any trafficking with the theological enemy. It does imply, however, that on many questions of political and social order the individual Catholic may find himself more in sympathy with the viewpoint commonly associated with liberalism than with the sterile reaction to liberalism common among many of his fellow Catholics. Hence the "liberal Catholic" category to which he is frequently assigned. . . .

What the "liberal Catholic" pleads for is that Catholics should become as passionately dedicated to human dignity and freedom as the liberal has been. Liberalism may have fought its battles for the wrong reasons. The Catholic's mission should therefore be to redeem its struggle by supplying the right ones.

(1952)

## SOCIALISM AND CATHOLICISM
## ARE IRRECONCILABLE

### PIUS XI

THE question arises, or is unwarrantably proposed in certain quarters, whether the principles of Christian truth also could not be somewhat

298

moderated and attenuated, so as to meet Socialism, as it were, halfway upon common ground. Some are engaged by the empty hope of gaining in this way the Socialists to our cause. But such hopes are vain. . . .

But what if, in questions of class war and private ownership, Socialism were to become so mitigated and amended, that nothing reprehensible could any longer be found in it? Would it by that very fact have laid aside its character of hostility to the Christian religion? This is a question which holds many minds in suspense. . . . We pronounce as follows: whether Socialism be considered as a doctrine, or as a historical fact, or as a movement, if it really remains Socialism, it cannot be brought into harmony with the dogmas of the Catholic Church, even after it has yielded to truth and justice in the points We have mentioned; the reason being that it conceives human society in a way utterly alien to Christian truth.

According to Christian doctrine, Man, endowed with a social nature, is placed here on earth in order that he may spend his life in society, and under an authority ordained by God, that he may develop and evolve to the full all his faculties to the praise and glory of his Creator; and that, by fulfilling faithfully the duties of his station, he may attain to temporal and eternal happiness. Socialism, on the contrary, entirely ignorant of or unconcerned about this sublime end both of individuals and of society, affirms that living in community was instituted merely for the sake of advantages which it brings to mankind. . . .

The Socialists argue that economic production, of which they see only the material side, must necessarily be carried on collectively, and that because of this necessity men must surrender and submit themselves wholly to society with a view to the production of wealth. Indeed, the possession of the greatest possible amount of temporal goods is esteemed so highly, than man's higher goods, not excepting liberty, must, they claim, be subordinated and even sacrificed to the exigencies of efficient production. . . . Society, therefore, as the Socialist conceives it, is, on the one hand, impossible and unthinkable without the use of compulsion of the most excessive kind; on the other it fosters a false liberty, since in such a scheme no place is found for true social authority, which is not based on temporal and material advantages, but descends from God alone, the Creator and Last End of all things.

If, like all errors, Socialism contains a certain element of truth (and this the Sovereign Pontiffs have never denied), it is nevertheless founded upon a doctrine of human society peculiarly its own, which is opposed to true Christianity. "Religious Socialism," "Christian Socialism" are expressions implying a contradiction in terms. No one can be at the same time a sincere Catholic and a true Socialist.

All that We have thus far laid down and established by Our sovereign authority bears application also to a certain new Socialist phenomenon, hitherto little known, but nowadays common to many sections of Socialism. Its main aim is the formation of minds and manners. Under the appearance of friendship, it attracts little children in particular and attaches them to itself, though its activity extends to all the people, to make them convinced Socialists, upon whom to build society modeled on Socialistic principles. . . .

The formidable dangers which this form of Socialism brings in its train seem to be ignored or underestimated by those who are little concerned to resist it with strength and zeal, as the gravity of the situation demands.

It is the duty of Our pastoral office to warn these men of the grave danger which threatens. Let us bear in mind that the parent of this cultural Socialism was Liberalism, and that its offspring will be Bolshevism.

(May 15, 1931)

## "COMMUNISM IS INTRINSICALLY
## WRONG"

### PIUS XI

ACCORDING to this doctrine [Communism] there is in the world only one reality, matter, the blind forces of which evolve into plant, animal and man. Even human society is nothing but a phenomenon and form of matter, evolving in the same way. By a law of inexorable necessity and through a perpetual conflict of forces, matter moves towards the final synthesis of a classless society. In such a doctrine, as is evident, there is no room for the idea of God; there is no difference between matter and spirit, between soul and body; there is neither survival of the soul after death nor any hope in a future life. Insisting on the dialectical aspect of their materialism, the Communists claim that the conflict which carries the world towards its final synthesis can be accelerated by man. Hence they endeavor to sharpen the antagonisms which arise between the various classes of society. Thus the class-struggle with its consequent violent hate and destruction takes on the aspect of a crusade for the progress of humanity. On the other hand, all other forces whatever, as long as they resist such systematic violence, must be annihilated as hostile to the human race.

Communism, moreover, strips man of his liberty, robs human personality of all of its dignity, and removes all the moral restraints that check the eruptions of blind impulse. There is no recognition of any right of the individual in his relations to the collectivity; no natural right is accorded to human personality, which is a mere cogwheel in the Communist system. . . . Nor is the individual granted any property rights over material goods or the means of production for inasmuch as these are the source of further wealth, their possession would give one man power over another. Precisely on this score, all forms of private property must be eradicated, for they are at the origin of all economic enslavement. . . .

It is a system full of errors and sophisms. It is in opposition both to reason and to divine Revelation. It subverts the social order, because it means the destruction of its foundations; because it ignores the true origin and purpose of the State; because it denies the rights, dignity and liberty of human personality. . . .

It can surprise no one that the Communist fallacy should be spreading in a world already to a large extent de-Christianized. . . .

The enslavement of man despoiled of his rights, the denial of the transcendental origin of the State and its authority, the horrible abuse of public power in the service of a collectivistic terrorism, are the very contrary of all that corresponds with natural ethics and the will of the Creator. . . .

The doctrine of the Church . . . alone in the social as in all other fields can offer real light and assure salvation in the face of Communistic ideology. But this doctrine must be consistently reduced to practice in everyday life. . . . We cherish the firm hope that the fanaticism with which the sons of darkness work day and night at their materialistic and atheistic propaganda will at least serve the holy purpose of stimulating the sons of light to a like and even greater zeal for the honor of the Divine Majesty.

What then must be done, what remedies must be employed to defend Christ and Christian civilization from this pernicious enemy? . . .

As in all the stormy periods of the history of the Church, the fundamental remedy today lies in a sincere renewal of private and public life according to the principles of the Gospel by all those who belong to the Fold of Christ, that they may be in truth the salt of the earth to preserve human society from total corruption. . . .

Communism is intrinsically wrong, and no one who would save Christian civilization may collaborate with it in any undertaking whatsoever.

(March 19, 1937)

"IF the hand you hold out to us is that of the starving, we will give you bread both of body and soul; if that of the wounded, we will bear on our shoulders this fraternal sorrow; if that of the blind, we will guide you towards the light; if that of the despairing disinherited, we will give you peace, joy, hope, and love; but if the hand that you offer is that of the traitor, of the seducer, of the enemy of souls, then in the name of Christ who saved our souls with His Blood we will reject your gesture.

M. LE COUR GRANDMAISON (1938)

# TYRANTS FEAR GOOD MEN

### ST. THOMAS AQUINAS

THE disregard of the common good is greater under an oligarchy than under a democracy, where, after all, the welfare of the majority has been attempted. But sorriest of all is a tyrant where the advantage of one man is sought. As the rule of a king is best, so the rule of a tyrant is worst.

Security is banished and everything is uncertain when people are cut off from law and depend on the will, I would even say the greed, of another. A tyrant oppresses the bodies of his subjects, but, what is more damnable, he threatens their spiritual growth, for he is set on his own power, not their progress. He is suspicious of any dignity they may possess that will prejudice his own iniquitous domination. A tyrant is more fearful of good men than of bad men, for he dreads their strange virtue.

Fearful lest they grow strong and so stout of heart as no longer to brook his wicked despotism, but resolve in companionship to enjoy the fruits of peace, a tyrant is constrained to destroy good men's confidence in one another, lest they band together to throw off his yoke. Therefore he sows discord among them, and encourages dissensions and litigation. He forbids celebrations that make for good fellowship, weddings and feastings and suchlike that are wont to promote familiarity and mutual loyalty.

When they are brought up under such a régime of fear men inevitably degenerate. They become mean-spirited and averse from many and strenuous feats.

(ca. 1270)

# FASCISM

### THE REV. JOHN A. RYAN

FASCISM contradicts the Catholic doctrine on the authority, functions, and purpose of the State, on the natural rights of the individual, and on the means which the State may rightfully use; it rejects the principles of political democracy; and it promotes a spirit of excessive nationalism which is not conducive to international peace. In other words, the Fascist theory is a pragmatic combination of Absolutism, Machiavellianism, Toryism, and Chauvinism.

(ca. 1939)

# EVIL FALLACIES OF COMMUNISM

### MOST REV. FULTON J. SHEEN

IN order to understand the philosophy of Marx one must know at least the general philosophy of Hegel. For Hegel the evolution of the universe is the unfolding of the Idea which is always on its way to self-knowledge. The motive-force of this evolution or progress is through the development of opposites or contradictories. All ideas develop by contradiction and pass through three phases. This development he called dialectics, a term which not only means logic, but also discussion. In a conversation, for example, first one side of the question, and then another will be presented and finally as a result of the conflict of both, one will arrive at a solution. The first stage in the development of the Idea Hegel called the *thesis* or affirmation. This thesis contains within itself its opposite or contradictory which is called the *antithesis*. The third stage which results from the inter-action of both is called the *synthesis,* that is, the uniting of the truth contained in both the thesis and the antithesis. A very imperfect ex-ample of this dialectics which has been used by modern Communists is to call the male of the species the thesis, the female the antithesis, and the human race the synthesis. Another even more imperfect ex-ample used by them is to call the day of twenty-four hours the synthesis resulting from the thesis and antithesis, day and night. A better ex-ample is that of drunkenness which as a *thesis* produces sickness which is *antithesis*. From both results temperance which is the *synthesis*.

Marx was not so much concerned with ideas as he was with the dialectics of ideas. Hegel applied dialectics to ideas; Marx chose to apply it to matter, or in his own words "to stand dialectics on its head" (*Capital,* London, 1930, Vol. 2, p. 873). Marx came to this conclusion from reading Feuerbach's *Essence of Christianity,* which sought to demolish the idealistic basis of theology of Hegel and others. Feuer-bach claimed that there is nothing but matter. "Man is what he eats," said Feuerbach. Marx liked Feuerbach's insistence on matter; and he liked Hegel's dialectical method, but not his idealism. By marrying the dialectical method of Hegel to Feuerbachean materialism, Dia-lectical Materialism was born. Hegel saw contradiction at the heart of all ideas; Marx saw contradiction or dialectics at the heart of all reality. In other words, reality is essentially revolutionary. What dia-lectics is to thought (Hegel), that revolution is to matter (Marx).

The application of Hegel's dialectics to matter gave Marx a new outlook on the universe. Instead of matter being looked upon as dead, inert and lifeless, with no other motion than that communicated to it from the outside, Marx saw it as essentially active and endowed with its own movement. Just as Hegel's dialectics applied to ideas was called dialectical idealism, so Marx's dialectics applied to matter is called Dialectical Materialism. . . .

We are now in the second phase of Marx's Dialectical Materialism, namely its application to society. Just as Hegel said that all ideas are made up of contradictory elements Marx now said that society is made up of such contradictory elements, namely the classes. Classes are de-termined by their role in production and not by religion, race, family, or fatherland. There are only two classes in society, the exploiters and the exploited, which are in contradiction one with the other. No class has existence except in antagonism to another class, for history is nothing but the struggle of the two classes. . . .

The changes by which society passed from the one phase of social development to another is not gradual but violent, for the reason that the political, legal and moral systems generated during them have a power of endurance. Furthermore, each class clings to its privileges and refuses to abandon its authority without a struggle. The only way that a political change can take place is for the exploited class to violently break down this resistance, in order to appropriate itself to continually changing economic obstructions. . . .

Dialectical Materialism is not a philosophy based on facts, but rather a theory imposed on them. It was born of an attempt, as Marx himself admitted in the "first thesis on Feuerbach" of a desire to escape the immateriality of idealism. If Marx had lived at any other time than when he did live, and if he had not been perplexed by the artificial problem of Hegel and Feuerbach, he never would have formed a philosophy by the union of both. It is a philosophy born of philosophers, not of the world.

Historically, it is not true that the economic is the basis of religion, politics, art, culture, and morality. Other interests are often prior to the economic, for example, health, happiness, knowledge, art, leisure, religion. Marx himself was never controlled by economic motives. *He did not earn his own living,* and if it were not for Engels he would have starved. Furthermore, Arab expansion was not due to economic pressure in Arabia. The Crusades had nothing to do with economics in their motivation; Columbus did not discover America because he needed a new source of economic income. The Renaissance which left its imprint on modern civilization was primarily a literary, philosophical, artistic and scientific movement rather than an economic one. The French revolution was a struggle for political equality and only secondarily for economic equality. In our own times race has become a more potent element in Europe than economics, and throughout the world the loyalty of Catholic working men to their religion proves that something else besides tools determines their love of God. A French worker ought to feel he has more in common with a Russian worker than with French Capitalists, but there is not such feeling. The Communists must admit that the birth of Karl Marx depended on other factors than those of the purely economic order.

According to Communists, changes in tools or methods of production are the causes for all other changes, political, social and religious. But why are there *changes in the methods of production?* Communism does not answer this question. Marx says they change when a new economic situation arises. This is untrue. Economic changes take place more often because of inventions, and inventions are due to *intelligence*. Therefore the economic is not always the cause. It was science and not economics which made industry develop. Furthermore, scientists and inventors do not work for the sake of production; as a matter of fact they are very often disinterested in the economic side of life. When Marx left out brains as an important factor in history he failed to use his own. . . .

Economic determinism puts the economic above the human. It makes man exist for production instead of production for man. Man thus becomes the slave of the economic instead of the economic being the instrument of man. Economic production is not the distinguishing mark of man; production is like walking, it is a means to an end and what the end is will often vary from man to man. . . .

Economic determinism is a denial of free will. If social, religious and political institutions are determined by the methods of production, then man's free will is equivalently denied. If the Communists say that man's will is not determined, but only conditioned by economics, then economic determinism is no longer true. They cannot eat their caviar and have it. Either there is no economic determinism or there is no freedom.

If economic determinism were true, and we were all determined by economic necessity to end in Communism, why does Communism carry on propaganda? If Communism is inevitable, why do anything about it? If the sun of Communism is going to rise in the East tomorrow why organize a "League for Peace and Democracy" to make it rise? If nothing can stop Communism then why should Earl Browder be so anxious to get out of Leavenworth Penitentiary in order to spread it? Then why "purges" in Russia? Why indignation against "wreckers" which is just as absurd as the anger of a child against a toy that will not work? The answer is, in *practice*, Communism admits free will while in theory it denies it—just one of the many contradictions which make Communism unacceptable to anyone who thinks.

Among other difficulties inherent in Dialectical Materialism the following may be mentioned: a) Once the classless class is established what happens to the dialectics? Is Communism exempt from the very law which it brought into being? If it is, then Dialectical Materialism is not the necessary law of history. b) Does not Communism create as its antithesis, viz., Fascism? This is what it is creating today but Marx did not see its possibility. c) Dialectical Materialism does not as Communism asserts disprove the first principles of thought. The mere fact that it is in the process of becoming, A can coexist with a partial realization of B which was implied potentially in A, is no evidence that A is not B. . . .

Communism is right in only one thing, and that is it protests against concentration of wealth in the hands of the few; it is wrong in its reform because it carries that concentration to a point where nobody owns the means of production except the State, though they humbug the workers into believing that they own it. Putting all the productive property into the hands of the collectivity is no solution of the problem of property. Among the many defects of the system, these few might be mentioned:

a) It is difficult to see why our economic and social problems would be any easier to solve after a revolution than before. . . . To say that we must first have a revolution and a civil war between classes with all its bloodshed and ruin before we can ever have peace is just like saying that before we can have health we must have pneumonia, typhoid fever, cancer and ulcers. When a husband and wife are quarreling it is no solution to say that if you burn their house and purge their children, they will live happily ever after. . . .

b) Communism forgets that there is no magic in the transfer of the title of property from a few Capitalists to a few Red Commissars. Like most violent reformers they reform the wrong thing. The truth of the matter is that the cause of our ills is not in property, but in the person who owns it; hence, there will never be a radical transformation of society unless there is a spiritual regeneration of persons through a rebirth of Justice and Charity. But outlawing religion, Communism makes this impossible. Thinking that if we transfer the ownership of all property into the hands of a few Red Commissars, we will do away with economic injustice, greed, and exploitation, is just like thinking that if you register an automobile in the State of Illinois instead of the State of New York it will never backfire nor run out of gas.

c) Communism can give us no assurance that the workers will be the chief beneficiaries of State-owned combines than they will be under a Capitalist-owned combine. The point is not who owns the property, but who divides the spoils. This is always a problem when administration is distinct from ownership. Putting all property into the hands of the State may do away with private property but it will not do away with lust. It only transfers the lust from ownership to privilege. . . .

Once the collectivity becomes the sole owner of productive goods of all descriptions, it can do whatever it likes with the individuals. Once you begin taking your jobs, your education, your food, your work, your clothing, and your housing from the State, it will only be a matter of a few visits from the police until you take your thinking from the State and that is the end of liberty.

This is the basic defect of Communism—the destruction of liberty. Power follows property. Put all productive property in the hands of the State and you take freedom out of the souls of men.

(1939)

# XI

# The Material World

*Its origin. Its prehistoric disaster. Its suffering, evil, and sin.
Its godlessness. Christianity in history. The Church and the
world crisis. The insufficiency of earthly life.*

## THE SEED OF THE UNIVERSE

### ST. AUGUSTINE

As in the seed there are invisibly and at one time all the things which
in the course of time will grow into a tree, so the universe must be
conceived—since God created all things at the same time—as having
had at the same time all the things which were made in it and with
it, when the day of creation came, not only the heavens with the sun
and the moon and the stars, whose species remains in their rotary
motion, and the earth and the deeps, which suffer changing movements, and joined together below produce the other part of the world;
but also those things which earth and water produced potentially and
causally, before in the course of time they came into being in the shape
in which they are now known to us in those works which God
"worketh until now" (John v,17).

(ca. A.D. 415)

# THE NECESSITY OF GOD
## IN THE WORLD

### MOST REV. FULTON J. SHEEN

THE problem is not to learn how long the universe has existed, but how to explain its existence. It is sometimes argued that if the world was recently made, it was necessary to have a God as its cause; but now that we know it was made millions of years ago, we can dispense with the necessity of a cause, for time itself is a cause. This argument is based upon the causal efficacy of time. There is no doubt that the efficiency of causes is increased with time; for example, a man who could not dig a ditch in an hour might very well be able to do it in a year, or a man who could not write a book in a day might possibly do it in a year. The fallacy of this argument, however, is that it assumes that time is the cause instead of the environment of certain causes. In each and every instance where the greater amount of time increases the efficacy of the cause, the cause is by its very nature adapted and capable of producing that effect, but an unsuitable cause will never produce that effect, regardless of how much time it be given. A hen might be given a thousand light years in which to hatch the soliloquy of Hamlet, but in twice that time it could not produce even the first line of the soliloquy. The same is true of the universe. It makes no difference how much time one gives mechanical causes, the problem is whether or not they are capable of producing *by their very nature such and such an effect*. To assume that if you give a thing time enough it will dispense with the necessity of a first cause, is like saying that if the handle of a brush were long enough it would paint by itself, or that if the crank of an automobile were long enough it would automatically become a self-starter. The hare has need of an origin just as much as the tortoise, for the philosophical problem is not whether things are going fast or slow; it is why they go at all.

Another intellectual subterfuge resorted to by those who attempt to escape the implications of the argument from evolution is based upon the primeval stuff from which the universe evolved. It assumes that it requires a greater cause to make big things than to make little things, and that the only reason a cause was posited in the creational outlook was that all things were made at once. Now, if it be assumed, they argue, that the universe began not with many and powerful things, but with some very small and tiny speck, we could dispense with the necessity of a creator or a first cause. It is well here to remember that the size of the original stuff of the universe has nothing whatever to do with the problem. It makes not the slightest bit of difference whether the universe began with an enormous mass of chaotic gas which broke up into detached condensations, or with just some small tiny spark, or even an original mass of protoplasm—the problem is still the same, namely, to account for its origin. Midgets have parents just as well as giants, and children just as well as men, and the cause of the offspring is judged, not by the *size* of the offspring, but by its nature. In the philosophical order, in like manner, a God is required just as much for the original spark as for a ready-made universe, for the cause is to be judged, not by the thing produced, but rather by the fact that the thing was made from nothing, and in this sense demands an infinite creator. . . .

The argument for motion is also independent of the question of the eternity of the world. It is argued by some that if the world were eternal, it would therefore dispense with the necessity of God. In answer to this objection, it must first of all be kept in mind that modern science rejects the idea of the eternity of the world. But what is more important is that the eternity of the world could never dispense with the necessity of a cause. The world might very well be eternal (though from revelation we know it is not), but it would still be eternally dependent on God. The time element is quite independent of the causal element. I can imagine an eternal seashore and also an eternal footprint on that seashore, but I can understand it only on condition that I think of someone who from all eternity had left that footprint. So too with the universe. Though it might always have been, it would always have depended on someone to account for its movement, its development, and its purpose. . . .

Why did God will to make the universe? The Archetypal Ideas He had concerning it did not constrain Him. God created the world. God is Good, and being Good He could not, as it were, contain Himself; consequently, He told the secret of His Goodness to nothingness and that was Creation. The world is the overflow of Divine Goodness. Begotten of the Goodness of God, the Goodness of God is in it. All the versatile motions and strivings of the universe are modes of procedure corresponding to the continuous activity of His Will. Because God is in things by his Love and Goodness, they all strive in part to

311

produce the same Goodness which called them into being. That is why everything in the world tends to diffuse itself. The sun is good and diffuses itself in light and heat; the tree is good and diffuses itself in the fruit; the rose is good and diffuses itself in its perfumes; animals are good and diffuse themselves in the generation of their kind. Man is good and diffuses himself in the generation of thought. Fecundity, or productiveness, is the law of the universe; things give because to them has been given. The giving is their completion, and by seeking their own perfection and goodness, they seek the Perfect Goodness which is God. That is why man finds a paradox in creatures and speaks of their "traitorous trueness and their loyal deceit." They are fickle to us and faithful to Him, because God is in them drawing all things *suaviter et fortiter* back to the Heart of His Infinite Goodness.

(1948)

# "BECOME CHRISTIANS NOT ASTRONOMERS"

### ST. AUGUSTINE

IT very often happens that there is some question as to the earth or the sky, or the other elements of this world—respecting which one who is not a Christian has knowledge derived from most certain reasoning or observation, and it is very disgraceful and mischievous and of all things to be carefully avoided, that a Christian speaking of such matters as being according to the Christian Scriptures, should be heard by an unbeliever talking such nonsense that the unbeliever perceiving him to be as wide from the mark as east from west, can hardly restrain himself from laughing. . . .

The Gospels do not tell us that our Lord said, "I will send you the Holy Ghost to teach you the course of the sun and the moon"; we should therefore endeavor to become Christians and not astronomers.

(ca. 415)

# HOLY SCRIPTURE DEFENDED AGAINST
# RATIONALIST ATTACKS

### LEO XIII

IN earlier times the contest was chiefly with those who, relying on private judgment and repudiating the divine traditions and teaching office of the Church, held the Scriptures to be the one source of revelation and the final appeal in matters of faith. Now we have to meet the rationalists, true children and inheritors of the older heretics, who, trusting in their turn to their own way of thinking, have rejected even the scraps and remnants of Christian belief which had been handed down to them. They deny that there is any such thing as revelation or inspiration, or Holy Scripture at all; they see, instead, only the forgeries and falsehoods of men; they set down the Scripture narratives as stupid fables and lying stories; the prophecies and oracles of God are to them either predictions made up after the events or forecasts formed by the light of nature; the miracles and wonders of God's power are not what they are said to be, but the startling effects of natural law, or else mere tricks and myths; and the apostolic Gospels and writing are not the work of the apostles at all. . . .

The Catholic interpreter [of Scripture], although he should show that those facts of natural science which investigators affirm to be now quite certain are not contrary to the Scripture rightly explained, must, nevertheless, always bear in mind that much which has been held and proved as certain has afterwards been called in question and rejected. And if writers on physics travel outside the boundaries of their own branch, and carry their erroneous teaching into the domain of philosophy, let them be handed over to philosophers for refutation . . .

It is a lamentable fact that there are many who with great labor carry out and publish investigations on the monuments of antiquity, the manners and institutions of nations, and other illustrative subjects, and whose chief purpose in all this is to find mistakes in the sacred writings and so to shake and weaken their authority. Some of these writers display not only extreme hostility but the greatest unfairness; in their eyes a profane book or ancient document is accepted without hesitation, whilst the Scripture, if they only find in it a suspicion of error, is set down with the slightest possible discussion as quite untrustworthy. It is true, no doubt, that copyists have made mistakes in the text of the Bible; this question, when it arises, should be carefully considered on its merits, and the fact not too easily admitted, but only in those passages where the proof is clear. It may also happen that the sense of a passage remains ambiguous, and in this case good hermeneutical methods will greatly assist in clearing up the obscurity. But it is absolutely wrong and forbidden either to narrow inspiration to certain parts only of Holy Scripture or to admit that the sacred writer has erred. . . . All the books which the Church receives as sacred and canonical are written wholly and entirely, with all their parts, at the dictation of the Holy Ghost; and so far is it from being possible that any error can co-exist with inspiration, that inspiration not only is essentially incompatible with error, but excludes and rejects it as absolutely and necessarily as it is impossible that God Himself, the Supreme Truth, can utter that which is not true. This is the ancient and unchanging faith of the Church. . . .

Because the Holy Ghost employed men as His instruments, we cannot, therefore, say that it was these inspired instruments who, perchance, have fallen into error, and not the primary Author. For, by supernatural power, He so moved and impelled them to write—He was so present to them—that the things which He ordered, and those only, they, first, rightly understood, then willed faithfully to write down, and finally expressed in apt words and with infallible truth. Otherwise, it could not be said that He was the Author of the entire Scripture. Such has always been the persuasion of the Fathers. . . .

It follows that those who maintain that an error is possible in any genuine passage of the sacred writings either pervert the Catholic notion of inspiration or make God the author of such an error. . . .

Let them loyally hold that God, the Creator and Ruler of all things, is also the Author of the Scriptures—and that, therefore, nothing can be proved either by physical science or archeology which can really contradict the Scriptures. If, then, apparent contradiction be met with, every effort should be made to remove it. Judicious theologians and commentators should be consulted as to what is the true or most probable meaning of the passage in discussion, and hostile arguments should be carefully weighed. Even if the difficulty is after all not cleared up and the discrepancy seems to remain, the contest must not be abandoned; truth cannot contradict truth, and we may be sure that some mistake has been made either in the interpretation of the sacred words or in the polemical discussion itself; and if no such mistake can be detected, we must then suspend judgment for the time being. . . . As no one should be so presumptuous as to think that he understands the whole of the Scripture, in which St. Augustine himself confessed that there was more that he did not know than that he knew, so, if he should come on anything that seems incapable of solution, he must take to heart the cautious rule of the same holy doctor: "It is better even to be oppressed by unknown but useful signs than to interpret them uselessly, and thus to throw off the yoke only to be caught in the trap of error."

(November 18, 1893)

# FINITE WORLD AND INFINITE GOD

ALFRED NOYES

A VERY common belief today is that which suggests that the physical insignificance of the earth is an argument against the Christian scheme in particular, and indeed against any idea that the Almighty and Infinite God can possibly be interested in anything so physically minute. . . . It would be enough to remember the fine saying of Galileo, that we impose limits on the infinite power of God when we believe that the enormous dimensions of the universe render his universal activity impossible. "The sun shines on the grapes and ripens them, as if it had nothing else whatever to do," he said, "and in the same way, God can care for every individual, though his universe be infinite." Indeed, from the point of view of any philosophy of real values the argument will not bear serious examination. It misses the whole meaning of the scheme, which involved just this descent of the Creator from the heights to the depths, through all His worlds; this complete rounding of the circle; this consummation of infinitude in a union of extremes. What may have happened, or may even now be happening in other worlds, we do not know; but the suggestion that Orion or Aldebaran might have offered a more majestic physical stage for the divine humility indicates a complete confusion of ideas. It misses even the symbolical significance of the divine birth amongst the beasts in an outlying manger. It misses the whole point of the plain narrative, whether it be true or false, that the palace was hostile; the simplest house was insecure; and there was no room at the Inn. It misses the whole point of the philosophy, which involved just that stooping from the heights to the depths. It was on these very

315

points that the moral sublimity and spiritual beauty of the whole story
turned, and to suggest that a physically larger stage would have been
more appropriate is—to say the least of it—naive.

(1934)

# THE WORLD'S FALL AND RESCUE

## JOHN HENRY CARDINAL NEWMAN

To consider the world in its length and breadth, its various history,
the many races of man, their starts, their fortunes, their mutual aliena-
tion, their conflicts; and then their ways, habits, governments, forms
of worship; their enterprises, their aimless courses, their random
achievements and acquirements, the impotent conclusion of long-
standing facts, the tokens so faint and broken of a super-intending
design, the blind evolution of what turn out to be great powers or
truths, the progress of things, as if from unreasoning elements, not
towards final causes, the greatness and littleness of man, his far-
reaching aims, his short duration, the curtain hung over his futurity,
the disappointments of life, the defeat of good, the success of evil,
physical pain, mental anguish, the prevalence and intensity of sin,
the pervading idolatries, the corruptions, the dreary hopeless irreli-
gion, that condition of the whole race, so fearfully yet exactly described in the Apostle's words, *having no hope and without God in
the world,*—all this is a vision to dizzy and appal; and inflicts upon
the mind the sense of a profound mystery, which is absolutely beyond
human solution.

What shall be said to this heart-piercing, reason-bewildering fact?
I can only answer, that either there is no Creator, or this living society
of men is in a true sense discarded from His presence. . . . *If* there
be a God, *since* there is a God, the human race is implicated in some
terrible aboriginal calamity. It is out of joint with the purposes of its
Creator. This is a fact, a fact as true as the fact of its existence; and
thus the doctrine of what is theologically called original sin becomes
to me almost as certain as that the world exists, and as the existence
of God. . . .

Supposing then it to be the Will of the Creator to interfere in human affairs, and to make provisions for retaining in the world a

316

knowledge of Himself, so definite and distinct as to be proof against the energy of human skepticism, in such a case,—I am far from saying that there was no other way,—but there is nothing to surprise the mind, if He should think fit to introduce a power into the world, invested with the prerogative of infallibility in religious matters. Such a provision would be a direct, immediate, active, and prompt means of withstanding the difficulty; it would be an instrument suited to the need; and, when I find that this is the very claim of the Catholic Church, not only do I feel no difficulty in admitting the idea, but there is a fitness in it, which recommends it to my mind. And thus I am brought to speak of the Church's infallibility, as a provision, adapted by the mercy of the Creator, to preserve religion in the world, and to restrain that freedom of thought, which of course in itself is one of the greatest of our natural gifts, and to rescue it from its own suicidal excesses.

(1864)

# EVIL: THE PERVERSION OF NATURE

## ST. AUGUSTINE

IN Scripture they are called God's enemies who oppose His rule, not by nature, but by vice; having no power to hurt Him, but only themselves. For they are His enemies, not through their power to hurt, but by their will to oppose Him. For God is unchangeable, and wholly proof against injury. Therefore the vice which makes those who are called His enemies resist Him, is an evil not to God, but to themselves. And to them it is an evil, solely because it corrupts the good of their nature. It is not nature, therefore, but vice, which is contrary to God. For that which is evil is contrary to the good. And who will deny that God is the supreme good? Vice, therefore, is contrary to God, as evil to good. Further, the nature it vitiates is a good, and therefore to this good also it is contrary. But while it is contrary to God only as evil to good, it is contrary to the nature it vitiates, both as evil and as hurtful. For to God, no evils are hurtful; but only to natures mutable and corruptible, though, by the testimony of the vices themselves, originally good. For were they not good, vices could not hurt them. . . .

It is impossible that there should be a harmless vice. Whence we

317

gather, that though vice cannot injure the unchangeable good, it can injure nothing but good; because it does not exist where it does not injure. This, then, may be thus formulated: Vice cannot be in the highest good, and cannot be but in some good. Things solely good, therefore, can in some circumstances exist; things solely evil, never; for even those natures which are vitiated by an evil will, so far indeed as they are vitiated, are evil, but in so far as they are natures they are good. And when a vitiated nature is punished, besides the good it has in being a nature, it has this also, that it is not unpunished. For this is just, and certainly everything just is a good. For no one is punished for natural, but for voluntary vices. For even the vice which by the force of habit and long continuance has become a second nature, had its origin in the will.

(A.D. 440)

# THE MYSTERY OF EVIL

### FRIEDRICH SCHLEGEL

THE greatest historical mystery—the deepest and most complicated enigma of the world—is the fact that God permits evil; and the explanation and solution can only be found in the unfettered freedom of man, who is destined to lead a life of struggle, being exposed to the influences of two contending powers ever since the earthly mission of Adam began. Here, we see, is the real, the whole business of man—this divinely ordained trial of the faculty of freedom which was imparted to the firstling of creation, to God's image, and must continuously be tested in the conflict with and victory over temptation and all hostile spirits. Only the man who recognizes, in its, at first, inconceivably wide extent, the permission given by God to evil (the whole magnitude of the power given to the wicked principle, in accordance with God's inscrutable decrees, from the curse of Cain, and the sign of that curse, uninterruptedly transmitted through all the labyrinths of error and of grossly mishandled truth, through all the false religions of Heathenism and through all the ages of extreme moral corruption and of crime forever repeated and forever growing in malignancy, to the final period when the anti-Christian principle, the spirit of evil, shall usurp dominion over the whole world, and when mankind, sufficiently prepared for the ordeal, shall be summoned to the final decisive trial, the last great conflict with the enemy in all the fulness of his power), is able to understand the great phenomena of history, which are of a complexity often dark and strange, though he, too, can penetrate only a little way into the hidden and mysterious ways of Providence.

He who regards everything in humanity and its progress from a merely natural or rationalist point of view and seeks to explain all in accordance with such views may not be without a certain instinctive feeling that an all-ruling Providence exists and entertain a kind of pious deference to its secret ways and high designs; but since he is without a deep insight into the ways of Providence and does not see clearly, manifestly and fully the power of evil, he must always rest on the surface of events and historical facts, content with outward appearances and neither comprehending the meaning of the whole nor understanding the import of any part. Yes, the matter of greatest moment is to observe the Spirit of God revealing itself in history, enlightening and directing the judgments of men, saving and guiding mankind, and, even here below, admonishing, judging and chastising nations and generations. This threefold law of the world, these three mighty principles which dominate the historical development of mankind,—the hidden ways of a Providence which delivers and emancipates the human race; the free-will of man, compelled to make a decisive choice in the struggle of life, in all of its acts and in the feelings to which it gives rise; and the power given by God to the evil principle—cannot be posited as absolutely necessary, as are the phenomena of nature or the laws of human reason. It is, rather, in the characteristic marks of particular events and historical facts that the visible traces of invisible power and design, of high and hidden wisdom, must be sought for.

(1829)

Dionysius says that evil is neither an existent nor a good.

I answer by explaining that one opposite is known from the other, as darkness from light. Hence the meaning of evil depends on the meaning of good. Now everything desirable is good, and since every nature loves its own being and perfection, it must be said that the being and perfection of any nature has the force of good. Consequently

319

it cannot be that evil signifies a being, or form, or nature. We are left,
therefore, to draw the conclusion that evil signifies some absence of
good.

ST. THOMAS AQUINAS (1272)

# THE MYSTERY OF EVIL
# AND SUFFERING

### THE REV. BRUNO WEBB, O.S.B.

THE Catholic theology of evil is condensed in the parable of the Prodigal Son. First came sin, a moral evil, that is to say an evil arising from
the abuse of man's free will. From sin followed suffering, a physical
evil, as its natural and inevitable effect. But, finally, the last state of
the Prodigal was better than the first, since from his suffering was
drawn a good far greater than that which he originally possessed.

First, then, came sin—that is the origin of all evil. And if, as Revelation tells us, all sins, and the first of all sins, namely the sin of Lucifer,
imply the rejection of the supernatural gift of grace, it is a foregone
conclusion that merely natural reason, that is to say pure philosophy,
although great use of it is made in dealing with this problem of evil,
cannot by itself present us with the ultimate solution, since pure philosophy as such makes no claim to know anything of the supernatural.
Many people have only a vague notion of what sin is. They see the
pain and distress that is in the world; they are stirred by the injustices
of man against man, of class against class, and of nation against nation. The world understands sin against one's fellow-men, but it is
far slower to understand sin against God. We hear much to-day of
the rights of free peoples and the honor of nations, but how much of
the rights and honor of God? Sin is the one supreme evil in the world,
it is the evil from which all other evils eventually flow; indeed it is
the only evil that ultimately matters at all, for while all other evils,
our earthly suffering included, end with time, sin can continue into
the world to come as an everlasting separation of the soul from God.
Yet even this is not the principal reason why sin is the supreme evil.
The evil of sin consists in its being the fully wilful rejection of God,
it is, as it were, an attempt to annihilate God, and, were this possible,
it would do so. Sin is in a sense an infinite evil, because it is an outrage
against the infinite sanctity and goodness of God. It is only in so far

320

as we understand who God is that we can understand what sin is; it is only in so far as we realize that God is one supreme Reality that we can realize that sin is the one supreme evil; and it is only so far as we understand that sin is the one supreme evil that we shall understand those other and far lesser evils in the world, and suffering in particular, that flow eventually from sin. . . .

Suffering and pain of any kind is, of its very nature, the signal that something has gone wrong. Consider any individual organism such as the human body. Each of its organs, heart, brain, eye, ear, stomach, muscles and so on, is limited by the other organs. Were any of these the only organ it would have to perform all the functions of life, whereas in fact each organ is limited to its own particular function by the fact that there are other organs to perform the other functions of the body. So long as this mutual limitation remains normal no suffering ensues, just the reverse. Mutual limitation in this case makes for harmony and the efficiency of the whole. It is only when one of the organs *fails* in its function that suffering appears. The same is true of nature as a whole. Where there is suffering something has gone wrong, it cannot follow merely upon the mutual limitation of the different parts that go to make up the universe even when these are endowed with feeling.

The reason is this: limitation is a mere negation, whereas any physical evil or disorder, of which suffering is the sure signal, is not a mere negation, but a privation, a failure, a defect. A negation is the absence of some perfection in the case when that perfection is in no way owing to the thing in question, such, for instance, as sightlessness in a stone; whereas a privation or defect is the absence of some perfection which should be present, such as blindness in an animal. In both cases there is absence of vision, but in the case of the stone there is no reason for vision being present and its absence is the mere limitation or negation in that stone of this further perfection, there is nothing lacking which should be there as when vision is lacking in the animal. Now all physical evil, which alone can give rise to suffering, is a privation, not a mere negation; it is the absence of some perfection which should be present; it is the sure sign, not of merely limited order, but of disorder.

(1941)

# CHRISTIAN REALISM TOWARD
# SUFFERING AND EVIL

### FRIEDRICH VON HÜGEL

CHRISTIANITY, without ever a hesitation, from the first and every-where, refused to hold, or even to tolerate, either the one or the other of the two only attempts at self-persuasion which, then as now, possess souls that suffer whilst they have not yet found the deepest. Christianity refused all Epicureanism,—since man cannot find his deepest by fleeing from pain and suffering, and by seeking pleasure and pleasures, however dainty and refined. And it refused all Stoicism,—since pain, suffering, evil are not fancies and prejudices, but real, very real; and since man's greatest action and disposition is not self-sufficing-ness or aloofness, but self-donation and love. Christianity refuted those theories, not by means of another theory of its own, but simply by exhibiting a Life and lives—the Life of the Crucified, and lives which continually re-live, in their endless various lesser degrees and ways, such a combination of gain in giving and of joy in suffering. Christianity thus gave to souls the faith and strength to grasp life's nettle. It raised them, in their deepest dispositions and innermost will, above the pitiful oscillations and artificialities of even the greatest of the Pagans in this central matter,—between eluding, ignoring pain and suffering, and animal-like, seeking life in its fleeting, momentary pleasures; or trying the nobler yet impossible course,—the making out that physical, mental, moral pain and evil are nothing real, and the suppressing of emotion, sympathy and pity as things unworthy of the adult soul. Christianity did neither. It pointed to Jesus with the terror of death upon Him in Gethsemane; with a cry of desola-tion upon the Cross on Calvary; it allowed the soul, it encouraged the soul to sob itself out. It not only taught men frankly to face and recognize physical and mental pain, death, and all other, especially all moral evils and sufferings as very real; it actually showed men the presence and gravity of a host of pains, evils and miseries which they had, up to then, quite ignored or at least greatly minimized. And yet, with all this—in spite of all such material for despair the final note of Christianity was and is still, one of trust, of love, of transcendent joy. It is no accident, but of the very essence of the mys-tery and of the power of faith, it springs from the reality of God and of His action within men's souls, that, as the nobly joyous last chapters of Isaiah (Chap. xl to the end) contain also those wondrous utterances of the man of sorrows, so also the serenity of the Mount of the Beatitudes leads, in the Gospels, to the darkness of Calvary.

Pray believe me here: it is to Christianity that we owe our deepest insight into the wondrously wide and varied range throughout the world, as we know it, of pain, suffering, evil; just as to Christianity we owe the richest enforcement of the fact that, in spite of all this, God is, and that He is good and loving. And this enforcement Christianity achieves, at its best, by actually inspiring soul after soul, to believe, to love, to live this wondrous faith.

(1925)

# PAIN, THE ALTRUISM OF NATURE

### THE REV. PATRICK A. SHEEHAN

I KNOW no philosophical talisman for anguish or sorrow, except that final hope of suffering humanity: All things have an end. But, nevertheless, it may be in our painless moments a soothing thought that suffering is not the unreasoning and inconsiderate infliction on helpless human beings of pain from the hands of a supreme and arbitrary power; but that behind it there may be grave motives and far-reaching designs which our imperfect knowledge may feebly grasp, if we cannot always hold fast to them as a consolatory remedy for our weakness and our woes.

It is strange that men will not see how suffering is the inevitable accompaniment of our state of existence. Whether man has fallen from a state of perfection according to Christian truth and belief, keeping still some vague tradition of that happy condition in his eternal dream of the perfectability of the race; or, whether, in the evolutionist theory, he is supposed to be struggling upwards from primary elements towards more spacious conditions and final developments, it must be admitted that this his intermediate state is a state of imperfection, with all the blunted senses, stunted faculties, darkened intellect, and weakened will, that denote a fallen or struggling being. In such a state, suffering is almost inevitable. Death must be preluded by disease; and the aspiring soul must beat its wings in fruitless efforts to touch an ideal that is ever present, and ever unattainable. Hence, the sublime dissatisfaction that ever haunts the dreams of mortals,—the never-satisfied craving and hunger after an indefinable something that ever eludes us, and that is not to be attained, no matter how frequently we change the surroundings of life and seek to satisfy our unquenchable desires. Hence come mental pain and anxiety,—"the looking before and after and pining for what is not." . . .

Again, there can be no progress without pain. In pain are we brought forth into the world; in pain do we grow and increase; in pain, perhaps painless pain, do we die. But never a forward step is taken by man or society without pain and suffering. The whole development of human character is wrought, and can only be wrought, by self-denial and suffering, by the patient bearing of weary burdens. . . .

Now each tiniest item of creation works outward and upward, subserving some higher species. Its energies are not limited to its own existence or welfare; nor even to the continuance and preservation of its own kind. It is the Altruism of Nature—the design of making all things cooperate in one single plan; each working for some higher existence than its own, and subserving some higher and hidden purpose far beyond its ken. . . . Every human life has some ulterior purpose, as yet but dimly guessed, but yet most certainly to be revealed. And, as the rabbit or guinea-pig in the hands of the scientist knows nothing in its pain of the vast purposes it subserves, and only knows that it is passing through a mysterious trial under the hands of some superior and powerful being, so we, too, are ignorant of the purposes which we serve throughout the universe of God by the mysterious agency of labor and pain and suffering. . . .

We also may be the means, through labor, agony, and even death, of communicating larger knowledge, nay, perhaps wider help, to beings of whose existence we can form but a vague comprehension, but who are far beyond us as we are beyond the beasts that perish and are dumb. And may there not be some supreme science, some synthesis of all earthly sciences, such as we are always seeking after, but never attaining; and that all this human pain and suffering under which we blindly labor, and which sometimes seems to us such an affliction of unnecessary cruelty on the part of an all-powerful but capricious Being, are contributory to the perfecting of that science?

(1916)

# A GOD-LESS WORLD

## ETIENNE GILSON

A WORLD which has lost the Christian God cannot but resemble a world which had not yet found him. Just like the world of Thales and of Plato, our own modern world is "full of gods." There are blind Evolution, clear-sighted Orthogenesis, benevolent Progress, and others which it is more advisable not to mention by name. Why unnecessarily hurt the feelings of men who, today, render them a cult? It is however important for us to realize that mankind is doomed to live more and more under the spell of a new scientific, social, and political mythology, unless we resolutely exorcise these befuddled notions whose influence on modern life is becoming appalling. Millions of men are starving and bleeding to death because two or three of these pseudo-scientific or pseudo-social deified abstractions are now at war. For when gods fight among themselves, men have to die. Could we not make an effort to realize that evolution is to be largely what we will make it to be? That Progress is not an automatically self-achieving law but something to be patiently achieved by the will of men? That Equality is not an actually given fact but an ideal to be progressively approached by means of justice? That Democracy is not the leading goddess of some societies but a magnificent promise to be fulfilled by all through their obstinate will for friendship, if they are strong enough to make it last for generations after generations?

(1941)


# HISTORY'S SPIRITUAL ASPECT

## PETER WUST

WE are today, one and all, too apt to forget the fact that history, in its deepest sense, does not consist merely of secular happenings, but that it is always at the same time a sacred process, a spiritual happening. For it is only on the surface that history is a *motio physica* of wars, battles, national disorders, political catastrophies, and so on. Below, in the depths that are accessible to the mind alone, it is a truly majestic *motio metaphysica voluntatis,* a passionate stirring will-drama of the spirit. And, if this is so, then the really decisive factor in this will-drama will be that tremendous tension which continually exists in one form or another between the organism, compound of all human wills, and the absolute Will of God.

(1931)

## HISTORY AND THE KINGDOM OF GOD

JACQUES MARITAIN

To my mind it is a betrayal at once of man and of God not to understand that history is a movement towards the Kingdom of God and not to wish for the coming of that Kingdom. But it is absurd to think that it will come *in and as a part of* history, where good and evil are inextricably intertwined. Prepared by the growth of history, and by the progressive mixing and refining of the human being that it involves, it will come *at the end* of history, at that hour of the resurrection of the dead to which all history leads. . . .

We find ourselves faced with three forms of thought: of which the first is that of the *Kingdom of God,* the city which is at once *earthly and heavenly,* where God is king and He will be all in all. The Jews looked for the Kingdom in time. For the Christian it is outside time: it is an eternal Kingdom, whose place will be in the new world of the resurrection of the dead. Inasmuch, then, as it is the idea of a veritable Kingdom, of a polity where God is king, and is, as such, distinguished from the idea of the Church, as was shown by Erik Petersen in a remarkable little book written before his conversion to Catholicism, this idea of the Kingdom of God is eschatological, an idea concerned with the end of time. It does not belong to the things of earthly time, but to what will be thereafter.

But what comes after time is prepared in time: the Kingdom of God constitutes the ultimate prepared for by the movement of all history and in which it concludes, towards which it converges, on the one hand, the history of the Church and the spiritual world; and on the other, the history of the secular world and the political city: with this difference, that the Church is already the commencement of the Kingdom of God in its beginning in time, the 'crucified Kingdom' which in the end shall be revealed; while the history of the secular world will only come to its ultimate end by means of substantial 'mutation,' described as the conflagration or burning up of the world, by which it will be born into the Kingdom. . . .

For Christianity, the truth about the world and the earthly city is that they are the kingdom at once of man, of God, and of the devil. This is the cause of the essential ambiguity of the world and history: it is the common ground of these three together. The world belongs to God by right of creation; to the devil by right of conquest, because of sin; to Christ by right of victory over the first conqueror, by his Passion. The task of the Christian in this world is to dispute his domain with the devil and wrench it from him. He must strive to this end, in which he will never wholly succeed while time endures. The world is saved indeed, it is delivered *in hope,* it is on the march towards the Kingdom of God, and that is why it is treachery towards that Kingdom not to seek with all our power,—in relation and proportion to the conditions of earthly history, but as effectively as possible, *quantum potes, tantum aude,*—a realization, or more truly, the refraction in this world of the exigencies of the Gospel. Nevertheless this realization, even a relative one, will always, in one way or another, be deficient and disputed in this world. At one and the same time this world is on the march,—it is the growing of the wheat—towards the Kingdom of God; it is also on the march,—it is the growth of the tares, inextricably mingled with the wheat,—towards the kingdom of reprobation.

(1936)

# CHRISTIAN FREEDOM AND
# TODAY'S WORLD

### CHRISTOPHER DAWSON

THE true freedom of the world—the only freedom that can free man in the depths of his personality—depends on keeping open the channel of revelation, preserving the Word of Truth and communicating the Spirit of Life. These are the essential Christian freedoms, and it is for this that the Christian Church as a visible institution exists. If the channel becomes choked or the bridge broken, the world falls back into darkness and chaos and humanity once more becomes bound in that state of slavery which the ancient world saw as an impersonal chain of necessity but which Christian tradition conceived in terms of active personal evil as the Kingdom of Satan.

It is this wholesale loss of spiritual freedom that is the real danger that faces the world today. The plain fact which we see displayed before our eyes is that the power of man has grown so great that it has denied and shut out the power of the Spirit and that consequently it is destroying the world. We have seen how the new totalitarian orders all tend to become closed orders—spiritual as well as economic autarchies which leave no room for true Christian freedom. And we have no reason to suppose that a new democratic order which bases itself on the ideals of technocracy and economic planning would be fundamentally different in this respect, even though it avoids the grosser evils of the existing totalitarian systems. In so far as this is so, all these new orders are orders of death.

In face of this great danger Christianity still stands as the hope of the world. It is true that Christendom is weakened and divided. At first sight it seems like a valley of dry bones, the dry bones of dead controversies and moribund traditions, since Christians are more tied to the dead past, more dependent on antiquated modes of thought, more wedded to the old social and political order than the rest of the world. There is hardly a social abuse or intellectual fallacy that has not found its stoutest defenders in the ranks of the Christian orthodoxy. Nevertheless, in spite of all this, Christianity is still a living force in the modern world. It has still the promise of new life and spiritual freedom as at the beginning. . . . The nature of the new forces that threaten to enslave humanity will inevitably tend to make both Christians and non-Christians conscious of the essential truths of faith and spiritual reality on which the Church stands. The rise of the new totalitarian systems and ideologies is a religious as well as a political revolution. It destroys the traditional division of life into separate secular and religious spheres. It attempts to unify human life and to organize the total psychic and material energies of the community for common ends. And consequently it marks the end of the four centuries of religious development which followed the Reformation—a period that was characterized by the progressive individualization of consciousness, by religious separation and division and by the identification of spiritual freedom with religious individualism. The totalitarian revolution reverses this tendency and leaves no room for any kind of individualism, either secular or religious.

But it goes further than that and attacks spiritual freedom itself. It is therefore vital that Christians should not allow themselves to become confused and divided on this fundamental issue. Christians are agreed that the spiritual anarchy of unbridled individualism is contrary to the whole Christian tradition of faith and order, however much they may differ in their definitions. But on the other hand they must be still more united in defending the vital principles of Christian freedom which is the fundamental law of spiritual action. For what we are defending are not only man's rights but the rights of God. If the channels are closed by which the word of Christ and the power of the Spirit are communicated to man corporately and individually, the world must fall back into the state of darkness and slavery which Christ came to destroy. It is, of course, true that the opposition and conflict between the Two Cities runs through the whole of human history, but hitherto a limit had been set to it by the limitation of human power and knowledge. But today the scientific development of the techniques of social control have created a new situation in which for the first time in history it has become possible to make the human soul itself a cog in the mechanism of planned organization. This is the challenge that Christians have to face today, and they can do so only by returning to the foundations—the organic principles of spiritual life and spiritual freedom which are the laws of the Church's life.

(1942)

IF the world purifies the Christians by shedding their blood, the blood of Christians will at the same time purify also the world. It is perhaps from this double purification that the new Christendom that is to come will be born.

JACQUES MARITAIN (1936)

# THE CHURCH AND THE WORLD CRISIS

### EMANUEL CARDINAL SUHARD

ALL agree that our times are an age of transition. The suffering which affects the whole world, the dangers which threaten its future, the strong currents which sweep over it are less the consequences of a catastrophe than the warning signs of an imminent new birth. Or more exactly, the present uneasiness is neither a sickness nor a decadence of the world: it is a crisis of growth. . . .

Barriers are collapsing in this expanding world, walls crumbling under the tremendous pressure of this new tide which overthrows and levels everything. . . .

The modern man in the making seems to proceed from an organic unity and an internal principle of life. The same can be said of the City he is building for himself. The most apparent feature of this new humanism is its technical character. Born of discovery and the machine, it owes its universal framework to them. It turns to them and counts on them to promote the new order. Day by day, scientific knowledge displaces classical culture. Man's interest is shifting its object. It is giving up pure thought for effective action.

This human effort is not individual. Henceforth each one needs everyone else. The unit of work is no longer the artisan but the team. Relationships are forming which go beyond the horizons of the province and the nation in order to reach the human scale; a communal humanism, a universal civilization. . . .

Society, especially Western society, is going through a structural reform which is breaking the continuity of traditions, upsetting the play of established rules, and questioning consecrated values. The confusion, the sense of maladjustment which results in every realm justifies the feeling so often expressed in the ambiguous phrase: "The world is revolution."

It is at this juncture that the fundamental question arises: Who is going to infuse a soul into this common civilization, into this world now compartmentalized? Who will infuse the soul into this sudden unity which has come about quicker than our thought, into this planetary humanism for which we were not prepared? Who will produce the synthesis of this new universe? Who will be its Principle and its Inspiration?

Unbelievers affirm that it will not be the Church, for the very simple reason that the Church is dying. . . .

Believers too have asked themselves the question. And their reply is clear: No, the Church is not dead. No, the new world will not come into being without her. But this is true only on certain conditions.

. . . The position of Catholics—and the numerous critiques to which they have devoted themselves in recent years—can be reduced, we believe, to two essential attitudes.

The first is to remain on the defensive. In their arguments they stand up to their opponents without flinching. The adherents of this attitude reply to aggressive atheism with a dogmatism of defence. It is not the Church which is in agony or at fault but the modern world—or simply the world—for it is "modern" only in our eyes. The problems to which it refers in order to justify its divorce from the Church are in no way original. They can be found in past crises. "There is nothing new under the sun." The problems are the same, only their names change. The *Church* is not behind the times. It is man who sins or reasons badly. Like all systems this one will have its day. Let the storm pass. Truth always triumphs in the end. The Church has known other crises, she is not afraid of this one.

The great danger the Church is running today, they say, is in wishing to adapt herself. She must resist this perpetual temptation. It is not for her to adapt her teaching but for civilizations to assimilate it. . . . The Church is not of this world. She is the kingdom of God. Far from trying the impossible task of bridging the gap which separates her from the world, she should steadfastly remain outside and above its successive fluctuations. The only attitude for the Church is to break with the world. . . .

Those who criticize the Church for her lack of effectiveness in temporal affairs urge her to an exactly opposite reform. The Church—in the West—has not evolved with civil society. She has remained frozen in feudal forms which worked in times past. In our time instead of being fused with society as she was in the Middle Ages when the parish and the commune had the same extension and the same life, the Church is "absent" from the City. She hovers over humanity instead of being incarnate in its flesh and blood. In her message to men she has everything she needs, nay, more than she needs to animate the contemporary structures and to draw up plans for the future, but she does not use her resources. She lets strangers, or adversaries, take the decisive initiative on questions of doctrine, culture or action. When she acts or speaks it is often too late. In scientific research, social legislation, or humanism she has few innovators. It is not in this way that she will win the world to Christ. The Church still has time to hold her place—and even the first—in the formation of the future. But on one condition: She must become incarnate: "God became man in order that man become God." Then, and only then, will the Church come to life again. . . .

As a result of their daily experience with the deChristianized masses, many apostles, both priest and laymen, have concluded that modification—usually secondary, but pressing ones—are necessary for effective evangelization. They want a concrete and adapted religious teaching to replace the present preaching and catechizing which are too far from the Gospels. From theology, which is not a thing completed like Revelation, they want—without sacrificing anything—an attempt at synthesis and realism which will place the major dogmas of Christianity at the center and within the reach of the spiritual life of this century. . . .

Who is right? The answer is of great importance. It will determine the practical attitude of the majority of Catholics—for they have not taken sides. . . . Loyal to both, they stand aloof. As citizens of the world they feel themselves a part of it and responsible for its destiny. As sons of God, they understand their mysterious incorporation in His church and their transcendent vocation. To avoid betrayal they refuse to choose and commit themselves.

Meanwhile, they observe the anxiety and suffer because of it. They see clearly that the world crisis reacts inevitably on the Church which has her roots in it. They do not fear for her and her final triumph. But they wonder how she can pull through the present and how they can help her. . . To avoid bewilderment, they take refuge either in prayer or in some form of diversion.

To stiffen, to adapt herself, or to wait? Who is right? What is the meaning of this crisis? What do these initiatives and anxieties signify? An agony or growing pains? An autumn or a springtime of the Church? . .

Concerning the crisis we will say only this: insofar as it reveals a division among Catholics, it is an evil and ought to stop. The continuation of the mutual excommunications between brothers in Jesus Christ would constitute a scandal and an obstacle to going ahead. In proportion, however, as these parallel though opposite attitudes evidence an intense love of the Church they are a proof of her vitality, the sign of growing pains. This multiplication of ideas and undertakings is more reassuring than a stagnant satisfaction. We would like both to calm the anguish we observe among too many Catholics confronted with the times ahead, and to trouble the deceptive security into which too many of the faithful settle. We would like to show that both the only explanation of the present crisis and the only criterion of certitude and of action for the Christian today rest in the profound nature of the Church as her dogma and her history reveal them to us. . . .

The Church is not limited to what can be seen of her from without. Even her temporal visage bears witness of the eternal youth of Him who conquered death. Where those outside the Church see an agony, believers, without any risk of error, discern a renaissance. If the Church is the tree grown from the mustard seed it is normal that she experience, like it, the succession of seasons—autumns and springs.

The second conclusion is no less clear: to deny the Church one of these two elements is to destroy her. Thus we see the error common to both attitudes—contradictory though they be—which an exaggerated conservatism and an exaggerated progressivism would constitute: a denial of this incarnation of the Church. The first defends the transcendence and perennial duration of the Church but does not accept her contingence and her temporal growth; the second, to assure the development of her terrestrial forms forgets her eternal essence.

The truth is richer. It is not a question of choice but rather of uniting and conciliating, while leaving to each element its respective value. This is a precious teaching for the present commitments of the Christian. "Permanent incarnation of the Savior" the Church perpetuates His mystery. In Him two natures were united: He was man and God. In the same way two worlds are closely united in the Church: the invisible reality and the visible Society, the community of the faithful. If we forget one of these two aspects we suppress the Church. Without a visible organization, without institutions, a hierarchy, the sacraments, etc., Christ is no longer incarnate on earth, the Church is no longer a body. But on the other hand, to stop at the juridical organization and go no further than external appearances is to replace the Body of Christ by a corpse of the Church. . . .

Excessive traditionalism forgets one of the factors of the problem, and thus ends up in the same contradiction as modernism. While the latter made a norm of every value of today, the former makes of yesterday's forms the ideal of the present. This is a serious mistake of which Catholics should be doubly careful, first because this negative attitude of distrust of legitimate changes hampers the forward march of the Church, delays its penetration of the world, and risks furnishing pretexts for inaction to the average faithful, but especially because this habit of suspicion if it assumes a systematic form, would not be Christian. It would add a subtle danger of private interpretation to a lack of intellectual charity. . . .

The only effective course for the Church in the face of evil is to fight the world by starting a crusade against the adversaries of Christ, to answer attacks and even to launch offensives. To yield or to resign oneself perpetually to calumnies and injustices is to forget the violence of Christ towards the Pharisees. We must conquer the world, they say, with its own arms instead of compromising with it and losing without results.

Here again the Church recalls her mystery. It is true that she is "bound to the Eternal" by an alliance which is not of this world. It is true that she is the "spotless Jerusalem" which makes no pacts with Samaria. But it is not because she is divine that she should oppose the world. Her transcendence is not of this order. It is not because she is composed of the chosen people that she should harden her heart against those not yet in the Fold but "in the valley and shadow of death." The Church is not a party. Christians are not partisans. The Church will not win the world by opposing it as one force opposes another. No doubt every error calls for a refutation and every injustice a correction. . . . The Church never surrenders her principles. She never swerves from her sacred intransigeance. But will she adopt her adversaries' way of doing things? Will she, in order not to concur in their errors, try to impose her Truth and Faith by way of authority? . . .

The commitment which the Church ought to make today is much too important for her to be satisfied with a passing and local compromise. A vast synthesis is needed, capable of giving Christians the twofold answer they are seeking, a humanly effective action and a completely Catholic doctrine. Here again the theology and history of the Church will make possible the realization of this valid doctrine. . . .

The whole work will be of long duration and will not be the work of one man. The time has come when the greatest service that can be rendered the Church and her children is to make the "Christian summa" of the world in formation. The greatest error of the Christians of the twentieth century, and the one its children would not forgive them, would be to let the world take shape and unite without them, without God—or against Him; to be satisfied with recipes and tactics for their apostolate. We do not wish to make this error. It will perhaps be the great honor of our time to have started what others will carry through: a humanism in proportion to the world and God's plan. On this condition, and only on this condition, can the Church develop and become in a near future what she was in the Middle Ages for the West: the spiritual center of the world. The atheistic and anti-Christian civilization, which is spreading in our time, can give way to a sacred culture, to a Christian transfiguration of life.

334

Need we add that this task is incumbent on the intellectuals, as it was in the time of the great Doctors of the Church? They must bend every possible effort to the creation of a Christian society in which the kingdom of God will be sought above all else. The first apostolate, at the present crossroads, is in the realm of Thought. The Church is at this turning point where she can lose all, or win all, according to the spirituality she offers mankind.

(1948)

# THE INSUFFICIENCY OF EARTHLY LIFE

### JOHN HENRY CARDINAL NEWMAN

WE are ever expecting great things from life, from our internal consciousness every moment of our having souls; and we are ever being disappointed, on considering what we have gained from times past, or can hope from time to come. And life is ever promising and never fulfilling; and hence, however long it be, our days are few and evil. . . .

Our earthly life then gives promise of what it does not accomplish. It promises immortality, yet it is mortal; it contains life in death and eternity in time; and it attracts us by beginnings which faith alone brings to an end. . . .

There is something in moral truth and goodness, in faith, in firmness, in heavenly-mindedness, in meekness, in courage, in loving-kindness, to which this world's circumstances are quite unequal, for which the longest life is insufficient, which makes the highest opportunities of this world disappointing, which must burst the prison of this world to have its appropriate range. So that when a good man dies, one is led to say, "He has not half showed himself, he has had nothing to exercise him; his days are gone like a shadow, and he is withered like grass." . . .

Such being the unprofitableness of this life, viewed in itself, it is plain how we should regard it while we go through it. We should remember that it is scarcely more than an accident of our being—that it is no part of ourselves, who are immortal; that we are immortal spirits, independent of time and space, and that this life is but a sort of outward stage, on which we act for a time, and which is only sufficient and only intended to answer the purpose of trying whether we will serve God or no. We should consider ourselves to be in this world in no fuller sense than players in any game are in the game. . . .

To those who live by faith, every thing they see speaks of that future world; the very glories of nature, the sun, moon, stars, and the richness and the beauty of the earth, are as types and figures witnessing and teaching the invisible things of God. All that we see is destined one day to burst forth into a heavenly bloom, and to be transfigured into immortal glory. Heaven at present is out of sight, but in due time, as snow melts and discovers what it lay upon, so will this invisible creation fade away before those greater splendours which are behind it, and on which at present it depends. . . . For this glorious manifestation the whole creation is at present in travail, earnestly desiring that it may be accomplished in its season.

(1843)

# XII

# The Spiritual World

*The use of time. Eternal life. Faith, reason, and conscience.
The nature and joy of prayer. Christianity's message. The
contemplative life. Monasticism's contribution to civilization.
Miracles. Sin, contrition, and punishment. Salvation for non-
Catholics. "Remember the last things."*

WHY humble yourself and bend to false gods? Why bow your captive
body before helpless images and moulded earth? Why grovel in the
prostration of death, like the serpent whom ye worship? Why rush
into the downfall of the devil, his fall the cause of yours, and he your
companion? . . . Believe and live; you have been our persecutors
in time; in eternity, be companions of our joy.

ST. CYPRIAN, TO A HEATHEN MAGISTRATE,
(ca. A.D. 200)

## THE USE OF TIME

### THE REV. ANTONIN SERTILLANGES, O.P.

TIME contains all that is most sublime in what is passing, and it is the
harbinger of eternity. Time is not merely an extension; it possesses
depth because of our link with immortality. It could be only through
our own fault that the disillusioned line of Leconte de Lisle would be
fulfilled: "Time has not kept its promise divine."

Time does not betray; let us not be its traitors. Let us love and revere
it. Let us not be of the number of those who "kill" it by not using it
at all; of those who squander it by wasting it on empty nothings; of

those who overtax it and become its "executioners" as well as their own. Time, since it is itself an internal regulator of things, demands regularity. Time requires seriousness and depth, for by its nature it is a surface undulation below which is the immutable substance of things, and whose profoundest depths are the eternal Being.

In order to relish the full meaning of time, one must soar above it, take a position on the heights, and meditate on the eternal. Then, time is seen to be in concordance and participating in eternity as its "moving image."

(1950)

# MAN'S ACTIONS SHOULD BE POINTED TOWARD ETERNAL LIFE

### BLAISE PASCAL

WE do not require great education of the mind to understand that here is no real and lasting satisfaction; that our pleasures are only vanity; that our evils are infinite; and lastly, that death, which threatens us every moment, must infallibly place us within a few years under the dreadful necessity of being for ever either annihilated or unhappy.

There is nothing more real than this, nothing more terrible. Be we as heroic as we like, that is the end which awaits the noblest life in the world. Let us reflect on this, and then say whether it is not beyond doubt that there is no good in this life but in the hope of another; that we are happy only in proportion as we draw near it; and that, as there are no more woes for those who have complete assurance of eternity, so there is no more happiness for those who have no insight into it. . . .

For it is not to be doubted that the duration of this life is but a moment; that the state of death is eternal, whatever may be its nature; and that thus all our actions and thoughts must take different directions according to the state of that eternity, that it is impossible to take one step with sense and judgment, unless we regulate our course by the truth of that point which ought to be our ultimate end.

There is nothing clearer than this; and thus, according to the principles of reason, the conduct of men is wholly unreasonable, if they do not take another course.

(1661)

# INTELLECT AND FAITH

### ST. THOMAS AQUINAS

FAITH signifies the assent of the intellect to that which is believed. Now the intellect assents to a thing in two ways. First, through being moved to assent by its very object, which is known either by itself (as in the case of first principles, which are held by the habit of understanding), or through something else already known (as in the case of conclusions, which are held by the habit of science). Secondly, the intellect assents to something, not through being sufficiently moved to this assent by its proper object, but through act of choice, whereby it turns voluntarily to one side rather than to the other. Now if this be accompanied by doubt and fear of the opposite side, there will be opinion; while, if there be certainty and no fear of the other side, there will be faith.

Now those things are said to be seen which, of themselves, move the intellect or the senses to knowledge of them. Therefore it is evident that neither faith nor opinion can be of things seen either by the senses or by the intellect.

(1272)

# THE CHRISTIAN CONCEPT OF FAITH

### BROTHER BENIGNUS, F.S.C.

MY assent to a scientific proposition on the word of a scientist is superficially similar to my assent to a religious proposition on the word of God, since in both cases I believe on the word of one who knows; but the two acts are really worlds apart. I assent to the scientific proposition because it has been demonstrated and verified by men, and could be by me; I assent to the religious proposition while knowing that neither I nor any man can demonstrate or verify it in this life. "Faith is of things which appear not," and any explanation of it which would strive to make it similar to an assent whose object is demonstrable would falsify its very nature. . . .

The Christian stand on faith is perfectly rational, given its premises. Man's reason is limited, and consequently there are truths about God which man can neither demonstrate nor comprehend. If God has chosen to reveal these truths, natural reason itself demands that assent be given to them. It would be a mark of stupidity for man, seeking the beatitude for which God has destined him, to ignore the easiest and most certain way of it. This certain way is the way of faith in God's word; for reason flounders in error and uncertainty when it seeks by itself to discover the ultimate purpose of human life. What the Angelic Doctor [St. Thomas Aquinas] wrote in the thirteenth century can be supported by much more evidence today:

"No one can attain to such knowledge without danger, since human investigation, because of the weakness of our intellect, is prone to error; and this is clearly shown by reference to those philosophers who, in attempting to find out the purpose of human life by way of reason, did not find in themselves the true method, and so fell into many and shameful errors; and so greatly did they differ among themselves that scarcely two or three among them all were in agreement on any one question; yet, on the other hand, we see that by faith many peoples are brought to the acceptance of one common belief."

(1947)

THE light of faith makes us see what we believe. For just as, by the habits of the other virtues, man sees what is becoming to him in respect of that habit, so, by the habit of faith, the human mind is inclined to assent to such things as are becoming to a right faith, and not to assent to others.

ST. THOMAS AQUINAS (1272)


# FAITH IS A FREE ACT

### AUBREY DE VERE

WHEN man believes Divine Truth, on Divine Faith, he believes voluntarily as well as reasonably, and therefore meritoriously. It is the special dignity of God's *rational* creature that that union with his Creator for which he was made was effected neither passively on his part nor involuntarily, but through a personal co-operation with grace, which, though the humblest, is also the highest exercise of his most Godlike power—free-will. In mere intellect there is often, as in the animal part of our being, something that resembles mechanism—witness our involuntary "association of ideas." In our ordinary and worldly life there is also an element of bondage, for we act, though only within certain limits, under the suasion of downward-tending inclinations, and with a preference determined in part by the balance of earthly interests. But the Soul remains free; and the Will, the spiritual within us, when it is a "good-will" becomes the highest expression of our freedom, lifting the reason into its loftiest sphere, and delivering the heart from the thraldom of inferior motives. The obedience of this nobler Will to grace is the "fiat" which unites man with God; and faith, the light of the soul, is the child of that union. The Creator's primal *Fiat lux* was an act of supreme authority; the creature's *Fiat voluntas tua* is an act of humility, and irradiates the world within.

Faith, so far from being belief on compulsion, is, in the highest sense, a spiritual *act,* though also more than reasonable. There is no difficulty in recognizing this truth except to those who have been entangled by sophisms, and cannot discern what is divinely simple. The unbeliever unconsciously assumes that the frank acceptance of a creed is much the same sort of thing whether the creed be true or false. He thus implicitly implies that truth does not exist; for if it exists it cannot but wield a discriminating power. Religion affirms the contrary—viz. that objective truth does exist, and that God's *reasonable* creature was created in a dignity so high, and after his Fall was renewed by grace so admirable, that his well-being consists in communion with Truth, whose claim he has been made capable of recognizing.

(1887)

# FAITH AND REASON

## JOHN HENRY CARDINAL NEWMAN

TRUE faith is what may be called colourless, like air or water; it is but the medium through which the soul sees Christ; and the soul as little really rests upon it and contemplates it, as the eye can see the air. When, then, men are bent on holding it (as it were) in their hands, curiously inspecting, analyzing, and so aiming at it, they are obliged to colour and thicken it, that it may be seen and touched. That is, they substitute for it something or other, a feeling, notion, sentiment, conviction, or act of reason, which they may hang over, and dote upon. They rather aim at experiences (as they are called) within them, than at Him that is without them. . . .

Faith is a process of the Reason, in which so much of the grounds of inference cannot be exhibited, so much lies in the character of the mind itself, in its general view of things, its estimate of the probable and the improbable, its impressions concerning God's will, and its anticipations derived from its own inbred wishes, that it will ever seem to the world irrational and despicable;—till, that is, the event confirms it. . . .

Faith is an intellectual act; right Faith is an intellectual act, done in a certain moral disposition. Faith is an act of Reason, viz. a reasoning upon presumptions; right Faith is a reasoning upon holy, devout, and enlightened presumptions. Faith ventures and hazards; right Faith ventures and hazards deliberately, seriously, soberly, piously, and humbly, counting the cost and delighting in the sacrifice.

(1843)

# ACCEPTANCE OF ALL THAT
# THE CHURCH TEACHES

## ST. THOMAS AQUINAS

Now the formal object of faith is the First Truth, as manifested in Holy Scripture and the teaching of the Church, which proceeds from the First Truth. Consequently, whoever does not adhere, as to an infallible and divine rule, to the teaching of the Church, which proceeds from the First Truth manifested in Holy Scripture, has not the habit of faith, but holds that which is of faith otherwise than by faith. So, too, it is evident that a man whose mind holds a conclusion, without knowing how it is proved, has not a scientific knowledge, but merely an opinion about it. Now it is evident that he who adheres to the teaching of the Church, as to an infallible rule, assents to whatever the Church teaches. Otherwise, if, of the things taught by the Church, he holds what he chooses to hold and rejects what he chooses to reject, he no longer adheres to the teaching of the Church as to an infallible rule, but to his own will. Hence it is manifest that a heretic who obstinately disbelieves one article of faith, is not prepared to follow the teaching of the Church in all things; but if he is not obstinate, he is no longer in heresy but only in error. Therefore it is clear that . . . a heretic in regard to one article has no faith in the other articles, but only a kind of opinion in accordance with his own will.

(1272)

IF a man says to me, I would understand in order that I may believe, I answer, Believe that you may understand. . . .

"I would understand in order that I may believe." Certainly, what I am now saying, I say with the object that those may believe who do not yet believe. Nevertheless unless they understand what I am saying, they cannot believe. Hence what he says is in some part true, "I would understand in order that I may believe." And I, too, am right when I say, as does the Prophet (Is.vii, 9, sec.LXX), Nay, believe that thou mayest believe my words; believe, in order that thou mayest understand the word of God.

ST. AUGUSTINE (ca. 410)

## "CONSCIENCE MUST STAND SUPREME"

### THE REV. COLUMBA CARY-ELWES, O.S.B.

No man may surrender his conscience except to truth, whether he be Catholic, Protestant, Theist, Hindu or Moslem. That is the inexorable law of our nature; and he who does surrender his will to anything else is a slave who deserves our pity. For conscience is the power of the practical judgment to discern what it is right to do in given circumstances, and what it is right to do can only be discovered by our intellect; it is a form of truth. To surrender our judgement, or conscience, to force or to some imagined danger, to passion, is to surrender the soul, its reason and its will, to something unworthy of it. . . .

No non-Catholic should submit to the authority of the Church until his conscience tells him it is reasonable to do so. Faith is not blind, and the Church maintains that the evidence for her claims is enough for certitude, given an unbiased mind. Even a Catholic should not remain a Catholic if his conscience tells him he should not. But here the Church, as she claims that the evidence is sufficient for certitude, maintains that a Catholic who was properly instructed could not in fact arrive at such a conclusion without fault. The fault might be in

343

trusting too much to his own reasoning and not relying upon grace for support; more often it would be in the moral sphere, due to the difficulty of living according to the Church's exacting laws. But the fact remains that conscience must stand supreme all the time for Catholics quite as much as for any other human soul. . . .

All men have the support of God's guidance in their souls no matter what their religion, and any man who humbly asks for help may be assured that he will be granted it provided he takes all the ordinary means for finding out God's will in his regard. That was the reason why God implanted intelligence within us. But the snare of this method of direct guidance alone is that our desires get entangled in the answer. The wish is father to the thought, and never more so than in those moral questions which beset the soul like a storm. Few men are good judges in their own cause. . . .

We are upon the frontiers of a new age; we are feeling in the night between two civilizations. It may be that we shall come out into an age of barbarism; we may emerge upon an ordered plain in which the rule of Christ holds sway. Which it will be depends primarily upon our thoughts; for it is precisely in thought that the uncertainties of our day consist.

Men have long since abandoned truly Christian ideas, on authority, on morality, on justice, on economics. They have invented other ways, the rationalist way, the romantic way, the liberal way, the scientific way, and lastly the dictator's way. And only too often these ways have been shown to lead to a hell upon earth for someone; for the poor or for a minority, or indeed for a majority.

The Christian answer is never out-of-date; it remains as true as when Christ first propounded it. But each age needs a new application of these same truths. The problems are different and therefore require new answers, even though by the application of the same principles. But modern man has forgotten those first principles upon which his civilization has been based.

(1951)

EVERY judgment of conscience, be it right or wrong, be it about things evil in themselves or morally indifferent, is obligatory, in such wise that he who acts against his conscience always sins.

ST. THOMAS AQUINAS (ca. 1270)

# THE JOY OF PRAYER

## GEORGES BERNANOS

THE usual notion of prayer is so absurd. How can those who know nothing about it, who pray little or not at all, dare speak so frivolously of prayer? A Carthusian, a Trappist will work for years to make of himself a man of prayer, and then any fool who comes along sets himself up as a judge of this lifelong effort. If it were really what they suppose, a kind of chatter, the dialogue of a madman with his shadow, or even less—a vain and superstitious sort of petition to be given the good things of this world, how could innumerable people find until their dying day, I won't even say such great "comfort"—since they put no faith in the solace of the senses—but sheer, robust, vigorous, abundant joy in prayer? Oh, of course, "suggestion," say the scientists. Certainly they could never have known old monks, wise, shrewd, unerring in judgment, and yet aglow with passionate insight, so very tender in their humanity. What miracle enables these semi-lunatics, these prisoners of their own dreams, those sleep-walkers, apparently to enter more deeply each day into the pain of others? An odd sort of dream, an unusual opiate which, far from turning him back into himself and isolating him from his fellows, united the individual with mankind in the spirit of universal charity!

This seems a very daring comparison. I apologize for advancing it, yet perhaps it might satisfy many people who find it hard to think for themselves, unless the thought has first been halted by some unexpected, surprising image. Could a sane man set himself up as a judge of music because he sometimes touched a keyboard with the tips of his fingers? And surely if a Bach fugue, a Beethoven symphony leave him cold, if he has to content himself with watching on the face of another listener the reflected pleasure of a supreme, inaccessible delight, such a man has only himself to blame.

But alas! We take the psychiatrist's word for it. The unanimous testimony of saints is held as of little or no account. They may all affirm that this kind of deepening of spirit is unlike any other experience, that instead of showing us more and more of our own complexity it ends in sudden total illumination, opening out upon azure light—they can be dismissed with a few shrugs. Yet when has any man of prayer told us that prayer has failed him?

(1938)

# THE CONTEMPLATIVE LIFE CAN
# BE LED BY ALL

### THOMAS MERTON

THE term "contemplative life" is one that is much mistreated. It is more often used than defined, and that is why arguments about the respective merits of "active" and "contemplative" orders generally end nowhere. I am not talking here about the contemplative orders, but about the contemplative life. It is a life that can be led and, in fact, must eventually be led by every good Christian. It is the life for which we were created, and which will eventually be our everlasting joy in heaven. By the grace of Christ we can begin to lead that life even on earth, and many in fact do so begin. Some of them are in cloisters, because the vows and rules of religious orders and congregations make the necessary work of preparation easy and, as it were, almost a matter of course. But many more "contemplatives" are out in the world. A lot of them may be found in places like Harlem and wherever people suffer, and perhaps many of these have never even heard the word "contemplative." And yet, on the other hand, not all of those who are in contemplative orders are contemplatives. Through their own fault they miss the end of their vocation.

The contemplative life is a life entirely occupied with God—with love and knowledge of God. It can be considered from three points of view, as it were in three degrees. There is first of all possible a kind of natural contemplation of God—that of the artist, the philosopher, and of the most advanced pagan religions. Then there is the contemplative life in the usual sense of the word: a life in which a baptized Christian, making full use of all the means which the Church puts at his disposal—Sacraments, Liturgy, penance, prayer, meditation, spiritual reading and so on—strives to conform his will with God's will and to see and love God in all things and thus to dispose himself for union with Him. This is *active* contemplation, in which grace indeed is the principle of all the supernatural value and ordination of our acts, but in which much of the initiative belongs to our own powers, prompted and sustained by grace. This form of the contemplative life prepares us for contemplation properly so called: the life of *infused* or *passive* or *mystical* contemplation.

Infused contemplation is nothing but the fullness of the Christian

346

life—the flowering of grace and the gifts and beatitudes which perfect the work of the three theological virtues.

Far from being something esoteric and dangerous, infused contemplation is given us as the normal term of the Christian life even on earth. *"Omnis qui ad Dominum convertitur contemplativam vitam desiderat,"* said St. Gregory the Great and he was using contemplation in our sense: to live on the desire of God alone; to have one's mind divested of all earthly things and united, in so far as human weakness permits, with Christ. And he adds that the contemplative life begins on earth in order to continue, more perfectly, in heaven. Saint Thomas echoed him with his famous phrase: *"Quaedam inchoatio beatitudinis."* Saint Bonaventure goes farther than any of the other Doctors of the Church in his insistence that all Christians should desire infused contemplation. And in his second conference on the Hexaemeron, applying Christ's words in Matthew 12:42, he says that the Queen of the South who left her own land and traveled far to hear the wisdom of Solomon will rise up in judgment against our generation which refuses the treasures of infused wisdom, preferring the far lesser riches of worldly wisdom and philosophy.

Infused contemplation is an experimental knowledge of God's goodness "tasted" and "possessed" by a vital contact in the depths of the soul. By infused love, we are given an immediate grasp of God's own substance, and rest in the obscure and profound sense of His presence and transcendent actions within our inmost selves, yielding ourselves altogether to the work of His transforming Spirit.

(1948)

# CHRISTIANITY'S MESSAGE

### FRANCOIS MAURIAC

When I hear great voices propounding from the pulpit questions concerning society and confronting the Gospel with the problems of the State, the relations between capital and labor, between the civil power and the Church, I have no doubt of the urgency of coming to grips with such questions.

Yet I cannot help suspecting that a great number among that vast congregation—vast since it also included the unseen radio listeners—

must be sharing my feelings, mingled with great admiration, of having been slightly deceived; for surely they ask for one thing alone, and only come crowding around the pulpit to hear one thing—that we have a Father in Heaven, that we have been redeemed, that our sins will be forgiven.

Do you think that in the secrecy of their hearts they want to hear about syndicates? No, of course they don't. They want to hear about forgiveness and redemption.

(1950)

# MONASTICISM'S CONTRIBUTION
# TO CIVILIZATION

### CHARLES RENE COUNT DE MONTALEMBERT

From the middle of the fifth century the cenobitical institution, proceeding from the Thebaid, had occupied one by one all the provinces of the Roman Empire and encamped upon every frontier to await and win over the Barbarians. The immense services which this institution rendered to the Church, and the new and necessary force which it lent to society, lying inert between the avenging embrace of the Germans and the despicable languor of expiring imperialism, could already be appreciated.

The monks were, after the Papacy, the direct instruments of the salvation and honor of Europe. They rendered her capable of gigantic and supernatural effort against the inveterate paganism of the old world and the torrential impetuosity of the northern invaders. Contemporaries themselves perceived it; no one disputed the solemn testimony of the priest Rufinus, who was not himself a monk but had long studied and observed them: "There is no doubt that without these humble penitents the world could not have gone on existing." . . .

The lovers of solitude, the men of penitence, sacrifice, and voluntary humiliation, alone knew how to live, hope, resist and stand fast. To those who reproach the monastic spirit with enervating, debasing and making sluggards of men, let it suffice to recall what the monks were in those days of desolation and despair. They alone showed themselves equal to all needs and proof against all terrors. Human courage has never been more tried than among the monks; it has never displayed greater resources or a deeper constancy; and it has never shown itself more manly and unshakable.

The monks opposed to the successive waves of the invading Barbarians an insurmountable barrier of virtue, courage, patience and genius; and when all external resistance was found useless and impossible, it became apparent that they had formed, for all the germs of civilization and of the future, shelters which the floods might pass over but could not engulf. In the midst of the deluge which annihilated the Roman Europe and the world of antiquity, they concentrated themselves in a high and pure sphere which was destined to survive all that chaos and be the center from which new life would come into a new world.

Their courage was surpassed only by their charity—by their gentle and sympathetic compassion with all those whom, they saw, burdened with the miseries which overwhelmed the earth. They loved their neighbors passionately because they loved God more than themselves. They derived the secret of this love and this supernatural energy from Christian self-renouncement, from the voluntary expiation of their own faults and those of others. In opposing the three eternal bases of monastic life—poverty, chastity and obedience—to the orgies of luxury, debauchery and pride, they created a contrast which was also a remedy. By sacrificing in a spirit of penance all permitted privileges, such as marriage, property and the free disposition of their time and their lives, they became the guardians and saviors of those who lawfully desired to retain these legitimate possessions, and who saw no way in which such things could be safeguarded from irremediable outrage in a social order so desperate.

But we must not be under a misapprehension on this matter. They never dreamed of making their exceptional life the common rule. They knew that it could only be the privilege of certain souls, more completely transfixed than others by the blood of Christ. They did not presume to compel all to accept the evangelical counsels as precepts. They remained faithful to the interpretations of the sacred texts which had been unchanged from the time of the first Popes until the present day. Their leaders always resisted the excesses of intemperate zeal which characterized the Gnostics and others, who would have rendered what was possible for some obligatory upon all. No doubt one could cite certain events, or certain lives, which appear to lean toward excess. But there are excesses which are inseparable from the force and vigor of all great movements of the spirit, and which only serve to reveal the existence of a vital and fertile current. In their hearts, on the whole, they remained aloof from all unregulated exaltation, and firmly attached alike to apostolic traditions and to the infallible prudence of the Church. They had no tendency to transform the whole world into a cloister, though this accusation has been brought against them. They wanted only to create and maintain, despite all the storms and defeats which characterized the world they knew, the home, the place of refuge, the school of a peace and power mightier than the world.

That is why they brought so great an influence to bear upon the world thereafter. They had fled from men in vain, for men followed them. Everything of the good heart, the lofty mind and the clear intellect which survived in this broken-down society rallied round the monks, as if to escape from universal ruin. Their spirit breathed from the far places of the desert upon towns, upon schools, and even upon palaces, lighting them anew with some rays of vigor and reason. The distraught people sought them out, listened to them and admired them, understanding them little, to be sure, and imitating them even less. Yet their mere existence was the most energetic protest against pagan materialism, which had ended by depraving all souls and undermining the social constitution of the ancient world. They aroused in man all those intellectual and moral forces which could help him to bear up under the unparalleled catastrophies of the age. They taught him to struggle against that reign of sensuality which was to be so painfully expiated under the yoke of the Barbarians. They showed him at one and the same time the road to heaven and the way to a future in this world—the sole future open to those long enervated races, namely regeneration by suffering voluntarily accepted and courageously borne.

(1870)

## MIRACLES

RT. REV. MSGR. RONALD KNOX

THERE is a significant story to be found in one of the less familiar by-ways of Old Testament history. When Israel had been oppressed for seven years under the tyrannous yoke of the Midianites, God would raise up a deliverer for His people; and His choice fell upon Gedeon, a hero of little estimation, till then, in the world's eyes; "Behold," he says, "my family is the meanest in Manasses, and I am the least in my father's house." Humility, rather than want of faith, made Gedeon ask for a sign, a miraculous sign, that this strange vocation was really meant for him. And Almighty God saw fit to indulge his request. Gedeon laid a fleece of wool on the ground, and left it there all night. The first night the fleece alone was wet with dew, when all the ground was dry; the next night, the fleece alone was dry, and there was dew on all the ground. An unfamiliar incident, and one which would hardly be remembered by ordinary Christian folk but for the providential accident that it serves us for a type of our Blessed Lady's Child-bearing; she, like, Gedeon's fleece, was the one spot in our benighted and parched world where the dew of Divine Grace could find a lodgment, when in the fulness of time we were set free from the tyranny of our sins.

I say, a significant story, because it seems to me that it throws into relief a very important consideration which we are apt to overlook when we discuss the subject of miracles. What consideration? Why, this—that those special exercises of Divine power which we call miracles are not in themselves greater, are not in themselves more sensational, are not in themselves more deserving of our gratitude than His ordinary operations in nature. It was a wonderful sight, doubtless, when after a sleepless night spent between hope and self-distrust, Gedeon went out at dawn to find the fleece wringing wet, glistening like silver in the grey light of morning. And yet, when he went out the next day, was there not a still more wonderful vision awaiting him. A whole world silvered with dew, diamonds shining from every blade of grass and every fallen leaf, the very gossamer in the fields a patch-work of filigree? You have seen as much yourself, maybe, on some early summer morning in the country. Oh no, there was nothing wonderful about it, of course; you were quite right; it was just dew . . . Nothing wonderful, because we're so accustomed to it, because we take it so for granted. When you saw that sight long ago, with the clear eyes of childhood, or with the transfiguring vision of first love, perhaps you caught the marvel of it; and since then, what exactly has happened? Is it that the dew-drenched world is less wonderful? Or that you have lost your faculty of wonder?

It is important to realize that the same power which covered a single fleece with dew one night covered a whole landscape with dew the next night. And which was the marvel? Which showed the greater exercise of power, which signalized God's bounty in greater profusion? The first night, or the second? Because in the second instance we can account for the phenomenon, whereas in the first instance we cannot account for the phenomenon, we call the first instance a miracle. But if we had not lost the child's faculty of wonder, we should see the same hand at work on the second night as on the first, only with more widespread effect, only with richer largesse. The same hand, the same power, only exercised in a different way. The same power which sent the stars rolling on their courses gives sudden health to some poor cripple at Lourdes, and we say, "Impossible!" Th  feeding of the Five Thousand, *that* taxes our powers of belief to the utmost. And yet, as St. Augustine pointed out long ago, what is the feeding of the five thousand compared with that patient process by which vast plains of wheat shoot up and bud and mature, under God's hand, to make the slices of bread which you forgot to say grace over yesterday? The same hand, the same power.

A miracle, though it ought to mean any event, natural or supernatural, which claims our wonder, is the term technically applied to a particular class of the wonderful works of God. God ordinarily brings events to pass in the natural world by means of secondary causes. When He suspends for a moment the action of those secondary causes, we call it a miracle. . . .

Everything which revelation or natural theology can tell us about the character of God, everything which Science can teach us about the uniformity of Nature, fortifies us in the belief that miracles are a very exceptional feature in God's ordinance of the world, designed to meet exceptional needs. We are not to multiply miracles beyond what is necessary. To take a very simple way of illustrating that, let me suggest that Almighty God would not do a sensible miracle in circumstances where there was nobody there to see or to be conscious of the experience. Miracles are a message from Him addressed to man; they would not occur unless man were present to witness them. I think it is not presuming too much upon our human philosophy to suggest that.

They are a message addressed from God to Man. And, although they may have various secondary purposes—the relief of human pain, the satisfaction of human needs, the vindication of innocence against injustice, and so on—they have all one primary purpose, and that is to be an evidence—if the word had not become vulgarized in our day, I would say an advertisement—of His Almighty Power. To prove that He does govern the world; to prove that the Catholic Church is His Church, bearing the seal of His Commission; to prove that this or that man or woman is a Saint, one of His special friends, and therefore worthy of special honor from the faithful—that is the sort of motive which is a sufficient motive to call this special exercise of His power into play.

But, you say, if miracles are only an evidence of God's power, surely they must be unnecessary? Have we not just agreed that His natural operations are, in themselves, more wonderful even than miracles? Why cannot we be content, then, to learn His Omnipotence from the lightning and from the sunset, from the multitudinous perfections of creation, from the delicate workmanship of leaf and petal, from the patterns which the frost traces on our windows? Having left us such witness of Himself, having set upon our world this seal of creative wisdom, would He do more than that? Would He try to arrest our attention by breaking His own laws, as the more vulgar kind of modern music arrests our attention by working discords into its harmony? Must He sacrifice consistency, to advertise Omnipotence?

The answer to that objection is twofold. In the first place, God does not do miracles *merely* to display His power, merely to show that He can do them. He does miracles, because He wants to draw our attention to this or that sanctified career. What is more important, than that we should take notice of a Saint? And who is more anxious that we should take no notice of him, than the Saint himself? The very humility of the Saints would defeat God's purposes for them, if He did not take His own steps to shed lustre upon their self-effacing virtues. It is miracle that gives us the assurance: "Behold My servant, whom I have chosen." . . .

Miracles are God's signature, appended to His masterpiece of creation; not because they ought to be needed, but because they are needed. And if you doubt it, tell me of any religion that has really affected millions of men, really stirred their hearts, that did not claim miracles for its sanction. . . .

You will hear people say, "We, in our day, believe the Gospel in spite of the miracles it records, not because of them. To us, miracles make it harder, not easier, to accept the Christian faith." Now, if you examine that statement for a moment, you will see that it rests on a very silly confusion. In order to believe the Gospel, you must do two things. You must first of all convince yourself that the narrative which the Evangelists have left us is true; and then you must decide whether the Church is right in inferring, from the narrative, that the Hero of the story was Incarnate God. Now, it's quite true to say that the miracles which are recorded in the Gospel don't make it easier for us to believe *in the truth of the narrative*. But then, who ever thought they would? Who ever, in his wildest dreams, imagined that a document was MORE likely to be historically accurate because it represented its Hero as walking on the water, instead of walking on the land? The suggestion is ridiculous. No, the value of miracle comes in when we reach the second process, the process of proving that the Church is right in representing the Hero of the Gospels as Incarnate God. Now, is anybody going to be such a fool as to tell us that miracles make it harder for us, instead of easier for us, to believe that? Is anybody going to say: "What! Did Christ walk on the water? Then of course He can't have been God! Did Christ rise from the dead? Then of course He can't be God"? Obviously, if the Gospels give us satisfactory evidence that Our Lord walked on the water and rose from the dead, then that is the best possible proof that the claim He made was true. . . .

The Gospels deal with a situation in which miracles are not only natural; they are necessary. Our Lord was not proving that He was a prophet, was not proving that He was a man entrusted with a divine mission. He was proving that He had been personally present when the foundations of the earth were laid, when the morning stars sang their praises together, and all the sons of God made a joyful melody. He was proving that He had existed from all eternity, the Co-equal Word of the Omnipotent Father. Was He to prove this by earnest moral exhortations, by devoted missionary zeal, by patient endurance of indignities? Put Raphael down at a street-corner as a pavement-artist, what proof can he give of his identity but to paint like Raphael? Bring God down to earth, what proof can He give of His Godhead but to command the elements like God? . . .

The Catholic Church has believed in miracles, not as something that used to happen a long time ago in Palestine, but as something that may happen anywhere, any day, given the proper conditions. . . .

We are bound to believe in the Bible miracles, because they are in the Bible; we are not bound as Catholics to believe in this or that miracle of later times. We're bound to believe that St. Peter the Apostle walked on the water, because the Gospel tells us that he did. We are not *bound* to believe that St. Peter of Alcantara walked across a river dry-shod, although that story is told of him. But in this discussion I have taken the liberty of dividing my subject not into Bible miracles and ecclesiastical miracles, but into Gospel miracles and ecclesiastical miracles. We have considered the miracles which Our Lord did Himself, during His lifetime. We have to consider now the miracles which He has done and still does through the agency of His Saints, now that His feet tread no longer the ways of our earth. . . .

If you turn to the Acts of the Apostles, you find yourself confronted with miracle. If you turn to St. Paul's epistles, you find him justifying his own apostolic position by appealing to miracle. And wherever you turn in reading the lives of the Saints, from John the Evangelist in the first century to John Vianney in the nineteenth, you will spoil the whole lesson of them and lose the whole flavor of them if you try to leave out of sight this miraculous element in the story. . . .

We find, as a matter of history and as a matter of common experience, that these signs are only vouchsafed by Almighty God at distant and irregular intervals, for the most part in connection with the lives and deaths of men and women of recognizable holiness. We take the facts as we find them; we admit that miracles are not common. We admit that stories of miracles have to be accepted with reserve, and the evidence for them carefully weighed. But we do not admit that miracles never happen. We refuse to admit that, because it happens to be clean contrary to the evidence. . . .

All this talk of an opposition between science and miracle is merest hypocrisy. The fact is that you cannot believe in a miracle unless you believe in science. Supposing you saw a man suddenly lifted up two feet in the air. When you had satisfied yourself that it was not done by wires or mirrors, what verdict would you pass on the performance? Only two verdicts are possible. One is to say, "Why, this must be a miracle! That man is a solid body, and like all solid bodies he is attracted towards the earth's center. No natural obstacle is counteracting the law of attraction; no scientific explanation is possible; it must, therefore, be a miracle." That is one possible attitude; and the other possible attitude is this, to say, "There! I knew it! These scientists do not know their job! Here have they been telling me for years that a solid body is attracted towards the center of the earth, by a fixed law of nature; and now I can see for myself that it is not true. A solid body is just as likely to rise in the air as not. Henceforth, no science for me; I will not believe in a word the fellows say." Which of those two attitudes is the more respectful towards science? The attitude which can witness a miracle and still preserve its faith in Sir Isaac Newton? Or the attitude which calls Sir Isaac Newton a liar because once, in exceptional circumstances, his principle, valid in itself, has been superseded by a higher principle? . . .

We do not resent scientific investigation into our stories of miracle; rather, we welcome it. We do not say that in a given case miracle is theologically certain; we only say that it is, so far, the best account we can give of the facts. We differ from our critics only in this, that we say, "It may be a miracle, or it may not," whereas they say, "Whatever it is, it certainly is not a miracle." Which side approaches the subject with an open mind, and in a spirit of inquiry? Which side approaches the subject encumbered with the burden of dogmatic prepossessions? Which side faces the facts?

(1928)


# WHY MAN SHOULD LIVE
## ACCORDING TO GOD

### ST. AUGUSTINE

WHEN man lives according to man, not according to God, he is like the devil. Because not even an angel might live according to an angel, but only according to God, if he was to abide in the truth, and speak God's truth and not his own lie. . . . When, then, a man lives according to the truth, he lives not according to himself, but according to God; for He was God who said, "I am the truth." When, therefore, man lives according to himself—that is, according to man, not according to God—assuredly he lives according to a lie; not that man himself is a lie, for God is his author and creator, who is certainly not the author and creator of a lie, but because man was made upright, that he might not live according to himself, but according to Him that made him—in other words, that he might do His will and not his own; and not to live as he was made to live, that is a lie. For he certainly desires to be blessed even by not living so that he may be blessed. And what is a lie if this desire be not? Wherefore it is not without meaning said that all sin is a lie. For no sin is committed save by that desire or will by which we desire that it be well with us, and shrink from it being ill with us. That, therefore, is a lie which we do in order that it may be well with us, but which makes us more miserable than

356

we were. And why is this, but because the source of man's happiness lies only in God, whom he abandons when he sins, and not in himself, by living according to whom he sins?

(A.D. 426)

WHEN God punishes sinners, He does not inflict His evil on them, but leaves them to their own evil. . . . When therefore God punishes, He punishes as a judge those who transgress the law, not by bringing evil upon them from Himself, but by driving them on to that which they have chosen, to fill up the sum of their misery.

ST. AUGUSTINE (ca. 415)

GOOD and evil should be set in the context of what is proper to man as man. This is his rational life. Therefore a good or bad human act is tested by its agreement or otherwise with reason instructed by the divine law, whose principles may be inborn, acquired, or infused.

ST. THOMAS AQUINAS (ca. 1270)

# SIN

### THE REV. JOHN B. HARNEY, C.S.P.

SIN . . . is not chiefly the external act of theft, or adultery, or murder, or any other evil deed that man may do, but it is the immaterial act of his will by which he freely chooses and determines to do something that he knows or fully believes to be contrary to the law of God. . . . The core of sin is in the heart of him who wills it, not in any physical action by which he makes it manifest. Its external completion is but the husk and shell, adding little more than intensity as a rule to its wickedness. . . .

To have a clear and accurate realization of what constitutes a mortal sin we must consider carefully much more than the deed, the words, or the desires which are objectively against the laws of God. The individuals against whom they seem to stand are not always accountable or responsible for them in the same measure and degree. That is obvious and is universally admitted in the case of those apparent culprits who are insane or are plainly delirious at the time that they say or do what is objectively reprehensible. It is also quite certain that

357

many other people who seem to be normal are at times partially or even wholly irresponsible for various misdeeds done while they were hardly more than half conscious, or were laboring under some serious mental handicap. It is always difficult to estimate the extent, the importance, and the actual value of those extenuating circumstances. Happily, it is rarely our duty to do that for others. We can and we must do it for ourselves. We know all the facts. One principle, however, must always be kept clearly in mind. It is this. No man does or can commit a mortal sin unless he *knows,* or *strongly suspects* that the contemplated action is mortally sinful, and yet decides to do it. To act while uncertain on that point is to sin gravely.

It has already been indicated that there can be no question of sin unless one's intellect and one's will are both involved in the act under consideration. Those two spiritual powers are separate and distinct faculties of our souls, with wholly different objectives and functions. They are, however, very intimately related. Neither can carry on, even momentarily without the other. Of these two, the intellect is always the first to act, for the will is a blind, unseeing faculty. Its function is to choose, to decide, to determine. It cannot inaugurate any activity of the soul or of the body, but must wait until a signal of one sort or another has been given to the intellect. That signal may come from outside the man, a ray of light, a noise, a spoken word. It may come from within him, the twitching of a nerve, the stirring of an appetite, a recollection, a dream. It may be clear or vague, strong or weak, but it must be at least enough to make an impression on the intellect; otherwise, the will cannot come into play. But once that signal has been perceived, however faintly, the will springs into action and thenceforth remains in charge of the intellect's subsequent activity. . . .

Our intellects do not always give our wills right and sound advice. Quite frequently they approve what is wrong and evil. Occasionally they condemn what is right and good. In either case they play a part in every decision of the will, for while it is free, and is able to throw aside even the soundest of intellectual judgments, it does not, nor can it choose what is wholly evil in every way and from every point of view, but only what is set before it as good and desirable in some way. . . .

Ignorance, especially of basic religious truths and moral principles, is plainly not an excuse for many of the gravest sins. When it is presented in extenuation of patent wrongdoing we must therefore inquire into its character and origin. . . .

The ignorance of a man who could easily have known the truth, who should have known it, who deliberately neglected or refused to become acquainted with it, is not an excuse for his misdeeds.

Happily, it is not for any among us to form definite judgments about any man except ourselves. The demand of Christ is clear and all-embracing: "Judge not, that you not be judged. For with what judgment you judge, you shall be judged, and with what measure you meet, it shall be measured to you again." (Matt. vii. 1-2). . . .

As *blameless* ignorance cancels responsibility for intrinsically evil desires, words, and deeds, so also does a lack of advertence to their real character. In this ignorance and inadvertence are alike. The latter may be aptly described as temporary, transient ignorance. It is a much more widespread evil. For the hundred who do not know right from wrong in many matters, there are a thousand who know but do not stop to think. They go blithely on their way; thinking, saying, desiring, doing many wrong things, often leaving a ghastly trail of ruin in their wake, but almost wholly unconscious of the harm they have done to others, and only dimly if at all aware of their sinfulness. . . .

Since God is infinitely perfect, we know that He does not pass one unvaried judgment on all human sins. We ourselves see that there are great differences between them; between the anger that prompts a man to commit a cold-blooded murder and the anger that stops with a hasty word of complaint; between a lie by which a man deliberately blasts another's reputation beyond cure or reparation and a harmless lie by which a schoolboy hopes to escape a scolding. All men perceive such differences, at least vaguely. What men see dimly, God sees unerringly. On that ground rests the distinction between *mortal* and *venial* sins—a distinction of tremendous importance. . . .

However, we must be very sharply on guard against two errors. The first is that of excusing, or minimizing our sins too readily on the score of ignorance. Quite frequently ignorance is an aggravation, rather than a diminution of guilt. A judge, for example, who has handed down an utterly wrong and harmful decision in a case of serious importance cannot be excused on the ground that he was ignorant of legal principles and precedents which *plainly* called for a very different verdict. It was his business and his strict duty to have known these things. His ignorance was not a mere misfortune; it was an instance and a proof of criminal negligence.

In very much the same way many men who sin gravely will be without excuse even though they may be able to say truthfully that they did not know they were sinning, or at any rate did not know that their sins were grievous. This is more likely to be the case with Catholics than any other group.

Those who began life with the gift of Divine faith; who have had the priests of the Church as their teachers and guides; who have had within easy reach but have wilfully failed to make use of the absolutely sound, reliable, and even infallible means which God has graciously given them of separating the wholesome wheat of truth from the huge heaps of chaff which clutter this world, ignorance will rarely be a legitimate or acceptable excuse. Instead, it is almost always an aggravation of the guilt that is inherent in their violations of God's laws. For if they are ignorant of His will, it is usually because they have not wished, have not sought, have not tried to keep their minds in accord with His truth, nor their wills in harmony with His laws, but have preferred darkness to light and ignorance to knowledge. For such as these the plea: "I did not know" is worthless. For others who have broken His law in blameless ignorance, it is of high value.

(1949)

## CONFESSION

### BLAISE PASCAL

THE Catholic religion does not bind us to confess our sins indiscriminately to everybody; it allows them to remain hidden from all other men save one, to whom she bids us reveal the innermost recesses of our heart, and show ourselves as we are. There is only this one man in the world whom she orders us to undeceive, and she binds him to an inviolable secrecy, which makes this knowledge to him as if it were not. Can we imagine anything more charitable and pleasant? And yet the corruption of man is such that he finds even this law harsh; and it is one of the main reasons which has caused a great part of Europe to rebel against the Church.

How unjust and unreasonable is the heart of man, which feels it disagreeable to be obliged to do in regard to one man what in some measure it were right to do to all men! For is it right that we should deceive men?

(1661)

# THE ANALYST AND THE CONFESSOR

### THE REV. VICTOR WHITE, O.P.

WE have only to take a look at what actually takes place in the confessional, and what actually takes place in the analyst's office to see that the differences, even on the surface, are very marked indeed; and a closer acquaintance with their respective aims and presuppositions will further widen the chasm that divides them. We shall soon learn that the analyst who plays the confessor will be as bad an analyst as the confessor who plays the analyst will be a bad confessor, and we shall be put on our guard against the dangerous type of apologetic which might be understood as offering the confessional as a substitute for psychotherapy; dangerous because of the disappointment it must arouse in those who know no better than to suppose it to be a cure for psychoneurosis. . . .

Sin, truly, is an evil; and psychotherapy is also concerned, as is every therapy, with an evil. Moreover, both the sacrament and the analysis are concerned to remedy the evil. But the evil with which each is concerned is essentially different, even mutually opposed. Sin is defined as an evil human act; that is, a human activity which lacks the goodness and rightness it should have in conformity with divine law. In theological language it is *malum culpae*, "the evil men *do*." It is, of its very nature as a human act, in some measure voluntary; and a sin is sinful in the precise measure in which it is willed. A psychoneurosis, on the contrary, is a certain *malum poenae*—"an evil men *suffer*" or *"undergo."* It is a sickness, and as such something essentially involuntary, and usually contrary to the sufferer's will both in itself and in its symptoms and manifestations. It is something that *happens* to us, not something we do; though it may lead us to action, these actions are neurotic symptoms in the precise measure in which they are involuntary. We may say that while the sacrament of penance deals with certain evil results of human *freedom*, psychotherapy deals with certain results of human *compulsions;* with thoughts, feelings, emotions, conflicts, patterns of behavior which the patient "cannot help," which are uncontrollable by his will and usually clean contrary to it. Confession presupposes the power to sin and to turn from sin and seek forgiveness; analysis usually presupposes necessity and impotence and seeks liberation and freedom. In short: the primary and direct concern of the sacrament is with willful *misdeeds;* the primary and direct concern of analysis is with a certain kind of involuntary *misfortune.* . . .

From this basic difference spring others which are hardly less striking. Sin, being essentially voluntary, is also essentially conscious, while it is of the very definition of any analytical psychotherapy that it is concerned, at least no less, with the unconscious. Sacramental confession, as we have already remarked, is concerned solely with actual sins committed after baptism; it is not concerned with inherited sin, whose remedy lies within the province of baptism itself. In contrast, psychotherapy cannot confine itself to factors acquired in the patient's own lifetime, still less limit itself to any definite date in the patient's history. It can on no account neglect inherited factors and dispositions; least of all can any depth-analysis which, under whatever name, recognises a "collective unconscious" as an important factor in mental health and sickness. . . .

The "confession" required of the penitent and the "confession" required of the analysant are two very different things. . . . What a penitent is expected to confess is very clearly defined and restricted to sins committed since his baptism or his previous confession. No such limitation can bind the analysant. Though no analyst who knows his business will want to exclude such material, he will still less seek to limit his patient's "confessions" to his real or alleged misdeeds. And he will be concerned with them, not precisely as moral offenses, but as causes or symptoms of neurosis, and as providing—together with the patient's conscious or unconscious attitudes to them—important elements in the total picture of the personality with which he has to do. The patient's "good deeds" will interest him no less than his "bad" ones (confessors are notoriously, and rightly, impatient with rehearsals of the "penitent's" virtues!) while dreams, free associations, spontaneous reactions and other manifestations of the unconscious will interest him still more. His business is less with what the patient does than why he does it. Only from this totally different standpoint may there be some overlapping, but never complete identity, between sacramental and analytical "confession." The psychological processes demanded by each differ correspondingly: the former requires a certain concentration of conscious memory and the orderly recital of a selection of its contents; the second, contrariwise, a mental and physical relaxation which permits the free flow of uncontrolled phantasy and the suspension of regular "directed" mental activity. The uncomfortable confessional box with its hard kneeler, and the couch or armchair of the analyst's office, admirably express and promote the two very different kinds of "confession" for which each is appointed.

Psychological analysis knows nothing of contrition or satisfaction as predetermined acts to be required of the patient: it would fail entirely of its purpose were it to lay down in advance the conscious attitude which the analysant was to adopt to his material. This can no more be predetermined than can the material itself. . . .

There is still considerable disagreement among analysts as to what their own precise role in analysis should be. But few, even of those who most strongly advocate his "active" intervention in the process, would maintain that the ultimate remedy comes from the analyst rather than the analysant and his own response to his own material. None certainly would claim divine power and authority to forgive sin.

So the differences between sacramental confession as understood and practiced in the Catholic Church and psychological analysis as known and practiced today are considerable and profound. Are we then to conclude that there are no connections between them, and that they are so wholly diverse that they can hardly be spoken of in the same breath?

To say this would, we think, be a grave mistake. We may not overlook either the psychological value of sacramental confession or the "religious" features of many an analysis and the close connections which may be found between them. . . .

While sacramental confession (including contrition and amendment) does not deal directly with psychoneurosis, we need not be surprised to find cases in which it is indirectly therapeutic; indirectly in so far as it may remove one of its causes. But it is perhaps as prevention rather than cure that sacramental confession, especially if practiced with regularity and with frank and unflinching self-examination, may serve the ends, if not of psychotherapy, then at least of mental hygiene and prophylaxis. Analytic experience witnesses to the very great extent to which unconsciousness of the "shadow" side of life contributes to the formation and persistence of neurotic complexes. A patient's failure to meet consciously and deliberately the challenges ("temptations" or "tests" in Catholic parlance) which life brings to him, whether from his own character or his environment or their mutual impact; shady compromises, never fully faced, with life's conflicting demands; a consequent narcissistic idealization of ego and corresponding neglect of the less acceptable traits of his character: all these, notoriously, are a common breeding ground of neurosis. Frequent and honest self-examination, and the necessity of formulating its findings in the confessional, may alone do much to promote a more complete self-awareness, and to prevent these less pleasing features of a personality from sinking into unconsciousness, where alone they will generate neurotic symptoms. Hence, while sacramental confession is not ordained to cure, it may do much to prevent, the disorders with which psychotherapy is concerned. We say "It may"; indeed it should. But other factors, inherited or environmental, may enter in to prevent its exercising this particular efficacy; and indeed in certain cases (notably those known to Catholics by the tragic symptoms of "scruples") it may increase rather than prevent the virulence of the disease.

On the other hand, while psychological analysis is not ordained to forgive sin, it may do much to free the patient from those compulsions which make both sin and repentance from sin—and even any clear-eyed self-examination—impossible.

It should also be remarked that, although psychological analysis cannot demand contrition of the patient, it is seldom successful unless it brings about something which, at the very least, is not unlike it: a radical change of the patient's conscious outlook, a *metanoia* or change of mind, and with it of his moral valuations and behavior. It is a truism that if an analysis does not change the patient's outlook on life, his whole mentality in greater or less degree, it achieves nothing. The very enlargement of consciousness involves a shifting of his whole center of awareness, and with it of his standard of values. This change, however, is not something that he brings to analysis, but something which emerges from the process and its material themselves. Numerous case histories show striking resemblances not only between the results of analysis with those of religious and moral conversions, but also in the very symbols which eventually emerge from unconscious sources to induce the transformation. . . .

While man is limited to the appointed channels of grace and forgiveness, God is not so limited; and there seems to be no foregone reason why the theologian can deny to dream-symbolism the *ex opere operantis* efficacy he must allow to the sacraments of the Old Law, the baptism by John, the sacramentals of the Church or—it may be added—the dream symbols of the Scriptures. Though little can be affirmed or denied with certainty, the resemblances are sometimes too impressive to be totally ignored.

The most that can be said in summary is that although sacramental confession and psychological analysis are two wholly different things, pursuing two different but interrelated purposes; the purposes of the one may sometimes happen (*per accidens*) to be attained through the other. But when the prevention, or more rarely the cure, of psychoneurosis sometimes results from sacramental confession, this arises from the conscious human activities which it involves. If, however, divine grace and forgiveness are sometimes attained through the processes of psychological analysis, this can only be from the patient's response to God's uncovenanted mercies through the inner life of the soul.

(1948)

SINCE the will of God is the universal cause of all things, it is impossible that the divine will should not produce its effect. Hence, whatever seems to withdraw itself from the divine will according to one order, will be brought back to it according to another; as, for example, a sinner, who, in so far as he can, withdraws himself from the divine will by sinning, falls under the order of the divine will as long as, through its justice, he is punished.

ST. THOMAS AQUINAS (1272)

## SALVATION FOR NON-CATHOLICS

### THE REV. W. DEVIVIER, S.J.

AMONG infidels, heretics and schismatics the Catholic doctrine excludes from salvation for not having embraced the true faith only those who have not known revealed truth because they did not *wish* to know it, and those who knowing it sufficiently have *refused* to embrace it. Those alone are *de facto* bound to enter the Church who know the Church to be the necessary means of salvation. . . .

With regard to persons born in Protestant countries and validly baptized, who from want of instruction and opportunity, have never come to the knowledge that the Catholic Church is the only true Church of Christ, if they have never committed a mortal sin, or have atoned for their sins by perfect contrition united to a sincere desire of doing all that God may require of them, they will be saved in the ordinary way, as members of the Catholic Church. Such persons are in reality Catholics; they have entered the Church by valid baptism and are only outwardly separated from her communion by *inculpable* error. . . .

Such persons who are in error *inculpably,* observe the moral law as made known to them by the light of reason, and serve God to the best of their ability, according to the light which they possess, and are ready to do all that Heaven may desire of them will certainly be saved. They may never receive the baptism of water but for them what is called in the Catholic Church the baptism of desire is sufficient. Their efforts to please God include the desire to know the true Faith and willingness to embrace it; and as to sanctifying grace, which is also necessary for salvation, God, Who is unwilling that men should perish, when they do their utmost to please Him, infuses into their souls, in the course of their lives or at the moment of their death, the same sanctifying grace that is conferred by the baptism of water. . . . Their salvation is not according to the ordinary course of Providence, but the result of an extraordinary grace conferred in view of the merits of Christ. By the Baptism of desire they become members of the true Church of Christ, the Catholic Church and are saved only as members of her communion.

(1924)


## "REMEMBER THE LAST THINGS"

### ST. THOMAS MORE

*Memorare novissima, et in aeternum non peccabis.*
Remember the last things, and thou shalt never sin.
Ecclus. 7

IF there were any question among men whether the words of Holy Scripture or the doctrine of any secular author were of greater force and effect to the weal and profit of man's soul (though we should let pass so many short and weighty words spoken by the mouth of our

Saviour Christ Himself, to Whose heavenly wisdom the wit of none earthly creature can be comparable) yet this only text written by the wise man in the seventh chapter of Ecclesiasticus is such that it containeth more fruitful advice and counsel to the forming and framing of man's manners in virtue and avoiding sin, than many whole and great volumes of the best of the old philosophers or any other that ever wrote in secular literature.

Long would it be to take the best of their words and compare it with these words of holy Writ. Let us consider the fruit and profit of this in itself: which thing, well advised and pondered, shall well declare that of none whole volume of secular literature shall arise so very fruitful doctrine. For what would a man give for a sure medicine that were of such strength that it should all his life keep from sickness, [especially] if he might by the avoiding of sickness be sure to continue his life one hundred years? So is it now that these words giveth us all a sure medicine (if we [postpone] not the receiving) by which we shall keep from sickness, not the body, which none health may long keep from death (for die we must in few years, live we never so long), but the soul, which here preserved from the sickness of sin, shall after this eternally live in joy and be preserved from the deadly life of everlasting pain.

The physician sendeth his bill to the apothecary, and therein writeth sometimes a costly receipt of many strange herbs and roots, fetched out of far countries, long-lain drugs, all the strength worn out, and some none such to be got. But this physician sendeth his bill to thyself, no strange thing therein, nothing costly to buy, nothing far to fetch, but to be gathered all times of the year in the garden of thine own soul.

Let us hear, then, what wholesome receipt this is. "Remember," saith this bill, "thy last things, and thou shalt never sin in this world." Here is first a short medicine containing only four herbs, common and well known, that is to wit, death, doom, pain, and joy.

This short medicine is of a marvellous force, able to keep us all our life from sin. The physician cannot give not one medicine to every man to keep him from sickness, but to divers men divers, by reason of the diversity of divers complexions. This medicine serveth every man. The physician doth but guess and conjecture that his receipt shall do good: but this medicine is undoubtedly sure. . . . .

Many things know we that we seldom think on: and in the things of the soul, the knowledge without the remembrance little profiteth.

What availeth it to know that there is a God, which thou not only believest by faith but also knowest by reason, what availeth that thou knowest Him, if thou think little of Him. The busy minding of thy four last things, and the deep consideration of thereof, is the thing that shall keep thee from sin. And if thou put it in essay and make a proof, thou shalt well find, by that thou shalt have no lust to sin for the time that thou thinkest deeply on them, that if our frailty could endure never to remit or slacken in the deep devising of them, we should never have delight or pleasure in any sinful thing.

(1557)

# Index of Authors

## WITH BIOGRAPHICAL NOTES AND SOURCES

Adam, Karl (1876–    ), prof. of Catholic theology, Univ. of Tübingen, Germany:
*The Spirit of Catholicism* (tr. Justin McCann, O.S.B.), 249

Allers, Rudolph (1883–    ), reader in psychiatry, Univ. of Vienna; prof. of psychology, Catholic Univ. of America since 1938:
*The Psychology of Character* (tr. E. B. Strauss), 73, 76

Alter, Karl Joseph (1885–    ), Archbishop of Cincinnati, Ohio, since 1950:
Commencement Address, Xavier Univ., Cincinnati, printed in *The Tablet*, Brooklyn, N.Y., March 14, 1953, 154

Anonymous, Knights of Columbus pamphlets:
*Let Us Judge Catholics by the Bible,* 227
*What Do You Mean— Only One Church?*, 222
*Yes, I Condemned the Catholic Church,* 213

Anonymous: "Epistle to Diognetus" (Diognetus was a pagan whom the writer of the Epistle exhorted to become a Christian), *The Apostolic Fathers* (tr. Kirsopp Lake), 89

Anselm of Canterbury, St. (1033–1109), a Doctor of the Church, born in Italy, died in England, influenced Catholic philosophy:
*Bibliotheca,* July, 1851, 2

Antonino, Antoninius, St. (1389–1459), Archbishop of Florence, Italy:

*Summa Theologica Moralis,* 136

Aquinas, St. Thomas (ca.1225–1274), Italian Dominican, known as the Angelic Doctor and the Prince of Scholastics, ranks with Aristotle and St. Augustine because of his contribution to human thought in his systematic survey of Catholic theology in his *Summa Theologica;* founder of the Thomistic school of philosophy and theology. One of the Church's greatest minds:
*Philosophical Texts of,* sel. and trans. by Thomas Gilbey, O.P.:
*Opus. X, de Causis,* lect. i, xi
*Summa Theologica,* Ia. Iv. 3, 38
*Summa Theologica,* Ia. Xc. 3, 45
*Summa Theologica,* Ia. Xlviii. i, 319
III *Contra Gentes,* 80, 127
III *Quodlibet,* 27, 344
VIII, *Quodlibet,* 274
Opusc. XXIX, *de Perfectione Vitae Spiritualis,* 7, 131
Opusc. XI, *de Regimine Principum,* 3, 302
Disputations, 11 *de Malo,* 4, 357
Trans. by and quoted in *Philosophy of Religion,* by Fulton J. Sheen:
*Summa Theologica,* i. q. 79, a. 4, 44
*Summa Theologica,* dist. I, q. 37, a. 1, 38
*Summa Theologica,* i, q. 16, a. 5, 20
*Summa Theologica,* I–II, q. 2, a. 8c, 49
*Summa Theologica,* I–II, q. 91, 258
*Contra Gentiles,* lib. iii, cap. 71, 19

369

Catholic Bishops of the United States, Statements signed in their names and issued by the Administrative Board of the National Catholic Welfare Council, composed of representative members of the American Hierarchy, 112, 135, 157, 288

Cavanaugh, John J. (1899–    ), president of Univ. of Notre Dame, 1946–52; Dir. Notre Dame Univ. Fndn.:
*The Blasphemous Thing,* 148

Clancy, William P. (contemporary), formerly on faculty of Univ. of Notre Dame, now engaged in writing:
*The Commonweal,* July 11, 1952, 296

Claudel, Paul (1868–1955), French poet, playwright and diplomat: *Ways and Crossways* (tr. John O'Connor), 39, 123

Clement, St. (died about A.D. 215), the third Bishop of Rome (A.D. 96–A.D. 98), traditionally believed to be the third pope:
*Documents of the Christian Church,* ed. by Henry Bettenson, "Epistle to the Corinthians," 173

Commission on American Citizenship of The Catholic Univ. of America, Most Rev. Francis J. Haas, Chairman of Executive Committee, Rt. Rev. George Johnson, Director:
*Better Men for Better Times,* 70, 120, 272

Cox, Ignatius Wiley (1883–    ), prof. of Ethics and Religion, Fordham Univ., New York: *God, Man and Redemption,* 15, 46

Cushing, Richard James (1895–    ), Archbishop of Boston, Mass., 1944; created a Cardinal in 1958:
*Sermon,* Boston, April 14, 1952, printed in *The Tablet,* Brooklyn, N.Y., April 19, 1952, 144

Cyprian, St. (Thascius Caecilius Cyprianus) (ca. 200–258), first Christian bishop to suffer martyrdom when, as Bishop of Carthage, he was beheaded:
*De Unitate,* 238
*Ad Demetr.* quoted by Cardinal Newman in *Development of Christian Doctrine,* 337

D'Arcy, Martin Cyril (188?–    ), English philosopher and author, frequent visitor to U.S.:
*The Mind and Heart of Love,* 69

Dawson, Christopher (1889–    ), English educator, former editor of *The Dublin Review,* author of important works on cultural history and religion:
*Dublin Review,* July, 1942, 327
*Progress and Religion,* 197
*Beyond Politics,* 217
*Essays in Order,* 72, 219

De Vere, Aubrey Thomas (1814–1902), Irish poet, became a Catholic in 1851:
*Essays—Chiefly on Poetry,* vol. 2, 9, 30, 69, 340

Devivier, Walter (1833–1924), French theologian and writer on apologetics:
*Christian Apologetics,* (tr. Joseph C. Sasia, S.J.), vol. 2, 205, 365

Donoso Cortès, Juan marqués de Valdegamas (1803–1853), private secretary to Queen Marie Cristina of Spain, Spanish Minister to Berlin and Ambassador to France:
*An Essay on Catholicism, Authority and Order* (tr. Madeleine Vincent Goddard), 191

du Noüy, Lecomte (1883–1947), famous French scientist, lawyer and philosopher; worked with Alexis Carrel; 1920–27 associate member of Rockefeller Institute:
*Human Destiny,* 78

England, John (1788–1842), Bishop of Charleston, S.C., 1820–1842:
*Works,* vol. 4, p. 172—Speech before U.S. House of Representatives, January 8, 1826, 271

Facey, Paul W. (contemporary), on faculty of Holy Cross College, Worcester, Mass.:
*Education for International Understanding,* ed. by R. C. Hartnett, S.J., 162

Finlay, Peter (1851–  ?  ), educator, lecturer, and writer; prof. of theology,

Finlay, Peter (*continued*)
Dublin College of Univ. of Ireland: *The Church of Christ*, 219

Frenay, Adolphe Dominic (1899–    ), German-born educator and writer, engaged in educational and pastoral work in U.S. since 1922:
*Is Life Worth Living?*, 79

Furfey, Paul Hanly (1896–    ), leading writer on Catholic sociology, head of Dept. of Sociology, Catholic Univ. of America:
"Some Trends in Modern Social Theory," American Catholic Philosophical Assn., 4th Annual Meeting, 1929, 124

Gibbons, James Cardinal (1834–1921), the second American-born Cardinal (in 1886), occupied conspicuous place in American life; Archbishop of Baltimore, Md.:
*Faith of Our Fathers*, 197
*Pastoral Letter*, 89
*Retrospect of Fifty Years*, 284

Gill, Eric (1882–1940), English sculptor, engraver, designer; author of many books and papers on art and related subjects; became a Catholic in 1913:
*Art Nonsense and Other Essays*, 47
*Autobiography*, 209

Gillis, James Martin (1876–1957), author, radio speaker, lecturer, editor; for 12 years engaged in missionary work in U.S.; 1922 to 1949 editor of *The Catholic World*; conducts weekly column that appears in 47 Catholic newspapers:
*The Catholic World*, 136, 252
*If Not Christianity, What?*, 4

Gilson, Etienne Henry (1884–    ), foremost living Catholic authority on medieval philosophy; born in Paris, taught in French universities; prof. at Harvard 1926–29; Director of Pontifical Institute of Medieval Studies, Toronto, Canada; lectures and writes in both French and English:
*The Spirit of Medieval Philosophy*, 58
*The Unity of Philosophical Experience*, 24
*God and Philosophy*, 3, 9, 35, 325

Lecture, St. Michael's College, Toronto Univ., publ. in *The Ensign*, March 15 and 22, 1952, 139

Grandmaison, M. Le Cour (contemporary), member of French Parliament:
quoted in *The London Universe*, Feb. 4, 1938, 302

Haas, Francis J. (1889–1953), prof. at Catholic Univ. of America; Bishop of Grand Rapids, Mich., since 1943:
*The Modern Social and Economic Order: A Symposium*, 134

Hanrahan, Daniel U. (contemporary), pastor of Sacred Heart Church, Cambria Heights, New York, N.Y.:
*Sermon*, Red Mass, Brooklyn, N.Y., Sept. 27, 1951, printed in *The Tablet*, Brooklyn, N.Y., Sept. 29, 1951, 115

Harney, John B. (1875–1957), 1929–1934 served as Superior of the Paulist Fathers; prominent pamphleteer:
*Sin*, 357

Hartnett, Robert Clinton (1904–    ), former editor-in-chief of *America* and of *The Catholic Mind*, now on faculty of Loyola Univ., Chicago:
*Equal Rights for Children*, 150
*Radio Address*, Jan. 20, 1952, printed in *The Catholic Mind*, Sept. 1952, 167

Healy, Martin J. (contemporary), prof. of dogmatic theology, Seminary of the Immaculate Conception, Huntington, N.Y.; author of popular works: *My Way of Life*, 86

Hedley, John Cuthbert (1837–1915), Bishop of Newport, England, 1881 to his death; editor of *The Dublin Review*; prolific writer:
*The Light of Life*, 45

Hildebrand, Dietrich von (1889–    ), head of philosophy dept., Fordham Univ., New York; born in Italy, raised in Germany, fled Nazis, came to U.S. in 1940:
*Transformation in Christ*, 60, 71, 184

Hollis, Christopher (1902–    ), director of *The Tablet*, (London, England), author of many books and articles in field of history and biography; became a Catholic in 1922; studied and lectured at Univ. of Notre Dame in U.S.; served in R.A.F., World War II; elected to Parliament:

*The Noble Castle,* 24, 185

Horrigan, Alfred Frederick (1914–  ), pres. of Bellarmine College, Louisville, Ky.; formerly editor of *The Record,* and still frequent contributor to its columns:

*The Record,* May 9, 1952, 125

Hugel, Baron Friedrich von (1852–1925) eminent philosopher of religion:

*Essays and Addresses on the Philosophy of Religion,* 322

Hughes, Emmet John (1920–  ), press attache U.S. Embassy at Madrid, Spain 1942–46; *Time* magazine correspondent; on President Eisenhower's executive staff; consultant to Rockefeller nonprofit fndns:

*The Church and the Liberal Society,* 225, 291

Hull, Ernest Reginald (1863–1952), editor of *The Bombay Examiner,* 1903–1924; Archivist and Secretary to Archbishop of Bombay, 1924–31; returned to England to edit and write many books; became a Catholic in 1882:

*What the Catholic Church is,* 229
*What She Teaches,* 240

Ignatius of Antioch, St. (fl. A.D. 112), according to tradition he was the little child Christ placed in the midst of His Disciples for an example. He was converted by St. John the Evangelist and consecrated Bishop by St. Peter:

*Documents of the Christian Church,* ed. by Henry Bettenson, "Epistle to the Smyrnaeans," 238

Ignatius Loyola, St. (1491–1556), founder of the Society of Jesus, son of the Spanish ducal house of Loyola:

*The Spiritual Exercises,* 45

Ireland, John (1838–1918), born in Ireland, came to U.S. in boyhood, studied for priesthood in France, ordained 1861; archbishop of St. Paul, Minn., 1884 to death:

*Address,* Milwaukee, Wisc., Aug. 11, 1913, reprinted in *The Catholic Mind,* 290

Irenaeus, St. (?125–ca. 200), associate of the Apostles; apparently studied at Rome under St. Justin Martyr, later went to Gaul and became a Bishop; one of the Apostolic Fathers:

*Against the Heresies,* 174

Quoted by Cardinal Newman in his *The Development of Christian Doctrine,* 174

Jerome, St. (ca. 340–420), one of the four great Latin Doctors of the Church, translator of the Vulgate:

*Epistula liii ad Paulinum,* 231

Jerrold, Douglas (1893–  ), English author and book-publishing executive:

*The Future of Freedom,* 184

Jordan, Edward B. (1884–1951), on faculty of Catholic Univ. of America:

quoted in J.A. O Brien's *The Origin of Man,* 44

Kehoe, Patrick H. (1887–  ):

*Augustinian Studies,* "The Church and Evolution," 37

Kerby, William J. (1868– ?  ), one of most influential Catholic sociologists and pioneer of organized Catholic charities in U.S.:

*The Encyclopedia of Social Reform,* ed. by W. D. P. Bliss, 121

Knox, Ronald Arbuthnot (1888–1957), became a Catholic in 1917; Catholic chaplain at Oxford Univ. 1925–39; influential apologist, satirist, writer of detective novels, translator of Bible:

*Miracles,* 350

Lacordaire, Jean Baptiste Henri Dominique (1802–1861), great French pulpit orator and member of the French Academy:

*Quotation,* 245

La Farge, John (1880–  ), assoc. editor of *America,* formerly engaged in teaching, pastoral, and mission work;

of Labor Day, 1949, *Sermon* at Gary, Ind., 135

Mauriac, François (1885– ), highly regarded French poet, playwright, and novelist:

*The Tablet,* Brooklyn, N.Y., May 10, 1952, 347

*A Woman of the Pharisees,* (tr. Gerard Hopkins), 100

Mercier, Désiré Joseph (1851–1926), prof. of Thomistic philosophy at Louvain; Archbishop of Malines and primate of Belgium; made a Cardinal in 1907; spokesman for Belgians during German occupation World War I:

*Cardinal Mercier's Retreat to His Priests,* (tr. J. M. O'Kavanagh), 16, 48, 50, 56, 245

Merton, Thomas (name in religion, Father Louis, O.C.S.O.) (1915– ), born in France, became a Catholic in 1939, joined the Trappists in 1942, ordained in 1949:

*Figures For an Apocalypse,* 346

Montalembert, Charles René Count de (1810–1870), French journalist and politician, outspoken defender of the Church:

*Monks of the West,* 348

Mooney, Edward (1882–1958), spiritual director of North American College at Rome, 1923–36; Apostolic Delegate to India 1926, to Japan 1931; Bishop of Rochester, N.Y. 1933, first Archbishop of Detroit 1937, created a Cardinal 1946:

*The Catholic Mind,* August, 1944, text *Address* at Detroit civic mass meeting, June 7, 1944, 108

*Address,* Milwaukee, Wisc., 1938, 283

Moore, Thomas Verner (1877– ), prof. of psychology and psychiatry at Catholic Univ. of America; joined Paulist Fathers in 1896, became a Benedictine in 1923, now a Carthusian in Spain:

*Personal and Mental Hygiene,* 81

More, St. Thomas (1478–1535), English statesman, poet, and author; Lord Chancellor and friend of King Henry VIII, who ordered his execution when he refused to accept the King's ecclesiastical supremacy over the Pope:

*English Works of,* 366

Murray, John Courtney (1904– ), born in New York, N.Y.; ordained 1933; prof. of theology, Woodstock College; ed. of *Theological Studies:*

*Annals* (of American Academy of Political Social Science), March, 1948, 289

Murray, Rosalind (Mrs. A. J. Toynbee), (1890– ), daughter of Gilbert Murray, became a Catholic in 1932:

*The Good Pagan's Failure,* 122, 210

Newman, John Henry (1801–1890), Anglican clergyman who became a Catholic in 1845; rector of Catholic Univ. of Dublin 1851–58; created a Cardinal in 1878; one of the greatest modern writers on Catholic theological subjects:

*A Letter to the Duke of Norfolk,* 236

*Parochial and Plain Sermons,* 18, 335

*Grammar of Assent,* 22, 29, 62

*The Idea of a University,* 22

*The Development of Christian Doctrine,* 177

*Sermons on Subjects of the Day,* 194

*Discourses Addressed to Mixed Congregations,* 212

*Apologia Pro Vita Sua,* 235, 316

*Oxford Univ. Sermons,* 341

*Biglietto Speech,* 296

Nicholas I, St., Pope (858–867), one of most remarkable men of his age; governed ably as Pope for nine dark years:

*Documents of the Christian Church,* selected and edited by Henry Bettenson, Letter "Preposueramus quidem" to Emperor Michael, 254

Noyes, Alfred (1880–1958), English poet, essayist, and critic, became a Catholic in 1925:

*The Unknown God,* 50, 315

O'Boyle, Patrick A. (1896–1960), Archbishop of Washington, D.C. since 1948, Chancellor of Cath. Univ. of America:

Sturzo, Don Luigi (1871–1959), Italian priest, student of political and social life, author of several books:
*The True Life* (tr. Barbara Barclay Carter), 51

Suhard, Emanuel (1874–1949), Archbishop of Reims 1925–40; created a Cardinal in 1935; Archbishop of Paris 1940 to his death:
*Growth or Decline? The Church Today* (tr. James J. Corbett), 329

Teresa of Avila, St. (1515–1582), Carmelite nun, mystic and religious superior of great ability:
*Complete Works of,* 3 vols. (tr. E. Allison Peers) vol. 3, 74

Tertullian (ca. 160–230), great ecclesiastical writer and Christian apologist after his conversion from paganism; late in life sided with the Montanists against Rome:
*Apologetic and Practical Treatises,* (tr. C. Dodgson), 104

Third Lateran Council:
*Decree,* 141

Third Plenary Council of Catholic Archbishops and Bishops of the United States, at Baltimore, Md.:
*Statement,* 276

Vann, Gerald (1906–    ), on staff of Blackfriars School, Laxton, England; widely known for his books and periodical contributions:
*The Heart of Man,* 97

Vatican Council, The:
*Statement,* 232

Vincent of Lerins, St. (fl. 434, AD.), of a noble family, abandoned military career to become a monk on island of Lerins off France, where he engaged in writing on Church controversies of the day:
*Cambridge Patristic Texts,* ed. by Maxon, 175

Webb, Bruno (contemporary English Benedictine priest):
*Why Does God Permit Evil?,* 320

White, Victor (1902–    ), English psychologist and essayist, formerly ed. of Dominican monthly *Blackfriars,* prof. of Dogmatic Theology, Blackfriars, Oxford, England:
*The Commonweal,* July 23, 1948, 361

Windle, Sir Bertram C. A. (1858–1929), scientist and writer on science and Catholic apologetics:
*A Century of Scientific Thought,* 218

Woodlock, Thomas F. (?–1945), editor of *The Wall Street Journal,* author:
*The Catholic Pattern,* 192, 211

Wright, John J. (1909–    ), Aux. Bishop of Boston; Bishop of Worcester, Mass.; now Bishop of Pittsburg:
*The Tablet,* Brooklyn, N.Y., Nov. 17, 1951, text of *Sermon,* Bishop Molloy Retreat League, 206

Wust, Peter (1884–1937), German Catholic philosopher:
*Essays in Order,* 73, 325

Zahm, John Augustine (1851–1921), Provincial of the Congregation of the Holy Cross, in the U.S., prof. and head of Scientific Dept. at Univ. of Notre Dame:
*Bible, Science and Faith,* 38

# APOLLO EDITIONS